ISIS IN A GLOBAL EMPIRE

In *Isis in a Global Empire*, Lindsey Mazurek explores the growing popularity of Egyptian gods and its impact on Greek identity in the Roman Empire. Bringing together archaeological, art historical, and textual evidence, she demonstrates how the diverse devotees of gods such as Isis and Sarapis considered Greek ethnicity in ways that differed significantly from those of the Greek male elites whose opinions have long shaped our understanding of Roman Greece. These ideas were expressed in various ways – sculptures of Egyptian deities rendered in a Greek style, hymns to Isis that grounded her in Greek geography and mythology, funerary portraits that depicted devotees dressed as Isis, and sanctuaries that used natural and artistic features to evoke stereotypes of the Nile. Mazurek's volume offers a fresh, material history of ancient globalization, one that highlights the role that religion played in the self-identification of provincial Romans and their place in the Mediterranean world.

LINDSEY A. MAZUREK is Assistant Professor of Classical Studies at Indiana University, Bloomington and co-editor of *Across the Corrupting Sea: Post-Braudelian Approaches to the Ancient Eastern Mediterranean*. Her scholarship has been supported by the Loeb Classical Library Foundation, the Archaeological Institute of America, the Hardt Foundation, and the National Endowment for the Humanities.

ISIS IN A GLOBAL EMPIRE

GREEK IDENTITY THROUGH EGYPTIAN RELIGION IN ROMAN GREECE

LINDSEY A. MAZUREK

Indiana University, Bloomington

Shaftesbury Road, Cambridge CB2 8EA, United Kingdom

One Liberty Plaza, 20th Floor, New York, NY 10006, USA

477 Williamstown Road, Port Melbourne, VIC 3207, Australia

314–321, 3rd Floor, Plot 3, Splendor Forum, Jasola District Centre, New Delhi – 110025, India

103 Penang Road, #05–06/07, Visioncrest Commercial, Singapore 238467

Cambridge University Press is part of Cambridge University Press & Assessment, a department of the University of Cambridge.

We share the University's mission to contribute to society through the pursuit of education, learning and research at the highest international levels of excellence.

www.cambridge.org
Information on this title: www.cambridge.org/9781009016902

DOI: 10.1017/9781009032209

© Cambridge University Press & Assessment 2022

This publication is in copyright. Subject to statutory exception and to the provisions of relevant collective licensing agreements, no reproduction of any part may take place without the written permission of Cambridge University Press & Assessment.

First published 2022
First paperback edition 2024

A catalogue record for this publication is available from the British Library

ISBN   978-1-316-51701-7   Hardback
ISBN   978-1-009-01690-2   Paperback

Cambridge University Press & Assessment has no responsibility for the persistence or accuracy of URLs for external or third-party internet websites referred to in this publication and does not guarantee that any content on such websites is, or will remain, accurate or appropriate.

....

Publication of this book has been aided by a grant from the von Bothmer Publication Fund of the Archaeological Institute of America.

CONTENTS

List of Illustrations	page vii
Acknowledgments	xi
1 EGYPTIAN RELIGION AND THE PROBLEM OF GREEKNESS	1
2 BUILDING GROUPNESS: ISIS' DEVOTEES AND THEIR COMMUNITIES	29
3 DETERRITORIALIZING THEOLOGY? BRINGING THE EGYPTIAN GODS TO GREECE	59
4 SELF-UNDERSTANDING: VISUALIZING ISIS IN STONE	88
5 SELF-FASHIONING: DRESSING THE DEVOTEES OF ISIS IN ATHENIAN PORTRAITS	120
6 SELF-LOCATION: ISIAC SANCTUARIES AND NILOTIC FICTIONS	145
7 CONCLUSION: GRAECIA CAPTA, AEGYPTA CAPTA	186
Appendix: Catalogue of Sculpture Associated with the Thessaloniki Sarapeum	195
Notes	201
Bibliography	245
Index	275
Color plates can be found between pages 144 and 145	

ILLUSTRATIONS

PLATES

1 Mosaic depicting Rome and the personifications of several provinces from the House of Africa in Thysdrus, second half of the 2nd century CE
2 Personification of Egypt from Plate 1
3 Calendar mosaic from Thysdrus depicting the month of November, 3rd century CE
4 Votive relief of Ignatia Herennia dedicated to Hermanubis, featuring relief footprints in two different sizes, late 2nd–early 3rd century CE
5 Nilotic wall painting from the Casa del Medico at Pompeii, 1st century CE
6 Group of sculptures depicting Isis, Kerberos, and Sarapis from the Sanctuary of the Egyptian Gods at Gortyna, 3rd century CE
7 Statue of Aphrodite of the Louvre-Naples type from the Thessaloniki Sarapeum, 2nd century CE
8 Head of Isis with corkscrew curls from Thessaloniki, Antonine period
9 Statuette of Harpokrates from the Thessaloniki Sarapeum, second half of the 2nd century CE
10 Interior of the Tomb of Iarhai in Palmyra, 2nd century CE
11 Wall painting of an Isiac priest making an offering to a statue of Harpokrates from the portico of Pompeii's Iseum, mid-1st century CE
12 The Iseum at Dion, 1st century BCE–4th century CE
13 Section VI 6 A of the Nilotic panels of colored *sectile* glass from Kenchreai, 4th century CE
14 Replica of Isis and Osiris statues displayed in situ at the North Pylon of the Sanctuary of the Egyptian Gods at Marathon

FIGURES

1	Relief from the Hadrianeum in Rome depicting the province of Egypt, later Antonine period	*page* 2
2	Statue of Isis in diagonally draped *diplax* costume, thought to be from Rome, Hadrianic period	3

LIST OF ILLUSTRATIONS

3	Map of Greece	5
4	The Arch of Hadrian at Athens, dedicated 131–132 CE	11
5	Temple of Olympian Zeus at Athens, dedicated 131–132 CE	12
6	Portrait of a man in chiton and himation, Antonine period	24
7	Grave relief of Alexandra of Oe, wife of Ktetos, from Athens, mid-2nd century CE	30
8	Votive relief dedicated to Osiris μύστης, 2nd century BCE	43
9	Axiometric reconstruction drawing of the Iseum at Dion	46
10	Statue of Aphrodite Hypolympidia from her temple in Dion's Iseum, 150–100 BCE	48
11	Axiometric reconstruction drawing of the temple to Aphrodite Hypolimpidia in the Dion Iseum	49
12	Statue bases for Anthestia Maxima, daughter of Publius, Severan period	49
13	Plan of the Inopos Quarter and the Terrace of the Foreign Gods on Delos.	68
14	Excavation photograph of the central court, staircase, and ekklesiasterion of Sarapieion A, viewed from the southwest	83
15	Votive relief depicting two footprints, dedicated by several freedwomen (?) of Caecilia Polla, Roman period	84
16	Votive relief of Marcus Agellius found in the Thessaloniki Sarapeum and featuring an ear, early 1st century BCE	85
17	Statue of Sarapis *débout* from the Sanctuary of the Egyptian Gods at Gortyna, 3rd century CE	91
18	Statue of a seated Sarapis from the Sanctuary of the Egyptian Gods at Gortyna, 2nd century CE	92
19	Statue of a seated Sarapis from Sarapieion B on Delos, 2nd–1st century BCE	93
20	Statuette of Isis in the *Knotenpalla* costume, Roman period	95
21	Statuette of Isis in the *Knotenpalla* costume from Delos, 2nd–1st century BCE	97
22	Statue of Isis in the *diplax* costume from the Sanctuary of the Egyptian Gods at Gortyna, 3rd century CE	98
23	Statue of Isis Tyche from the northern shrine of Dion's Iseum, 2nd century CE	99
24	Terracotta statuette of Isis *lactans* from Herculaneum, 1st century CE	100
25	Reconstructed plan of the Thessaloniki Sarapeum	103
26	Statue of a female goddess, perhaps Artemis of the Ariccia type or Athena, from the Thessaloniki Sarapeum, 2nd century CE	105
27	Head of Sarapis, later 2nd century CE	107
28	Head of Sarapis found in the Vasiloglou plot near the Thessaloniki Sarapeum, 2nd century CE	108
29	Head of Isis from the Thessaloniki Sarapeum, 3rd century BCE	109
30	Detail of right side of Figure 29	111
31	Torso of a statuette of Athena Parthenos from the Thessaloniki Sarapeum, 2nd century CE	113
32	Black basalt statuette of a sphinx found in the Thessaloniki Sarapeum, late Ptolemaic period	118

LIST OF ILLUSTRATIONS

33	Grave stele of Sosibia, daughter of Eubios, of the dēme of Kephisia, 160–170 CE	121
34	Funerary relief for Maqi, son of M'ani, from Palmyra, ca. 200 CE	123
35	Funerary bust for a woman from Palmyra, 3rd century CE	124
36	Funerary relief of Yarkhai, son of Ogga, and his female relative Balya, mid-2nd century CE	125
37	Tower tombs of Palmyra, 1st century BCE	128
38	Portrait mummy of an adolescent male in Greek clothing from Hawara, 100–120 CE	130
39	Grave stela of Musaios (male), Amaryllis (female, center), and an unnamed woman of Large Herculaneum type (right), Trajanic period	132
40	Grave stela of a couple from Athens (area of modern Pireaus and Salaminos Streets), late 2nd century CE	133
41	Votive relief depicting Isis *Dikaiosyne*, early 1st century BCE	136
42	Funerary relief of Kallo of Eupuridon and Synpheron of Miletus (right) from Athens, Flavian period	138
43	Portrait bust of a young boy with Isiac tonsure found in the House of Leda at Dion, 2nd century CE and recarved in the 3rd century CE to create the tonsure hairstyle	140
44	Portrait bust of C. Norbanus Sorex from the Pompeii Iseum, mid-1st century CE	141
45	Grave relief of Mousa, daughter of Dionysios, from Halai found in the Herodou Attikou shaft of the Athenian Metro excavations, ca. 150 CE	142
46	Statue of Osiris found at the Sanctuary of the Egyptian Gods at Marathon, third quarter of the 2nd century CE	154
47	Statue of Osiris from the North Pylon of the Sanctuary of the Egyptian Gods at Marathon, third quarter of the 2nd century CE	155
48	Statue of Isis from the North Pylon of the Sanctuary of the Egyptian Gods at Marathon, third quarter of the 2nd century CE	156
49	Plan of the Sanctuary of the Egyptian Gods at Marathon	157
50	Portrait bust of Polydeukion found in Room A of the Sanctuary of the Egyptian Gods' East Court, ca. 160 CE	158
51	The South Pylon of the West Court, viewed from the south	159
52	The First Pylon of the temple complex at Philae in Egypt	160
53	View of central pyramidal feature of the West Court from the east	161
54	Statue of a sphinx from the Sanctuary of the Egyptian Gods at Marathon, third quarter of the 2nd century CE	162
55	Excavation photo showing the findspots of the sphinx, a statue of Isis tentatively associated with the East Pylon, and seventy oversized lamps in Room B	163
56	Statue of Isis *unica*, tentatively associated with the East Pylon of the Sanctuary of the Egyptian Gods at Marathon, third quarter of the 2nd century CE	164

57	Detail of Figure 56 showing the Egyptianizing crook implement held in the right hand	165
58	Statue of Isis-Demeter from the South Pylon of the Sanctuary of the Egyptian Gods at Marathon, third quarter of the 2nd century CE	167
59	Statue of Isis-Aphrodite from the West Pylon of the Sanctuary of the Egyptian Gods, third quarter of the 2nd century CE	168
60	Excavation photograph depicting the statue of Isis-Demeter tipped off of its base	169
61	Statue of Osiris from the South Pylon of the Sanctuary of the Egyptian Gods, third quarter of the 2nd century CE	171
62	Statue of Osiris-Antinoos from Hadrian's Villa at Tivoli, Hadrianic period	173
63	Statuette of Horus in falcon form from the Sanctuary of the Egyptian Gods at Marathon, third quarter of the 2nd century CE	174
64	Bust of Herodes Atticus, thought to be from Marathon, third quarter of the 2nd century CE	176
65	Bust of emperor Marcus Aurelius in cuirass, thought to be from Marathon, mid-2nd century CE	177
66	Water crypt in the Sanctuary of the Egyptian Gods at Gortyna	179
67	Central water feature within the Iseum at Dion	181
68	Sima with crocodile spouts from the Praetorium at Gortyna, 4th century CE	182

ACKNOWLEDGMENTS

At the end of a long project, there is much pleasure in pausing to remember all of the people and institutions that helped me along the way. Initial research was funded by a Julian Price Fellowship from Duke University's Graduate School and a Postdoctoral Fellowship in Humanities and Social Sciences in the departments of Classics and History at the Memorial University of Newfoundland. The final stages of field research were supported by funding from fellowships from the Loeb Classical Library Foundation and the College of Arts and Sciences and Department of History at the University of Oregon. A residential fellowship from the Oregon Humanities Center allowed me to finalize the initial manuscript. I thank all of them and the many institutions and photographers who allowed me to publish the images that appear in this book.

This project began as a doctoral dissertation in the Department of Art, Art History and Visual Studies at Duke University. The wonderful faculty, staff, and graduate students there challenged and inspired me to think about the ancient world in new ways, and enthusiastically supported every new venture. I am particularly grateful to Sara Galletti, Annabel Wharton, and Caroline Bruzelius for their teaching, advice, and support. The classics community at the University of North Carolina-Chapel Hill always welcomed me, and I am particularly fortunate to have learned from Monika Trümper-Ritter, Lidewijde de Jong, Mary Sturgeon, Jennifer Gates-Foster, and Richard Talbert.

Throughout my academic career, the staff at the American School of Classical Studies at Athens, particularly Ioanna Damanaki, made my research in Greece possible. Thanks to those who facilitated my access to sculptures and sites discussed here, particularly the museum and site staff at the Portland Museum of Art, Getty Villa, National Archaeological Museum, National Epigraphic Museum, and Agora Museum in Athens, the Ephorate of Antiquities of the City of Athens, and the archaeological museums at Delos, Dion, Gortyna, Heraklion, Isthmia, Marathon, Messene, and Thessaloniki. The School of Religion at the University of Southern California hosted me as a visiting scholar in spring 2017, and Ken Lapatin kindly allowed me to use the library at the Getty Villa and research some of the villa's objects during that period, which sparked the ideas that became Chapter 5.

My colleagues at Indiana University, especially Cynthia Bannon, Bill Beck, Nick Blackwell, Kenny Draper, Julie Mebane, and our indomitable chair Matt Christ, have supported my work in countless ways and seen me through to the bitter end of this project. I am grateful for their advice and friendship. I would also like to thank all of my former colleagues at the University of Oregon, particularly chair Brett Rushforth, who went to great lengths to support me and my project. Much of the book was drafted and revised in the University of Oregon's Center on Diversity and Community's and Indiana University's weekly faculty writing circles, and I owe much to my fellow writers and organizers Lara Bovilsky, Laura Plummer, and Michelle Moyd for keeping me motivated and focused as I wrote.

As the project developed, first as a dissertation and then as a book, many people provided generous guidance. Marica Cassis helped me get my academic career off the ground and encouraged me to pursue this project as a book. I owe a tremendous debt to Kate Topper, who has mentored me for the past few years and, along with Ellen Perry and Lowell Bowditch, workshopped my manuscript in August 2019 at the University of Oregon, funded by the Vice-Provost of Equity and Inclusion. They were an ideal set of readers, and this book is much better because of their careful thinking and critiques. Elizabeth Baltes, Steve Beda, Sean Burrus, Valentino Gasparrini, Anneliese Heinz, Patricia Eunji Kim, Eva Mol, Amanda Lazarus, Paraskevi Martzavou, and Stephanie Pearson all read and commented on chapter drafts, and the book is much better for their advice. Others, including Tolly Boatwright, Jacquelyn Clements, Iphigenia Dekoulakou, Christopher Dickenson, Pelly Fotiadi, Bethany Hucks, Rebecca Futo-Kennedy, Anna Kouremenos, Emilie Luse, Ian Moyer, Kathryn McBride, Ian Moyer, Giorgos Spyropoulos, Estelle Strazdins, Molly Swetnam-Burland, Kris Trego, Richard Veymiers, Caroline Vout, and Elizabeth Wolfram-Thill shared their time, expertise, images, and unpublished work with me. Lecture audiences at Brown University, Florida State University, and DEREE-The American College of Greece, as well as audiences at the Mediterranean Seminar, Arachne Conference, the Greek Art in Context Conference, TRAC 2018, and many meetings of the Archaeological Institute of America have provided invaluable feedback on my research. Ann-Marie Yasin provided crucial advice when I was at an intellectual crossroads, and I am grateful for the direction she gave me and this project.

Thanks also to my wonderful editor, Beatrice Rehl, and the editorial and production staff at Cambridge University Press. I was especially fortunate to have reviewers (especially Caitlín Barrett, who revealed herself as Reviewer 1) who provided generous, thorough, thought-provoking, and inspiring comments. I am also grateful to the Archaeological Institute of America's Von Bothmer Publication Fund, which supported the book's illustration program.

ACKNOWLEDGMENTS

Chapter 5 is a revised and expanded version of an article published in *Hesperia*, and Chapter 6 has its origins in an article published in the *American Journal of Archaeology*, and I thank editors Jane Carter and Jennifer Sacher for allowing me to reprint parts of those works.

My friends and family have provided tremendous support and love throughout. Thank you to Clara Bosak-Schroeder, Carolyn Fish, Diana Garvin, Devin Grammon, Kate Petcosky-Kulkarni, Kathryn Langenfeld, Suzanne Lye, Lauren Pinchin, and Amy Pistone for always offering your help and making me laugh. My parents, Ralph and Stacey Mazurek, and godparents, Tom and Kim Fogarty, have listened to me talk about Isis and the Roman Empire more times than any person should ever have to suffer. Last but not least, my wonderful husband, Noah Eber-Schmid, read many drafts, provided moral support through revisions, and talked me through the depths of critical theory over many long walks with our dogs. His love, support, and enthusiasm have seen me through many of the most difficult parts of this project, and I am so grateful to share my life with him.

My final and greatest thanks go to Cavan Concannon and Sheila Dillon, without whom this book would have never been finished. Cavan has been a research partner, friend, and mentor to me for many years, and I look forward to many more years of working together to untangle the Mediterranean's rhizomes. Sheila was my dissertation adviser at Duke, and through the years has given me her advice, her thorough and thoughtful editing, her support, her wisdom, and, always, the truth. She has made me a better thinker, a better writer, a better scholar, and a better mentor. I am lucky to have worked with her and profoundly grateful for all she has done to support me.

This book is dedicated to all of the women who have gotten me here.

CHAPTER ONE

EGYPTIAN RELIGION AND THE PROBLEM OF GREEKNESS

ISIS IN GREECE: FRAMING THE QUESTION

When Greeks and Romans thought of Egypt, what images came to mind? In a floor mosaic from a house in Thysdrus in Africa Proconsularis, six provincial personifications are grouped around the central figure of Roma, producing an allegory of Rome's Mediterranean-wide power (Plate 1).[1] The province of Egypt wears a yellow short-sleeved chiton with a blue mantle tied diagonally across the chest, a variation on Isis' signature knotted mantle costume (Plate 2). Like Isis, she has her hair arranged in tight corkscrew curls or locks, and an Isiac *sistrum*, a rattle used to make music during Egyptian rites, leans against her left shoulder. What is remarkable here is the collapse between religious and ethnic iconography: Egypt is Isis, and her defining feature is her cult.

The eclectic combination of geographic personification, ethnic identity, and religious iconography in the mosaic is consistent with personifications of Egypt from elsewhere in the empire. In a frieze depicting Roman provinces on the Temple of the Deified Hadrian in Rome's Campus Martius,[2] Sapelli identifies one personification, which wears a crown with rosettes and a long, fringed mantle, as Egypt (Figure 1). Similarly, a relief depicting the *Ethnous Aigyption* ("the Egyptian people") from the Julio-Claudian Sebasteion at Aphrodisias also uses cult-specific dress and iconography to epitomize Egypt.[3]

These three personifications of Egypt rely on the assumption that religion could serve as an effective and legible symbol of Egypt writ large (Figure 2).[4]

1. Relief from the Hadrianeum in Rome depicting the province of Egypt, later Antonine period. Rome: Palazzo Massimo alle Terme inv. 428497. By concession of the Ministerio per i beni e le attività culturali e per il turismo – Museo Nazionale Romano.

Greek and Roman peoples would have encountered Egyptian migrants and diaspora communities, and in practice the boundaries between ethnicities are never as clear-cut as they are in theory. But the presence of Egyptians in Greece does not mean that exoticizing and imaginative Greco-Roman stereotypes about Egypt disappeared.[5] Cultural anxieties informed how people saw the world constructed in the edges and shadows of the Hellenistic and Roman Empires. Violence and tension often result from migration. Ethnic and cultural boundaries persist, even if only as human constructs. Proximity does not always breed tolerance or cultural competency, and in many cases the opposite is true.

Noticing these connections opens up a challenging question for the study of Greece, a region where nearly every city had a sanctuary to the Egyptian gods: What does it mean for a Greek under the Roman Empire to become a devotee of an Egyptian religion? Many scholars who have worked on Roman Greece, particularly those who have focused on the Second Sophistic,[6] have highlighted the resurging importance of Classical Greek culture in this period. In these works, which form the core of previous studies on Greekness in the

2. Statue of Isis in diagonally draped *diplax* costume, thought to be from Rome, Hadrianic period. London: British Museum inv. 1805,0703.11. © The Trustees of the British Museum.

Roman Empire, Greek ethnicity was founded on a collapsed temporality that brought an idealized and supposed pure version of the golden age of Athens into the Roman present.[7] Given the ethnic connotations attached to the Egyptian gods, why was the cult so popular and successful? More importantly, how did Egyptian religion impact the Greek devotees' understanding of their position in the Mediterranean world?

This book explores the worship of Egyptian deities in Roman-ruled Greece and the impacts of those cults on ideas of Greek ethnicity. Through their participation in these cults, I argue, Isis devotees constructed a variant form of Greekness, one that broke open Greece's purportedly closed cultural system and located Isis and Sarapis in Greek mythologies, places, and cultures.[8] I consider this new idea of Greekness dissonant but not discrete. That is, devotees probably considered themselves Greeks, even if their translations of Isis and Sarapis produced a variant form of Greek ethnicity embedded in the cults' ideas about Greece, Egypt, and cultural primacy in the Roman Empire.[9]

This form of Greekness was divided by other intersecting factors, including gender, origins, and economic status. Though dissonant, the group was probably large: nearly a quarter of known Athenian funerary reliefs from the Roman period depict at least one person in Isiac cult costume.[10] There is no way to know if this sample is representative, but it does suggest the existence of a large, vibrant community of Isis devotees.

Despite the cults' popularity, no study of Imperial-period Greece has incorporated Isiac difference or other forms of discrepant experience or intersectionality into their analyses.[11] This book offers a new perspective on the formation and expression of minority forms of ethnicity in the Roman Empire. In contrast with these earlier, inward-looking approaches to Greek ethnicity, I suggest that some Greeks also looked out to the rest of the Mediterranean world to define themselves. Through a careful interdisciplinary study of Isiac cult, I challenge the notion of a singular Greekness in Roman Achaia and Macedonia by highlighting an understudied group that inflected its version of Greek ethnicity with foreign practices and ideas. The wealth of epigraphic, literary, artistic, and archaeological evidence associated with the cults in Greece allows for a fine-grained investigation of how local and regional communities adapted and remade globalizing phenomena.

My approach is grounded in the idea that identities are not monolithic or static but rather form over time and rely on continual processes of self-fashioning and self-location to produce ethnic forms of self-understanding. I organize my discussion around key concepts derived from Brubaker's critiques of ethnicity and identity. In his *Ethnicity without Groups* (2004), Brubaker advocates an approach founded on processes of identification that he calls group-making, self-understanding, self-fashioning, and self-location. These concepts are defined more fully at the end of this chapter and in Chapters 2, 4, 5, and 6, where they are applied to the analysis of case studies, but they are inherently interrelated and contribute jointly to the production of identity and, I argue, to the impact on the textual and material products that result from these communities.

Within the discipline of Isiac studies, excellent studies of Egyptianizing material culture from Italy have appeared, but comparable studies of Greece and other provinces have been largely overlooked.[12] Recent work by Versluys, Swetnam-Burland, Barrett, and Mol has brought more holistic and theoretical approaches to the study of Egyptianizing material culture in Italy, raising questions about the cults' relationships to globalization, power, viewership, and geography.[13] This innovative research has advanced the discipline by integrating the subject of Isiac cults into more prominent dialogues concerning imperialism and cultural change in the disciplines of Roman archaeology and history. But this focus on Italy leaves open the question of how the Egyptian cults interacted with provincial identities and experiences. By looking at Greek material produced under the Roman Empire, my work directs attention to a new geographic area: the provinces.[14]

Though my focus is material culture from religious contexts, particularly sculpture and architecture, this is not a work of religious history. Rather, this book is a work of materially oriented ethnic history: it examines the ways in which cultural and religious changes impacted traditional narratives of Greekness, and how material and textual objects intervened in these shifts. I work from the assumption that objects play an active and constitutive role in culture's formation and change – that objects have the power to affect human ideas and behavior.[15] My interpretations of material culture, however, require a careful study of the epigraphic and literary evidence. For this reason, the first half of the book focuses on texts related to Isaic cults, as they are critical for establishing the circular and dynamic ways in which, I argue, devotees would have understood and used the objects under discussion in the later chapters.

In terms of geography, I focus on the provinces of Achaia and Macedonia, but I also engage with evidence from the Aegean and Mediterranean islands, particularly with the sanctuaries, inscriptions, and sculptures of Kos, Crete, and Rhodes (Figure 3). My decision to omit Asia Minor reflects my opinion

3. Map of Greece. Ancient World Mapping Center © 2022 (awmc.unc.edu). Used by permission.

that the region's long and close political connections with Egypt, dating back well into the Bronze Age, may have resulted in a different kind of familiarity with and understanding of Egyptian religion and culture. I expect that the history of Asia Minor's understanding of Greekness in the Roman Empire, as complicated by Isiac cult and local identities fashioned at the city and provincial levels, merits its own study.

In order to construct a narrative that is as textured as possible, I include material from the Hellenistic period through the 3rd century CE. Most examples date to the 1st century through the late 2nd century CE, when the cults were at their height. Wherever possible, I have privileged material with archaeological context over better-known objects. In describing the sanctuaries, I retain the original scholarly nomenclature of the sites, which depends on the language used in early 20th-century academic publications. Consequently, French-excavated Delos has a Sarapieion while German- and Greek-studied Thessaloniki has a Sarapeum.

I focus primarily on material excavated in sanctuaries in order to ensure a heightened focus on the intersection of religion and culture. The funerary portraits that are the subject of Chapter 5 are the exception, but they, I argue, depict the subject in cultic dress connected to specific rituals and consequently emphasize a religious identity. Determining whether an object is religious or not is a difficult task,[16] and I work from the assumption that most monumental architecture and sculpture from a sanctuary site are at least partly religious in nature. This is not to draw a sharp line between the world of cult and the rest of human experience. Recent work by Swetnam-Burland, Mol, and Pearson highlights the fact that not all Egyptianizing material culture is connected with the cult,[17] but my view of the ancient world relies, in part, on the assumption that cult and other aspects of daily life are inseparable.[18] Objects used for ritual could have more prosaic uses in other spatial or even temporal contexts. Ritual activities have an impact on devotees' view of the world around them while also informing their use of Egyptianizing iconography and symbols.

Instead of treating cultural entities like Greekness, Romanness, and Egyptianness as bounded groups whose meanings persist over the long term, I argue that Greek devotees of Isis, through their participation in Egyptian cult, constructed a transcultural form of Greekness that met the challenges of an increasingly connected Roman Empire.[19] I will use the term "Greek" to refer to a commonly held cultural ideal to which a person living in the provinces of Achaia and Macedonia under the Roman Empire could reasonably ascribe. This term is not meant to obscure the existence of migrants and others who might identify with different ethnicities, but to describe those who have chosen, consciously or unconsciously, to participate in the practices of Greekness.[20] I use this term not absolutely, for I do not believe there existed a single, stable, reified group of Greeks. Rather, I keep the term for ease of expression, and ask the reader to grant me this shorthand.

SETTING THE SCENE: GREECE UNDER ROMAN RULE

The period under discussion is one in which Roman Imperial power impacted day-to-day life in unpredictable and sporadic ways.[21] Roman power first appeared in the region in the 3rd century BCE, and the intensification of Roman control in the 1st century BCE reshaped Greek identity profoundly. Throughout the Hellenistic/Republican period, Greece was a battleground on which Roman troops fought their wars. As their control increased, Roman administrators plundered Greece's artistic and cultural wealth and left cities like Corinth and Athens in disrepair. During the reign of Augustus, tensions flared into small, sporadic rebellions. At the same time, Roman administrators began to use the language of continuity and memory, often expressed through material culture, to build a new narrative of Roman rule as the logical outcome of the Greek past. But Greek communities had agency in the construction of these memories as well. Local communities could come up with their own framing narratives about Roman institutions, power, and people and their relationships with Greek culture and history. As I argue throughout this book, those narratives most often centered Greek culture, ranking it above other provinces in cultural value.

As a corrective to the often halcyon discussions of Roman control in Achaia and Macedonia, in this work I highlight aspects of violence, power, and domination in Greece's colonial experience. Other histories might minimize this violence,[22] but it is important to my argument to place Isiac cults in this context of conquest and foreign rule. While Greece probably had an easier transition to Roman rule than many other provinces, the violence inherent in Roman colonization should not be overlooked.

As early as the 3rd century BCE, the Mithridatic, Syrian, Macedonian, and Achaean Wars placed Roman soldiers in Greece intermittently and resulted in Rome's conquest of Greece. The brutality of these conflicts, sporadic though they were, had major consequences for particular communities. For example, during the Fourth Macedonian War, Corinth sided with Philip VI, the pretender to the Macedonian throne.[23] Strabo disparagingly describes Corinthian conduct in the war, claiming that the city's inhabitants threw mud at passing Roman envoys. Perhaps as a consequence of such behavior, the Roman general Lucius Mummius razed the city of Corinth in 146 BCE and subsequently bestowed the land upon the Sikyonians.[24] Corinth's famous paintings were destroyed, its monumental inscriptions were smashed, and its men were killed.[25] Cicero visited the city sometime between 79 and 77 BCE and described the Corinthians as living among the ruins of their once great city.[26] James demonstrates that after many public buildings in the city, including the North Stoa and the theater, were damaged, along with several public inscriptions, a small, loosely organized community of around 500–1,000 people remained in Corinth during the period between the sack and 44 BCE, when Julius Caesar refounded the city as a Roman colony.[27]

Similarly, Athens suffered a devastating sack at the hands of Sulla, and throughout the 1st century BCE suffered repeated ravages at the hands of Roman administrators. Verres removed gold from the Parthenon, L. Calpurnius Piso stole more treasures, and the damage from this constant pillaging by Republican officials was not adequately remedied until the end of the reign of Augustus.[28] Elsewhere during the Republican period, Rome intervened in interstate and even some minor intrastate affairs, including the matter of Athenian control over private sanctuaries on Delos, which suggests that Roman rule could extend to day-to-day operations within the Aegean.[29] This control was scattered and disorganized, however, and Greek cities continued to support Rome's dissidents and rivals, including Brutus and Marc Antony, during the civil wars at the end of the Republic.[30] During these wars, many battles were fought on Greek soil, including the Battle of Pharsalus in 48 BCE, the Battle of Philippi in 42 BCE, and the Battle of Actium in 31 BCE. These conflicts would have brought soldiers and bloodshed into the Greek countryside and damaged nearby cities and farms.

During the Imperial period, the Roman army maintained a small but mobile presence in Greece. The Legio IV Macedonia was based in the province of Macedonia during Augustus' reign, though it often traveled to the west to aid with Imperial campaigns. Many *coloniae* filled with veterans or Italian migrants were established in important cities like Corinth, Patras, and Dion, and these new arrivals often supplanted Greek elite families in political hierarchies.[31] Troops were stationed in Macedonia intermittently throughout the Julio-Claudian and Flavian periods, but the epigraphic evidence confirms that the Cohors I Flavia Bessorum was stationed in Macedonia sometime in ca. 100–120 CE. More troops were stationed there during Marcus Aurelius' war with the Costoboci, which must have signaled to later emperors that it was necessary to station at least two auxiliary cohorts in the province to protect the Via Egnatia.[32]

Even without a permanent base in Attica, the Roman army was still a visible part of life. Many soldiers appear in Roman-period Athenian inscriptions, which attests to frequent troop movements through the port.[33] Roman military and administrative control coincides with other cultural interventions in the region that shifted the balance of local power. Agrippa and Augustus organized a Panhellenic assembly and granted the majority of votes to Nikopolis, a city Augustus founded to commemorate his victory over Marc Antony and Cleopatra. This new institution shifted the intraregional power balance away from Thessaly, its historical and symbolic center, placing it instead in the hands of a new city filled with migrants.[34]

Throughout the late Julio-Claudian and the Flavian periods, emperors and wealthy elites continued to visit Greece and dedicate buildings and sculptures.

Many of their artistic and architectural activities reveal a desire to rewrite historical and material narratives to introduce Roman rule at earlier periods of Greek history. Caligula was said to have taken the Phidian statue of Zeus from Olympia for reuse in a new cult dedicated to himself at Rome,[35] and Nero famously inscribed his name on the Parthenon and caused all of the Panhellenic festivals to be held in the same year.[36]

These interventions were part of a broader pattern of reinventing the Greek past to suit contemporary needs.[37] Many monuments were reconstructed to strengthen Roman claims to membership in local Greek communities. Shear has identified a series of sixteen Classical and Hellenistic bronze portrait statues from the Athenian Akropolis that were refashioned to depict Roman consuls and elites, and Platt has identified two more from Oropos that were rededicated as Appius Claudius Pulcher and Marcus Agrippa.[38] These monuments are early examples of a revisionist cultural strategy used by Roman elites and emperors in the city throughout the Imperial period. Among the Athenian statue bases, seven had the name of the Classical-era subject erased, and nine contain a dedication to a Roman carved underneath or alongside the original Classical inscription, constructing an analogy between the two subjects.[39] The monuments were selected for their artists' signatures, including those of famous Classical sculptors like Praxiteles and Kritios and Nesiotes, which placed the monuments at an early date and established epigraphic connections to prominent 5th- and 4th-century BCE Athenians like Hegelochos, a veteran of the Persian Wars.[40] These statues, then, offered their Roman subjects an opportunity to insert themselves into earlier historical narratives and to claim equivalence with the Greek heroes whose portraits remained on the statue bases.

This retrospective approach became especially useful during the early Imperial period, when much of the city needed repairs after Sulla's sack and the neglect of the Late Republican era. Toward the end of his reign, Augustus, with Marcus Agrippa, rebuilt Athens in historically significant areas. In the Agora, they dedicated several new temples atop old sanctuaries, often bringing in Classical architectural elements from sites in the Attic countryside, enriching Athens while leaving the rest of Attica depleted.[41] Though earlier scholars saw these monuments as an infilling effort aimed at curtailing Athenian democracy, more recent work has documented the continuity between these new Roman monuments and the temples that preceded them.[42] These monuments, then, glossed over the history of Roman conquest and violence; instead, they support the argument that Romans played a constructive role in the creation of these touchstones of the Athenian landscape.

Some revisionist monuments, however, broke with the past entirely. Among the most intrusive was a monument to Augustus and Roma erected on the Akropolis. This small monopteral temple was probably dedicated by an elite Greek man from Marathon. It stood just a few meters to the east of and directly in line with the Parthenon's main entrance.⁴³ The dedication of this temple, one of the first dedicated to Augustus, might have been unpopular because of Augustus' punitive actions against the city early in his reign.⁴⁴ Scholars have compared the somewhat unusual monopteral design with representations of an unexecuted temple at Rome that would have commemorated Augustus' victory over the Parthians.⁴⁵ The effect of these monuments is thus twofold. It set Augustus and Rome among the city's most venerated Classical cults in the city and served as a constant reminder of Rome's conquest and control over the city.

Though the evidence suggests that local elites adapted quickly to Roman rule, these material interventions were remarkable enough to provoke occasional small acts of resistance.⁴⁶ In an evocative passage from the 2nd–3rd century CE historian Cassius Dio (54.7.2–4), a statue of Athena on the Akropolis responds to Augustus' decision to free Aegina from Athenian control in 22/21 BCE by turning to the west and spitting blood.⁴⁷ The passage clearly refers to Athena's displeasure at Roman colonial control, and by extension that of Athens – but the act of spitting blood suggests a grave and perhaps even a mortal injury. Hoff interprets Dio's account literally and suggests that the Athenians, who were angry at the loss of territory and tax revenue, moved the image and defaced it in protest.⁴⁸ Given the long history of active statues in Greek literature and thought, I argue that the passage is metaphorical and alludes to a conquered and weakened Athens.⁴⁹ As the residents of a city that was the site of repeated warfare throughout the 1st century BCE and the victims of restrictive Augustan regulation, many Athenians may have seen themselves as battered and broken, just like Athena's statue.

As Roman power over Greece solidified, such material narratives of historical continuity and the Romanness of the Greek past intensified. Elites and intellectuals in the Antonine period cultivated the definition of the boundaries of Greekness at both the institutional and individual levels. During his reign, the emperor Hadrian devoted special attention to Athens and invested in building and political projects that integrated the city's Classical past with the ideologies of the Roman present, including an arch that represented him as a founder of Athens by comparing him to the mythological hero Theseus (Figure 4).⁵⁰ Hadrian's Arch follows contemporary styles of monumental architecture in Greece and Asia Minor and features a theatral façade, which must have held at least three portrait statues above a single-bay arch. A mirrored pair of inscriptions, one on either side, divided Athens in two. On the western face of his arch, Hadrian inscribed: "This is the city of Hadrian, and not of Theseus." On the eastern side: "This is Athens, the ancient city of Theseus."⁵¹ The pairing of Hadrian and Theseus creates an equivalence between the two. More importantly, it suggests that Hadrian belongs among

4. The Arch of Hadrian at Athens, dedicated 131–132 CE. Photo: Carole Raddato (via Creative Commons license). © Hellenic Ministry of Culture & Sports/Archaeological Receipts Fund.

the mythological founders and heroes that lived long ago – either that he is one of them or that he has brought their legacy into the 2nd century CE.

Hadrian's Arch was built to accompany one of the emperor's most impressive building projects in the eastern Mediterranean: the completion of the colossal Temple of Olympian Zeus, located to the west of the city's Classical core. In 131/132, Hadrian selected this sanctuary, which contained bronze statues of *apoikia* (colonies), as the seat of a new political and cultural

5. Temple of Olympian Zeus at Athens, dedicated 131–132 CE. Photo: Carole Raddato (via Creative Commons license). © Hellenic Ministry of Culture & Sports/Archaeological Receipts Fund.

organization, the Panhellenion (Figure 5). Setting Athens as the center of the Panhellenion (in lieu of larger and more prominent cities like Alexandria or Ephesus) highlighted Achaia's new position as the home of Greekness and Greek culture.[52] Though its precise purpose is not clear, the Panhellenion was a group of cities that could claim membership in the Greek world and in Greek ethnicity.[53] Membership conferred significant symbolic, political, and cultural benefits from the Roman rulers, which led many cities in the east to develop new myths and histories in arguing for their inclusion.[54]

As an institution, then, the Panhellenion tasked itself with the process of determining who "counted" as a Greek. Most cities outside of mainland Greece argued for inclusion based on their relationship with a Greek *metropolis*, the majority of which were in Achaia, Crete-and-Kyrene, and Asia, by claiming mytho-historical bonds from the distant past.[55] But there were other ways into the Panhellenion. Greek ethnicity could be claimed, so long as these arguments relied on familiar people, places, and characters. For example, Aizanoi in Phrygia claimed Azan, son of Arcas, as its founder, and through Arcas, a relationship with the Arcadians, who claimed that Elatus, another son of Arcas, was the representative of the Lapiths in Thessaly.[56] Through this torturous mythology Aizanoi could claim a relationship with the Thessalians, one of the oldest and most significant groups in early constructions of Greekness.[57] These arguments of shared blood based on colonial foundations of the distant past rely on the assumption that the Greekness of these cities had persisted into the Roman present, a key aspect of Greekness in the High Empire.

The building that housed the Panhellenion, however, might also represent resistance to Roman hegemony. Whitmarsh argues that we can interpret Pausanias' (1.18.6) description of the temple's art and architecture as instances of localism, which he categorizes as a type of opposition to Roman imperialism. Pausanias is careful to note that the statues of the *apoikia*, or colonies, are dedicated by the Greek cities themselves, not by Hadrian or the Roman Imperial administration. Pausanias' use of the word "colonies" may have been intentionally vague, in an allusion to a secondary local meaning, perhaps to earlier forms of Athenian colonization as well as Rome's rule over Greece in the 2nd century CE.[58] Whitmarsh thus reinforces Elsner in reading Pausanias' text as a deliberate framing of Greece. Rather than seeing Pausanias as a mere chronicler, Elsner argues that Pausanias transforms "landscape into discourse."[59] Viewed in this light, the Temple of Olympian Zeus is a house built by and for Greek people and purposes that simultaneously housed a Roman institution centered on the concept of idealized Greekness.

VIEWERSHIP, OBJECTS, AND THE SEARCH FOR ETHNICITY

How, then, can we untangle the threads that composed the Greekness of Isis devotees in the Roman Empire? Greeks in the Roman period certainly thought of themselves as an ethnic group, and few would have thought of Greekness otherwise.[60] While some have suggested that we remove ethnicity from the discussion of Egyptian religion altogether,[61] this perspective flattens our understanding of the influence of cults on other aspects of life. Ethnicity in antiquity is fundamentally a question about how origins are intertwined with a sense of self and belonging. When we ask questions about ethnicity, we are trying to understand how selves were formed and perceived in the ancient world. These questions allow us to interrogate who is represented by a work of art, and to consider how and when certain types of communal belongings are communicated.[62] Isiac devotees belonged to a community identified with a set of deities grounded in Egypt as a place and culture, and devotees expended tremendous effort to negotiate these geographic and cultural conflicts.

In this section and the next, I trace out the twin methodological approaches I have employed throughout the book. The first deals with ethnicity and its relationships with texts and objects. In this book, I define ethnicity as a social group that creates and enforces a boundary based on criteria agreed upon by those who identify with the group (usually cultural praxis, material culture, descent, and/or shared geography, in varying combinations) and often, but not always, recognized by those outside the group. Ethnicities are most evident in places and times of contact, exchange, and conflict. In most cases, there is an actual or putative shared homeland, and the idea and memory of that homeland binds members together even when they are elsewhere. Most importantly, ethnicity can compel actions, whether through social pressure, unifying ideas or beliefs, or shared understandings of history or mythology.

My definition is grounded in earlier work on Greek ethnicity, particularly the work of Hall. Hall defined ethnicity as: (1) a social grouping; (2) constructed through the manipulation of genetic, linguistic, religious, or cultural features to form ascriptive boundaries; and (3) associated with a specific territory and a shared myth of descent, which may be putative and must be defined through consensus.[63] This definition is useful but speaks more clearly to the concerns of ethnicity in the Classical period. Vlassopoulos rightly argues that ethnicity is better ascribed to minority groups than to hegemonic ones and thus criticizes the use of the term for the study of normative Greekness in Greece.[64] Morgan prefers a more generalized definition of ethnicity that focuses on "the way in which social groups consciously choose to assert their identity and to define and constitute themselves in relation to others in any given set of circumstances."[65] While Morgan's definition describes some general features of ethnicity, it could also describe any kind of identity that motivates collective action.[66]

Among scholars of ancient ethnicities, there has been considerable debate about the role of objects in creating, delineating, and expressing ethnicity. Even more controversial is the issue of whether we can reconstruct ethnic identity from archaeological evidence.[67] Archaeologists are able to group finds into formal types, to recognize styles, and to establish relative chronologies, but the significance of these categories is not always clear.[68] How, then, can we find ethnicity in objects? Some scholars have rejected the premise entirely, claiming that material culture cannot provide insights into the internalized ideas and feelings that produce ethnic groups.[69] But this critique ignores the agency of material culture. Instead of treating objects as passive reflectors of ideologies, more recent work in Roman archaeology and art history has recognized the constitutive role that objects play in the creation of identity and culture.[70] Objects motivate human responses, communicate inference and interpretation, and direct our eyes and motion. Material culture constructs distinctions between communities and provides a means for humans to express their understanding of themselves and their world to others, particularly in contexts where multiple ethnic groups are present.[71] My view of material agency, however, focuses on the dynamic interplay between human and object.[72] Both humans and objects have agency in the construction of ethnicity and culture, and this book focuses on the ways in which devotees exploit, understand, employ, and react to material culture. By treating material culture as an active part of the process of creating, defining, and expressing group belonging and meaning, we can gain access to some of the interior and exterior processes and experiences of Greek ethnicity.

Traditionally, many archaeologists and art historians have preferred to call such distinctions "cultural identities" or "local identities."[73] Yet Brubaker has argued that there are so many different types of identity (cultural, social, political, ethnic, sexual, local, etc.), that the term itself has almost no intrinsic meaning.[74] Further, the terms cultural/local lower the stakes in understanding these meaningful forms of difference. Upon closer examination, much in what has been called "cultural identity" should be called ethnicity. In her studies of Archaic and early Classical Morgantina, Antonaccio demonstrates that indigenous Siculan-Geometric pottery types flourished alongside traditionally Greek material like Greek-inscribed coins, Doric and Ionian stone architecture, and, in later periods, red-figure pottery.[75] That is, these distinctive material cultures existed alongside each other, emphasizing the difference between the two and, in turn, creating what Antonaccio has called a new, hybrid material culture.[76] The objects expressed differences in foodways and storage in a context when indigenous Italic and colonizing Greek, creating what S. Jones might call an "objectification of cultural difference" that is the basis of her archaeology of ethnicity.[77] In Roman archaeology and art history, identity writ large has been a dominant heuristic for the study of Rome and its provinces, but Pitts argues that most scholarship uses identity as a stand-in for the problematic concept of Romanization,[78] and thus is subject to its main flaws: an emphasis on how *Romanitas* was exported to the provinces and how provincial communities received it.[79] More recent work has defined identity in ways that grant more agency to provincial peoples and focus on other forms of identity in the ancient world, including Greekness. For example, in her book on local identity in the Roman Empire, Revell embeds her definition of identity within a discussion of Romanization while describing identity as multiple, fluid, and situational, and focusing on how individuals responded to prevailing social structures.[80] The question she asks, then, means that nearly everything could be construed as Roman or not-Roman, creating a static binary between two poles that would exclude communities like the one under study.

If Egyptian cults stand at the intersection of Greekness and Egyptianness, how can we model ethnicity as something other than a static essentialist category? As a partial answer to this question, I argue that a more precise terminology could help us better assess how the inhabitants of the Roman provinces of Achaia and Macedonia defined their ethnic groups and subgroups. Instead of assessing identity as an independent concept, Brubaker proposes a more process-based vocabulary that highlights the choices that individuals and communities make in order to ascribe to certain categories and ethnicities. Several scholars of the ancient world, notably Geary, Rebillard, Andrade, and

Mattingly, have begun to adapt Brubaker's critiques of identity by treating identity formation as a dynamic and relational process, and recent work by Barrett applies Brubaker's work to the study of Egyptianizing wall painting at Pompeii.[81] By analyzing identity as a series of decisions manifested in texts and objects, these recent works have advanced the study of identity and ethnicity. Not all aspects of identity, especially those that stem from others' judgments, are choices, but individuals and groups have the power to decide how to respond to, express, and value identity.[82] More precise characterizations of the decision process might provide even clearer insights into the religious, cultural, and historical contingencies that informed the construction of Greekness under the Roman Empire.

This precision also requires a more careful consideration of the intersection of ethnicity with other aspects of human identity, including gender, geographic mobility, citizenship, socio-economic class, and religion. In this book, I have focused particularly on the intersections of ethnicity and religion, and elements of gender and class further inflect my account. Crenshaw coined the term intersectionality to explore the ways in which an individual's multiple identities inflect each other.[83] Intersectional frameworks demand that we replace essentialist identity categories with the recognition that no aspect of human identity can be understood on its own but must be studied in a holistic context. Most importantly, Crenshaw and other critical race feminist scholars have emphasized the power that intersectional identities offer individuals and communities.[84] It is impossible to recover these kinds of details for the ancient world, but we can trace some aspects of how Isis devotees felt about their cults by looking at what they invested in joining, belonging, and expressing their membership in these kinds of ethno-religious communities.

It is also critical that we look at these shifts as the products of globalization. Defined broadly, globalization is a series of processes by which localities and people become increasingly interconnected and interdependent. Globalized approaches rely on analyses of connectedness, unevenness, and asymmetry in order to describe and explain local experiences within Imperial contexts.[85] In a general study of ancient globalization, Jennings identified a list of processes that constitute globalizations: time-space compression, standardization, simultaneous homogeneity and heterogeneity, deterritorialization (the appearance of objects with geographic attachments outside of their home regions), unevenness, and the deeper embedding of local culture.[86] Many of these appear in the Roman context, but some of the more frequently studied processes include increasing connectivity, unequal responses, the translation and reinterpretation of globally available forms for local use, and the lessening of place-specific and culturally specific connections. The processes of identification that I use in this book, as defined briefly in the section "The Problem of Greekness," intersect with and respond to these globalizing phenomena.

Though my emphasis is on material culture, my approach is necessarily holistic. Ignoring texts in favor of solely archaeological or artistic evidence also produces flawed and incomplete readings. Texts offer directions on "where to look" in the material record to find evidence of ethnic ideology and practice.[87] Building on the work of scholars like Elsner, Platt, and Squire, I work from the assumption that reading texts, experiencing cultic rituals, and viewing art all informed how devotees understood Isiac cults.[88] None of these experiences, however, necessarily held primacy over the other, and over time a devotee or group of devotees might change their ideas and understandings of the cults as they read, saw, and experienced more. This approach recognizes that viewing art and other forms of material culture could intervene in devotees' understanding of rituals and cultic texts to produce layered, unstable readings of material culture.

As part of this approach, I bring together evidence from literature, inscriptions, sculpture, and architecture to address more holistically the intersections between cult, globalization, and ethnicity. From a textual perspective, Second Sophistic authors like Plutarch and Apuleius represent Isis and Sarapis as fulfilling functions previously held by canonical Greek divinities, contextualizing Egyptian religion within Greek philosophical and cultural paradigms that form the core of Greek antiquity. Similar themes also appear frequently in epigraphic hymns dedicated to Isis and Sarapis, which suggests that these texts developed through engagement with the cults' practices and ideas. In artistic media, Greek communities opted, in most cases, to depict Isis and Sarapis in Greek styles and Greek materials, constructing visual arguments for their enmeshment in the Greek pantheon. These representational decisions embedded Egyptian religion and its foreign associations firmly within Greek myth-history and ethnic ideals, producing a more transcultural and connected form of Greekness situated within the concerns of the Roman Mediterranean.

THE PROBLEM OF GREEKNESS

The second methodological issue concerns the definition of Greekness. Greekness has been defined repeatedly in previous scholarship, but there may have been more definitions available at a given time than has been assumed. Scholars have identified two main boundary criteria used in ancient periods: descent from Greeks, whether biological or mythological; and specific cultural actions like speaking Greek, participating in Greek religious activities or social institutions, or pursuing a Greek education. Traditionally, descent criteria have been associated with earlier historical periods, and cultural criteria have been associated with later periods. But a more careful study suggests that there was never a broad consensus about what made a Greek.[89] As early as the Classical period, there existed transregional forms of Greekness that prioritized cultural practices over descent.⁹⁰ It is true that cultural criteria were used more frequently in the Roman period, and the Roman Empire affected how people thought about Greekness.⁹¹ But these concerns also grew out of longstanding discussions about Greek ethnicity. Isiac cult would have added another layer of complexity to these already heated debates. The problem with Greekness, then, is that multiple definitions existed in competition at the same time as many people and institutions were policing the boundaries of this ethnicity.

The Beginnings

Earlier Iron Age and Archaic communities in the Greek *oikoumenē* had episodic and partial cultural, religious, and political group identities.⁹² Early writers like Homer, as well as Archaic and Classical historians like Herodotus, Thucydides, and Xenophon, use the terms *ethnos/ethnē*, but their meaning in these early periods is debated. While it is most often used to describe a form of political order that may be distinct from the *polis*, *ethnos/ethnē* might be used well into the Classical period to describe almost any kind of group, including women (Pind., *Ol.* 1.66), animals (bees in Hom., *Il.* 2.87), named groups of people like Lykians (*Il.* 12.330), or the dead (*Od.* 10.526). This textual evidence suggests that, rather than referring to a less organized political entity, the term originally did not have an inherently political or cultural meaning at all.⁹³

Hall makes a compelling case for dating the origin of Greekness as a broad ethnic identity to the period of the Persian Wars (499–478 BCE).⁹⁴ The broad military alliance that united against the Persian invasion produced a useful polarity, the barbarian, against which Greekness could be defined.⁹⁵ Hall's definition corresponds to a version of Greekness as follows: a social grouping of people that ascribes to the same sets of myths of common descent and kinship, and association with a specific territory and history. More importantly, that group is defined in opposition to something else; in this case, against Persianism. Even in this period of heightened Greekness, however, individuals and institutions contested the meaning of Greekness and where its boundaries would be drawn. During the early 5th century BCE, Herodotus tells us, the Macedonian king, Alexander I, attempted to enter the Panhellenic games at Olympia, but some of his competitors objected that he was not a Hellene. Though the Macedonians spoke a dialect of Greek and had much in common with their southern neighbors, their Greekness was a matter of some debate.⁹⁶ A group of judges that Hall identifies as the *hellanodikai* judged Alexander to be Greek based on the argument that the Macedonian royal family, the Argeadai, were descended from the Argives and from Herakles.⁹⁷ The ability to demonstrate sufficient knowledge of Greek myth-history, rather than a realistic claim to biological descent, was probably enough to convince the judges to allow the king to compete and claim Macedonia's membership in the Greek community.

Shortly thereafter, Greekness could also be defined in the second sense, as a set of practices. This shift occurs as Panhellenism rises in importance, offering new pathways to Greekness. In 380 BCE, the Athenian orator Isocrates circulated a text that offered a version of Greek identity based more on education and culture (*paideia*). In particular, he notes that the name Hellene refers not to descent or family (*genos*, *physis*) but to an attitude (*dianoia*) held by people who share in Greek culture (*paideusis*).[98] Isocrates' admittedly Athenocentric view of Greekness is not necessarily meant to lessen the divide between Greek and barbarian. Rather, Isocrates restricts Greekness to those who have been educated in the Athenian manner, turning education into a sort of ethnic initiation available only to a handful. Still, this definition reframes Greekness as a series of actions and experiences that produce a shared worldview.[99] Elsewhere, Isocrates also highlights the territorial dimension of Greekness, describing Athens as the sole *polis* in the entire region of Hellas (*Antid.* 299). Hall argues that Isocrates is here visualizing Greece as a "continuous geographic entity radiating out from Athens" that unifies all the disparate groups of Greece and places them in a single territory.[100]

Isocrates' work also speaks to the broadening perception that Greek culture could benefit all who participated.[101] In the *Panathenaikos*, Isocrates suggests that the various subgroups of Greeks are all of the same origin (90), even while arguing that Athens has a right and duty to reign supreme over them all. But this same origin refers to kinship models of ethnicity (*Panath.* 164, 200; *Ad Philippum* 108, 126; *Paneg.* 43), which indicates that Isocrates has not entirely abandoned descent as a key component of Greek ethnicity.[102] Similarly, in the Peloponnese, the newly freed Messenians created an ethnicity through narratives of descent from mythological heroes, particularly Herakles, and the establishment of new cults for gods like Asklepios. These new deities built a connection with the city's Spartan past while also preserving the Spartans as a group against which Messenian identity could be defined.[103] Even in this early period, then, both cultural and descent definitions of Greekness are in use.

Hellenistic Greekness: The Case of Ptolemaic Egypt

As more and more of Asia and Africa came under Macedonian rule, cultural definitions of Greekness came to the forefront and shifted ethnic identity to become a form of moral character. This shift suggests that ruling elites wanted to open the boundaries of Greekness and find new ways to integrate their subjects into new imperial projects. Migration and settlement also played an important role. Soldiers from Alexander's army, which included Macedonians and mercenaries from around the Mediterranean, settled in these conquered lands and founded new colonies and kingdoms that used Greek language and cultural norms.[104]

This book is about Greece, not Egypt, but it is worth pausing to explore how Greekness and Egyptianness were constructed in Egypt, where papyri provide more detailed evidence about how ethnic categories were formed in the Hellenistic period. Though Greek communities had long thrived in Egypt, their power had been limited prior to Alexander's conquest in 332 BCE, which likely accelerated an ongoing integration process.[105] As part of these changes, Ptolemaic bureaucrats strove to reify existing ethnic distinctions between Greeks and Egyptians into legal categories.[106] Egypt was reorganized around four cities (Alexandria, Ptolemais, Naukratis, and Paraetonion) that were either new foundations or home to large communities of Greek merchants or immigrants. Citizens of these *poleis*, often referred to as *Hellenes*, had many legal benefits, such as exemption from the poll tax, and de facto social benefits, such as access to elite cultural institutions like the *gymnasium* and *ephēbeia*.[107] Citizenship was determined by descent from citizen parents and membership in a *dēme*, identifiers that were often used in documentary papyri.[108] There, the ethnic term *Hellēne* was used more and more frequently to describe a person's identity and language, and an emphasis on Greek kinship and unity appeared in diplomatic, religious, and historical writing.[109] But people of Egyptian descent could gain citizenship and other ethnically named statuses in special circumstances, usually through military service, marriage, or civic benefaction.[110] These Egyptian elites appear frequently in the historical record, like Manetho, an Egyptian priest who served the first Ptolemaic kings and wrote several works in Greek, including a now-lost history of Egypt.

Outside of these four cities, individuals of Greek descent lived alongside Egyptians in villages or small cities that lacked political independence and consequently did not have access to the same benefits of citizenship.[111] Residents of these rural communities married across ethnic lines and often used multiple names and languages.[112] Those of Greek descent had some access to elite institutions like the *gymnasium* and could use these institutions to advance themselves. Despite the fact that these people were descended from Greek immigrants and spoke Greek, the Ptolemaic legal system often referred to them as Egyptians. This produced a legal situation in which some of those who identified as Greeks would not be seen as such by the state.[113]

This situation continued into the Roman period, when these distinctions were further reified by the intensification of legal administration. The Roman population of Egypt consisted of a small number of Roman citizens who migrated to Egypt, and some local elites and veterans to whom Rome granted citizenship. This meant that some people categorized as Romans in legal documents had Egyptian ancestry.[114] Roman administrators referred to all others as Egyptians because they were subject to Egyptian laws. This shift had a major impact on the day-to-day lives of people living in Roman Egypt. Marriage between Roman citizens and Egyptians was forbidden, and apart from the citizens of Alexandria, all "Egyptians" were subject to the poll tax. But in the capital of each *nome*, called a *metropolis*, a small group of elites paid a reduced rate, and members of the metropolitan *gymnasium* had similar privileges, particularly after the 1st century CE, when they were allowed to take up local civic and regional offices.[115] In turn, access to the *gymnasium* became more closely regulated, though it remained a voluntary institution.[116] These changes meant that elite status was no longer firmly tied to ethnic identity, weakening the importance of these terms even further.

A handful of people, however, retained the identity of *Hellēnes* in legal documents. In a letter of 55 CE, the Emperor Nero referred to 6,475 Hellenes in the Arsinoite *nome* and granted them special privileges.[117] In his study of the names of these 6,475, Bagnall notes that while the majority are Greek, they are not the same kinds of names that appear in mainland Greece. Instead, the majority have some connection to Egypt, such as Anoubion, Horion, or Sarapion, or could possibly refer to gods worshiped by both Egyptians and Greeks, including Herakleides or Apollonios.[118] Rowlandson takes this as evidence that these may have been people who also considered themselves Egyptian and who saw no conflict between Greekness and Egyptianness.[119] During the reign of Hadrian, the citizens of his new city, Antinoopolis, were called the *Neoi Hellēnes*, or New Greeks, though they were drawn from the Greek citizens of Ptolemais and the Arsinoite *nome* and thus had preexisting claims on Greekness.[120]

The cases of Hellenistic and Roman Egypt illustrate the constantly shifting boundaries of Greekness in the Hellenistic and Roman periods. By the Roman period, Greekness operated as a nebulous title used sporadically to refer to elite groups or people for whom exceptions to the rule would be made. Noting these changes, Vandorpe emphasizes the importance of distinguishing between state-defined categories, self-ascription, and ethnic labeling.[121] Individuals may not have had much control over how the state labeled them, and those labels may not have reflected the actual ways in which individuals understood themselves or their place in society. By reorienting away from external categories and toward more ascriptive actions, as I propose in the section "Chapter Outlines," we can gain a better understanding of the problems and nuances of Greekness.

Defining and Contesting Greekness in Roman Greece

While the meaning of Greekness was shifting in Roman Egypt, individuals in Achaia and Macedonia also began to police Greekness on a case-by-case basis. These debates make it clear that the precise boundaries of Greece and Greek ethnicity were of great concern. For many, Greece was a place that lived in the past.[122] Many of the best known and best studied Greek texts from this period, particularly in the 2nd century CE, adopted a retrospective version of Greekness, one in which Greeks were not subjugated by foreign rulers but were rather the inheritors of a venerated Classical tradition. This perspective gave Greece, and Athens in particular, status within the empire. Aelius Aristides, whose *Panathenaic Oration* claims that Greece is at the center of the whole world,[123] was not alone in his view that Greece was the center of the Mediterranean, but its power was primarily cultural. Political power was still concentrated in Rome, and Greek ports were less important than those in Sicily, Gaul, and North Africa. Though the majority of texts describe Greekness as a set of practices and processes, kinship and descent would never fully disappear as criteria for Greek ethnicity.[124] This tension produced an environment deeply concerned about Greekness: what it was, where its boundaries were, who counted as a Greek, who did not count – and what Greekness meant.

By the 1st century BCE, the Greek-speaking literary critic Dionysius of Halicarnassus defined Greekness (*to hellēnikon*) as speaking the Greek language, having a Greek way of life, acknowledging the same gods, and having reasonable laws (1.89.4). But Greekness had also expanded beyond its original geographic and genetic confines. Several writers describe personal or cultural attributes that define Greekness, including political knowledge, care for the arts, and an understanding of how to live (Strabo 2.5.26), and a good education and refined behavior (Cass. Dio 36.24, 26, 43; Philostr., *VA* 1.16; Plut., *Quomodo adul.* 9–30).[125] Similarly, Dio Chrysostomus (*Or.* 44.10; *To Prusia*) encourages the Prusians to make their city Greek by educating their children well and turning their energies and abilities to greater and finer things, a command that connects Greekness with the higher orders of human thought and action. Turning from the cultural to the territorial, the itinerant Apollonius of Tyre argues that Greece is everywhere for the wise man (Philostr., *VA* 1.35). Apollonius' approach gestures toward a global form of Greekness not tied to Greece's geography but accessible to all worthy men in any place and time.

In many texts, Greekness is linked with *paideia*, or "education," and students and teachers were often called Greeks irrespective of their origins. In a passage from the *Lives of the Sophists*, one sophist agrees to come with his "Greeks" (*VS* 571), a term that Whitmarsh and others argue refers generally to students.[126] This process of teaching and learning asks the student to replicate the values and practices of the teacher and transforms young men into adults that participate in established social and cultural hierarchies.[127] Possessing *paideia* meant that someone had mastered the canon of Greek literature and had learned a certain mode of behavior, "certain cognitive, ritual, ethical, and/or professional standards" that might help him feel a new sense of kinship with Greekness.[128] In this way, *paideia* created a sense of difference between Greek and other cultures and juxtaposed Greekness to all other forms of ethnicity.[129] Most importantly, *paideia* came to belong to Greece alone. Romans could not obtain this education in masculinity, elitism, and Greekness in Italy, but needed to go to Athens and other Greek intellectual centers to obtain it.[130] *Paideia*, then, offered outsiders a way to become Greek, to access the status and antiquity that Greekness might confer.[131] This emphasis on actions and becoming produced a constantly shifting dialectic in which Greekness' limits were repeatedly redefined.

Even as Greekness expanded geographically, many tried to control the supposed purity of Greek ethnicity. In Plutarch's *On the Education of Children*, he warns that enslaved companions of children must be fluent Greek speakers in order to keep Greek children from "being colored by" their base barbarian-ness.[132] Whitmarsh makes much of the verb *sunanachrēnnumenoi* in this passage, which derives from the word for color (*chrēma*). This term can refer both to the idea of influence and skin color, which links concerns about language with anxieties about skin color and racial purity.[133]

The debates I have outlined so far in this chapter have focused on external identifications; that is, how an individual was identified by others. As I discuss in Chapters 2 and 5, insiders and outsiders evaluated group membership based on the perceived correctness of an individual's performance of ethnic identity as a way to maintain boundaries.[134] But equally important is the self-perception of the individual, and the evidence suggests that a wide variety of people ascribed to Greekness, perhaps to gain access to the cultural prestige bestowed by Greekness.[135]

Favorinus, a rhetorician from Arelate in Gaul Narbonensis who became one of the leading figures of the Second Sophistic, described himself as fluent in the thought, manners, and dress of Greek culture.[136] The lengths to which he must go to claim that Greekness, however, suggest that his status was not secure. In his *Corinthian Oration*, Favorinus complains that the city has taken down his portrait statue; he goes on to use an array of local mythological knowledge to demonstrate his superior claims to Greekness and to argue for the image's restoration. He begins with the story of Arion and the dolphin and a visit from Solon and the sage Periander as an introduction to his own return to the city and his knowledge of local mythology (2–7). He further connects his image with allusions to Jason and the Argonauts, and Daedalus' craftsmanship; and ultimately credits the Corinthians with the Greek victory at Salamis during the Persian Wars (8–19). His ultimate argument for its restitution is his own Greekness, stating that by adopting Greek manners he has exceeded the best of the Greeks, who are increasingly turning toward Roman ways (25). His statue must be returned to its proper place so that he might serve as an

6. Portrait of a man in chiton and himation, Antonine period. Athens: Agora Museum inv. S 936. Photo: American School of Classical Studies at Athens: Agora Excavations.

exemplar of Greekness for others, demonstrating that culture is no less worthy than birth as a way to access Greekness (26–27).[137]

We should not ignore what Favorinus lost. In his biography of Favorinus (*V S* 489), Philostratus never lets the reader forget that Favorinus was born a Gaul and lived as a Greek. The statue would have been part of Favorinus' claim on the Greekness that he fought so hard to protect. It is likely that the now-lost image depicted the orator in the Greek-style chiton and himation used to depict intellectuals in Roman Greece (Figure 6).[138] Depicting himself in this costume would have been key to Favorinus' claim of Greek ethnicity. Dio notes the importance of dress and hairstyle and argues that these are two of the factors that marked out a true Hellene.[139] As a permanent reminder set up in front of Corinth's library, the statue reified his status as a Greek intellectual deserving of high public honors, as a participant in the social economies of honor, civic participation, and belonging that took form in Greek honorific portraiture.[140] Its loss made his position within these networks more tenuous.

As Favorinus' experience shows, there existed degrees of Greekness and several ways to claim it. A man might see himself as a Greek, but that did not mean that others had to agree. An individual could excel in Greekness and compete with others to highlight their connection and familiarity with Greek culture, but

Greekness could also be lost through improper behavior or through speaking mixed or improper forms of Greek.[141]

Greekness was also historically contingent. The ways in which Romans and those from around the Mediterranean laid claim to it changed depending on institutional, political, cultural, and social norms. Yet what stayed the same were the methods that cities and individuals used to claim membership in this community: engagement with Greek culture through processes of culture and *paideia* and the renegotiation of deep history, including myth-history, to construct or support kinship relationships. The focus on retrospective and mythological arguments of Greek greatness intersected with the demands of Imperial institutions like the Panhellenion but also with more subtle pressures like the popularity of Classical Athenian literature and philosophy among Roman elites and emperors. But this view of Greekness is only one option, and I argue that other Greeknesses existed alongside the small cadre of elite intellectuals who comprised the Second Sophistic.[142] Scholarly emphasis has been placed on a peaceful and largely intellectual dialectic between conceptions of Greekness and Romanness, past and present. These ancient authors, upon whom modern scholarship has focused for the last twenty years, form a small and interconnected circle. Philostratus' biographies name only a handful of men across multiple generations.[143] What about everyone else?

CHAPTER OUTLINES

This book offers another perspective on Greekness – focused on devotees of the Egyptian cults, a minority group who lived, worked, and potentially even worshiped alongside these sophists and other Greeks. In the chapters to follow, I explore a series of historically and socially contingent choices made about the boundaries and sense of belonging used to define a concept of Greekness for a limited community. I reject the premise that Greeks in the Roman Empire participated only nominally in other cultures and ethnic concepts, as has been suggested for Romanness,[144] but argue instead that certain actions, like joining a cult, had ethnic implications that Greeks resolved through several identification mechanisms. The form of ethnicity I reconstruct applies to those who involved themselves in Egyptian religion but may offer a new way to consider other minority perspectives on ethnicity in the ancient world.

Before determining how Isiac communities reckoned with their ethnicity, we must first determine that Isiac communities existed and that they were meaningful to their members. Relying on epigraphic and literary evidence, I argue in Chapter 2 that several aspects of cult practice, including day-to-day administrative functions, internal private associations, and opportunities to differentiate from Greek society as a whole, aimed at constructing a sense of groupness for devotees. Processes of group-making reify social boundaries and call into being the idea of a unified community defined by common ideals, experiences, and actions. Over time, groups must continually create their meaning and reinforce their sense of belonging through continued activity.[145] The idea of group-making that frames Chapter 2 recognizes that Isiac communities relied on continual practice and repeated social action to stay meaningful. This identification also operated on multiple levels. At a local level, Isiac identity could intersect with other identifiers like family to strengthen devotees' ties to the cult. At a regional level, the cults' migration history provided ritual and social links that contributed to a sense that individual communities belonged to a larger group of Greek Isis devotees.

Self-understanding is a set of internal processes and decisions that structures a sense of belonging within a community. If, as Hall has argued, ethnicity is constructed by a group that ascribes to a shared myth of common belonging that provides a boundary, self-understanding describes the ideas that underwrite these myths. It describes the ways in which ideas and systems of belief informed how communities gave themselves shape and meaning, and how they defined themselves in opposition to other groups and among their members.[146] In turn, these definitions shaped the decisions people made and how outsiders perceived the group. I reconstruct Isiac self-understanding in Chapters 3 and 4 by exploring the dynamic interrelationships produced by devotees in reading and hearing cultic texts and experiencing cult images. Chapter 3 focuses on texts. Through a careful rereading of Isiac epigraphic hymns, I argue that Egyptian religion in Greece relied on a culturally ambivalent version of Isis embedded in the deep Greek past. The Greek Isis comes from an imagined Egypt founded in experimentation and wonder, crosses boundaries, overlaps mythologically and cosmologically with Greek goddesses like Demeter and Athena, and appears frequently in Greece. Her visits to Greece, however, are couched in broader narratives of the cult's history of travel and assimilation with Greek deities. Though the cults never create a shared sense of devotees' origins, these new myths about the descent of Isis and Sarapis and their familial bonds stand in for the biological groupness essential to Hall's definition of Greek ethnicity. I argue that these texts construct a pancultural Isis who is, paradoxically, Greek at her very core.

Chapter 4 turns to statues of Isis and Sarapis. I consider questions of style and materiality to examine how Isis and Sarapis were represented sculpturally in Greek cult centers. Focusing on the Sarapeum at Thessaloniki, I combine epigraphic and sculptural evidence to suggest that devotees preferred cult images that embedded Isis and Sarapis in Greek religious and artistic paradigms. When seen alongside the hymns, I argue, Greek-style statues of Isis both mediate her Egyptianness and promote cult-specific interpretations of other images. That is, Greek devotees might begin to see statues of cognate deities like Aphrodite, Demeter, or Athena as avatars of Isis. Materiality also contributes to this reading. Though many sanctuaries in Italy and throughout the empire held large numbers of imported cult objects and sculptures, current archaeological evidence suggests that most Greek sanctuaries might have contained few or none. The stark contrast gestures toward a different set of priorities. I demonstrate that Greek devotees had a marked preference instead for images of Isis and Sarapis carved in Greek styles and materials. Isis is here embodied as a Greek version of herself. These images, I hypothesize, used style as a method for visualizing an Egyptian goddess as part of Greece's heritage. I conclude with a discussion of the materiality of these statues and argue that the marble itself further participates in a Greek desire to ground Isis and Sarapis in Greece. Greek materials and styles, then, function as the prism through which Isiac universalism functioned.

In Chapter 5, I consider how Isis devotees fashioned themselves through sculpted portraits displayed in the cemeteries of Roman Athens. Self-fashioning describes the ways in which self-understandings produce material and conceptual signifiers of membership. The process is simultaneously inward and outward looking and is fundamentally tied to the experience and adornment of the body. By analyzing funerary depictions of Isiac men and women in cultic costumes, I demonstrate that these images allow devotees to incorporate aspects of alterity and foreignness into normative modes of Greek portraiture. As communities defined their boundaries, certain images and symbols became part of the ascribing process. The particular use of each symbol and its use in combination with other symbols would allow individuals to signal membership in particular communities. I suggest that the Athenian portraits use Isiac iconography to allude to a possible ritual experience shared by many devotees, but they also establish the subject as different from other Athenian women by following a pattern used in provincial portraiture across the Mediterranean. These images, I argue, have both a cult-specific and a provincial meaning that fashions two different but complementary forms of self. By examining the use of these images and symbols on the bodies of cult members, as evidenced in portraiture, self-fashioning considers how the accretion of iconographies allows individuals to navigate competing ethnic claims and construct novel and liminal forms of identity.

I conclude with the concept of self-location, which can refer to processes used to place the person or community within existing spatial, socio-political, or cultural hierarchies. These settings provide information about how communities organize their innate geographies, where they see themselves in relation to others, and how this information underpins actions and reactions. In Chapter 6, I examine how Isiac sanctuaries in Greece create imagined geographies of Egypt that local communities could possess and control. First, I consider the Sanctuary of the Egyptian Gods at Marathon, part of the family estate of the famed Roman sophist Herodes Atticus, where the sanctuary combines references to the Emperor Hadrian's Villa at Tivoli, archaizing sculpture, and architecture meant to recall early pyramids and Egyptian temples. The Marathon sanctuary thus engages with its patron's interests in the project of the Roman Empire but adapts them in ways that emphasize Greek control over an imagined version of another province. Next, I examine how other cult communities used natural landscape and water features to construct a Nilotic world that locates an imagined form of Egypt in a Greek city. This type of self-location, in which Greek devotees find ways to recreate Nilotic visions of Egypt within the frame of Greek territory and landscape, offers these communities a way to assert control over the Egyptianness inherent in the cult, to domesticate and deterritorialize Isis, and to continue ongoing dialogues about the role of Egypt in Greece's past, present, and future.

My argument is that devotees of Isis in Roman Greece fashioned their ideas of themselves in ways that emphasized their own importance on a global scale as a counterpoint to their asymmetric experiences of power and cultural influence. These decisions navigated the complicated intersections of Greekness, a historically and regionally situated ethnic concept, and Egyptian cults, which many would have associated, to some extent, with Egyptian ethnicity and the multivalent and often exoticizing images found in Greco-Roman literature and art. The ways in which individuals and communities made these arguments, however, followed Greek norms of cultural value. In order to legitimate and raise the status of Egyptian religion, much of the text and iconography the cult produced tended to find ways to insert Isis into the deep Greek past, into Greek materials and places that recast and complicate her ethnic identity. For devotees, then, the cult and its version of Egypt and Egyptian deities offered a way to experiment with alterity while maintaining the primacy of Greekness in the world of the Roman Empire.

CHAPTER TWO

BUILDING GROUPNESS

Isis' Devotees and Their Communities

People like to belong to things small enough to feel.
A. Giridharadas[1]

This tomb belongs to a woman who died in an amazing fashion after living a venerable life, as all would agree. If you ask her name, it is Dionysia, she who would be judged happy if all the divine favors she received were known. For from the age of fifteen years old, Isis Pantokrator allowed her to be a servant and to arrange the Isiac garments. Then, when she reached the age of sixty, she was called to be a temple servant in a holy manner, for a lustral bath washed her beautiful skin and, when combing her sacred locks, she arranged them with moist perfumes. And when she went to the altar, she prayed, and went to the stars, revered by all, as if she left us to join the demigods in a holy way. Dionysia, farewell![2]
    2nd–3rd century CE funerary inscription from Megalopolis

This epitaph commemorates a woman who was devoted to the goddess for over forty-five years and died while praying at the altar, with her hair arranged to make her resemble Isis (Figure 7). But there is no indication that Dionysia was a priestess, and while Martzavou argues that she should be identified as an initiate,[3] we do not know what it meant to be initiated into the Isiac cults, how many people pursued that path, or how meaningful the rituals were to those that participated in them.

Did a devotion to the Egyptian gods produce a meaningful new identity? While the answer to this question is not available to us, the evidence suggests that this is what most cultic communities in Greece were structured to produce. I argue that these Egyptian cults offered regular social and ritual mechanisms that promoted identification with the gods and with other

7. Grave relief of Alexandra of Oe, wife of Ktetos, from Athens, mid-2nd century CE. Athens: National Archaeological Museum inv. 1774. Photo: Giovanni Dall'Orto (via Creative Commons license). © Hellenic Ministry of Culture & Sports/Archaeological Receipts Fund.

devotees. In Brubaker's terminology, Isiac communities aspired to *groupness*, a fragile and contingent state in which there exists a mutually oriented, bounded collectivity with a sense of shared identity, solidarity, and capacity for shared action.[4] Groupness can also be seen as a set of actions designed to construct an identity that can be defined or set apart in some fundamental way.

Groupness has several advantages over more static concepts. First, it does not presuppose the existence of a group, with all of its attendant assumptions of agency and shared interests. Instead, it focuses on the series of choices, processes, and networks of connection that produce affective senses of belonging. Groupness recognizes that communities are produced through repeated actions, by creating structures and actions that generate and sustain a sense of unity.⁵ Most importantly, it forefronts the various textures and gradations of belonging: some devotees may have had a casual affiliation with the cult, while others may have practiced more actively. Groupness is flexible enough to describe differentiated experiences and levels of engagement.

Isiac groupness can be seen also as a product of imperialism. As empires developed and grew to encompass the entire Mediterranean in the Hellenistic and Roman periods, identities often fractured in response, producing smaller, better defined groups, and the Isiac cults benefited from the effect of this pressure.⁶ By establishing mechanisms of differentiation, such as initiations, cultic regulations, and secret knowledge, these communities attempted to construct themselves and create boundaries that would be reified over time.

If identification entails a series of choices, then we must find the places and practices that offered participants those choices. First, I consider how devotees would have come into contact with the cults via shared affective experiences that differentiated them from outsiders. Cultic associations, festivals, and regulations further mediated devotees' experiences of their bodies and placed them within a cultic hierarchy. Then I consider Lucius' experience in Apuleius' *Metamorphoses* 11 as a likely example of initiation into Isiac cults. Next, I consider how Isiac identity intersected with other meaningful forms of groupness. Focusing on a series of repeated dedications within the Iseum at Dion, I argue that these two powerful forms of belonging – cult affiliation and family – could become entangled; that families could identify closely with the cult over several generations.

I conclude with a question: Did Isis devotees identify with one another beyond the confines of individual sanctuaries and communities? Scholars have increasingly highlighted the importance of local context.⁷ While this approach rightly recognizes that Isiac cults often follow local norms, particularly in the structure and naming of cult offices and priesthoods,⁸ we must also recognize the historical and ideological interrelationships that bound translocal communities together. To trace these connections, I study the migration history of Isiac devotees and how it produced a sense of belonging that bound them together across Greece. Taken as a whole, the evidence suggests that the cult combined an eclectic mix of Greek (and a few Egyptian) socio-religious practices in ways that offered meaningful identification to those who joined. Consequently, I argue that, as they were practiced in Roman Greece, the cults offered a sense of connection with a larger Isiac community across the region that could, and did, intersect with prevailing forms of Greekness.

CONSTRUCTING GROUPNESS: JOINING, BELONGING, AND AGENCY

Joining the Isiac cults required one to opt in, which Veymiers has described as the "Isiac choice."⁹ While it is not clear what motivated individuals to join,

I argue that many aspects of cultic life, from initiatory rituals and festivals to smaller internal social groups like associations, provided participants with what Brubaker calls group-making activities. These include delineating and defining the community, promoting shared action, and facilitating a sense of commonality. The aggregation of these priesthoods, social connections, and repeated actions would have produced a sense of shared cultic identity that informed how devotees lived, socialized, and in some cases even buried their dead.[10] Though many of the social features discussed here, including initiation, voluntary associations, and cultic regulations, appear in other forms of Greek religious practice, their eclectic and intensive usage among Isaic devotees suggests a cult structure that emphasized mutual internal orientation and a sense of solidarity with the community.[11]

I view religion as a broader perspective that affects how devotees experience and react to other parts of their lives. According to Smart, religion is also a worldview, a system of "belief which, through symbols and actions, mobilized the feelings and wills of human beings."[12] Though useful for illuminating the affective power of religion, Smart's definition is not grounded in Roman evidence. Rüpke suggests that we define religion not in terms of organizations, rites, or institutions but rather as a form of "communicative action" in which Romans attempt to contact their gods and, in turn, engage with each other about the nature and practice of that communication.[13] Though it is true that this approach has much in common with earlier approaches to Roman religion, particularly in its emphasis on ritual practice,[14] Rüpke's definition advances the discussion by allowing for individual beliefs, emotions, choices, and motivations to play a major role in our understanding of Roman religion.[15] More importantly, it highlights how gods function as symbols through which people communicate and are unified.

Here I am defining an Isaic devotee as someone who engages in cultic practices with some regularity, even if that regularity is infrequent. Barrett has highlighted the importance of distinguishing between cultic practices, attitudes toward the gods and cults, and religious identities grounded in those practices. She outlines four categories of involvement: initiation into the cults; engagement in ritual practices in temple or domestic contexts; believing in the existence of Egyptian deities and understanding their nature and powers; and holding positive opinions about Egyptian cults.[16] My idea of a devotee includes the first two categories but not the last two, as the majority of those who merely thought well of the cults or believed the Egyptian gods existed would not necessarily engage with Egyptian cults at a level that involved identification or developing groupness.

Devotees, then, were probably among the cults' more observant members, and Latin terminology suggests that ancient peoples saw repeated religious action as a defining personal characteristic. Textual evidence indicates that many devotees in Latin-speaking areas, including those engaged in Isiac rites in *Met.* 11, are described as *religiosus*.[17] These include individuals who march in processions, participate in daily rituals, and in some cases, those who had completed initiation rites. The related term *religio* refers to repeated actions that fulfill one's obligations to the gods, which is closely tied to the frequent emphasis on orthopraxy in earlier scholarly literature.[18] The *religiosi*, then, are those who do Isiac things. This emic emphasis on practice underscores the value of looking to religious actions and agency as a way of defining belonging and identity.

Of course, the extent to which any individual devotee identified with the cult could have varied, and we will never know with certainty how many people were initiates or devotees, or even what options there were for less active forms of participation. Could, for example, a devotee attend major festivals but skip the more mundane worship, in the way that one can be a "Christmas and Easter Catholic" today? Our evidence is not fine-grained enough to determine how often devotees needed to engage with the cults in order to sustain an Isiac religious identity. But, as I argue here, the cult was structured in ways that would encourage devotees to feel a sense of belonging within the group. The repeated engagement with other Isiac devotees through ritual practices, festivals, associations, and other forms of socialized experiences of time and groupness would have reoriented some aspect of the devotee's sense of self.

Apuleius as a Source for Isiac Rituals

Before diving into the discussion, it is necessary to address the reliability of one of the main sources of evidence in this book. The use of Apuleius' *Metamorphoses* is a matter of scholarly debate and even of controversy, particularly for scholars of the ancient novel. Written in the mid-2nd century CE (ca. 125–170 CE), the *Metamorphoses* tells the story of a man from Corinth named Lucius who is turned into an ass by a witch and wanders through Greece in search of a cure that will turn him back into a man. The first ten books tell of his adventures, often with comic effect. The last, Book 11, diverges in both content and tone: it tells how Isis saves Lucius, who participates in several Isiac festivals, undergoes initiation into the cult, and travels to Rome to pursue further initiations. Apuleius' depictions are vivid and detailed and offer invaluable evidence for the reconstruction of Isiac cults.

Three interrelated questions arise concerning the use of Apuleius as a source for Isiac cults. The first is whether we should see Apuleius' representation of the cults as serious or satirical. This issue involves a larger, tonal problem in the *Metamorphoses*. Though the novel's first ten books are unquestionably humorous (with a likely Platonic bent), Book 11, which features the only discussion of Isis in all of Apuleius' works, appears to be more serious.[19] The division is often referred to as the "unity problem." Several scholars have argued that we are missing the joke in Book 11. Tilg has argued that Book 11 combines the comedic and the serious, and that while this section has major Platonic underpinnings, its religious aspects are mostly metaphors for Apuleius' own literary achievement.[20] Winkler suggests that the entire novel is a "philosophical comedy about religious knowledge," and that Book 11 depicts the general structure and experience of gaining religious knowledge rather than describing specific Isiac practices. Further, the ending of Book 11, in which Apuleius travels to Rome for further initiations, suggests to some that it may depict, through a series of several unnecessary initiations, how Lucius is fleeced of his money.[21]

Several works more grounded in historical and cultural approaches have recently pushed back against this interpretation. Méthy has argued that Apuleius' treatment of Isis is religious rather than philosophical and that references to Isis pervade the entire novel, not just the final book.[22] Similarly, Finkelpearl argues against the existence of a unity problem, noting several thematic connections between Book 11 and the rest of the novel, including stories of rebirth, transformation, and multiplicity. The distinction between the two parts of the novel, in her view, is not as sharp, and the first ten books are more serious than previously assumed.[23] In my view, the issue of unity remains a serious problem for the study of the work as a whole and merits further research. But a satirical interpretation of Book 11 does not undermine its reliability as a source for religious evidence: satire is inherently grounded in reality, and the jokes are only funny if they are based in the truth.

Second, how much did Apuleius actually know about Isiac cults? This is the least controversial question. Even those with a pessimistic view of the unity problem admit that Apuleius was knowledgeable about Isiac cults and that his descriptions reflect actual cult practices.[24] Apuleius' descriptions of Kenchreai reconcile with the archaeological evidence and our historical understanding of Antonine-period Greece; and while his account does not always agree with other forms of evidence, he seems familiar with many details of cult practices.[25] His description of the cultic calendar is close to what we know from the epigraphic evidence.[26] It may not have been difficult to learn about Isiac rites and ideas: the cults were popular and prevalent in many cities, and it is not unlikely that many, if not most, inhabitants of the Roman Empire knew someone who was a devotee. Apuleius uses epithets and key terms that regularly appear in Isiac inscriptions across the Mediterranean,[27] and it is clear that he and other writers had access to Isiac hymns that convey an organized set of beliefs about the nature of the Egyptian gods. Scholars have matched his descriptions of ritual actors with visual depictions, particularly in Roman wall painting, and the performative processions he describes would have been visible to the casual passerby as well as to initiates.[28]

More controversial is whether Apuleius gained this knowledge through firsthand experience. This debate is grounded in the question of whether the novel (or at least, Book 11) is autobiographical. Griffiths and Martzavou argue that Apuleius himself underwent Isiac initiations.[29] The best evidence for this is *Apologia* 23, 55, where Apuleius states that he was initiated into a cult at Kenchreai; from this account it appears that he spent considerable time in the sanctuary as a devotee.[30] He does not name the cult he joined explicitly, however, and it is possible that he joined the cult of another deity, or that the claim served a rhetorical or philosophical purpose. Merkelbach, taking a credulous approach, interprets the text as an initiatory novel conveying a hidden meaning accessible only to other initiates.[31] For the purposes of this book, which is concerned with understanding Isiac cult practices and their impacts on Greek identity, I am less concerned with this question. Even if he was not a devotee, Apuleius would seem to fall into the category of those who were knowledgeable about the Egyptian gods and their cults.

The third major question is how broadly we can apply Apuleius' account to actual practice. Is his depiction of Isiac experience representative of cultic practice throughout time and space? This question has not been considered as frequently as the others, but it is just as important. Gordon argues that we must consider Book 11 as embedded within a tightly bounded context. Even if Apuleius' account were completely true, and if Apuleius himself was initiated, his account could reflect only a set of rites practiced ca. 170 CE at one sanctuary. It might not describe the initiatory rites generally practiced throughout Roman Greece.[32]

Even with all of these problems, it is impossible to ignore such a detailed account. Every scholar who has considered Isiac cults in any depth has included the *Metamorphoses* in their analysis, and ultimately, since there is no comparable source, Apuleius' veracity is a matter of scholarly judgment.[33] I use his descriptions of Isiac rituals here with caution but with some confidence that research in the history and archaeology of religion has borne out his representations, even if only within a limited scope.

RITES AS SOCIAL STRUCTURES: DEFINING EXPERIENCES OF TIME AND PLACE

Festivals

Literary and epigraphic evidence attests to a calendar of Isiac rites that could have restructured devotees' experiences of time and their social worlds. Like most cults in antiquity, the Isiac cult had its own internal calendar of festivals.[34] At several sites, these festivals marked the beginning of the seasons, which would have added to the sense of anticipation devotees felt as they prepared themselves to move into new parts of the year. The two best attested festivals are the *Navigium Isidis*, celebrated at the beginning of spring, perhaps in early March,[35] and the *Isia*, celebrated at the end of October or early November.[36] In a work from ca. 346 CE, the poet Firmicus Maternus links the *Isia* with the planting season and the annual cycle of growth,[37] a calendar that resonated not only in the Isiac community but also with the general public. In a calendar mosaic from Thysdrus, the month of November is illustrated by a man dressed as Anubis carrying a *caduceus* alongside two *pterophores* wearing a winged cap and a version of male Isiac dress in which the garment is wrapped around the chest (Plate 3).[38] The iconography refers to the *Isia* festival's reenactment of the myth of Isis and Osiris.[39]

Relying primarily on references from Seneca and Juvenal, Alvar reconstructs the festival as taking place over at least four days.[40] The first part involved a passion of Isis, in which devotees searched for Osiris and rejoiced when his body was found. An epigraphic hymn from Thessaloniki alludes to Isis' joy at the discovery of Osiris' body, which suggests that this or a performance of a similar myth was part of that community's practice.[41] In Plutarch's account, which does not reconcile well with that of the Latin poets, the priests went down to the sea, took a golden casket from the *cista* that held the head of Osiris, and poured water into it, at which moment the devotees cried out in joy. Then a statuette of Osiris was made, dressed, and venerated.[42] After the first phase, at least at Rome, there followed another three days of rejoicing, culminating in another festival called the Hilaria.

Alongside their temporal structures, these festivals also reified and displayed the cults' internal social order. The Navigium Isidis festival was celebrated in a procession down to the sea and the launching of a ritual barque (*Met.* 11.9–11). In Apuleius' account, many members of the cultic community participated, which turned the public procession into a demonstration of the cults' hierarchies and internal groupings.[43] The first group of devotees wear costumes of magistrates and local mythological heroes in a parody of local culture. Then, women in white garments carry mirrors and mime the actions of caring for the cult statue, perhaps a reference to the temple servants who handled the goddess's toilette. Lamp-bearers followed, then musicians and pipers dedicated to Sarapis, and finally a group of male and female initiates, dressed in pure white linen decorated with stars and silks, shaking their *sistra*. Behind them came a group of priests carrying sacred objects, including a sacred lamp, model altars, a golden palm tree, the wand of Mercury, a model of a left hand (which symbolized equity), a *situla*, a winnowing fan, and an amphora. Statues of the gods and sacred objects, carried by worshippers, came next, including a statue of Anubis, a cow, a *cista*, and an aniconic statue of the Supreme Deity covered in hieroglyphs. The finale was the chief priest, carrying a *sistrum* and a wreath of roses (*Met.* 11.16).[44]

These types of performative processions construct a sense of collective belonging through shared objects, actions, and emotions.[45] As Mol and Versluys have argued, Egyptianizing objects – and the ways that they were used – created a sense of the extraordinary, constructed a sense of transformation, and built a sense of shared community among devotees.[46] For outsiders, these processions, with their unusual dress, bright colors, loud and strange musical instruments, and performative secrecy, could have contributed to prevailing exoticizing stereotypes about the cult. But processions like these also offered opportunities for the community to visualize its own social contours. For example, the Panathenaic procession of Classical Athens, which featured discrete groups of individuals arranged according to religious and social function, has been interpreted as a mechanism that reified social orders.[47] Processions of this type, then, would have defined the group both for members and for outsiders and contributed to the process of group-making.

Cult Associations as Social Groups

Several of the participants in Apuleius' procession have been identified as belonging to voluntary cult associations and priesthoods known from epigraphic sources. We know that such associations were active as early as the beginning of the 3rd century BCE and attracted members well into the 3rd century CE, though they declined in prominence during the Imperial period. While most sanctuaries were supervised by a single priest who gained the position either by inheritance or by civic appointment,[48] associations offered other opportunities for devotees to gain status and form intracommunity bonds. We might see them as providing an intermediate position between devotee and priest, one that grants a special status to select members within a broader cult community.[49] Arnaoutoglou concludes that these associations: are found in cities that are easily accessible to traders and travelers; include mostly men while not fully excluding women; appeal primarily to the middle classes; and include both citizens and a mix of migrants from all over the Mediterranean.[50] Delos and Thessaloniki, with their rich epigraphic records, had several large and diverse groups, including *therapeutes*, who raised money for improvements to the sanctuary; *melanophors*, so named probably because they wore black garments in certain rituals or processions; and *enatists* and *dekaists*, whose function is unclear.[51] In many places, associations dedicated plaques inside the sanctuary that listed the names of their members, thus delineating a boundary between members and nonmembers. In the more structured groups, members met outside the festival calendar and daily rituals for smaller gatherings that were, in some places, organized around communal dining.[52] Others may have met less frequently.

Because these associations regimented their participants' daily lives through meetings and activities, they helped establish durable ties within the sanctuary community. Several associations seem to have been named for the regular performance of particular tasks, a feature that was perhaps specific to Isiac cults.[53] The names of these associations allude to their activities, as in the case of the *pyrophoroi* or lamp-bearers from Delos and *hieraphoroi* or bearers of sacred objects from Thessaloniki. Several groups would have to perform these tasks frequently. Groups of *stoliasts* and *hypostoliasts*, known from Athens and Eretria, were apparently charged with the dressing of the cult images, which was probably performed frequently, perhaps even daily.[54] Similarly, an inscription from 2nd–3rd-century CE Epidauros includes daily care for the cult of Aphrodite-Isis that requires the *pyrophoros* to visit the temple twice a day, call out the goddess's name, light each lamp and the sacred chandelier, and set the lamps in particular places in the sanctuary.[55] The *pyrophoros* returned in the evening for more work, though the complete list of tasks has been lost. Joining these associations would have entailed a regular commitment to perform tasks alongside other members, which could have facilitated close social connections. Even for those who did not join an association, these activities would have injected a sense of life and regularity into the sanctuary, giving other devotees a schedule of activities to anticipate and view.

The social ties could also promote a deeper solidarity with the gods themselves. Some associations were organized around the veneration of specific deities, particularly Isis, Sarapis, and Anubis. Most popular were the Sarapiastai, who are known from many sites throughout the Mediterranean, including Rhamnous, Athens, Keos, Kamiros, Lindos, Rhodes, Thasos, Methymna, and Delos in the 3rd–2nd century BCE, and at Kos in the 1st century CE.[56] Cities on the islands of Kos, Rhodes, and Thasos also had active groups of Isiastai, while the Anoubiasts were mentioned less frequently. The earliest attestation on Rhodes dates to the 2nd century BCE, and the latest to 10 CE.[57] Remarkably, two of the attestations from Roman-period Kos served as boundary markers for special grave plots, one for the Isiastai and another for the *thiasos* of the Anoubiasts.[58] Organizing burials in this way – by membership in a voluntary association of individuals especially devoted to a single deity – would suggest that members of these groups derived great meaning and self-definition from belonging to the group. More importantly, these burial plots would have reified the boundaries of group membership over the long term and offered a visible place for its members to assert their sense of belonging to future generations.

The case of the Anubophores suggests that some associations offered opportunities to identify closely with the Egyptian gods. Members dressed up as the jackal-headed god himself to participate in certain religious rituals, which could have offered practitioners the opportunity to collapse the self with the god.[59] Though the only secure attestation of the group comes from Viennes in modern France,[60] some scholars have interpreted an inscribed relief stele from

Thessaloniki as evidence of an Anubophore who led a group of Hermanubis worshippers.[61] Further, there is an association of Anoubiasts known from Delos, and a mid-1st-century CE inscription from Teithras identifies one Demophilos, son of Dionysius from Sounion, who gets to carry the ἡγεμών (lord), whom Bricault identifies as Anubis.[62] Apuleius describes a devotee carrying an image of Anubis in his account of the Navigium (*Met.* 11.11). He initially describes the Anubis-bearer as the god himself, claiming that the god "deigned to walk with human feet" and only later clarifies that a man is carrying a cult image.[63] Like the burial plots, performative roles like the Anubophore would have allowed practitioners to exhibit their close connection with the deity to the cultic community at large, and perhaps even to the wider civic community.

Regulations as Common Social Action

Religious restrictions and prohibitions enforced within the sanctuary controlled personal aspects of devotees' lives and adhering to them would have promoted identification during rituals and festivals. Among the earliest is a set of restrictions from Sarapieion C on Delos. A small plaque, dated to the period before 166 BCE, prohibits entry to those who have (recently?) drunk wine or are wearing *anthina* – short, brightly colored garments that must have been insufficiently sober for the sanctuary.[64] A pair of plaques from Sarapieion A on Delos prohibits women and men in wool garments from entering a temple, probably a small chapel, dedicated by a Roman named Lucius Granius.[65] Another rule from early 2nd-century BCE Megalopolis outlines an onerous set of purification rituals required for women alongside rules about purifications after eating goats and sheep.[66] Here, women who have given birth must wait nine days to enter the temple, those who have aborted a pregnancy forty-four days, those who have menstruated seven days, and those who have eaten goat or mutton three days. Those who have engaged in sexual intercourse or eaten other foods are required to wash the entire body before entering.[67] Given the importance of goat and mutton in the Greek diet, as well as the basic human need for sex, these restrictions would have required a degree of sacrifice and commitment that was outside of the norm.

Though most of these rules appear in the 3rd–2nd century BCE, some of them date to the Roman period. A late 1st-century BCE set of rules from Teithras in Attica prohibits the same person from serving as *zakoros* twice.[68] The column bearing the inscription is damaged and the rest of the rules are lost. The extant text makes it clear, however, that violators were not permitted to enter the sanctuary or to make offerings to the gods without the permission of the Boule, like the enforcement mechanism outlined in the Megalopolis decree. Pausanias, in his description of the Temple of Isis at Tithorea, claims that only those who have been called by the goddess herself are permitted to enter (10.32, 13).[69] Lucius abstains from unholy foods several times in preparation for his initiation (*Met.* 11.22, 23), in an echo of the Megalopolitan prohibition against mutton and goat meat.

In following these rules, devotees chose to participate in the cult according to the dictates of the priests and other cult functionaries. The extent of the impact of the rules would have depended on the frequency of visits to the sanctuary. The regulations often exert control over dress and the body, which is normal for sanctuary communities across the Greek world.[70] In the case of dress, they provide the visible evidence marking an individual as part of the community. Regulations concerning the body sometimes encourage non-normative patterns of diet and behavior, like the Delian prohibition against drinking wine or the Megalopolitan rules about diet. In effect, the regulations impose a structure on devotees' lives that requires them to count down the days until their next ritual experience. These rules, then, delimit the cultic community and establish criteria for inclusion and exclusion.

Building and Ordering Belonging

These rules would have established the rhythms and patterns of daily life for the sake of shared activities, a key feature of groupness. Chief among them were the cultic regulations and ritual calendars, which forced devotees to regulate normal daily activities like sex, drinking, and wearing linen in order to render the body sufficiently pure to enter the sanctuary. These regulations informed devotees' choices to reorient their most intimate behaviors to conform to the cult's expectations. While some devotees, particularly those who served the cult in priestly or other functionary roles, would have visited the sanctuary often, the custom of more casual participants is unknown. Even for these, however, the rules would have created a heightened sense of belonging and anticipation during festivals like the Isia or Navigium Isidis, which required the devotee's presence in the sanctuary.[71] The divergence from normative dress, diet, and sexual activity would have oriented devotees toward others who shared the same restrictions.

Similarly, associations, with their repeated activities, might have relied on this new orientation to produce shared actions. If these associations, as I argue here, formed an important part of members' social connections and self-identification, they would have also served as a place for people of different social classes, legal status, and ethnic origins to meet and work together,[72] constructing a group identity that was layered upon these other meaningful ways of self-understanding and self-location. Not all devotees would have chosen to follow the rules or join an association, which may have resulted in decreased identification with the cult. But most communities were still offering these opportunities to opt into the cult, which suggests that many saw the cult as a place to find something "small enough to feel."

Groupness as Event: Initiation as Cultic Paideia

Initiation was the telos of a devotee's ritual life, offering the initiate a profound education in the mythology of these mysterious cults, serving not only as "rites of institution" but also as a means for conveying the cults' values and history to new members.[73] As devotees learned more, they crossed the social and ritual boundaries that defined the cult, identifying more deeply with the cultic community. At the same time, initiation reified a sense of commonality and defined a boundary between those who had completed them and those who had not. Although it is unlikely that everyone completed the initiation process, we may assume that those who chose to do so gained entry to a closely guarded body of knowledge that admitted them to a small, elite, and highly structured community.

Lucius' initiation at Kenchreai began with a dream message from Isis, who told the soon-to-be initiate on what day the rites should take place, which priest should oversee them, and how much the procedure should cost.[74] Lucius was thus called to the cult, which increased his sense of belonging.[75] Upon waking, Lucius went to see the priest, who took Lucius into the temple and gave him certain practical instructions set forth in a holy book. Next, Lucius procured the specified ritual objects for his initiation, which included a white linen robe. Just prior to the initiation, Lucius purified himself by bathing in the neighborhood baths and abstaining from meat and wine for several days. After the ritual cleansing, Lucius began the three-day initiation process.

On the first night, community members brought gifts to the new initiate. Lucius dressed himself in a sacred costume of linen. Alvar suggests that the first initiatory ritual would have revealed the tale of Osiris' nocturnal journey through the underworld to heaven in his role as a solar deity,[76] quite possibly through some sort of ritual dramatic performance of the myth. The reenactment of this myth played a major role in the Egyptian Isia festival, and the ritual plays and processions practiced here also featured prominently in Egyptian festivals.[77] On the morning of the second day, Lucius is revealed to his community in divine guise,[78] dressed in a linen cloak and solar crown, carrying a torch and standing on a dais directly in front of the cult statue. As a simulacrum of the sacred object, Lucius became the object of the sacred gaze, receiving veneration in the place of the statue.[79] Unfortunately, the activities of the second and third days were not treated in such extensive detail, suggesting that these rites may have been considered too secret to share or less interesting to the *Metamorphoses*'s readers.

Only a handful of likely initiates can be identified in Hellenistic Greece, and the evidence for the Roman period is even more obscure.[80] Though references to individual *mystes*, or initiates, appear in cultic texts as early as ca. 100 BCE, direct references to the mysteries as a series of rites do not appear until the 1st–2nd century CE.[81] There are mentions of *mystes* in inscriptions from 2nd-century BCE Bithynia and 2nd-century CE Tralles,[82] and single funerary inscriptions from 1st-century and 2nd-century CE Rome, Brindisium, and Forum Popilii that describe the deceased as initiates.[83] There are some indications of initiatory rituals in Greece. Plutarch argues that the true *Isiakos* is not the man who shaves his head and wears linen, but the one who has "legitimately received what is set forth in the ceremonies connected with these gods, uses reason in investigating and in studying the truth contained therein."[84] In several hymns found throughout the eastern Mediterranean, Isis is described as composing texts that are sacred to the *mystes*, sometimes in concert with other deities.[85]

The evidence for initiation is scattered across time and space, and it is difficult to determine if the practice was widespread. A figural stele from Thessaloniki, which dates to the second half of the 2nd century BCE, is dedicated to Osiris *mystes*, an epithet that references the Isiac hymns mentioned above and their use in ritual practices (Figure 8).[86] The stele depicts a mortal man draped in a himation and leaning his head on his bent right arm while standing on a rectangular object. He receives veneration from the devotees standing beneath him: a man carrying a *situla* and a veiled woman with long curly hair who carries a *sistrum* in her right hand, facing a semi-nude mortal man. Though early interpretations suggested that the central figure was a statue, and that the relief consequently depicted a standard image of religious veneration, more recent studies have identified him as a mortal devotee.[87] The figure's feet are not visible on top of the rectangular object, which indicates that a person rather than a statue is depicted, though his unusual pose suggests that he is perhaps trying to imitate a statue. Apuleius' account of Isiac initiation includes a similar rite, discussed in more detail in Chapter 5, which lends further credence to the use of the *Metamorphoses* as a source for reconstructing Isiac rituals. Another inscription on a statue base from the 2nd century CE mentions Isis Orgia, another epithet linked with mystery cult and initiation.[88] These two objects suggest that initiation was part of the rites practiced at Thessaloniki, potentially as early as the end of the 2nd century BCE.

By reconsidering initiation as a group-making pedagogical process, we can see how the community introduced the initiate to secret knowledge in order to build a sense of commonality. Lucius began his Isiac education by receiving instructions from a sacred book; he continued on the first night of the initiation, when the tale of Osiris' nightly journey through the underworld was revealed:[89]

> Listen then, but believe, for my account is true. I approached the boundary of death and treading on Proserpina's threshold, I was carried through all the elements, after which I returned. At dead of night I saw

8. Votive relief dedicated to Osiris μύστης, 2nd century BCE. Thessaloniki: Archaeological Museum inv. MΘ 997, IG X 2, 107. Photo courtesy of the Thessaloniki Archaeological Museum. © Hellenic Ministry of Culture & Sports/Archaeological Receipts Fund.

> the sun flashing with bright effulgence. I approached close to the gods above and the gods below and worshipped them face to face.[90]

Experiencing this myth through reenactment offered initiates a way to explore the complex theological metaphor connecting the sun and rebirth in Egyptian religion while also allowing them to share in an exclusive experience.[91] These highly performative and emotional experiences would have reinforced a sense of solidarity and delineated another, smaller group within the community.

These rituals offered new devotees the opportunity to learn about the Egyptian gods, while more advanced devotees might reinforce their knowledge with ritual experiences. Consequently, the rituals also served as a kind of community-reinforcing *paideia*. There is a parallel here between Lucius' cult-based education and the role of education in the construction of Second Sophistic Greekness. These acts often required the devotee to reenact mythologies, and thus encouraged a close connection and communication with the deities.[92] From dressing up as a statue of the goddess to receiving veneration from his peers, Lucius' actions represent an active, repeated choice to identify with the Egyptian gods and their cult.[93] It is important to note here the affective power of this moment: the wondrous sights, the sounds of ritual music in performance, the sense of wearing unfamiliar clothes and behaving in unusual ways, and the disorienting experiences of light and dark. Engaging in these rituals helped to remove Lucius from his everyday experience and establish himself within a new group.

These rituals marked a transition and formalized the boundaries of Lucius' religious identity. During the initiation process he has crossed an embodied social boundary, a conceptual line that separates Isiac from non-Isiac, devotee from initiate, by performing specific acts.[94] The point here is not that engaging in Isiac ritual required Lucius to abandon his previous life, but rather that the rite was designed to create a sense of having passed through some kind of boundary into a new world, whether that world was primarily social or religious.[95] Through initiation, then, an initiate added something new to his worldview by strengthening his connection with other devotees.

What, then, was the effect of initiation on initiates' identification? It is difficult to read Apuleius' account and argue that these rituals would have had no impact on those that completed them. To the extent that we are able to reconstruct them, the rituals involved acquiring secret knowledge through cultic *paideia*, which would have required initiates to delineate who was allowed to have the knowledge. Other rituals involved assuming the place of Isis and other deities, which, in tandem with other forms of direct communication with the divine, would have deepened the initiate's sense of solidarity with other initiates and with the deities themselves. Still, it is unlikely that all of the people who dedicated in the sanctuaries or paid for festival equipment or even served in low-level positions were initiated. Rather, initiates probably formed a smaller elite group within each sanctuary's broader cultic community. But it is important to note how sparse this evidence is. At most sites in Greece, there is no evidence for Isiac initiation rites, and it is possible that they were sporadic and site-specific.

Though devotees continued to participate in Greek civic and social life, Isiac initiations may have also produced a fundamental reorientation of the self. Joining the cult represented a continued choice to devote energy, time, and capital to cultic activity, to become part of a community, and to commit to following the rules and practices that defined a new sense of self. Some of the cults' ideological features (described in fuller detail in Chapter 3), including the emphasis on epiphany in many foundation stories, the shared sense of secrecy, and the idea that each community was part of a larger whole, gave meaning to the concept of Isiac groupness. Many of these features would have been accessible to all participants in Isiac cults, initiate or not.

PRACTICING FAMILY AND COMMUNITY AT ROMAN DION

How did devotees' involvement in Isiac cults intersect with other forms of identity? In the case of Dion, whose exceptional preservation allows us to consider inscriptions and sculpture in a secure archaeological context, I argue that the Iseum provided a venue for two families to identify themselves with the cult through repeated dedication and display. Taken alongside epigraphic evidence from the region, the two families' dedicatory activities at Dion's Iseum promoted a sense of commonality within the sanctuary's community and a link between family and cult that was constructed and preserved across time and space.

After the Battle of Actium in 31 BCE, Octavian named the small city of Dion a colony (Colonia Julia Augusta Diensis). Once used for primarily ritual purposes, the city prospered under Roman rule, particularly in the 2nd and 3rd century CE. In 1978, under the direction of Pandermalis, a sanctuary dedicated to the Egyptian gods was found on the site of a 1951 discovery, just outside the city wall on the southeast side.[96] The first temple on the site, probably dedicated to Artemis Eilytheia, was constructed in the mid-Hellenistic period, but visitors to the site today find a well-preserved enclosed sanctuary of the 2nd century CE with significant later restorations and renovations.[97] The sanctuary consists of four small *naiskoi* clustered at the west end of an open sanctuary square, with smaller rooms for meeting, dining, and storage fronted by columned porticoes flanking the square's north and south sides (Figure 9). A central architectural feature running east–west across the square has been identified as a water basin. This sanctuary remained in use until it was destroyed by an earthquake, probably in late antiquity. Attempts to repair the buildings were abandoned after the sanctuary was flooded. The inundation deposited over 2 m of sediment at the site – ultimately preserving the sanctuary's architecture and sculpture. The water presented major challenges during excavations and made stratigraphic excavation impossible. Many sculptures were found still standing on their bases or fallen from their likely display contexts, resulting in an unusually high level of preservation.[98]

The Anthestii

Among the remains are many epigraphic and sculptural dedications dedicated by members of the Anthestii, a large clan that used the sanctuary throughout

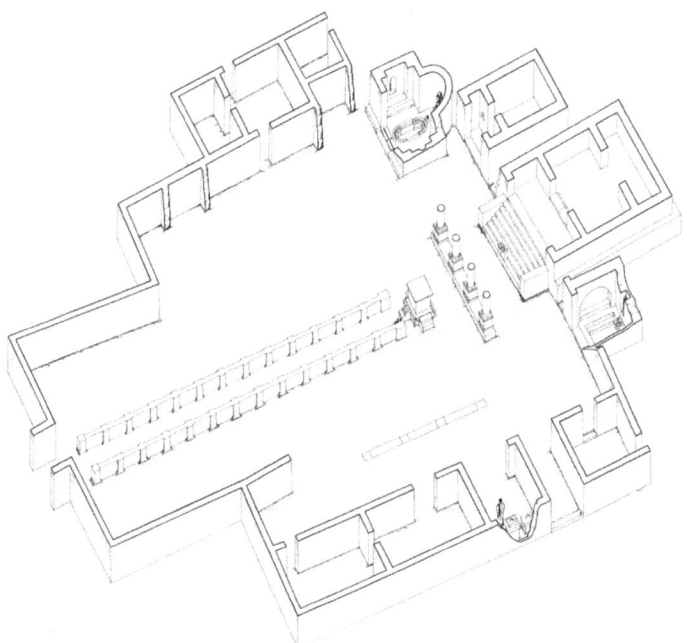

9. Axiometric reconstruction drawing of the Iseum at Dion. Reproduced from Pandermalis 2016, fig. 8. Courtesy of the Aristotle University of Thessaloniki, Dion Excavation Archive.

the Roman period as a site for dedication and display. The family is attested throughout the empire at Rome and Pompeii, in the Aegean Islands, and in much of Imperial-period Greece; its Macedonian branch has been identified as a family of *negotiatores*.[99] The Anthestii were part of a mass migration of Italians to Macedonia throughout the late Republic, appearing in some places as early as the mid-2nd century BCE, though they did not immigrate in significant numbers until the 1st century BCE.[100] Most of them settled in Amphipolis and Thessaloniki, the region's largest port cities; they may have been responsible for introducing Isiac cult to the region.[101] The Anthestii, by way of Delos, may have been among these early adopters. An epigraph of one Markia Anthestia, believed to be a member of the Anthestii, was found in Delos' Sarapieion C and dates to the end of the 2nd century BCE.[102] Another, a marble stele from Amphipolis, commemorates a crown awarded in 67/66 BCE to Aulus Anthestius for his excellence as a trierarch.[103] Because Aulus is honored by a group of *hypostoloi*, Veymiers has argued that he must have some relationship with Isiac cults.

At Dion, later generations of Anthestii and their freedmen continued their devotion to Isis by dedicating at the city's Iseum.[104] A Severan-period inscription details major renovations funded by Publius Anthestius Amphio, a successful freedman who held important civic offices, and his wife, Anthestia

Iucunda.[105] The inscription was found in a small building just to the north of the main temple of Isis and indicates that their renovations included two porticoes, the *alae* (rooms flanking the central court), and a covered passageway. A quick glance at the sanctuary's plan demonstrates how much these renovations would have changed the devotees' experience of the sanctuary space. These new structures enclosed much of the sanctuary square and framed it with space for dedication and display.

Two nearly identical inscriptions, one in Greek, the other in Latin, were found in the same building; they commemorate Anthestia Iucunda's dedication to Aphrodite Hypolympidia and the *colonia*.[106] The same woman reinstalled a later 2nd-century BCE cult statue of the goddess that stood in a small temple just to the south of the main temple, and her name appears on the statue's 2nd-century CE base, repeating the same text found on the two marble bases described above (Figure 10).[107] The Aphrodite Hypolympidia temple connects to the *alae* that Anthestia built, and it is likely that visitors experienced these structures as part of the same complex.

The rededication of this statue illustrates Anthestia Iucunda's power in both the city and the cultic community. The image, which dates stylistically to 150–100 BCE,[108] could have been commissioned in the early phases of the construction of the sanctuary to Isis (Figure 11). But it is unclear whether the cult of Aphrodite Hypolympidia existed before the Imperial period. The goddess is not known elsewhere in Dion or Macedonia, and there is no evidence to suggest that Aphrodite Hypolympidia was worshiped in the earlier phase of the sanctuary.[109] So where did this statue originally stand? It is possible that the statue came from another sanctuary in the city and that it was transferred as part of Anthestia's renovations – an event that would suggest that Anthestia, a wealthy freedwoman from a powerful clan, had enough influence in Dion to move from the original location both a precious statue of great antiquity and the cult of a local goddess. Similarly, the move would have meant that she possessed sufficient power within the cultic community to introduce a new deity. If the statue belonged to the sanctuary already, however, rededication would still have offered Anthestia a means for asserting and gaining status, as the restoration of a 400-year-old statue of a local goddess named for neighboring Mt. Olympus might have been construed as an especially pious gesture. Further, the replication of the text in several buildings within the sanctuary amplified the prominence of her dedication. The statue is thus part of a politics of reuse – of using the past to claim status and prominence through piety – that might have represented Anthestia's renovations as a rededication or refoundation of the sanctuary.

Anthestia also used the sanctuary to promote herself and other female members of her family. A base for a portrait statue of Anthestia Iucunda was

10. Statue of Aphrodite Hypolympidia from her temple in Dion's Iseum, 150–100 BCE. Dion: Archaeological Museum inv. MΔ 4+383. © Hellenic Ministry of Culture & Sports/ Archaeological Receipts Fund.

discovered in the same wing mentioned in the renovation inscription. The base preserves a bilingual inscription that indicates that the wives of the colonists and immigrants (*colonarum et incolarum coniuges*/Κολώνων καὶ παροίκων) dedicated the portrait to Anthestia.[110] Next to this statue base another was found, a large gray marble base with a smaller white marble base on top, intended for a portrait statue of Anthestia Maxima, daughter of Publius and, presumably, of Anthestia Iucunda (Figure 12). The smaller base preserves

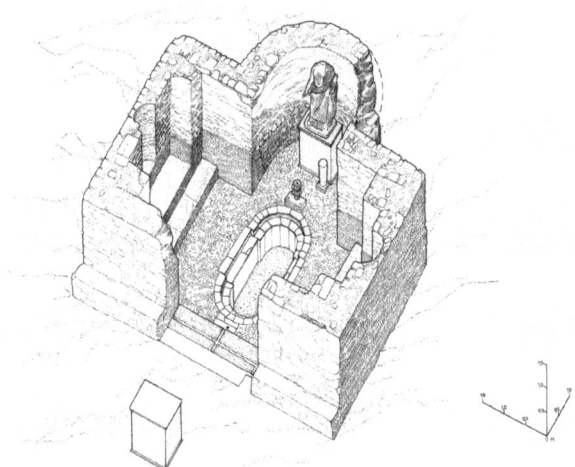

11. Axiometric reconstruction drawing of the temple to Aphrodite Hypolimpidia in the Dion Iseum. Reproduced from Pandermalis 2016, fig. 9. Courtesy of the Aristotle University of Thessaloniki, Dion Excavation Archive.

12. Statue bases for Anthestia Maxima, daughter of Publius, Severan period. Dion: Archaeological Museum inv. MΔ 414+415. © Hellenic Ministry of Culture & Sports/Archaeological Receipts Fund.

a Latin inscription, while the larger base's inscription is in Greek, but both provide the same information: that Anthestia's portrait was dedicated to Sarapis, Isis, and Anubis, and that Anthestia was being honored for the excellence of her parents.

Because of the difficulty of excavation and establishing a date for these inscriptions, it is not clear if all three were put up at the same time. The variety in base heights, design, materials, and construction suggests that this was not a planned group but an accretion of images over several years. Anthestia Maxima may have been honored after her mother was, and for her own activities on behalf of the cult, even if the statue was paid for by her parents. A third base in the shape of an altar held a portrait of Ioulia Phrougiane Alexandra, paid for by the city.[111] The statue is a fairly typical, well-executed depiction of a Roman matron, dressed in a chiton with a large mantle wrapped around both arms, with a somewhat aged and individualized face, and heavy braids wrapped around her head – with no Isiac attributes.[112] Alexandra's relationship with the Anthestii, if she had any at all, is unknown. It is possible that the monument was placed here later to set her among the cultic community's most powerful and vaunted members. But the location of the mother and daughter pair in this part of the sanctuary suggests that the purpose of this room was to advertise the family's strong relationship with the cult and the continued excellence of these women.

Portraits of women throughout the Imperial Greek world were often intended to highlight the excellence of a family and, particularly in their inscriptions, to define a woman's place in familial networks.[113] The inscriptions in this case honor female civic dedicators. Anthestia Iucunda's statue was dedicated by a group of women described in relation to the colony, the *colonarum et incolarum coniuges*, and Anthestia Maxima's statue was dedicated by her parents, a dedication in which Anthestia Iucunda was likely involved. Alexandra's monument was granted by the city of Dion, a special but not unusual honor for an eminent woman.[114] Thus, most of the dedications fall into a small group of images dedicated by women,[115] but in both cases the women are situated within a broader familial context. Anthestia Iucunda is described as the freedwoman of Publius, which links her to her clan, and Anthestia Maxima is identified primarily as Publius' daughter. These types of inscriptions and portrait monuments participated in a local economy of honors, and the accretion of texts and images within specific areas of the sanctuary would have amplified the fame of the Anthestii over the long term. These portraits and reliefs, then, helped to locate the family's status claims within the sanctuary.

The Herennii

The Anthestii were not the only family that made a series of dedications at the sanctuary. The names of two Herennii women have been found in votives that date generally to the Imperial period. A large merchant family of Italian origin, the Herennii first appear in Macedonia in an agonistic list from Chalkis in around 100 BCE,[116] and other members appear in many key sites in Macedonia during the late Republic and Imperial periods. Most notably, two inscriptions from the Thessaloniki Sarapeum indicate that members of the family were active in the Egyptian cults there. The first, a fragmentary marble plaque, mentions one "Marcus Herennius Kyn [...] "; it dates to 42–32 BCE.[117] The second, which dates to ca. 22/21 BCE, is a white marble stele that records the dedication of Marcus Erennios Philonikos.[118] Herennii names also appear on coins from Dion and Pella and on inscriptions in Thessaloniki as late as the 3rd century CE, which indicates that the family held important offices throughout Imperial Macedonia.[119]

One inscription, carved on a pilaster, mentions a woman named Herennia Pagilla, daughter of Marcus.[120] The pilaster stands on the steps of the sanctuary's main temple to Isis Lochia, one of several small votives dedicated there.[121] Dedicated by the decurions and funded at public expense, the monument honors the parents of Herennia Pagilla. The text is carved on a base that supported a relief with two footprints, a common type of votive found in many Isiac sanctuaries around the Mediterranean, with a particular concentration in Macedonia and Hellenistic Delos.[122] That relief was dedicated by a priest named Gaius Hostius Philon, "according to divine injunction" (κατ'ἐπιταγήν), a common formula that may indicate that the god or goddess appeared to the dedicant.[123] The relief itself depicts the imprint of two feet, the left one significantly larger than the right. While the relationship between the two objects is not clear, Herennia Pagilla's base is much wider than the footprint relief and features scoring, at least one dowel hole, and a central channel that suggests the base was intended to hold a different object, perhaps a statue base or crowning block. The epigraphy is not datable beyond the Imperial period, and it is unclear when Philon's footprint relief was set on Herennia Pagilla's base. Still, it is likely that viewers who saw the two inscriptions displayed as one monument might have assumed that Herennia Pagilla and Philon were related. Another relief found on the footsteps of the temple of Isis Lochia within the sanctuary also features two footprints, one larger and one smaller (Plate 4). The dedicant, Ignatia Herennia, who uses the same κατ'ἐπιταγήν formula as Gaios Hostios Philon, dedicates her relief to Hermanubis, a deity unknown at Dion but popular in Thessaloniki and Delos, which further supports the case for a link between these three communities.[124]

These two families dominate the epigraphy of Dion's Iseum. Of the nineteen inscriptions found in the Iseum, only eight have no obvious familial or proximal relationship with either family.[125] Of these, three were dedicated to Isis Lochia, the goddess on whose temple steps most of the objects stood. This epithet of the goddess was popular in Macedonia but absent from the Herennii and Anthestii dedications.[126] Two were footprint and ear reliefs of a type similar to those used by the Herennii and Anthestii.[127] The consistency in these dedications suggests that local norms played a major role in the dedicants' decisions about the type and placement of votives within the sanctuary. These inscriptions, like many of the rest from the Iseum, are not datable beyond the Roman period; it is thus impossible to determine the order in which they were set up, and it is certainly possible that more inscriptions originally stood in this area. Still, it is clear that both families saw the sanctuary as a locus for claiming elite status in the town and used local norms and forms of dedication for that purpose. In turn, their dedications contributed to the sanctuary's sense of place by regularizing and popularizing specific monument types and venues for dedication.

The dedicatory patterns of the two clans suggest that joining the Isiac cult was profoundly meaningful for the Anthestii and the Herennii. In several other places, many members of the same family joined the same association, which, while not uncommon for private associations generally, might indicate that the family considered Isiac cult and its smaller groups an important part of their self-definition. A list of the *therapeutes* from Maroneia included a set of siblings and a father and son pair.[128] The association of Osiriasts in 2nd-century CE Kos includes two pairs of brothers,[129] and another 1st-century CE dedication of Archikydes, together with the *eranistai Isiastai*, honoring his father, Charmophantos.[130] A list of the *koinon* of the *diakonoi* in 1st-century BCE Ambrakia includes a father and son named Krates and Herakleitos.[131] These dedications might indicate that familial identity and religious identity overlapped for these clans, with sons following fathers and daughters following mothers into the cult. This particular interpretation indicates a certain level of personalization – that a smaller group of devotees could develop a stronger bond with a deity or set of deities and pass on the devotion as a legacy to future generations.

TYING THE WEB: MIGRATION AND A GLOBAL GREEK ISIAC COMMUNITY

The previous sections highlight the diverse textures and tempo of local social life within the Isiac cults. Communities chose elements from a constellation of local norms, regional socio-religious structures, and, as I discuss here and in Chapter 3, ideas and practices available throughout the Mediterranean. These localized choices produced a dynamic and diverse range of cult practices and structures that must have changed over time in response to historical events. Still, I argue, some elements of the cult were shared widely, resulting in the standardization of cult practices across Greece. These consistencies helped construct a sense of solidarity that transcended the local scale and governed common, repeated actions across the region.

Human Migrations

The cult's early history of migration and textual transmission suggest that there existed a sense of commonality between communities. Indeed, migration was probably key to the cult's dissemination and success. The Egyptian cults in Imperial Greece were the product of several waves of migration, from Egypt to the Aegean Sea, to mainland ports and into the hinterlands. The Egyptian cults first arrived in the Greek islands in the late 4th century BCE along major trade routes. By the end of the 3rd century BCE, cult centers were active in many of Greece's port cities, becoming an active part of the religious landscape.[132] Many of the early participants in the Isiac cult have been identified as having Egyptian origins. One Egyptian, a priest named Apollonios, brought a statue of Sarapis with him when he immigrated to Delos at the end of the 4th century BCE.[133] At Eretria, the earliest inscription found on the site is a block found in situ in Court C of the Temple to Isis that records a dedication to Isis by a group of Egyptians at the end of the 4th or the beginning of the 3rd century BCE.[134] Krateso, a priestess of Isis who died at Amphipolis sometime in the early Hellenistic period, may have come from Egypt as well, though it is also possible that she was of Greek origin.[135] At Argos, a 3rd-century BCE inscription lists a woman with an Egyptian name, Thaeis, as a dedicator of the earliest known Egyptian sanctuary on the site, which may indicate that she was one of the cult's founders.[136] A painted grave stele from Demetrias depicts Ouapheres, son of Horus, dated to the latter half of the 3rd century BCE. Ouapheres is shown with a shaved head, dressed in a white linen chiton and himation – a set of identifiers for Egyptian priests.[137] The text explicitly names the deceased's hometown as Posiritis, which Stamatopoulou identified as the Egyptian *nome* of Busiris.[138]

It is not clear why so many Egyptians founded or joined in the foundation of early Greek sanctuaries to these gods. A well-known inscription from 4th-century Athens records that the *demos* permitted the merchants from Kition in southern Cyprus to build a sanctuary of Aphrodite.[139] The grant is justified based on an argument of equivalence, that the Egyptians had been granted permission to set up their own sanctuary to Isis. Perhaps these early foundations were a useful place for Egyptian migrants to meet, practice familiar rituals, and preserve their own communal ties. Over time, however, people from elsewhere joined these sanctuaries, which, at least in some places, produced communities of diverse ethnic backgrounds. But the cults' narratives of Egyptianness persisted,[140] more often in ways that appropriated, imagined, and recontextualized Egyptian culture.

As migration continued, the connections between far-flung communities intensified. Though Delos is not the cult's sole origin point, its excellent epigraphic record allows us to track the diasporic movement of Isiac Delians.

Many residents left the island in the second half of the Hellenistic period, first after Athens expelled many of the islanders in 166 BCE, and again after the island was largely depopulated in the late 1st century BCE. Their migrations brought key aspects of Isiac cult into other areas of Greece and the Mediterranean and may have promoted ties between distant cultic communities.[141] Martzavou has argued convincingly that patterns in dedicatory inscriptions suggest that the Delian diaspora also brought Isiac communities to places like Eretria, Thessaloniki, and, in later years (ca. 1st century CE), Gortyna and Amphipolis. She offers a "trickle down" model of diffusion, suggesting that Delian expatriates, particularly traders of Italian origin, arrived in popular early Imperial port cities and founded cults closely modeled on Delian practices and hierarchies. These Delian expatriates often went to cities that already had Egyptian sanctuaries, and, just as for the first wave of Egyptian migrants, Egyptian cult may have offered them a locus for integration.[142] At Thessaloniki, for example, Martzavou finds the names of eleven *gentes* known at Delos, as well as similarities in material culture and sculpture that further highlight the relationship between these two communities.[143]

At several sites, Delian communities introduced their own practices into existing communities. Most notably, attestations of *navarchs*, an association or liturgical group that paid for a boat used in the Navigium Isidis festival, appear in places associated with Delian migrants, including Tinos,[144] Chalkis,[145] Eretria,[146] and Amphipolis.[147] An inscription from Thessaloniki mentions a member of the Salarii family, another clan associated with Egyptian cults across the Mediterranean, who dedicated a *hydreion*, a feature only known at Delos.[148] The Delian community, with its many competing sanctuaries and associations, was probably not homogenous in its worship of Isis. But the diaspora may have promoted a certain sense of commonality and a shared set of practices across a wide geographic span.

The Delian diaspora was not the only way the Egyptian cults spread across Greece. One inscription from the Thessaloniki Sarapeum details how a man named Xenainatos came to Thessaloniki to seek counsel from Sarapis, where he had a dream encounter with the god.[149] In this dream, Sarapis told Xenainatos to give a letter to Eurynomos, the son of Timastitheos. When he awoke, Xenainatos found a letter under his pillow and gave it to Eurynomos, who founded the cult and appointed its first priestess at Opous. This story connects the cult at Opous with a more established cult center in a major urban center, giving it a clear place in the network of Isiac cult communities around the Mediterranean. Much like the myths of Hellenic ancestry described in Chapter 1, these stories construct mytho-historical bonds between these two cult communities.

The recent scholarship suggests that we should reconsider the Isiac diaspora, in its movements large and small, as independent instances of the local appropriation of an internationally available culture.[150] The Opous inscription, along with the myth-history of Egyptian founders at other sites and constant migration in the Hellenistic period, suggests that we see the cults' spread as instances of active engagement with existing cult practice at various centers, with the impetus for appropriation coming both from migrants' agency and from religious justifications like divine encounters. Both regional and Mediterranean-wide connectivity thus played an integral role in the spread of Egyptian cults, demonstrating how large- and small-scale trade and transport allowed a small, local cult to diffuse throughout the Mediterranean world.

Textual Migrations

These migrations may have produced some trans-Mediterranean standardization of ritual practices.[151] In the late Hellenistic and early Imperial periods, a set of unusual hymnic texts circulated among Isiac communities in Greece and Asia Minor. Called aretalogies, they describe Isis' personality and character in detail, explaining her familial connections and specific powers in an almost didactic fashion. I return to the content of the aretalogies in Chapter 3, but here I must address their transmission and use. The earliest example dates to the 3rd century BCE, and variations appeared throughout Latin and Greek literature into the 3rd century CE. Epigraphic aretalogies to Isis, dating from the 3rd century BCE to the 2nd century CE, are known from Ios, Thessaloniki, Maroneia, Kassandreia and Andros, and from Telmessos and Kyme in Asia Minor.[152] Related texts that offer praise to other Egyptian gods like Sarapis, Anubis, and Harpokrates have also been found, including one at Delos dedicated by the Egyptian founder Apollonios.[153] To date, no aretalogy has been found outside of Greece and the west coast of Asia Minor. These aretalogies also found a receptive home in Imperial literature, particularly among the intellectuals of the Second Sophistic. Diodorus Siculus' *Library of History*, Plutarch's *De Iside et Osiride*, and Book 11 of Apuleius' *Metamorphoses*, written in the 2nd century CE, contain passages that reproduce or adapt epigraphic aretalogies.

Several of these texts copy each other quite closely, and scholars have argued that they were read and displayed as part of the cult's rituals and also to attract new members.[154] As Martzavou has argued, the Kyme aretalogy stele's find-spot in a publicly accessible part of the sanctuary suggests that the uninitiated and even the casual passerby would have had access to aretalogical texts.[155] More recently, Moyer has demonstrated that the text of the only fully preserved aretalogy (the example from Kyme) displays consistency in punctuation and spacing with its copies at Thessaloniki and Telmessos, and to a lesser extent with the copies at Ios and Kassandreia. The dates of these texts seem to suggest that the format of the Isiac aretalogies became standardized across the region sometime in the late 1st century BCE or 1st century CE.[156] More importantly, Moyer argues that this punctuation provided a guide to the reader about the proper performance of the text.[157] If the texts were read in the same way at many sites, perhaps as part of a carefully choreographed ritual, they would have constructed a sense of uniformity and solidarity with a larger global Isiac community.

The consistency of the hymns indicate that many communities desired a sense of shared belonging with other Isis devotees, whether the scope of belonging was local or global. In many places, the cults share a series of Egyptian founders, though we have no way of knowing if the founders coordinated their actions. Similarly, aretalogical texts, which have some connection with Egyptian cult practice, played a defining role in the cults' ideologies and practices.[158] Roman imperialism facilitated these new connections by creating a world in which cultic texts and personnel could move with relative safety and ease. As people migrated across the Mediterranean in the Hellenistic and Roman periods, they brought specific practices with them and adapted them for their new homes. From there, local communities could reappropriate the cult again. The Opous inscription of Xenainatos describes just such an instance and demonstrates the value of a continued connection with the mother community. These ties are furthered through the distribution and performance of aretalogies. As we see in Chapter 3, these texts often reconstruct a universal form of Isis: by sharing and circulating the texts, each community can find membership within a larger community. While we should not overstate any claims of universality in Isiac cult, the history of migration and the repetition and performance of similar aretalogies indicate that there were social and ideological connections between sanctuary communities that produced a common religious culture.

SHAPING ISIAC GROUPNESS

In this chapter, I have argued that many of the cult's internal structures aim at constructing groupness. Ritual activities, including processes of initiation, celebration of festivals, and participation in voluntary associations, defined the group clearly for members and for outsiders. In many places, regulations, regular dedications, and caretaking rites further solidified the group. Isiac groupness could also entangle itself with other powerful forms of identification. At Dion, two families used the sanctuary for repeated dedication and display, a practice that suggests that families and other, smaller groups like migrants could incorporate cultic activities into their own processes of group-making.

In order to construct these arguments, I have brought together evidence from wide expanses of time and space. Because of the fragmentary and scattered nature of our evidence, it is difficult to fully understand the subtle ways in which the cult must have changed over time in response to both local and Mediterranean-wide pressures. My reading here presents a series of practices that may be representative of larger phenomena but could also reflect the practices of specific times and places. The cult was constantly recreated at new sites and individual members and leaders could fashion narratives of community that suited their needs. Some may have failed entirely. But those who engaged in the actions discussed in this chapter – those who came to festivals and made sacrifices and followed rules – would have felt themselves to be an Isis devotee. More importantly, the cult was structured in such a way as to encourage devotees to feel that belonging to the cult mattered.

Groupness was probably not uniform. The cults did not have sharp edges.[159] Devotee communities could be composed of individuals with varying levels of involvement, and belonging to the cult did not require devotees to divorce themselves from other cults or from Greek civic life. Egyptian cults were not a "religion" in the modern sense, which would require devotion to a single set of gods or cult practices, but a set of repeated actions and social affinities that produced a fragile sense of belonging.[160] For less devout members, their sense of groupness may have been more episodic: it may have required an external trigger, like a festival or social interaction with other devotees, to come fully into being. But situational identities can be meaningful. Under the right circumstances, even occasional or partial involvement could have made devotees feel like part of the group.

I also argue that there existed a sense of commonality between Isiac communities across Greece. The cults' history of migration produced ritual and social ties between communities that persisted over the expanses of time and space. Shared texts elucidating Isis' personality and nature appear at many sites throughout the region, indicating that a significant number of communities desired to engage with common ideas about their gods. This sense of commonality, constructed through shared, repeated actions, would have also contributed to a sense that this localized form of belonging to a single cult community also meant sharing in a broader form of groupness that spanned most of Greece and spread into Asia Minor. It is notable, on the other hand, that this network did not stretch into the western Mediterranean. There is no evidence in Italy of any cultic regulations or aretalogical hymns, two aspects that were key to creating Isiac groupness across Greece, as I have argued. This absence makes it difficult to place Italy in the same network of Isiac cult practices identified for Greek communities. While there must have been some commonalities in Isiac cults across the Mediterranean, there is no evidence yet to suggest that the same types of groupness existed in Pompeii or at other sites in Italy.[161]

How, then, did this new cultic identity impact how devotees negotiated ethnicity in Roman-colonized Greece? As I argue throughout the book, Greekness and Isiac cult had a dynamic relationship that produced a new interpretation of Isis centered on Greekness and the domestication of Egypt for Greek consumption. In Chapters 3–6, I explore the intersections and interpretations that produced this regional version of a global cult.

CHAPTER THREE

DETERRITORIALIZING THEOLOGY?

Bringing the Egyptian Gods to Greece

In Chapter 2, I examined how Isiac communities coalesced by building a larger community through local and regional ties. Key to these connections was a corpus of hymns called aretalogies, which defined Isis' personality, powers, family networks, and place in myth-history. The extant texts are copies or near-copies of each other; and Moyer has demonstrated that the texts are punctuated consistently, which suggests they were meant to be read in the same way, perhaps even as part of an ritual performance.[1] Not every Egyptian sanctuary in the ancient world preserves an Isiac aretalogy, and only two distinct types are known, but there are enough examples to suggest a pattern of shared characterizations of Isis from Egypt to the eastern Mediterranean and Asia Minor. In this chapter I examine the reception of Isiac aretalogies by cult devotees to investigate how cultic myth-history framed devotees' interpretations of Isis' origins and ethnic identity. I argue from the literary and epigraphic evidence that devotees relied on stories about Isis and Sarapis that contextualized Egyptian religion within Greek antiquity. In this way, the communities created a transcultural version of the Egyptian gods that belonged fundamentally to Greece.

Because the texts were displayed in sanctuaries, they must be understood as part of the cults' material culture. In the Greco-Roman world, perceptions about Egyptian cults were nested within other, prevailing ideas about Egypt, and these preconceptions would naturally have informed devotees' ideas about Isis. As early as the 5th century BCE, Greek historians like Herodotus were writing about Egypt, and by the time of the Roman Empire, Latin authors represent Egypt as a place of experimentation, wonder, and timelessness. These notions also frame many visual representations of Egypt in Roman wall painting – yet another medium in which devotees could encounter images of Egypt that, in turn, shaped their perceptions of Isis and Sarapis.

These dialogues between textual and visual evidence produced narratives about the Egyptian gods that weakened their perceived connection to Egypt.[2] Together they created an Isiac mode of viewership that primed devotees to see the gods as universal, multivalent, and available in many forms, as originating in Egypt and yet deeply connected to the Greek mythological past.[3] While these themes also underpinned more normative forms of Greco-Roman visuality,[4] Isis' cult was unique in the intensity with which the theological principles defined the cults' ritual and visual culture. Consequently, the cults' texts prepared devotees to interpret ritual and material culture in a way that placed Isis and Egyptian religion at the very foundation of Greek myth-history and reframed that myth-history in a more transcultural way, setting Greekness as a cultural thread that wound together the Mediterranean's disparate cultures.

I consider these implications first by examining how Greeks and Romans of the Imperial period thought about Egypt. In a brief survey of Greek-speaking authors from Herodotus to Plutarch, I argue that many would have come to the cult already primed to see Egypt as a place for experimentation. Then, I turn to the Isiac cults and explore how devotees framed the gods' journey from Egypt to Greece. I focus on the Chronicle of Sarapieion A, a hymnic, mytho-historical text from early 3rd-century BCE Delos that describes how the Memphite priest Apollonios brought the cult of Sarapis to Greece. I place three aspects of the text in context. First, I consider how the narrative of the founder Apollonios frames the cults as a product of boundary-crossing and emphasizes Sarapis' own abilities to transgress geographic space. This version of the Egyptian gods thus highlights his ability to lessen distances and cultural difference, a key aspect of most definitions of imperially produced ancient globalization.[5] Next, I look at the praises included in the second portion of the text (called the Hymn of Maiistas), which constructs a universalizing version of the gods. This new Isis had major consequences for our understanding of the cult in the Roman Empire: these texts loosened her ties to Egypt and rendered her a universally available deity. They also operated as a metaphor for an increasingly transcultural Mediterranean world in which foreign cultural features could be appropriated and remade for local use.[6]

Returning to the Chronicle of Sarapieion A, I conclude with another aspect of Isiac geography that brings the goddess into the embodied realm of Greece: epiphany. In many accounts, Isis and Sarapis frequently appear directly to viewers in Greek sanctuaries. These stories would have encouraged devotees to expect personal encounters with the gods, especially within the sanctuary, a notion that heightened the experience of viewing cult images. The cults' textual world, then, uproots the Egyptian gods and finds a new home for them in Greek mythology, history, geography, and ritual experience, prompting critical questions of cultural appropriation as we examine the cult's intersections with ancient globalization and ethnicity.

FROM THE AEGEAN TO THE NILE: KNOWLEDGE, STEREOTYPE, AND INTERACTION

Isis' Egyptianness was not a neutral cultural concept. Rather, it was associated with ideas and stereotypes that made it useful as an expression of a certain type of difference. In her discussion of Roman perceptions of Egypt, which focuses on the Italian peninsula, Swetnam-Burland points to the vacillation of Roman stereotypes of Egypt between the land of the present and the idealized and marvelous version of Egypt's pharaonic past, which was drawn primarily from commonly held stereotypes and "hearsay."[7] I am especially interested in the ways these literary texts imagine Egypt, and the kinds of images they construct. While previous scholarship emphasized Egypt's role as the ultimate other in Greek thought, more recent work has nuanced this perspective, suggesting that earlier cultural exchanges between Greece and Egypt created complex ideas of foreignness and familiarity. I argue that some Greco-Roman literature and material culture represented Egypt as a place for experimentation, exploration, and rewriting history.

Building Classical Ideals of Egypt

Greek authors found Egypt good to think with. In many texts, Egypt becomes a place to experiment with conflicting poles of dichotomies and explore in-between spaces. Egypt's positive qualities take center stage in many Classical Greek and especially Athenian texts, from the *Histories* of Herodotus to Isocrates' *Busiris* – particularly its long history and its role as a center and producer of wisdom and sacred information, and as the home of many natural wonders.[8] These attributes were of great value and interest to Greek audiences and shaped the ways in which Egyptians were represented. But these texts tend to reflect Athenian values and histories more accurately than their Egyptian counterparts.[9] Because Egypt was sufficiently distant from Athens – especially with respect to daily life – it served as a place in which to construct experimental histories that reframed mytho-historical figures like Solon and Busiris.[10]

The most famous treatment of Egypt in Greek literature is in Book 2 of Herodotus' *Histories* (5th century BCE), which takes an expansive ethnographic approach to Egypt and the Nile River. Understanding Herodotus' view of Egypt is challenging. Hartog's *The Mirror of Herodotus* emphasized the key role that inversion and cultural difference played in Herodotus' representations of Egypt.[11] Similarly, Vasunia's more critical study explores Herodotus' use of the conceptions of space and time to develop that contrast.[12] Recent work has shifted away from Hartog's approach, arguing instead for a more ambivalent approach that recognizes the agency of the Egyptians in creating Herodotus' narrative.[13] Moyer's arguments in particular have provided critical nuance to our understanding of Herodotus as a historian, highlighting his respectful engagement with Egyptian sources and priests, especially in those sections focused on Egyptian history and religion.[14] But Herodotus' account of Egypt as a place and in his representations of people outside the priestly class frequently emphasize the types of difference discussed by Hartog. This is to say that Herodotus has many Nile Rivers in his work, and my discussion here concerns just one facet of Herodotus' representation of Egypt. The sense of distance and difference discussed by Hartog and Vasunia becomes central to the conception of Egypt and the vision of the Egyptian experience in the work of later Greek and Roman authors.

As part of his ethnographic approach, Herodotus offers an inventory of Egyptian practices and traits, many of which invert Greek norms.[15] Some sections clearly establish Egyptian peoples as degenerate and inferior. In a particularly negative passage describing Egyptian funerary and embalming practices, he claims that the corpses of women who were especially beautiful and famous are held at home for three days so that the embalmers and other funerary workers do not have intercourse with the body (2.89).[16] The charge of necrophilia exploits the Greek suspicion of Egyptian funerary practices and the sexual aspects of Egyptian cult, as described below. Invoking the trope of the vulnerable yet beautiful female, this passage plays upon gendered stereotypes to draw a line of difference between the two cultures.

In most cases, however, these explorations of difference take on a lighter tone. In several passages of Book 2, Herodotus describes the drunkenness and lewd acts performed by nameless Egyptians that accompanied the festival of Bubastis, a custom surprising to many Greeks. As part of the festival, men and women travel together by boat, and the women lift their skirts and reveal themselves to onlookers on shore (2.60). Lateiner argues that Herodotus uses women to illustrate norms, set limits, and create contrasts between Greek and other.[17] Unnamed women urinate standing up in Egypt while men urinate sitting down, women are charged with supporting their parents while men are not obligated to do so, and women work in the marketplace while men stay home (2.35).[18] Herodotus frames this discussion in terms of Egyptians versus all others, which posits Greece and Greek customs as the norm and describes Egypt as part of a "ethnographic narrative of difference."[19] Though Greek customs are never explicitly mentioned, the contrast between these unnamed, generalized Egyptians and "all other peoples" is – which suggests that

Herodotus' Greek-speaking audiences would have seen these customs as very unlike their own.[20] These precisely embodied details, many of which describe practices rife with affective resonance, would have made these actions feel especially unsettling.

Throughout the Hellenistic period, Egypt continued to provide a point of reference by which Greekness and otherness could be explored through equivalence and comparison. In his *Library*, Diodorus Siculus discusses at length some alternative mythologies of characters like Herakles and Dionysus that include visits to Egypt.[21] He also remarks that Egyptian and Greek deities are often interchanged with or referenced by the name of their cognate god in the other culture.[22] These remarks on equivalences are not banal observations but are part of a process of connecting the two cultural traditions.[23] Elsewhere, he represents the Greek gods and heroes as inhabiting Egypt. At 1.19.2, Herakles stops a disastrous deluge of Nile floodwaters and returns the river to its normal course, saving Prometheus, who is the overseer of the district, from suicide.[24] Diodorus follows Herodotus in positing two Herakles, a Greek demigod and an Egyptian hero, but the narrative conflates the two. In another myth, we are told that Orpheus never visited Hades but actually visited Egypt and brought all of his sacred mysteries from Egypt into Greece (1.96.4–7). Gruen sees this tendency in Diodorus as part of a larger Hellenistic view of Egypt, active in the 1st century BCE, that advocated interdependence and argued for ethnic and cultural harmony between the two lands.[25] Just as Egyptians had consumed Greek myths and used them for Egyptian advantage, so too the Greeks consumed Egyptian myths, using them as a means of understanding themselves.

Like Herodotus, Diodorus also presents several aspects of Egyptian culture as an inversion of Greek culture. Some of these passages, including his discussions of Egyptians' excessive reverence for animals (1.83–90) and their strange burial practices and unusual reverence for funerary workers (1.91–92), largely follow Herodotean models. In other passages, however, he explores Egypt as a place to idealize and even to improve aspects of Greek culture.[26] In his discussion of Egyptian laws and courts, Diodorus creates equivalences between Greek and Egyptian politics that push back on Hellenistic and Roman models of kingship.[27] Despite his claims that Egyptians have the best laws, Diodorus is able to justify his arguments only through comparison.[28] For example, he compares Egyptian courts to those of the Areopagus in Athens and the *gerousia* of Sparta; and the geographic methods used to create the Egyptian court (ten judges each from Heliopolis, Thebes, and Memphis) echoes the selection of representatives from the demes in the Athenian *Boule*.[29] Like Athenian jurors, these judges receive sustenance from the state (1.71.4), but the Egyptian system has one major advantage over Greek systems. Because plaintiffs and defendants are required to submit their arguments in writing rather than presenting them orally, Diodorus argues, Egyptian judges are less likely to be swayed by emotion and are able to present verdicts based in fact (1.76.1–3). The Egyptian system that Diodorus recreates offers Egyptian methods as a solution to Greek problems. Key intellectual and political figures in Greek history like Lycurgus, Plato, Solon, Pythagoras, and Democritus integrated Egyptian thoughts and legal concepts into their own famous works (1.98). Egypt here is a source not only of primordial wisdom but of Classical practices that impacted the institutions that touched the everyday lives of Greeks and Romans. No Greek history would be complete without a thorough discussion of Egypt.

After Herodotus: Egypt in the Roman Mind

As the Roman Empire grew in prominence, traditional Greek ideas about Egypt continued to resonate in Latin literature. As Manolaraki has argued, Egypt's increasing participation in Greek and Roman affairs during the Hellenistic and Roman periods inspired Latin authors to map particular types of otherness and functions onto Egyptian landscapes.

> As Rome gradually absorbs Egypt and opens to Egypt's seductive exoticism, authors exploit the capacious symbolism of the Nile to articulate perennial ontological, epistemological, and ethical questions: these include the allure and threat of the unfamiliar; the collaborative dynamic between conquest and knowledge; the tension between political pedagogy and imperial authority; the ability and validity of human desire to master the unknowable; the humancentric personification of the natural world; the immanent presence of the divine; the transience of humans within space and time; the disconnection between human time and cosmic time; the process by which human meaning is mapped onto plain geology; and the relation between nature and artifice or reality and perception.[30]

The Nile often reconciles diametrically opposed concepts, constructing a middle ground in which the Roman and the Egyptian can coexist, an Imperial fantasy of effective global rule. Many Roman-period authors, including Tibullus, Dio Cassius, Pliny the Younger, Fronto, Plutarch, and Dio Chrysostomus, discuss episodes of Imperial intervention in Egypt in ways that highlight an ongoing concern with the status of Hellenism in the Mediterranean, the individual's place in the empire's vast social and geographic terrain, and the relationships between gods and men.[31]

Ideas about Egypt and the Nile changed according to Rome's political priorities. While Augustus was locked in combat with Marc Antony and Cleopatra (and during much of the Julio-Claudian period), Egypt was often negatively depicted: Augustus snubbed Egyptian religion and the famous tombs of the pharaohs during his visit to Alexandria;[32] Strabo wrote a colonizing description of the Nile in Roman terms;[33] Tibullus emphasized the barbarism and feminization of Egypt through the character of Osiris;[34] and then there were multitudes of criticisms of Cleopatra herself. Still, Egyptian objects and motifs remained popular, including the same narratives about Egypt's antiquity, natural wonders, and the otherness of its inhabitants.[35] These repeated inquiries suggest a deep if perhaps prurient interest in Egypt. In material culture, however, the picture is somewhat different. Egyptianizing iconography appears in wall painting on the Palatine even before the Battle of Actium, and in a wide range of media, from relief sculpture in Augustus' Forum to small cameo glass bottles.[36] Van Aerde has argued that the early date and widespread use of Egyptian themes and objects in Augustan art suggest that Egypt was already part of Rome's stylistic and cultural repertoire.[37] Material culture, then, reflects a similar level of interest, even if this interest involves Egypt as part of the empire, and global character.

These messages shifted somewhat during the Flavian period, when the emperors often employed Egyptian themes to legitimize their rule.[38] According to Tacitus and Suetonius, Vespasian learned of the death of his rival Vitellius from the Alexandrian oracle of Sarapis, and felt he owed a debt of loyalty to the Egyptian deity. In addition to renovating the Iseum Campanese in 80 CE, Domitian and his son dedicated a lavish sanctuary to the Egyptian gods at Benevento.[39] At around the same time, images of the Nile became popular in wall painting and mosaics. For example, forty-nine paintings depicting the Nile were found at Pompeii, mostly in private houses and gardens.[40] Though Pompeii and Rome have the highest concentration of Nilotic scenes, some examples were also found in Hellenistic and Roman Greece,[41] which suggests that this iconography may have also influenced how Greek devotees of Isis perceived Egypt. These fantastical scenes imagine the world of the Nile with its flora and fauna, particularly papyri, cranes, crocodiles, and hippopotami – peopling it with temples and dwarves.[42] Many of the paintings show Egypt in an apparently unflattering light. For example, in one painting from the pseudo-peristyle of the Casa del Medico at Pompeii, a group of dwarves defend their town against the ravages of two crocodiles and a hippopotamus, which has a dwarf in its jaws (Plate 5).[43] A warship full of dwarves sails away from buildings sketched in the background, and others swim away from the wild beasts. Another fresco from the same room depicts dwarves drinking, feasting, and engaging in sex acts.[44] Though these paintings seem to incorporate the more salacious aspects of Herodotus' portrayal, Barrett notes that many depict acts that were part of Egyptian religious practice or replicated established visual tropes in pharaonic and Ptolemaic Egyptian art, including representations of the Nile. But, like much of Roman art, these iconographies have been recombined and translated into something new.

These images miniaturize Egypt and grant their viewers control over how Egypt is constructed and who lives within it. More importantly, they domesticate Egypt. The Nile is now something that can be possessed and associated with leisure and comfort in the Roman home.[45]

During the Antonine and Severan eras, the Nile came to symbolize the excellence of Imperial rule and Egypt's connections with the rest of the empire. Hadrian tended to materialize his deep sorrow over Antinoos' death in the form of Egyptianizing material culture, which resulted in the construction of several Egyptianizing buildings at his villa at Tivoli and a general resurgence of interest in Egyptianizing themes in art across the Mediterranean.[46] One of the Nile's most fertile homes, however, was Second Sophistic literature. Plutarch, in one of his later philosophical works, *De Iside et Osiride*, used the Egyptian gods Isis and Osiris to reexamine Platonic ideas about the nature of the gods.[47] Here, the fantastical version of Egypt observed in earlier texts persists, as when Plutarch equates Isis with the fertility of the Nile Valley, and the river itself with Osiris' "effusion," such that their joining produces Egypt's natural bounty, and the annual inundation is constructed as a cosmic event (366a).[48]

By the 2nd century CE, however, the idea of Egypt need not always be linked with Egypt as a place, a process called deterritorialization. Deterritorialized objects and places have been uprooted from their original context, retaining only a tenuous connection to their point of origin. Because of this separation, they may be associated with new places or even remain entirely unmoored. Scholars regularly describe deterritorialization as a constituent process of globalization and the product of imperialism.[49] This process happens both to Isis and to Egypt itself, in varying degrees.[50] At *De Iside* 372e, Plutarch highlights Isis' changeability, explaining how she is called by many names and forms, and at 355e–356a the mythology of Isis' birth and life is recounted in ways that compare her to Greek deities. These discussions follow the surprising assertion that "Isis is a Greek word" (Ἑλληνικὸν γὰρ ἡ Ἰσίς ἐστι, 351f), which appears at the very beginning of the work. Plutarch argues that the Egyptian gods should be understood not only in terms of the marshes and lotus flowers of the Nile, because this would deprive the rest of the world of Isis, where others lack the Nile, or Buto, or Memphis (377c–d); rather, the gods are the same among all peoples, whether Greek or barbarian (377e–378a). The Egyptian gods now belong to a broader geographic landscape that is no longer limited to their traditional home in the Nile Valley.[51]

As a cultural concept, Egypt is becoming more flexible: it is no longer epitomized by its natural landscape. This new reading deracinates Isis and her companions, establishing them within the cosmopolitan Roman world. Isis and Sarapis are at home anywhere they travel, and those that bring them to new places only enhance the gods' power. These literary constructs feed into the origin myths of the Egyptian cults and provide the sense of a fantastic, timeless point of origin for these deities. Most importantly, they argue that those in power have the ability to possess far-off places and to experience Egypt without even traveling there. Uprooted and unmoored, Isis and Sarapis are available to be reconfigured for Greek use.

SARAPIS AS BOUNDARY CROSSER

The literary tropes discussed above illustrate one context in which the cults of the Egyptian gods traveled to Greece. Crossing geographic boundaries was an important part of both the history of the cults and how the gods were conceived. Isis was one of the oldest goddesses in Egypt; while most devotees on the Greek mainland would have associated Sarapis with Egypt as well, his origins are more obscure and likely more recent. His most obvious Egyptian precedents were the gods Apis and Osiris; he also assimilated aspects of Greek male divinities like Zeus to become an independent deity in the Ptolemaic period.[52] The worship of Sarapis and Isis in Greece, then, relied on a narrative of travel that traced the gods' departure from Egypt and arrival in Greece.

Greek devotees needed stories of the Egyptian gods that preserved their connection with Egypt while also binding them to Greek communities. The arrival of Sarapis in the Greek city of Delos is legitimized through a narrative of the migration of an individual priest, Apollonios of Memphis (hereafter referred to as Apollonios I), who established a house shrine now referred to as Sarapieion A in the Inopos Quarter of Delos. Near the sanctuary's main entrance, an incised votive marble column bears the Chronicle of Sarapieion A (early 3rd century BCE), which gives two complementary accounts of the sanctuary's past, as written by two priests named Apollonios and Maiistas.[53] The accounts differ in style, length, and detail but tell roughly the same story.

The Apollonios account presents its protagonist as the hero of a story that describes the obstacles raised to the cult's existence on Delos.[54] The first few lines of the Chronicle emphasize this sanctuary's deep connections with Egypt. Apollonios (hereafter II) presents himself as the author and his grandfather, Apollonios (hereafter I), as the protagonist. Apollonios (II) thus establishes two critical components of the Sarapieion A cult: that the original priest came from Egypt (Memphis, as the Hymn of Maiistas specifies on line 38), and that he passed the cult's priesthood down to his descendants. In the former case, the author is emphasizing the family's ethnic origins to establish a close connection with Egypt as the place of origin for the cult. The mention of family lineage in the latter case also establishes that Apollonios (II) inherited the priesthood from his father, Demetrios, who inherited it in turn from Apollonios (I). As Greek priesthoods were rarely passed down by inheritance,[55] this allusion demonstrates how the cult preserved Egyptian religious customs.

Though Delos was a cosmopolitan city with a mixed population, the Chronicle portrays Apollonios (II) and his cult as being in a vulnerable position. In order to further legitimize the cult for Apollonios (II)'s community, a proper sanctuary was needed. One night, Sarapis appeared to Apollonios (II) in a dream and told him to found a Sarapieion in a particular spot. The god smiled upon the project, enabling Apollonios (II) to complete the sanctuary in only six months. His troubles, however, were far from over. An outside group brought suit against him and Sarapieion A, demanding that the sanctuary be closed. This account is curious and may be unrelated to his grandfather Apollonios (I)'s status as an Egyptian. Roussel's 1916 report on the sanctuaries originally implied that the three Sarapieia on Delos – A, B, and C – served the same cultic community and did not compete with one another. Relying on archaeological and epigraphic evidence, Moyer convincingly argues that Sarapieia B and C were active already in the latter half of the 3rd century BCE, which means that all three sanctuaries operated at the same time – in direct competition with one another for devotee attention and dedications (Figure 13).[56]

The devotees of Sarapieion A successfully defended their sanctuary from its detractors, thus creating space for Egyptian religion on Greek soil.[57] In the Hymn of Maiistas (66), the author tells us that it was κακὸς φθόνος ("evil jealousy") that motivated his neighbors to sue, but what exactly this might

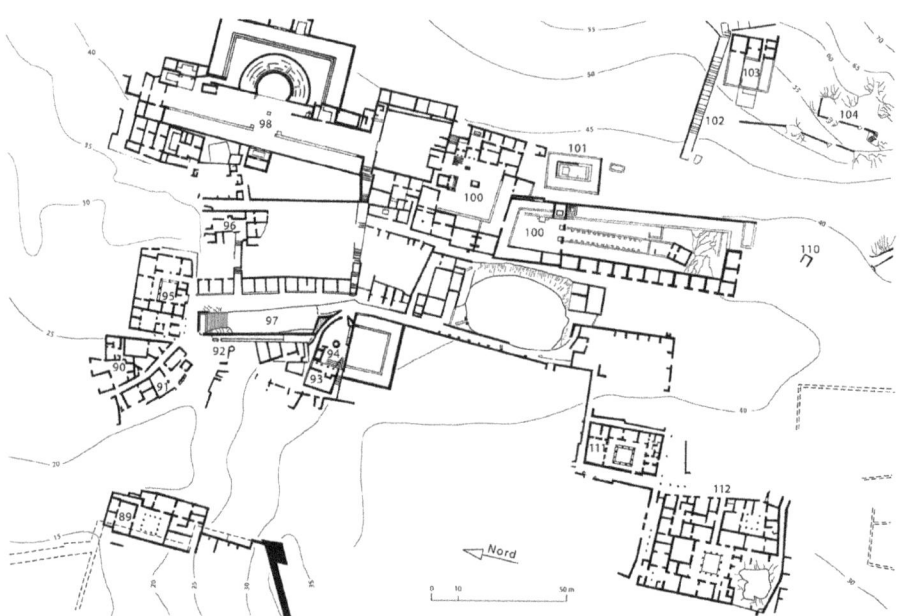

13. Plan of the Inopos Quarter and the Terrace of the Foreign Gods on Delos. Sarapieion A is marked as 91, Sarapieion B is 96, and Sarapieion C is 100. Courtesy École Française d'Athènes/ B. Sagnier.

mean is unclear.[58] Siard's theory that the water-starved residents of Delos may have been upset by the sanctuary's ad hoc (and probably illegal) construction of a channel to the Inopos River has gained considerable traction among scholars, recognizing the prominent role of water in the sanctuary's rituals that reconstructed a Nilotic experience for Greek devotees.[59]

Moyer, however, rejects Siard's theory. He argues that we should take the phrase κακὸς φθόνος literally – that intersanctuary competition and jealousy were the motivating factors behind the lawsuit. If we view the Chronicle's claims to Egyptian ancestry in this context, the author's repeated bid for authenticity can be seen as a way of superseding the other cult communities on the island – as a direct assertion of Egyptianness that emphasized the placement of a "real" Egyptian on Greek soil.[60] The names of other cult founders of presumably Egyptian origin – including Ouapheres, son of Horus, from Demetrias; Krateso from Amphipolis; and Thaies, wife of Agathokles, from Argos – have been found in inscriptions in Greece, suggesting that few had the connections and financial means to undertake the lengthy journey from Egypt to Greece in the Hellenistic period.[61] Preserving the memory of the ethnic and geographic boundaries that Apollonios and his gods crossed to arrive in Delos becomes a significant means of legitimizing the community's prominence.

This tale illustrates the extent to which Egyptian cults relied on establishing a sense of authentic connection between Egypt and the devotee communities. Though humans often see authenticity as a binary notion, the reality is much more nuanced. An authentic thing or event has a deep, real, and organic connection with the past – whether through origin, material, or narrative – and is seen as bringing that past into the present.[62] In a study of community responses to the Hilton of Cadboll Stone in the Museum of Scotland, Jones suggests that authenticity is a complex network of relationships between people, places, and objects.[63] That is, authenticity is created through narratives that place objects in close dialogue with or near desirable peoples and places. In discussions of ethnicity and culture, authentication is necessary for legitimization. Authenticity roots cultures in the tangible and intangible worlds and argues for their preservation.[64] The sense of permanence that accompanies authenticity often derives from the idea that these cultures are unchanging and exist primarily in the past.[65]

The Chronicle of Sarapieion A grants mythologies of distance, travel, and place a central role in the early history of Egyptian religion in Greece. While accounts of this type are rare, the Chronicle demonstrates that Delian devotees wanted to claim that their founders originated in Egypt and to build connections between the Mediterranean and Nile. Alongside these mortals traveled the Egyptian gods. Apollonios (I) brought with him a small statue of the god Sarapis, setting Egyptian religion in the same context of movement across geographic boundaries. The story of Sarapieion A was one of a departure from Egypt and a successful adoption in Isis' new Greek home. This transitory aspect of Sarapis' and Isis' history was another facet of their appeal. Like the migrants who brought them to Greece, these gods were seen as travelers in their own right, and their connections to peoples and places outside of Egypt became an essential part of how Greek communities conceptualized them.

FROM ONE, MANY: ISIS IN THE GREEK ARETALOGIES

The second portion of the Chronicle, the Hymn of Maiistas, begins with praise for Sarapis and Isis.[66] The divine works of Sarapis are innumerable and prodigious, and while some of them are sung in the cities of Egypt, all are praised in Greece. Then, as a god of health along with his wife Isis, Sarapis looks over all those who are good and pure of thought. These praises frame a longer version of the foundation story that presents each action as a personal victory for the god and ends with another set of encomia and thanksgivings. Sarapis has given great glory to his servants on Delos, and through his greatness, innumerable hymns will continue to be celebrated.

The column (again, dated to the early 3rd century BCE) thus offers an early version of an aretalogy for an Egyptian deity in Greece. The Isiac aretalogies were composed in 3rd century BCE–4th century CE; and epigraphic copies were dedicated in Isiac sanctuaries throughout Greece and Asia Minor. Except for a Latin adaptation in Apuleius' *Metamorphoses* 11, all are written in Greek. These texts praise the Egyptian gods, usually Isis, naming her family members and extolling her great virtues and deeds.[67] Examples from Maroneia, Telmessos, Andros, Kyme, Thessaloniki, Kassandreia, and Ios, dating from 1st century BCE–3rd century CE, have been identified as possible copies or adaptations of a single original text.[68] There are two primary strains, one written in the second person ("You are Isis") and another in the first ("I am Isis"), but both are largely consistent in terms of content and theme.[69] It is possible the texts originated in Egypt. The Kyme aretalogy claims to be a copy of a *stele* in Memphis, and Diodorus Siculus records a similar aretalogical text that he claims is from the Temple of Ptah in Memphis.[70] Scholars have also noted connections with a series of Isiac hymns from the Temple of Isis built by Ptolemy II at Philae.[71]

Recent research has given us a better understanding of the use and display of these texts. Only the Kyme aretalogy was found in situ, dedicated as a votive inside a public area of a sanctuary.[72] If the Kyme text is representative, it would suggest that people outside of the community had access to the text along with devotees. Most scholars agree that the texts were meant to be read out loud and repeated in rituals,[73] which would have provided another mode of transmission. Recitation would have prepared audiences for epiphanic experiences by inviting the god to listen and appear while also describing previous interventions and appearances.[74] Further, the repeated readings would have ingrained the universalizing ideas of the Egyptian deities deep into the memories of devotees.

Isiac aretalogical texts often follow a standard three-part schema.[75] In the first part, the aretalogies recount the essential characteristics of the god or goddess to whom the text is directed, usually Isis. The authors highlight her role as patroness of all the earth, inventor of language, and lawgiver to civilized peoples. In the second section, the author expounds on Isis' genealogy: her connections to Osiris, Horus/Harpokrates, and other gods associated with cosmic creation, such as Kronos. The final section tells of Isis' omnipotence and discoveries and emphasize her control over the heavens and seas. These passages often assert further that, having mastered fate, the goddess held complete dominion over all earthly affairs. Not all extant aretalogies conform to this structure, but their thematic and stylistic consistencies suggest these key principles that unified cultic practices and perhaps even beliefs across the region.

In many hymns, Isis is mentioned in conjunction with deities from all over the empire, particularly the Greek deities most familiar to the Greek-speaking communities that used the texts. One such text belonged to a set of Greek hymns incised on temple pillars in the sanctuary of Isis in modern Medinet Madi, Egypt.[76] The author was a priest of the 1st century BCE named Isidorus. The hymns describe Isis as a unifier of divinities and cultures across the Mediterranean: she subsumes all goddesses, domestic and foreign, under her aegis. In Hymn 1, Isidorus illustrates this principle by listing the goddesses through whom Isis receives veneration:

> All mortals who live on the boundless earth, Thracians, Hellenes, and all that are barbarians, call you by your beautiful name, greatly honored among all, each in his own tongue, each in his own land. The Syrians call you Astarte, Artemis, Anaia and the Lycian tribes call you Leto, the Sovereign. The Thracians call you also Mother of the Gods; the Hellenes call you Hera of the Great Throne and Aphrodite, and good Hestia and Thea and Demeter. But the Egyptians call you Thiouis, because you alone are all other goddesses named by the races of men.[77]

By enumerating the long list of peoples who worship Isis, Isidorus locates her among the disparate tribes of the Mediterranean world, marking two key aspects of her divine character. First, Isidorus notes that Isis has found many homes outside of Egypt, consciously highlighting her multiplicity and adaptability to a variety of cultural contexts. Like the history of travel embedded in the Chronicle of Sarapieion A, Isidorus' text separates Isis from Egypt, weakening her physical ties to the region and opening up the possibility of locating her in new geographic and cultural contexts. While Egypt is given pride of place in keeping with the inscription's location, identifying Isis as solely Egyptian would have raised significant issues.

Moving Isis out of Egypt had its consequences. For Egyptians and Greeks alike, Isis and her companions were deeply rooted in Egypt. For Egyptians, moreover, deities, ancestors, and other sacred characters were immanent in the landscape and the material world around them:[78] temples were seen as the sites of the gods' indwelling; cosmic concepts ordered the mortal Egyptian experience of the natural landscape; and divinities were present both in a literal sense, within divine objects, and in a metaphorical sense, through practices of cultural memory.[79] While Egyptian mythology speaks of the travels of Isis, most notably in her search for the body parts of Osiris, she is nevertheless deeply embedded in Egypt. Taking her out of Egypt complicated her core identity, and there is some evidence that the Egyptians of the Imperial Roman era saw this dislocation as problematic. Moyer notes in particular that the passage in Hymn 1 ends with overt references to Egypt and to Egyptian claims of special knowledge of the goddess. Her Egyptian name, Thiouis, meaning "sole" or "unique," references both her unifying character and the idea that Egyptian devotees have access to her deepest and truest nature.[80]

While Egypt holds pride of place in this list of avatars and cultural affiliations, the multitude of others deconstructs the boundaries between the deities. This universalizing aspect of Isis' nature is called henotheism. The modern term derives from the Greek phrase εἰς ὁ θεός (the single god), which appears in several inscriptions dedicated to Sarapis.[81] Henotheism is a theological system in which a particular divinity holds primacy over other gods, often by subsuming their attributes, powers, and identities. Devotees view the central god as original and all-powerful; all the other gods derive from the central god's henotheistic power.[82] Other deities in Hellenistic and Roman religions display henotheistic characteristics, most notably Hermes and Dionysos, but because of her explicitly universalizing and centralized role in the Isiac pantheon, Isis has the strongest claim to such a title.[83]

It is important to note the distinction between henotheism and monotheism. The henotheistic god is not the sole god but the best and most important. In the case of Isis, whose primacy was often expressed through the metaphor of motherhood, she was the creator of life and civilization and, by extension, of other divinities.[84] Her status as a mother-goddess, however, diverged from that of Demeter or Artemis Eilytheia in that she contained or subsumed her derivative divinities within her godhead. In some other Greek aretalogical texts, henotheistic properties were assigned to Sarapis and Harpokrates, which suggests that this aspect of the gods was not peculiar to Isis but a generic characteristic of the cult.

The henotheism of Isis in Greek texts derived from Egyptian precedents that make similar claims of universal control. Henotheistic principles belong to the earliest forms of Egyptian religion. Already by the end of the Middle Kingdom, Osiris occupies a central role as king of the gods, but the claim is not exclusive.[85] The title could be transferred to any deity, and many gods could be lord of all simultaneously. The central god's rule was also defined in spatial and temporal dimensions: he or she is lord of all the created world until the end of time.[86] This distribution of power relies on the idea of a single creator god who is manifested through the many other gods in the Egyptian pantheon.[87]

During the Ptolemaic and Roman periods, Isis received epithets in Egyptian hieroglyphic and Demotic texts that emphasized both her role as the patron of the king and her preeminence among other Egyptian deities.[88] These texts have much in common with the Greek aretalogies discussed below. In his study of some of the Demotic texts, Kockelmann notes that Isis is given Demotic epithets like "lady of love" that identify her with Greek goddesses, and that the general theological principles espoused in these texts are similar to those seen in the Greek epigraphic aretalogies.[89] He interprets these correspondences as a sign of interpenetration – evidence that Greek and Egyptian ideas about Isis' henotheistic personality were engaged in an ongoing and mutually influential discourse.[90] Similarly, Dousa notes, in his discussion of the mid-2nd century BCE Archive of Hor, the repeated emphasis on the role of Isis as queen of the gods and on her worldwide rule, even when Hor's own religious practice began to focus more directly on Thoth.[91] The henotheistic centrality of Isis, then, was a key part of how Egyptian devotees – Greek and Demotic speakers alike – conceptualized Isis in the Hellenistic and Roman periods.

There are some distinctions between Greek and Egyptian henotheism. In Egyptian religion, henotheism is more closely tied to the idea of kingliness, the notion that one god rules over all the others and is thus the most powerful and worthy of particular rule, while Greek texts place a stronger emphasis on the role of Isis as a mother. But the many similarities between Greek and Egyptian uses of henotheism suggest a Mediterranean-wide dialogue on the nature of the Egyptian gods. Many Greek and Demotic aretalogies of the Hellenistic period represent Isis as a unifier of various divinities under the aegis of a single goddess – Isis *unica*, as Dousa calls her – a concept that was also popular in Italy. A dedicatory inscription from a statue base in Capua describes what Dousa identifies as the "pantheistic dimensions" of the goddess, referring to her as "the one goddess Isis who is All."[92] In giving a uniform face to these various names, Isis blurs ethnic, theological, and cultural boundaries, becoming a goddess who belongs to all the peoples of the Mediterranean equally.

Isidorus' text also sets Isis in a transcultural framework. While the aretalogies at Medinet Madi mediate Greekness within broader concepts of globalization, some devotee communities went even further, representing Isis as an explicitly

Greek goddess. In an aretalogy from Maroneia, in Thrace, Isis is connected with several Greek deities and given credit for their foundational tasks.[93] The aretalogy appears in a fragmentary inscription on a marble votive stele dedicated in the 2nd century BCE.[94] Grandjean divides the extant text into three parts: the opening prayer, the description of the family of the god, and the list of divine attributes. Part one, the opening prayer (l.1–15), establishes the dedicatory context of the inscription, thanking Isis for her help in resolving the dedicator's eye problem.[95] Part two, the description of Isis' family (l.15–22), redefines her as the first daughter of the earth, the companion of Sarapis, and the cosmic counterpart of Selene.[96] So, while the Kyme aretalogy, for instance, combines the Greek and Egyptian gods, describing Isis as the oldest daughter of Kronos, the wife and sister of Osiris, the mother of Horus, and a companion of the Dog-Star Sothis (lines 5–10), the lineage in the Maroneia description redefines the goddess' ethnicity to assign her more primacy and align her more closely with Greece.[97]

The third and final part of the Maroneia aretalogy lists Isis' powers (l.22–44). Most of these attributes of Isis appear in other Greek aretalogies, including those from Kyme (line 7), Andros (lines 51–54), Diodorus Siculus (I.14.1), and Medinet Madi (I.8), indicating a general consistency in her theology across a broad swath of the eastern Mediterranean. At Maroneia, Isis is praised as a discoverer of writing (in tandem with Hermes), the inventor of justice and Greek and barbarian languages, a lawgiver, and the divinity who defined familial values (l.22–34).[98]

> [For] she, with Hermes, discovered writing. And some of it was sacred for initiates, and some of it was public for all. She established justice among us, in order that each of us might know how to live on equal terms, just as, because of our nature, death makes us equal. She established for some barbarian language, for others the Greek language, in order that the race might be differentiated not only as men from women, but also between all peoples. You established laws, but they were called *thesmoi* originally. Accordingly, cities enjoyed stability, having discovered not legalized violence but law without violence. You made it that parents were honored by their children, in that you cared for them not only as fathers, but also as gods. Accordingly, the favor is greater when a goddess also drew up as law what is necessary in nature.

There is much to parse in this passage, but the overall impression is that of a cultic community striving to contextualize Isis and Egyptian religion in the Greek mythological past. First, the goddess is credited with tasks normally associated with particular Greek deities: the creation of laws and justice (Athena) and the definition of familial roles and productive female fertility (Hera).

Isis next explicitly joins forces with Hermes, sharing credit with the Greek deity for a major civilizing force in Greek culture: the creation of writing and language, and with it the sacred writings used to initiate her devotees. Here, writing is described in ethnic terms: the author carefully separates out Greek and barbarian languages, emphasizing the significance of language for Greek self-definition.[99] The relationship between Greek language and cultural identification persists into the 2nd century CE. Language and performance, especially a facility with the archaizing Attic dialect, were important for the construction and definition of a transnational Greekness in Roman Greece, particularly for the authors of the Second Sophistic.[100] Learning the Greek language redefined the boundaries of membership in the Greek cultural community.[101] In casting Isis as a creator of ethnically bound languages, the Maroneia author establishes her as not only a unifier but also a definer of Greekness.

The last complete lines of the Maroneia text (I.34–41) argue for Isis' special connection to the landscape of Greece. Other aretalogies allude to Isis' preference for Greece, but none ground her so explicitly in Greek cities or sanctuaries.

> As a domicile, Egypt was loved by you. You particularly honored Athens within Greece. For there first you made the earth produce food: Triptolemos, yoking your sacred snakes, scattered the seed to all Greeks as he traveled in his chariot. Accordingly in Greece, we are keen to see Athens and in Athens, Eleusis, considering the city to be the ornament of Europe, and the sacred place the ornament of the city.[102]

First, the text describes Isis as residing in Egypt but sharing her patronage with Greece. Devoting just five words to Isis' Egyptian home, the author indicates an intention to minimize Isis' connections with Egypt. The next several lines (35–38) describe her deep connections with Greek soil, and particularly with Eleusis. Despite her foreign origins, then, Isis' Greek identity diverges from the visual and textual accounts described in the first section, deemphasizing the expression of foreignness in the text's construction of Isis.

The aretalogy, as preserved, concludes with a claim that cements Isis' relationship with Athens and the rest of Greece by describing her as a central goddess in the Eleusinian Mysteries.[103] First, the author promotes Triptolemos, an Eleusinian hero, as the first missionary of the Isiac religion. The final lines (39–41) of the fragment continue the theme, connecting Isis to Eleusis, Athens, and the City Eleusinion. Unlike the earlier example, the non sequitur here emphasizes the causality implied within the particle τοιγαροῦν (accordingly). Thus, two concepts that appeared to be unrelated became intimately intertwined: Triptolemos' crucial role in the diffusion of the Isis cult resulted in Isis' special role at Athens and Eleusis, and as such, recontextualized Isis as a Greek goddess who was expected to appear and participate at key sites on Greek soil.

Isis and her transculturality belonged, for many Greek devotees, to Greek myth-history from the very beginning; and her universality remained an important aspect of her divine character into the Roman period. The aretalogies framed Isis, and to a lesser extent her companions, as divinities who unified disparate divinities and cultures under a single godhead. As the creator of many basic human experiences and partner of Olympian deities, Isis was no longer a newcomer. Instead, these texts push the date of her arrival backward in time: they imply that Isis was part of the Greek pantheon from the beginning.

Despite chronological and geographic disparities, the Greek aretalogies repeat certain themes and formulae to construct a well-defined theology of the Egyptian gods. These 1st-century BCE texts and their myth-history exist in tension with the cults' 4th- and 3rd-century BCE history, challenging the goddess's connections with the priests that brought her to Greece. But the aretalogical version of Isis would persist well into the 3rd century CE, if not later, which indicates how powerful this idea was for devotees. These universal and polyvalent characteristics, I argue, permitted Isiac viewers to interpret material culture in a new and particularly expansive way, as part of a cult-specific psychology of recognition. Within a single cult image, devotees familiar with Isiac theology could read a whole pantheon of divinities into the numen of Isis.

Plutarch and Apuleius: Isis as a Middle Platonic Deity

Because of the henotheistic character of Isis, many Second Sophistic writers used Egyptian cults and their mythology as a central theme in their studies of Platonic philosophy. Several schools that were engaged in the reinterpretation of Platonic thought flourished in Greece during the High Empire, and much of their work on the nature of the divine focused on the knowability of the gods, describing the multivalent deities that resonate with the universalizing view found in the aretalogies.[104]

Perhaps the most famous example is, again, in Apuleius' *Metamorphoses* 11, set in the Greek city of Kenchreai near Corinth. Here Isiac aretalogies appear (in modified form) in the text of two of the prayers offered to Isis by the protagonist, Lucius.[105] At the beginning of Book 11, Lucius, who is still trapped in the form of a donkey, prays to Isis to help him. Referring to the Egyptian models, Lucius calls her the "uniform face (*facies uniformis*) of the gods and goddesses," the goddess that the whole world worshiped with different rituals and under different names.[106]

> O Queen of Heaven – whether you are Ceres, the primal and bountiful mother of crops, who, glad in the return of her daughter, removed the old nourishment from foraged acorn and showed gentle food to men, and now you honor the soil of Eleusis, or whether you are heavenly Venus, who, in the beginnings of nature, united the diversity of the sexes by creating love and, after bringing forth the human race with its

unceasing offspring, now are adored in the island shrine of Paphos. Or Diana, Apollo's sister, you who relieve the pangs of countless childbirths with your soothing remedies, venerated now at Ephesus; or dread Proserpina herself, she of the night-cries, who triple-faced combats the assault of spirits shutting them from earth above, who wanders the many sacred groves, propitiated by a host of rites ... by whatever name, with whatever ceremony, or by whatever visage we should invoke you.[107]

Once more, the idea of translating and unifying across cultures characterizes the divinity of Isis. Isis is equated to Ceres, Venus, Diana, and Proserpina; she is named as well by a catch-all term, *quoquo nomine ... quaqua facie*, that could refer to a variety of female deities. There can be little doubt that Apuleius drew from Isiac aretalogies to compose this passage. Lucius organizes these claims around the metaphor of the moon and its movement across the sky. Throughout Roman Imperial art – from the breastplate of the Prima Porta Augustus to the Arch of Galerius the tetrarch at Thessaloniki – the image of Caelus, a personification of the sky, represents Rome's rule over the known earth according to the *terra orbis* model of rulership that was the basis of Roman imperialism.[108] The invocation of Isis as *regina caeli* at *Met.* 11.2 refers to the globalizing tendencies of Roman imperialism. As the Queen of Heaven, Isis again floats, deterritorialized, above the earth, lacking a clear connection to Egypt but embedded in the global workings of the Roman Empire.

Apuleius' earthly pantheon, however, is smaller and geographically more intent upon establishing a Greek home for Isis. Her response to Lucius' prayer through her "single face" makes all the gods and goddesses available to the supplicant:[109] she identifies herself as the Phrygian Pessinuntine Mater Deum, the Attic Kekropian Minerva, the Cyprian Paphian Venus, the Cretan Dictynna Diana, the Sicilian Ortygian Proserpina, the Eleusinian Attic Ceres, the Rhamnousian Nemesis, Juno, Bellona, and Hecate – though only the Egyptians know her true name of Isis and worship her with the proper rites. Like Isidorus, Apuleius preserves her connection to Egypt. At the same time, while he uses Latin names for his divinities, he takes great care to locate these various manifestations of Isis within the Greek-speaking world: at Eleusis, a famed sanctuary near Athens, at Paphos on the island of Cyprus, and at Ephesus, in the heart of Asia Minor.

The choice agrees with the setting of this particular episode on the beaches of Kenchreai and the novel's location in Greece. In the context of the Greek cult's theology, however, and given Apuleius' origins in North Africa – the choice feels charged. Rather than prioritizing an Egyptian, North African, or even Roman version of the goddess, Apuleius reframes Isis with geographic specificity, setting her in a Greek landscape and, by extension, in a Greek cultural paradigm. Known on the international stage and fluent in Latin and Greek, Apuleius still frequently alludes to his African heritage, making reference, for example, to the Tanit sanctuary at Carthage at *Met.* 6.4 and the foundation of his education at Carthage at *Flor.* 18.18. In addition, several of his oratorical works seem to have been composed for a local audience.[110] The inclusion, at *Met.* 11.2, of these Greek sites for Isis, which would have little resonance for North African audiences, indicates that the *Metamorphoses* served a broader public. More importantly, Lucius' Greek-focused version of Isiac universalism suggests that the idea had spread throughout the Mediterranean by the 2nd century CE. By this point, many readers must have seen Isis' transcultural Greekness as a legitimate reading of the goddess, even if only for Hellenophile devotees like Lucius.

This Hellenocentric version of Isis reached a large audience through Apuleius' novel, including the Second Sophistic authors and intellectuals discussed in Chapter 1. Apuleius' ideas about Isiac cult probably owed much to the Platonic tradition of which he was an adherent: the tradition was deeply interested in Egyptian deities and mythologies.[111] Plutarch's *De Iside et Osiride* could have offered a model. The text follows the epigraphic aretalogies in promoting a polynymic and universalized vision of Isis and Osiris.[112] Addressed to the Delphic priestess Klea, to whom Plutarch addressed several short treatises of the *Moralia*, the *De Iside* offers a mythology of Isis' genesis and powers that presents Isis and Osiris as Platonic ideals of the good and places Isis and her companions in a Greek intellectual and cultural framework.[113] These readings, like those of Apuleius, imagine Isis and Sarapis as fundamental divine principles, setting the Egyptian gods at the foundation of Greek ideas of divinity.

Plutarch also portrays Osiris as dispersed yet eternal, emphasizing his ability to originate from all places – universalized, that is, in the Egyptian tradition – while simultaneously describing the god's story in Greek terms.[114] In the *De Iside*, Plutarch recounts one of Osiris' foundational myths as follows. Osiris' brother Seth kills and dismembers him in battle, scattering the pieces of the body around Egypt and the Levant. Isis, his sister and wife, traveling in disguise, gathers up the pieces and brings a newly whole Osiris back to life. At 378.69.1e–f, Plutarch rationalizes the more morbid and mournful rituals of the Egyptian cults by comparing them to the celebrations of Demeter's sorrows that are inherent in the Eleusinian Mysteries, following the pattern of integrating the two goddesses observed in the Maroneia aretalogy. Isis' mournful search for her deceased husband brings her to Byblos, where the local queen finds her crying and brings her into the royal household as a nurse (357.15a–16d). The passage clearly recalls Demeter's tears at Eleusis and her adoption into the royal household there: as in the Maroneia inscription, the Hellenizing impulse equates Isis to Demeter, framing her search within Demeter's own Eleusinian mythology.[115] Plutarch's approach represents a broader interest among Middle Platonists in equating Isis and Egyptian religion

FROM ONE, MANY: ISIS IN THE GREEK ARETALOGIES

to Greek counterparts that can be traced back to Herodotus.[116] Isis, in his mind, cannot be understood except through a Greek lens.

As for the Osiris myth, the metaphor of reunification in a single body is perfect for Plutarch's Platonic thinking. After Osiris' body is cyclically dismembered and scattered throughout the earth, Isis finds him and reassembles him into a revivified being, suggesting that the god and his soul are everlasting and imperishable (*De Is.* 373a, ἀίδιον εἶναι καὶ ἄφθαρτον). The reconstructed Osiris brings together the disparate parts of the world, where his body was scattered, into a single body – a perfect metaphor for universalism and Roman power. Isis, on the other hand, fills the parts of several Platonic roles, including those of the World Soul, the Demiurge, and the Receptacle, innovating on a long Greek philosophical tradition.[117] As the World Soul, Isis lives in parallel with the human experience, seeking the God in the material world and eventually directly encountering the God. As the Demiurge, Isis orders the world's chaos by reassembling Osiris' scattered body parts, becoming a creative energy in and of herself and bringing forth the image of the perceptible world.[118] Isis here generates universality and connection by mimicking the globalizing power of the Roman Empire.

As the Receptacle, Isis transmits being to another through her participation in the physical act of giving birth, creating life and assuming multiple forms.[119] This part of Isis' character suggested to Plutarch's reader that he should expect tremendous variability in Isis' image. Shortly after describing how statues of Isis have horns that resemble the crescent moon and wear dark garments,[120] Plutarch mentions Isis' physical changeability, describing her as having many names and many shapes.[121] Though the two concepts are not explicitly linked in Plutarch's text, Isis' multiform nature leads Plutarch to the conclusion that creation is the image of being in nature, alluding again to the Platonic Forms.[122] These disparate concepts are unified through the divinity, constructing a creative tension between Isis' innate diversity and unity that echoes the transcultural principles framed in the Isiac aretalogies.

Viewed through a philosophical lens, Isis and her companions prepare the viewer to encounter a single divine truth through multiple forms. Plutarch sets the Egyptian gods atop a hierarchy of divinities as abstracted paradigms of Truth and Good.[123] This ideal of Truth and Good resonates with the aretalogical emphasis on universalism, and Osiris and Isis thus represent these ideals of goodness among all the peoples of the Roman Empire. These ideal gods were represented for their devotees in turn, inviting a wide variety of styles and local influences upon their physical images. By worshiping the gods and contemplating their nature, the initiate could grow closer to the essential, ideal truth of the Egyptian gods and become one with them.[124] Still, Plutarch's Platonic approach serves largely to explain preexisting phenomena. Most of the ideas that Plutarch approaches through Platonic Forms, such as the abstraction of the ideal/divine and the idea of multiple physical forms as derivations of the ideal/divine, appear in basic forms in the aretalogical texts as early as the Hellenistic period. For an elite, well-educated initiate, Plutarch's text and his references to Greek philosophers throughout would have provided an ethnically and historically specific intellectual framework through which the educated initiate might interpret his religious experiences.

EPIPHANIC EXPECTATIONS IN ISIAC TEXTS AND OBJECTS

These texts and their focus on deterritorialization, universalism, and polysemy highlight the fact that the gods could assume a variety of forms that tended to place them in the Greek world, both metaphorically and physically. These ideas shift the Egyptian gods further away from their points of origin and reterritorialize them within Greek sanctuaries. Several of the Greek texts bring the gods to Greece's shores through episodes in which they appear directly to Greek devotees. Epiphany renders the gods in concrete forms, even if the forms are of various different sizes, shapes, and iconographies.[125]

The gods' appearances to their devotees provided the authority for the production of ideal images of the gods and goddesses,[126] resulting in artistic representations of the corporeal god. These epiphanic visions, in turn, probably drew from existing images in text and art. Translated into locally appropriate modes of representation, the gods reinforced the arguments for Isis' essentially Greek identity found in texts like the *De Iside* and the Maroneia aretalogy.[127] Readers would have seen the Egyptian gods as abstractions that could take myriad physical forms in both epiphanic experiences and artistic representations. Thus, polysemy provided a crucial foundation for Isiac viewership that was predicated on Isis' power to appear directly to her devotees. These site-specific epiphanic experiences also anchored Isis within particular spaces in Roman Greece, placing the gods in new networks of connection and meaning that complicated the narratives of foreignness inherent in her cult.

But where and how might these divine encounters take place? Most of our accounts of epiphanic experiences in Egyptian cults in Greece are connected to dreams. While dream-based encounters were common in Greek and Roman literature and religion,[128] certain types of dream oracles were more often associated with the Egyptian cults.[129] Moyer notes that 60 percent of inscriptions referring to dream oracles on post-independence Delos belong to the Egyptian cults; during the period of Delian independence (314–168 BCE), the proportion is close to 100 percent.[130] I argue that these accounts of dream oracles and other material evidence of epiphanic encounters motivated readers to anticipate their own encounters with the divine. In this section, I study the Hymn of Maiistas, the second part of the Chronicle of Sarapieion A, as an example of an Isiac dream oracle from Hellenistic Greece.[131] The text describes epiphanic encounters that likely took place inside the sanctuary. Contemplating the hymn in its original context formed a discursive practice that encouraged the reader to contemplate the gods and their presences and absences inside the sanctuary space.

Soteriological tendencies played a prominent role in the Egyptian cults on Delos, where the gods' interventionist aspect was an important part of the cults' foundation narrative.[132] Maiistas' tale recounts the same historical episode as Apollonios (II)'s account, but it includes more details about the cult's early foundation and takes a deeper interest in the miraculous nature of the dream oracles.[133] The author, Maiistas, names himself in the first line in order to distinguish the tale from the foregoing Apollonios account,[134] and shortly thereafter turns to the story of Apollonios (I) and the foundation of Egyptian cults on Delos. Maiistas tells the story as a prayer of thanksgiving, repeatedly calling attention to Sarapis' miraculous inspiration in Sarapieion A's foundation. For example, he credits Sarapis with bestowing divine glory upon Apollonios (I)'s cult images.[135] Maiistas also offers more details about the priestly family and their lives, noting that Apollonios (I) lived a long life, and presenting a more vivid account of Apollonios (II)'s dream prayers to Sarapis, which here includes a desire to found a temple so that the god will no longer wander over the earth (lines 51–53). The last section focuses on the trial, again emphasizing Sarapis' miraculous intervention. Not only did Sarapis reassure Apollonios (II) in a dream that a mortal could not successfully oppose a god, but he also intervened in the trial itself. By paralyzing the plaintiff's tongue, the god ensured victory for his supporters and a future for his own cult.

Sarapis appears directly to his devotees three times in Maiistas' account.[136] In the first encounter, Sarapis appears to a sleeping man, probably Apollonios (II)'s father Demetrios, and answers Demetrios' prayer for a statue to himself in the sanctuary.[137] Like many other accounts of divine epiphanies, Maiistas describes the encounter in vague terms. In his description of the second dream apparition, however, he offers more detail. Sarapis came to the sleeping priest and spoke directly to him, directing the dreamer to awaken, to walk to a portico entryway, and find a piece of paper that would tell him where to build a sanctuary to the god.[138] Sarapis' intervention worked: the dreamer, presumably a member of the Apollonios family, arose and found the piece of paper, which led him to the preordained spot.[139] As the Maiistas Chronicle tells us, the Isiac community successfully built their sanctuary according to the god's wishes, only to be sued by neighbors possessed of a κακὸς φθόνος (line 66). In response, Sarapis appears a third time, this time to Apollonios (II) in his sleep, to reassure Apollonios that he would prevail in the lawsuit.[140] As in the previous dream apparition, Sarapis' promises were fulfilled: the god stopped the tongues of Apollonios (II)'s adversaries in court, and the devotees retained their sanctuary.

These dream encounters perform multiple functions within the religious and cultural context of Hellenistic and Roman Delos. First, Maiistas' descriptions of the dream encounters emphasize a personal and embodied relationship with the god verified through later interactions with the material world, highlighting Sarapis' role as a sōter (savior). In each instance where Sarapis intervenes, the author praises Sarapis, using active and decisive terms such as τέλεσσας (44) and ἔτευξας (84) to describe the god's specific, concrete, and miraculous actions on behalf of his devotees. Sarapis here is a god of action who paid attention to the everyday needs of his followers in the mortal realm. Each of Sarapis' commands is accomplished through objects – the piece of paper, the new parcel of land for the sanctuary, and the opponents' stopped tongues. Most of these objects could be kept and displayed in a sanctuary or represented in artistic media.

These two accounts would have designated the cult, its officials, and its sanctuary as *loci* for divine encounters. In the first dream oracle, the encounter with the god happened within the sanctuary.[141] In the case of the other two oracles, the encounter was directly related to the sanctuary space. The second decreed where the sanctuary should be, making the space itself a gift of the god. The third helped Apollonios to defend that space against outside attackers and portends another miraculous intervention by Sarapis. Those that read these two texts on the column as they entered the sanctuary's main square might enhance their expectations of a divine encounter within the sanctuary, making them especially receptive to the sanctuary's visual rhetoric.[142] Maiistas' account, read together with Apollonios' more prosaic account, would lend authority to these ideas, since at least two people had witnessed them and recorded them in a permanent and public way. These two texts thus worked in tandem to reaffirm the mystic experience of the sanctuary space for cultic devotees throughout the sanctuary's life span. In the Chronicle's account, the sanctuary became a space that the gods frequented and inhabited, a place where the gods came to speak to men. If the gods visited their priests as frequently as the Chronicle of Sarapieion A claimed, participation in this religious community might provide devotees with a means to access the divine more directly.

The text thus invites its readers to transform the Greek sanctuary into a conceptual space filled with Egyptian divinity (Figure 14). In doing so, the viewer would be invited to consider Sarapis' own interventions in the same sanctuary space. Experiencing the sanctuary and its sculptures promoted the types of philosophical and theological contemplation that Plutarch thought critical to the Egyptian cults. As Plutarch wrote, "The name of her sanctuary also clearly offers recognition and knowledge of what really exists; for it is called the Iseion to indicate that we shall know what really exists if we approach the sanctuaries of the goddess with reason and reverence" (*De Is.* 352a).[143]

14. Excavation photograph of the central court, staircase, and ekklesiasterion of Sarapieion A, viewed from the southwest. Photo: École Française d'Athènes.

In the process of contemplating text, image, and sacred space all together, the reader undergoes that transformative experience with the divine truth that Plutarch associates with the Egyptian cults and their gods.[144] The texts discussed in this chapter prime the viewer to expect the Egyptian gods to appear in Greece at any moment, whether in material or immaterial form, and use the same mythologies of travel and deterritorialization to enhance devotees' expectations of Isiac sanctuaries. Epiphany provides a way to set the gods *in* Greece, embodying the transculturality at the cults' core.

At other sites, these epiphanic expectations could be created through other means. Throughout Greece and other parts of the Mediterranean, reliefs depicting ears and footprints have been found at Isiac sanctuaries. Footprint reliefs have been found at sites concentrated in Macedonia and Thrace, including Dion, Thessaloniki, Maroneia, and Beroia, and at sites throughout Greece, including Larissa and Charoneia.[145] Ears are known from Thessaloniki, Dion, Serres, and Stobi (now in North Macedonia).[146] These objects are Greek adaptations of Egyptian precedents that were primarily used to memorialize pilgrimages and to thank the gods for medical interventions (Figures 15 and 16).[147] Gasparini has recently interpreted the ear reliefs as a complex signifier representing the constant attention of the god and his or her presence in the sanctuary for key rituals, including the readings of the aretalogies and perhaps initiatory rites.[148] These reliefs, then, act as a synecdoche for the gods that place them permanently in the sanctuary. But, just like the Chronicle of

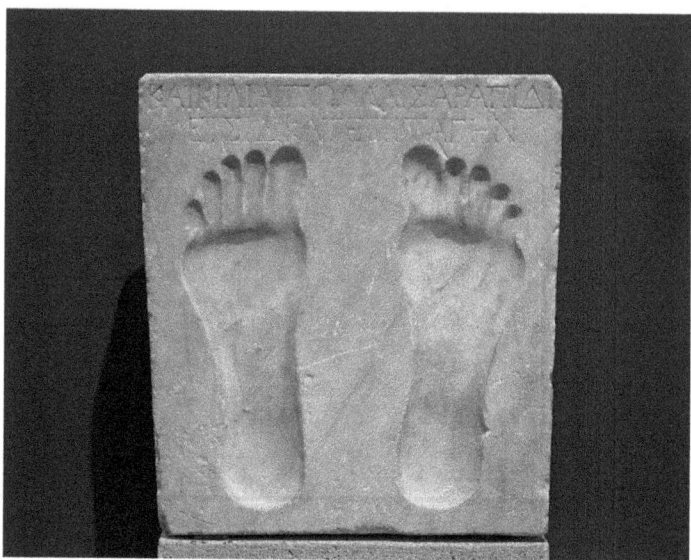

15. Votive relief depicting two footprints, dedicated by several freedwomen (?) of Caecilia Polla, Roman period. Thessaloniki: Archaeological Museum inv. MΘ 841. © Hellenic Ministry of Culture & Sports/Archaeological Receipts Fund.

Sarapieion A, they prepare and prime the viewers to find the gods inside the sanctuary.

The precise meaning of the footprint reliefs and the functions they play within the cult are debated.[149] The reliefs seem to be used in a variety of ways across the Mediterranean, and their functions may have been determined at a regional or even at a local level.[150] Interpretations range from commemorations of pilgrimage, marking moments and places where the gods stood in the sanctuary, recording instances of epiphany, and commemorating dream encounters with the gods. Most of these interpretations, however, describe some type of personal experiences of the divine, and most locate that encounter in the sanctuary. Especially challenging are several reliefs that include feet of multiple sizes, common at Dion, which led Bricault to argue that the larger feet represented those of the god.[151] Bricault's interpretations, however, return to the idea of footprint reliefs as markers of epiphanic experiences. In Greek literary sources, particularly Herodotus 4.82 and Lucian, *Verae Historiae* 1.7, certain footprints are associated with the activities of heroes like Hercules and Castor on earth.[152] The examples from Dion, discussed in Chapter 2, were found in situ lining the main temple's steps where viewers about to enter would encounter them. If they did commemorate epiphanies or similar experiences, Dion's devotees would have been reminded of these events as they entered the sanctuary's main temple.

These reliefs, then, serve as an index for the gods. In semiotics, an index is a form of representation that refers to something not through similarity or resemblance but because it stands in dynamic conversation with the object

16. Votive relief of Marcus Agellius found in the Thessaloniki Sarapeum and featuring an ear, early 1st century BCE. Thessaloniki: Archaeological Museum inv. MΘ 998. © Hellenic Ministry of Culture & Sports/Archaeological Receipts Fund.

and the memories it evokes in the viewer.[153] These reliefs remind the viewer that Egyptian deities come down and walk among their devotees, even if they are not currently present. They record previous instances of encounters and bring them into the present to create a discursive dynamic between god and human in past and present. In some ways, they operate in ways not dissimilar from Classical period *martyria* like the saltwater spring and olive tree on the Athenian Akropolis that commemorated Athena's and Poseidon's mythical contest over the patronage of Athens.[154] These objects are not meaningful on their own, but when considered in dialogue with Athenian foundation myths, they become a way of making the deep past tangible and real for viewers. Similarly, the Isiac footprint reliefs make a supernatural event feel immediate and authentic. They also bring mythological figures like Isis and Sarapis, who exist in deep mythological time, into the recent past and emphasize their power to collapse and transcend space and time.

BRINGING A GLOBAL GODDESS TO GREECE

The Greek Isis oscillates between her origins as an Egyptian goddess – deeply linked with Egyptian culture, religion, and geography – and a universal deity, deterritorialized and tied to metaphors of transculturalism, Imperial power, and Greekness. Most of the cults' Greek epigraphic aretalogies and related philosophical texts construct a new version of Isis and her companions: one that has traveled from Egypt to Greece, bringing goddesses from around the Mediterranean to take up residence in the Greek pantheon. This idea of Isiac polysemy reconciles well with the other major aspects of the cult, particularly with the gods' direct intervention in the daily lives of mortals. Since artists relied on accounts of these epiphanies to lend authority and authenticity to their visual representations of the divine presence,[155] these dreams and other divine encounters could have motivated the material culture produced for the Egyptian cults. In turn, these images helped viewers define the gods and may have helped shape their own sense of epiphany as they entered the sanctuary. Thus, we should not be surprised when the Egyptian gods, like their Greek counterparts, are depicted in diverse modes by local sculptors.[156] Ancient viewers, particularly those that embraced Egyptian cults, could have granted their images a great deal more polysemy than modern viewers might allow; they might have found Isis in what might seem to us like unexpected places.[157]

On a cultural level, Isiac universality allows the devotee to imagine a world without boundaries, in which an Egyptian goddess paradoxically has deep roots in Greece. Inherent in the Egyptian gods' identity were their Egyptian origins and the idea that these gods had migrated across natural and cultural barriers to arrive in the northern and eastern Mediterranean. This connection with the stereotypical and separate version of Egypt discussed in Greek and Latin literature granted Egyptian gods a certain alterity that remained relevant to devotees well into the High Empire.[158] The gods kept this alterity when they traveled and bestowed it upon their followers, as evidenced in the histories of individual Egyptian priests who carried the cult across the Mediterranean Sea into many different regions of Greece.

Isis' difference, however, is mediated within a longer tradition of Greekness, producing a goddess is simultaneously foreign and familiar. The aretalogical texts similarly valued the Egyptian gods' biographies of travel and movement, mythologizing the gods' departure from Egypt and locating them repeatedly in the culture and geography of Greece. The process of deterritorialization was fundamental to Isis' identity in Greek culture, emphasizing her status as foreigner and outsider within the Greek pantheon. The texts reframe Isis as a goddess who belongs to the very beginning of Greek myth-history, a goddess who regularly appears in Greece and supports the development of Greek cult communities. For these devotees, Isis' Egyptianness was subsumed within her Greekness, rendering her and her cult useful for reconsidering the role of Greek culture in the Mediterranean world.

For the Isiac cults, the multiplicity of Isis' ethnic identities demonstrated in literary texts and the aretalogical inscriptions suggest that polysemy would be a particularly appropriate method for interpreting Isiac divine images.[159] We should expect representations of the Egyptian gods to encourage many viewer interpretations, particularly those that find many gods within one image. Still, we cannot assume that Greeks looked at Isis only as another means to access Eleusinian Demeter and the other gods to which the aretalogical texts connected her. Rather, the goddess and her polysemic images offer a way for many ideal and cultural concepts to coexist, making a goddess like Isis an ideal *locus* for reimagining the long, intertwined, and globalized history of Greece and Egypt.

CHAPTER FOUR

SELF-UNDERSTANDING

Visualizing Isis in Stone

As cult communities developed and disseminated a shared set of iconographies for Egyptian deities, they also defined the gods' cultural politics. In order to represent these new divinities, Greek communities could have chosen from a wide range of possibilities, including: importing images of Isis from Egypt; recarving or modifying Egyptian imports to suit local standards; commissioning imitations of Egyptian sculptures from local sculptors; and carving statues of her as if she were a Greek goddess. Greek devotees, like their counterparts across the Mediterranean, preferred the last option.[1] Throughout the Hellenistic period, sculptors and devotees experimented, and by the 2nd century CE they were producing a broad, eclectic canon of types to represent Isis, Sarapis, and Harpokrates (Plate 6).[2] The resulting images navigate a complex web of meanings and associations. These statues borrow heavily from earlier Classical and Hellenistic models of Greek gods and goddesses.[3] But Egyptian elements, especially iconographies and attributes, remain. Statues of Isis often show her hair separated into distinctive locks, over which she frequently wears Egyptianizing headgear like the *basileion*,[4] a solar disc nestled between the cow horns of the goddess Hathor. In lieu of the Greek chiton and mantle, Isis' garments are often decorated with a trademark knot over the chest or floral garlands that are derived from pharaonic Egyptian precedents. All of this iconography marked her as different and lent an exoticism to Isis' images.

Other aspects of the images, however, planted the gods firmly in Greece. Statues of Isis and Sarapis were often set among sculptural assemblages that depicted the Greek gods. These conceptual groups relied on devotees' expectations of Isis and Sarapis, outlined in Chapter 3, to embed the gods even further into the material world of Greece by setting the Egyptian gods alongside Greek gods that looked similar. These aesthetic strategies (for, well into the Roman period, these images lie outside Greek norms) might have provided devotees with another method to contextualize Isis and Sarapis in Greek cultural paradigms while preserving the gods' attractive exoticism.[5] The result was a set of images that depicted Egyptian gods as culturally liminal. Artistic style thus became a form of cultural imagining, creating a space in which Isis and Sarapis can retain parts of their otherness while being paradoxically embedded in Greek materials and styles.

By defining their gods, devotees defined themselves. Several scholars have argued that communities created material worlds that reflected their ideas of self, and in turn these objects and landscapes intervened in the ongoing processes of identification.[6] As I argued in Chapter 2, devotees found meaning and identity through the cults, and these statues gave communities another opportunity to explore the ethnic implications of worshiping a foreign deity. Isis and Sarapis were not the first foreign deities worshiped in Greece, but their popularity and prevalence demanded a consistent and easily legible set of images that were effective across a great span of time and space. The method the Greeks chose, which integrated ethnically marked subjects and styles, cast Isis and Sarapis as rooted in Greek traditions while still being linked to Egypt.

I argue that these images also informed how devotees understood themselves. In order to parse more discretely the multiple processes that make up identification, I focus in this chapter and Chapters 5–6 on three distinct methods of creating and communicating Isiac identity in Roman Greece. This chapter focuses on the concept of self-understanding, which I define as a set of beliefs and ideologies that gave shape and meaning to the cult and its community for devotees, and in turn informed how outsiders perceived and described the cult.[7] Self-understanding is a form of commonality that provides meaning to a group, the shared ideas and symbols that gave shape to Isiac cult identity. This concept relies on the idea that devotees shared a collective form of selfhood that guided the ways in which they thought about, worshiped, and depicted the Egyptian deities. The ancient perception of self is socially correlated and closely linked to social status and the possession of wealth and other resources, including power.[8] Consequently, ancient self-understanding must involve a dialectic between internal narratives that drove actions and, in turn, visualized internal aspects of the cult for outsiders.[9] Internal and external understandings need not necessarily align;[10] rather, the dynamic tension between the two drives the constant renegotiation of self-understandings.

The result is an inherently reflexive, active method of self-formation that often directs the production of images and texts.

I begin this chapter with a survey of the major sculptural types used to depict Isis and Sarapis in Roman Greece. I argue that devotees chose new ways of depicting and displaying the gods that forged new relationships with existing Greek artistic traditions. The next section considers how the gods were displayed, using the Sarapeum at Thessaloniki as a case study. The large extant corpus of preserved statues offers a representative sample of the types of objects and texts that might be found in Egyptian sanctuaries across Roman Greece: statues of the Egyptian gods, statues of Greek gods, an imported Egyptian statuette, and a variety of epigraphic texts that illuminate how this devotee community visualized Isis. The breadth of this assemblage, when considered through the lens of an Isiac visuality, suggests a sanctuary that promoted a polysemic viewing experience. These images may have prompted devotees to identify familiar gods and their images with Isis, and in turn to reexamine the cult's continuing ties with Egypt.

THE NILE'S GODS IN WHITE MARBLE

Sarapis

Sarapis was the most popular of the Egyptian deities during the early Hellenistic period in the Greek world. Full-length statues most often depicted Sarapis as seated or standing (*debout*), but he was represented by an unusually large variety of types.[11] Generally, he has an idealized face, long, flowing locks of hair parted down the middle, and an ample beard divided into two sections, as seen in a characteristic 3rd-century CE example from the Egyptian sanctuary at Gortyna (Figure 17).[12] In this example, he wears a chiton and himation, though other statues of this type employ only the himation, and carries three of his main attributes, which can appear in multiple combinations. On his head he wears a cylindrical *modius* or *kalathos* (grain-measuring cup) decorated with images of grain. In his left hand he holds a tall scepter. Other examples hold a cornucopia in the left hand to symbolize Sarapis' role as a god of bounty. Along his right side sits a three-headed Kerberos that emphasizes his connections with Hades and the underworld. The missing right hand may have held a *patera*. Alongside these attributes, his drapery falls in a characteristic vertical fold running from the left shoulder to the plinth.[13] The fold and the *kalathos* are the only features that belong specifically to Sarapis, which can make fragmentary examples difficult to distinguish from those of other Greek gods.[14]

The *debout* type appeared in sanctuaries at Ephesus and Xanthos in Asia Minor,[15] the island of Amorgos,[16] and Carthage in Africa Proconsularis.[17] The type also appears in metal and terracotta statuettes found throughout the

17. Statue of Sarapis *débout* from the Sanctuary of the Egyptian Gods at Gortyna, 3rd century CE. Iraklion: Archaeological Museum inv. 259. © Hellenic Ministry of Culture & Sports/ Archaeological Receipts Fund.

empire. From Greece we have the 3rd-century CE example from Gortyna discussed above; two marble statuettes from Delos (one of them, Delos A 126, from Sarapieion C);[18] single examples from Athens;[19] Amorgos;[20] Thessaloniki;[21] a silver statuette from Paramythia in Epirus, now in the British Museum;[22] a possible further example from Athens;[23] and a relief from the smaller 4th-century CE Arch of Galerius in Thessaloniki.[24]

The iconography of the seated Sarapis type is more consistent than that of the Sarapis *débout* type. One example was found toppled off of its base just

18. Statue of a seated Sarapis from the Sanctuary of the Egyptian Gods at Gortyna, 2nd century CE. Aghii Deka: Apotheke inv. GO 201. © Hellenic Ministry of Culture & Sports/Archaeological Receipts Fund.

outside the southwest corner of the temple at Gortyna (Figure 18).[25] Sarapis wears a chiton and a himation that drapes over the left shoulder and across the lap. Some examples of the seated Sarapis wear a chiton, like another partial torso from Gortyna,[26] while others, mostly statuettes like the marble example from Sarapieion B on Delos, depict the god semi-nude (without the chiton) in a manner more consistent with enthroned representations of Zeus or Poseidon (Figure 19).[27] The god probably sat with his right arm on the throne and his left arm grasping a raised scepter.[28] Besides the examples from Gortyna, two others are known from Delos;[29] one each from Corinth,[30] Eleusis,[31] Olympia,[32] and Amphipolis;[33] and three examples from Rhodes.[34] At present, there are not enough examples of either type to determine a clear chronological or regional distribution pattern for Sarapis statues.

THE NILE'S GODS IN WHITE MARBLE 93

19. Statue of a seated Sarapis from Sarapieion B on Delos, 2nd–1st century BCE. Delos, Archaeological Museum inv. 1990+2004. Photo: École Française d'Athènes/Ph. Collet.

There is a considerable body of mythology surrounding the origins of Sarapis' cult image, but in each case, the statues' origins place it squarely within the Greek sculptural tradition.[35] The main accounts come from Plutarch's *De Iside et Osiride*, Tacitus' *Historiae*, Clement of Alexandria's *Protrepticus*, and Rufinus' *Historia Ecclesiastica*, but none of these tales reconcile easily.[36] Plutarch claims that the god himself called to Ptolemy I from Pontus, and the legendary scholar Timotheus and the Delphic oracle confirmed the god's mysterious identity (*De Is.* 361f–362a).[37] Tacitus offers a somewhat similar account, in which Ptolemy I dreamed of an "infernal" Zeus and then imported a sculpture of Pluto or Zeus from Sinope (*Hist.* 4.83–84). There is some evidence to suggest that Sinope is either an originator or early adopter of the type. A small terracotta votive associated with the so-called Temple of Sarapis at Sinope, though fragmentary, still depicts the god with idealized Greek-style facial features and the long, wavy hairstyles typical of Greek gods.[38] Clement attributes the cult image to a non-Athenian sculptor named Bryaxis who crafted the image from a panoply of valuable materials, including gold, silver, bronze, iron, lead, sapphire, hematite, emerald, and topaz, all mixed together to form a powder (*Protr.* 4.48). These precious materials are representative of disparate parts of the Mediterranean world. Pliny the Elder notes that emeralds are commonly mined in Scythia, Bactria, and at a mine near Koptos in Egypt (*NH* 37.17.65); the topaz and sapphire come from Ethiopia or India (*NH* 37.42.126–127); and lead comes from Lusitania and Gallaecia (*NH* 34.47.156–157). The act of grinding these disparate materials and using them as sculptural material is a metaphor for the universal expansion of Roman Imperial power and imbues Sarapis' original image with these qualities.

Most modern scholars follow Clement's account and assume that there existed a major sculpture of Sarapis by a sculptor named Bryaxis in the Sarapeum of Alexandria.[39] This image was one of the major artistic highlights of the Hellenistic city. Bryaxis' sculpture most likely depicted the god in a Greek style. Pliny (*NH* 34.42, 34.73) describes Bryaxis' other work in Greco-Roman terms, naming him as the sculptor of a famous Asklepios, a portrait of Seleukos, and five colossal sculptures of the gods in Rhodes. This record of sculptural production would suggest that Bryaxis normally designed for a Mediterranean-wide Greek market and was best recognized for working in that style.

In style and composition, Sarapis is depicted in a manner that closely follows the norms used for representing Greco-Roman gods like Asklepios and Zeus. The god's iconography and mode of representation fit easily within Greek and Hellenistic paradigms for representing gods and goddesses, which deemphasizes his foreign origins.[40] For example, though the *kalathos* is uncommon in Greek ideal sculpture, it can be associated with the worship of Demeter and Kore at Eleusis, and may perhaps have served to connect Sarapis with an Eleusinian version of Hades or Pluto.[41] The attributes these sculptors selected were designed to help viewers place Sarapis among more familiar deities and, through iconographic and formal analogy, understand his powers more clearly. Consequently, the cult statue of Sarapis should be considered along other "new" divine images produced in the early Hellenistic period.

But these images are not wholly new. Rather, they add new elements to existing forms to produce new and eclectic modes of representation.[42] The references to earlier forms, symbols, and styles make new subjects legible to an existing audience.[43] Sarapis' Greek image set the deity within an existing paradigm of masculine divinities that reminds the viewer of familiar deities like Zeus or Asklepios who took similar forms. Sometimes these images were even displayed together. For instance, Pausanias (7.26.7) mentions a Sarapis-Isis-Asklepios statue group in a temple at Aigeira.[44] Greek viewers would have been able to spot the similarities between Sarapis and the other key male divinities, and in turn these similarities would have helped viewers to interpret Sarapis as the most important male deity and as one whose powers included healing.

In particular, many scholars have noticed the striking similarities between Sarapis *débout* types and Asklepios' types. A Sarapis statuette from the Bardo Museum in Tunis depicts the god in his normal attire and hairstyle, standing while resting his left hand on a snake-wrapped staff (Figure 20).[45] The pose refers to Asklepios' Giustini types, which depict the god standing with his left hand on his hip and his right hand grasping a staff, often depicted with a snake wrapped around it.[46] The two are composed in a similar manner, using the

20. Statue of Sarapis-Asklepios from Leptis Magna, Roman period. Khoms: Leptis Magna Archaeological Museum. Photo: Bildarchiv Steffens/Bridgeman Images.

same arrangement of dress folds, the same pose, the same iconography, and a similar hairstyle. The visual connections between these two images underscore the theological similarities between the two gods: both are latecomers to the Greek pantheon, responsible for healing, associated with dreams and dream oracles, and expected to intervene in the affairs of mortals.[47] Adopting Asklepios as a visual model, then, makes a highly legible statement of who Sarapis is and what the Greek viewer might expect from him. Consequently, these images rely not only on viewers' knowledge of Sarapis' divine character from ancient texts but also an intermedial reading relationship between Sarapis and other male Greek deities.

Isis

Images of Isis tend to depict the goddess in a manner consistent with that of other Greek goddesses, but some of her iconography is more explicitly Egyptian or Egyptianizing. These attributes, I argue, placed Isis in a liminal position that highlighted both her Egyptian origins and her new home in the Greek pantheon. Originally, Isis was worshiped as the consort of Sarapis, but by the 1st century BCE she had become the more popular of the two deities and the center of Egyptian cult worship in Greece.[48] Isis has more variety in her types, and at least four of her main types appear in multiple examples in Greece. During the Hellenistic period, most ideal images of Isis depict the goddess in a distinctive mantle with a prominent knot over the chest, a garment that Eingartner has called the *Knotenpalla*.[49] The costume is strikingly different from those used in Greek sculpture and would have announced the goddess's foreignness to even the least attentive viewer.[50] Examples of this type are known from Delos,[51] Rhodes,[52] Chersonesos[53] and Kissamos[54] on Crete, Amphipolis,[55] Samos,[56] Sparta,[57] Knossos,[58] Dion,[59] Philippi,[60] and Marathon.[61] They date from the 2nd century BCE through the 3rd century CE. Another Antonine-era statue of Isis with a small-scale Anubis,[62] now in the Archaeological Museum of Rethymno, lacks archaeological provenance but probably comes from somewhere on Crete.[63]

The costume consists of two garments: a long chiton, often with long sleeves, and a mantle knotted at the center of the chest such that it hangs down and leaves the arms free.[64] The mantle is often fringed, and in some cases hangs down the back like a cape. The knot can be placed in several places (most commonly in the center of the chest or on the left side of the chest just below the shoulder) and can include from two to all four corners of the fabric (Figure 21). From the knot hangs a characteristic set of drapery folds that cascade down from the knot around the hips and upper thighs, which can be used to identify a *Knotenpalla* type even when the knot is not preserved.

In her free hands, Isis often holds attributes. The most common are the *sistrum* and the *situla*. The *sistrum* was used in pharaonic Egypt and consists of a cylindrical handle and a loop with two or three pieces of metal.[65] *Situlae* are breast-shaped vessels with a handle that were used for libations. The shape is unusual and the connection between this object type and pharaonic Egypt is not clear. The Isiac costume was often paired with a hairstyle that featured heavy corkscrew locks that hung down to the shoulders, often called Isis-locks in scholarly literature, and an exoticizing headdress that sat directly atop the head.[66] Several statue heads preserve dowel holes that would have held these extra attributes. The overall effect is exotic and diverges significantly from period norms.

Though scholars have debated the precise vehicle by which this costume might have arrived in Greece,[67] the *Knotenpalla* must derive from Egyptian precedents, particularly the representations of goddesses during the pharaonic period and later portraits of Ptolemaic queens.[68] Most of the known examples (those from Dion, Delos, Rhodes, Chersonesos, Kissamos, and Amphipolis) can be dated to the Hellenistic period and, apart from the asymmetric examples from Kissamos, Dion, and Chersonesos, show stylistic cohesion.[69] These examples are carved

21. Statuette of Isis in the *Knotenpalla* costume from Delos, 2nd–1st century BCE. Delos: Archaeological Museum inv. A 378. Photo: École Française d'Athènes/Ph. Collet.

in local marbles on a small scale, depicting the body in a simple yet fluid and fleshy manner; and they rely on simple chisel lines to represent the type's characteristic folds. The later examples, which date to the 2nd and 3rd century CE, are fewer and more varied. The Marathon example, which is discussed more fully in Chapter 6, is carved in an archaizing style, while the Sparta, Philippi, Rethymno, and Knossos examples are carved in a more contemporary style.

Eingartner has identified a second common type for Isis, called the *diplax* type, which deployed Isiac attributes alongside a more normative Greco-Roman style of dress (Figure 22).[70] In Greece, these images date to the 2nd

22. Statue of Isis in the *diplax* costume from the Sanctuary of the Egyptian Gods at Gortyna, 3rd century CE. Iraklion: Archaeological Museum inv. 260. © Hellenic Ministry of Culture & Sports/Archaeological Receipts Fund.

century and 3rd century CE and often come from Roman colonies or sites that had a large Italian population. In this type, Isis wears a chiton and a long mantle draped over the entire body, with the end of the drapery pulled over the right shoulder to create a diagonal line. Several examples feature a floral garland that hangs over the right shoulder down to the left thigh. In these images, Isis often wears a smaller, less elaborate headdress and carries the *situla* and *sistrum*. Though the *diplax* is much more popular in the western Mediterranean, there are examples from Gortyna,[71] Messene,[72] and Thessaloniki.[73] This type diverges less noticeably from normative Greek and Roman female types, but the exoticized Egyptian attributes preserve a critical expression of otherness.

There are also two other types used with some frequency in Greece: the Isis Tyche/Fortuna and the Isis *lactans* type. Like the *diplax* type, both generally follow Greek norms for representing female deities. The Isis Fortuna largely borrows from Tyche and Fortuna's standard chiton and mantle attire, the cornucopia, and occasionally the rudder, while adding Isiac attributes, particularly the *basileion* crown. The type was widely popular throughout the Roman Empire and in Hellenistic Greece, especially on Delos.[74] It is known in later Greece in marble in only one example from Dion (Figure 23),[75] but several bronze statuettes were found at Messene and at sites in Macedonia and western Thrace.[76]

23. Statue of Isis Tyche from the northern shrine of Dion's Iseum, 2nd century CE. Dion: Archaeological Museum inv. MΔ 5442. © Hellenic Ministry of Culture & Sports/ Archaeological Receipts Fund.

24. Terracotta statuette of Isis *lactans* from Herculaneum, 1st century CE. Naples: Museo Nazionale Archeologico inv. 76724. © Scala / Art Resource, NY.

The Isis *lactans*, which depicts the goddess seated, often on a throne and occasionally on a *cista*, appears within Greece in only one life-sized example at Messene but was very popular elsewhere in the empire (Figure 24).[77] The type integrates Isis' popular *kourotrophos* type in Egyptian sculpture, in which the infant Harpokrates sits on the goddess's lap, with Greek Demeter's more reserved seated form.[78] As early as the 5th century BCE, Herodotus notes the equivalence between Isis and Demeter within Egypt, but monuments depicting the syncretic Isis-Demeter are actually rare.[79] Scholars have long assumed that the cult statue of Demeter at Eleusis sat on a *cista* to reference the Eleusinian Mysteries,[80] and cists appear not infrequently on funerary reliefs for Isis devotees as well. The type is also known from bronze statuettes from Delphi[81] and Pherai,[82] a relief cut into the bedrock at Philippi,[83] and an ivory example from Attica.[84] This eclectic combination of Egyptian precedent and canonical Greek type connected Isis clearly with Demeter's more motherly aspects and the longstanding Greek iconography of the breastfeeding mother and infant.

Color and Legibility in Isiac Ideal Images

These images were also materially Greek. Apart from a few statuettes from Hellenistic Delos and Rhodes, there are no statues of Isis or Sarapis made of Egyptian stone known from a Greek sanctuary.[85] Still, Greek images of Isis rely on Egyptian and Egyptianizing attributes that seem to be used in a way that is generally consistent with their representation and use in Egypt.[86] Sculptors and patrons may have been familiar with these objects and their proper usage, either through participation in the cults' rites, knowledge of Egyptian religion, or seeing other images and rites of Isis and Sarapis in public contexts. Combining these elements borrowed from Egypt with Greek artistic style and materials creates a transcultural version of Isis that does not deny her connections with Egypt.

These images are made almost exclusively out of white marble, usually from local quarries or imported from regionally significant quarries like Mt. Pentelikon or Thasos. Though sculptors could paint statues to resemble imported stones,[87] there is no evidence to suggest that this is what occurred here. Instead, I argue, the white marble was part of the statues' meaning. During the early Roman Empire, imported stones were often used to commemorate victories and represent the empire's growing control over territories and resources. Greek marbles, which are mostly found in shades of white, held pride of place due to their connections with Classical Athenian monuments, and colored stones like Egyptian red granite and Numidian yellow marble were closely connected in literature with Roman control over their geographic origins.[88] Greek statues of Isis could have made arguments about the provinces' participation in this Imperial narrative. Instead, they choose to embody Isis in Greek materials, a choice that, I argue, is based on a need to privilege Greekness as the Mediterranean's most important culture.

These Greek bodies also made the gods legible to external audiences. The iconographic and formal features of these statues, including their poses and gestures, link Isis and Sarapis with cognate gods in the Greek pantheon.[89] These connections informed viewers who were not members of the cult about the Egyptian gods in ways that intersected with the aretalogies' lists of the gods' achievements and personalities. By incorporating these visual references, which would have been recognizable to Greek viewers steeped in their local tradition, sculptors and patrons could emphasize particular aspects of the Egyptian gods: the motherhood of Isis in the mother-and-child composition of the Isis *lactans*, or the kingliness of Sarapis in the enthroned statues. This dynamic tension between the Isiac and non-Isiac readings would have evoked multiple responses.⁹⁰ For viewers, then, the composition and material of the images primed them to find connections between the Greek gods they had known since birth and the new Egyptian gods they were coming to know.

The continued emphasis on Greek models and forms in sculpture, as well as the tendency to rely on earlier models, continued the mytho-historical narrative of the relationship of the Egyptian gods with Greek culture – longstanding, deep, and fundamental to the representation of the gods. Nagel has looked at these statues as examples of translation, of adapting and reinterpreting Egyptian religion for a new(er) audience.⁹¹ When statues of Egyptian gods integrate Egyptian attributes with Greek style, they often employ certain representational strategies that might have been used to rationalize the contrast. For Isis and Sarapis, who did not have earlier Greek models on which to build a new image, the past they are referencing is not wholly Egyptian. Just as in the Maroneia hymn discussed in Chapter 3, which rewrote basic Greek mythologies with Isis in the key roles normally assigned to Demeter and Athena, these images build aesthetic and visual meanings that rely on temporal fictions. As visualized in these sculptures, Isis and Sarapis are enduring members of a Greek pantheon and visual culture, able to rely on earlier models to make themselves understood.

POLYSEMY ON DISPLAY: THE SARAPEUM AT THESSALONIKI

Devotee communities tended to display their images of Isis and Sarapis alongside other images of Greek gods. In this section, I focus on the Sarapeum at Thessaloniki, a site that preserves over thirty-five pieces of sculpture. Except for a small imported statuette of the sphinx god Tutu,⁹² all of the votive dedications, divine images, and portrait statues are of local or Greek manufacture, and many depict Greek goddesses. While it is common for Greek sanctuaries to contain multiple deities and cult statues, I argue that Isiac devotees would have interpreted these disparate images differently. Viewers who knew Isiac texts and rites could have connected these images with the henotheistic and transcultural image of Isis depicted in the cult's texts, like the aretalogy found in the sanctuary.⁹³ Devotees could have understood these images as representations of multiple subjects at once, as Isis and Aphrodite or Isis and Athena. This viewership creates a form of polysemy, in which a single image is designed to provoke multiple interpretations. Framing Isis and her Greek counterparts in this way reconfigured Isis and made innovative claims about her deep connections to Greek culture by contextualizing her in a Hellenic visual landscape.

Excavation and Identification

The known Egyptian sanctuary at Thessaloniki, called a Sarapeum in the scholarly literature, lies under a private house near the intersection of

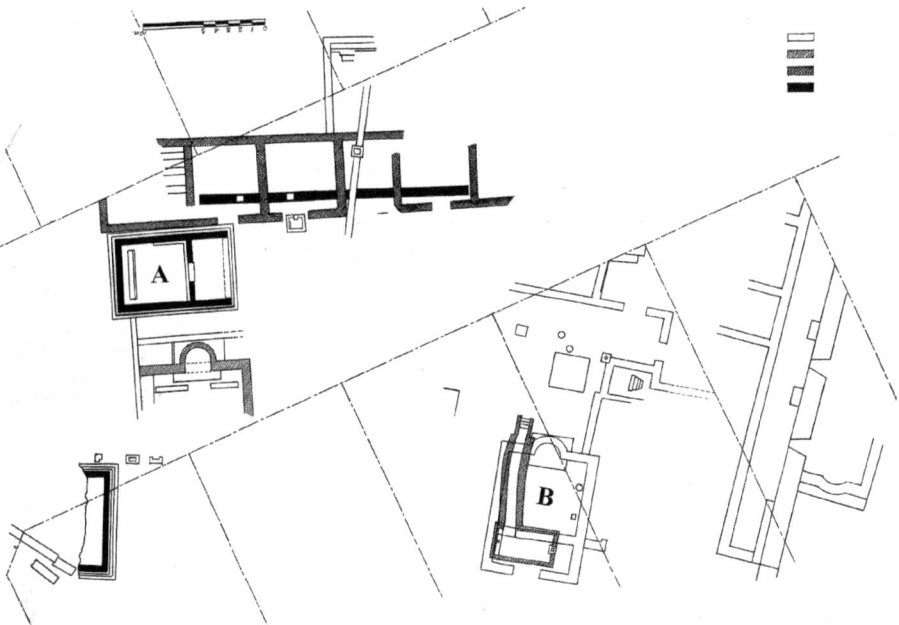

25. Reconstructed plan of the Thessaloniki Sarapeum. © Ephorate of Antiquities of Thessaloniki City.

modern-day Eleni Svonou and Karaoli and Dimitriou Streets. The precinct originally contained at least two smaller temples within a square surrounded by porticoes (Figure 25). The site first came to light during a major reorganization of the modern city, prompted by a fire on August 5, 1917.[94] After the end of World War I, Pelekides, then Ephor of Macedonia, explored the sanctuary in rescue excavations and oversaw work on the site in 1920, 1921, and 1926. The subjects of the sculpture (see Appendix) and repeated mentions of the Egyptian deities Isis, Sarapis, Anubis, and Harpokrates in regulatory and dedicatory inscriptions led Pelekides to identify the site as a sanctuary to the Egyptian gods. Most of Pelekides' excavation records have been lost. He published a one-page summary of his work during the 1920 season in the 1921 volume of *Bulletin de Correspondance Hellénique* and another one-page summary in the 1924 issue; a similarly brief summary of the third season appeared in the 1926 edition of *Archäologischer Anzeiger*.[95] After the completion of work in 1926, Pelekides composed a short report and a list of finds from the sanctuary. This report, now in the Historical Archive of the Archaeological Museum of Thessaloniki, mentions several objects that can be reconciled with objects now in the museum's collections. In 1939, Makaronas, working with Pelekides, continued the excavation on a neighboring plot, where he identified some of the sanctuary's architectural remains: another temple, a stoa, altars, and a crypt, as well as more inscriptions related to the Egyptian cults.

Like Pelekides, Makaronas produced a brief two-page report on his excavations; his notes are not preserved.[96]

Despite this missing documentation, museum inventories and records allow us to place statues in the sanctuary with some confidence. During his time as the Ephor of Macedonia, Pelekides modernized the system of excavation permits and attempted to create systematic catalogues for objects from Greek, French, and British rescue excavations.[97] Based on Koukouvou's recent historical study, it seems likely that these records would have been written by hand as the objects were being inventoried shortly after excavation. These records offer only brief mentions of the findspot (often just "the Sarapeum"), and some of the topographical references to particular plots are difficult to understand, but it does mean that we can trust that statues identified as part of the Sarapeum did in fact come from the sanctuary.

Reconstructing the sanctuary's architecture is more challenging. The only visual records of the architecture are a handful of excavation photographs and sketches from a notebook written by van Schoenebeck, a Danish archaeologist who visited the site a few times during his excavations of the Arch of Galerius.[98] Van Schoenebeck's notes contain only sketches and brief remarks, and their interpretation has sparked a great deal of debate.[99] Based on one of these sketches, Steimle reconstructed a porticoed sanctuary precinct filled with small temples.[100] Temple A (*Antentempel*) is a rectangular pronaos temple about 5 m wide, while Temple B (*Apsistempel*) is a square temple with a raised apse and large crypt that extends underneath the structure for most of its length. Part of a stoa was found to the northeast of Temple A, and the partial remains of a third temple of unknown size and form were found to the southwest of Temple A.[101] Van Schoenebeck's drawing does not indicate the relative size of these buildings. The sanctuary precinct must have been larger and included more buildings, but further information would require an intensive excavation that is unlikely to occur. Our only other evidence of the sanctuary's architecture comes from a model of Temple B produced shortly after the 1939 excavation and now on display at the Archaeological Museum of Thessaloniki. Though the model's origins and sources are not known, it generally depicts Temple B in a manner consistent with van Schoenebeck's notes.[102]

By combining van Schoenebeck's notes and Pelekides' report of 1940, as well as the Thessaloniki Archaeological Museum's inventories, it is possible to place a few objects inside the two temple structures.[103] In Temple A, Pelekides places a statue of a female goddess dating to the 3rd century BCE, a 1st-century BCE altar that was reused as a statue base for a statue of Isis Orgia in the 2nd century CE (MΘ 986), and a head of Sarapis.[104] Museum catalogues indicate that a black basalt sphinx (MΘ 4922), a statue of Aphrodite of the Louvre-Naples type (MΘ 831, Plate 7) and another Greek goddess (MΘ 832, Figure 26) of Roman date, two headless statues, and at least three votive reliefs featuring

26. Statue of a female goddess, perhaps Artemis of the Ariccia type or Athena, from the Thessaloniki Sarapeum, 2nd century CE. Thessaloniki: Archaeological Museum inv. MΘ 832. © Hellenic Ministry of Culture & Sports/Archaeological Receipts Fund.

ears also came from Temple A. (See Appendix.) Van Schoenebeck mentions the presence of the late Hellenistic archaizing herm (MΘ 1074) in Temple B's crypt, which has led scholars to believe that van Schoenebeck was describing one example within a larger collection of sculptures.[105] Steimle has critiqued these reconstructions because of the lack of detail in van Schoenebeck's notes about sculptural findspots. He points out that Makaronas' report indicates that only the herm was found in this space.[106] While I agree with Steimle that there is room for doubt regarding the exact findspots of most of these sculptures, comparison with other Egyptian sanctuaries in Roman Greece, like those in Rhodes, Marathon, and Messene, suggests that several late Roman Isiac communities used crypts to store caches of sculptures, though it is not clear that these objects were used in the crypts prior to their deposition.[107]

Steimle's study also offers some preliminary suggestions about the sanctuary's date. Based on epigraphic and sculptural evidence, the Egyptian cults were introduced to Thessaloniki shortly after the city's foundation in 316 BCE and were active into the 4th century CE.[108] The first inscription related to the Sarapeum dates to the end of the 3rd century BCE, and another inscription, from 187 BCE, indicates that Philip V took control of the sanctuary's finances and transitioned the sanctuary from private to public control.[109] The 1926 report indicates that Temple A consisted of a masonry foundation and upper levels of brick and small stone masonry, which Steimle interprets as a late Roman building on a Hellenistic foundation.[110] Temple B, in contrast, must date to the Roman period alone. The walls, made of brick and lime mortar, sat over a crypt that was supported by a barrel-vaulted concrete ceiling. A fragmentary inscription dated to the 2nd century CE describes the construction of a *dromos* for Osiris, which Wild connects with the construction of the crypt area. Relying on van Schoenebeck's notes, Steimle argues that the temple's brick superstructure follows late 3rd-century CE brickwork patterns, and the building probably dates to that period.[111] I offer here only an abbreviated summary of these arguments,[112] but it is clear that the sanctuary underwent renovations and additions at several points between its foundation and the 4th century CE.

Apart from the few findspots listed above, I do not assume certain knowledge of any particular findspot or display location within the sanctuary for any of the sculptures below. In studying these objects, I do not assume that viewers would have been able to see any particular statue while looking at another image. Instead, my reconstruction is based on the premise that a viewer moving through the sanctuary might encounter a significant proportion of the sanctuary's sculpture and be able to interpret these objects in dialogue with one another. Different types of viewers – entering for different purposes, at different times of day or year – would encounter different groups of images. The lack of detailed findspot information means that I have been forced to generalize here, but even very general interpretations can provide useful insight into the types of responses and readings these objects evoked in their viewers.

Ideal Statues in the Thessaloniki Sarapeum

There are three heads of Sarapis known from Thessaloniki: MΘ 897, MΘ 1017, and MΘ 1019. All three images depict the god with the same features that we have seen in other examples of Sarapis from Hellenistic and Roman

27. Head of Sarapis, later 2nd century CE. Thessaloniki: Archaeological Museum inv. MΘ 897. © Hellenic Ministry of Culture & Sports/Archaeological Receipts Fund.

Greece: long, curling hair, a tightly curled beard parted into two sections, and an idealized face. The first, MΘ 897, has been dated to the early to mid-Antonine period. It was found to the east of the Varelas plot in Olympou Street, not far from the Agora and associated with another potential sanctuary to the Egyptian gods (Figure 27).[113] Designed to be set into a larger statue, the Sarapis head depicts the god with loose, wavy locks. The hair is divided into large sausage curls at the back of the neck.[114] His beard features tight snail curls carved with the drill, creating the characteristic detailed locks of the latter part of the 2nd century CE. The head and neck were highly polished, and traces of red in the hair and beard suggest gilding or other coloration in these areas. The top of the head was cut flat, with a square hole in the center meant to hold the tenon of a tall *modius* that would have stood on top of the god's head.

The other two heads were found in or near the Sarapeum, but records make distinguishing them difficult. In his inventory, Makaronas suggested that a finely carved head of Sarapis dating to the Hellenistic period may have been part of a possible Hellenistic "cult statue" in the Sarapeum. But identifying the object to which Makaronas refers has been challenging.[115] For the purposes of this analysis, I do not assume that any of the statues discussed were cult statues,[116] but it is not unlikely that the renovations discussed above coincided with new sculptural dedications. Though the head MΘ 1017 was found in the Vasiloglou plot near the Sarapieion, its quality is far too low and the date (2nd century CE) far too late to be the head referred to in Makaronas' inventory (Figure 28).[117] Carved in an archaizing style used frequently in Roman sculpture,[118] the statue depicts the

28. Head of Sarapis found in the Vasiloglou plot near the Thessaloniki Sarapeum, 2nd century CE. Thessaloniki: Archaeological Museum inv. MΘ 1017. © Hellenic Ministry of Culture & Sports/Archaeological Receipts Fund.

god with simple, drilled curls and waves, a broad nose, and carefully defined eyes. Voutiras, however, has identified a 1st-century BCE statuette from the sanctuary as a votive statue of Sarapis *debout*.[119] The statuette, which preserves only the body, depicts the god standing with his left arm raised. He wears a thin, short-sleeved chiton and a long mantle that drapes across the hips and up to the left shoulder to create a dramatic diagonal. Though only preserved to a height of 45 cm, the statuette is consistent in iconography with other early examples.

Two heads of Isis came from the Sarapeum excavations.[120] The first, MΘ 1011, which dates to the 3rd century BCE, depicts Isis with a very subtle set of corkscrew curls set within a classicizing set of loose waves gently pulled halfway back to frame a naturalistic and idealized female face (Figure 29).[121]

29. Head of Isis from the Thessaloniki Sarapeum, 3rd century BCE. Thessaloniki: Archaeological Museum inv. MΘ 1011. © Hellenic Ministry of Culture & Sports/Archaeological Receipts Fund.

Her oval-shaped face is fleshy, with almond-shaped eyes, a broad nose, and a small mouth with a rounded chin, following Greco-Roman patterns of depicting Greek goddesses and mortal women with idealized and expressionless faces.[122] This head would have been attached to a stone or wooden body, and the drilled dowel hole at the top probably held an attribute, perhaps an Egyptianizing crown.[123]

Isis' hairstyle is very similar to normative types used for Greek goddesses and portraits except for the sausage locks that frame her neck. These curls offer a clue about the statue's origins. Unlike the hair of other Hellenistic female images, the curls are carved in a different technique: they are more deeply lined with the drill to create a sharper contrast between light and shadow than the hair covering the crown of the head.[124] The carving is clumsy and rather flat; it is difficult to make out when viewed from the front. When viewed from the left side, the curls are heavily undercut with a drill line on all sides, an unusual technique for the early Hellenistic period, and the geometry of the detail lines in the hair above the ears is simpler and more deeply rendered (Figure 30). By the 2nd century BCE, sculptural types for Isis were well established in Macedonia and the Mediterranean islands,[125] but at this early phase Isiac sculpture was still inchoate. Perhaps the sculptor was trying to adapt Isis' particular iconography to existing types used for divine representation in Classical and Hellenistic art and executed his experiment clumsily. It is also possible that the sculpture was recut from an image of another deity to serve as an image of Isis. In either case, this statue may represent part of an early trial-and-error phase in developing locally appropriate images for Egyptian gods.

The second head, MΘ 2490, depicts Isis in a deeply drilled Antonine style that integrated the corkscrew curls more gracefully (Plate 8).[126] Like the Hellenistic Isis, MΘ 2490 portrays Isis with a smooth, idealized face and loose, wavy hair parted down the middle and gathered in the back. Because the waves were carved with extensive drilling and detailed indications of strands, there is less of a contrast between the loose waves on the top of the head and the short, spiraling corkscrew curls at the bottom of the head. A diadem holds the hair in place, and a rounded depression on the left side of the head probably attached a crowning attribute to the top of the head.[127] The use of depressions on the sides of the head instead of a single hole or cutting centered at the crown of the head is unusual and may indicate that the missing attributes may have taken a distinctive form.

The statues were part of a large and lavish sculptural program that built various forms of familial relationships between deities. As well as images of Isis and Sarapis, the sanctuary contained one statue of their son, Harpokrates, represented as an almost nude boy, with defined pectoral and abdominal muscles but pudgy thighs and posterior (Plate 9). His hair is arranged into large, doughy waves and crowned with a vegetal wreath. He stands resting his

30. Detail of right side of Thessaloniki Archaeological Museum inv. MΘ 1011. © Hellenic Ministry of Culture & Sports/Archaeological Receipts Fund.

left arm on a tree stump and raising his right forefinger to touch the chin in a gesture well known from Egyptian figurines and sculptures.[128] In his left arm, Harpokrates carries a cornucopia. Originally another crown, now lost, stood above the wreath, which Despinis reconstructs as a form of the double crown of Egypt, the *pshent*, based on Harpokrates' iconography as it is represented in Greek terracotta figurines and Egyptian sculpture.[129]

On the whole, Harpokrates looks very similar to Eros. Some statues of Harpokrates from Greece, including a Harpokrates–Eros statuette from Messene,[130] preserve cuttings around the shoulder blades where wings were presumably attached in a clear instance of visual syncretism between the two child deities, highlighting Harpokrates' role as Isis' child. In a late 3rd-century to early 4th-century CE aretalogy from Chalkis, the author praises Harpokrates' creative role in the invention of music and hymns.[131] Harpokrates, however, holds more prominence than Eros. The Chalkis aretalogy grants him more power and spheres of influence, including the ability to determine seasons and the term of the year. Though the parallel is limited, the iconography still reinforces the familial connections with his parents, with whom he regularly receives dedications as part of a triad.

The Roman-period statues of Isis and Sarapis may have been displayed as a triad with the Harpokrates statue somewhere in the Thessaloniki sanctuary. Following the Egyptian cults' tendency to worship the gods in threes,[132] the trio of Isis, Sarapis, and Harpokrates appear in artistic representations throughout the Roman period, and are known epigraphically from several sites throughout Greece.[133] Isis and her male consort were displayed as a pair at 2nd-century and 3rd-century CE sanctuaries at Marathon and Gortyna.[134] Outside of Greece, a wall painting at Pompeii has been identified as portraying a small shrine containing Isis, Sarapis, and Harpokrates.[135] This grouping would have emphasized Isis' and Sarapis' roles as ideal spouses and parents, a key element of Isis' identity as described in the aretalogies. For example, in lines 17–19 of the Maroneia aretalogy, Isis and Sarapis' marriage is paired with Isis' role as the creator of marriage as an institution: "For you took Sarapis to live with you, and when you had made your marriage together, the world, provided with eyes, was lit up by your faces, Helios, and Selene."[136] Clearly, Isis' and Sarapis' roles as parents and a divine couple were key parts of their meaning for many Greek communities.

SYNNAOI THEOI: WORSHIPING EGYPTIAN AND GREEK GODS TOGETHER

This familial grouping would also emphasize the multifaceted relationships that Egyptian deities had with gods from around the Mediterranean. In addition to these statues of Egyptian deities, the Thessaloniki Sarapeum contained many images of Greek gods, as well as portraits of men and women carved in contemporary Greco-Roman styles. Part of a 2nd-century CE statuette of Athena was found in the Sarapieion (Figure 31).[137] The fragment preserves the upper part of the torso from the waist to the neck. The goddess wears her aegis, complete with gorgon head and coiled snakes, over a belted *peplos* with a long *kolpos* fold. The remnants of the arms indicate that the right arm pointed downward, the left was bent at a right angle with the forearm held forward, and the body twists slightly to the right to depict Athena in motion. Based on the reconstructed pose and the statue's technical details, Despinis argues that this statue was a 2nd-century CE copy of a Classical Athena Parthenos statue. The full-size statue MΘ 832 from Temple A (Figure 26) could also be an image of Athena, though it is also possible that statue depicts Artemis.[138]

31. Torso of a statuette of Athena Parthenos from the Thessaloniki Sarapeum, 2nd century CE. Thessaloniki: Archaeological Museum inv. MΘ 833. © Hellenic Ministry of Culture & Sports/Archaeological Receipts Fund.

In addition to the images of Athena, an Aphrodite statue from Temple A depicts the goddess in a thin, slinky chiton that has slipped off of the right shoulder, leaving the breast exposed (Plate 7).[139] The Louvre-Naples type, thought to be a copy of the cult statue of Venus Genetrix from the forum of Julius Caesar at Rome, is known from many examples around the empire.[140] The head and right arm are missing, and the right arm would have extended upward to raise the mantle over the left shoulder, probably to cover or veil herself. This image of the goddess highlighted Aphrodite's role as a goddess of sensuality and beauty by emphasizing her fleshy hips and thighs, her breasts, and the sheer drapery. Both Brinke and Andronikos have dated this statue to the 1st century CE, but Despinis argues that the statue has the same stylistic features of the Athena statue (Figure 26) and thus follows Pandermalis in dating the statue to the early 2nd century CE.[141]

Setting images of Isis and Sarapis in this sculptural assemblage provided a deeper Greek context for the Egyptian gods. The Greek goddesses represented in the Thessaloniki Sarapeum, which include Athena, Demeter, and Aphrodite, are also associated with Isis in aretalogical texts.[142] Given the size and quality of the Aphrodite and *peplophoros* statues and their display within a temple, these probably served as visual focal points alongside statues of the

Egyptian gods. The epigraphic evidence further supports the idea that the Greek gods were worshiped here as part of the group that shared the sanctuary. Several inscriptions found in Thessaloniki's Sarapeum and its environs honor the *synnaoi theoi*,[143] *theoi synbomoi*,[144] and *theoi entemenoi*.[145] Most of these are formulaic dedicatory inscriptions that name Sarapis, Isis, Anubis, and the *synnaoi theoi* as the recipients of small marble stelai or altars and date to the Hellenistic or early Roman period. In each of these inscriptions, however, the Egyptian gods are named individually while the sanctuary's other gods are lumped together under collective titles. This formulation may have been repeated as part of a hierarchy that classified Isis and Sarapis as ideal, henotheistic deities that stood above the other gods that shared the sanctuaries.

Sharing altars may have also served to expand the mythological family of the Egyptian gods to include canonical Greek deities. In her study of the introduction of Asklepios' cult to Piraeus in the last quarter of the 5th century BCE, Lamont examines a sacred law that prescribes the proper handling of sacrifices at specific altars and stelai dedicated to different gods who shared the *temenos* with Asklepios at his sanctuary in Piraeus.[146] She argues that the sharing of sacrificial altars and rituals with established deities was a key mechanism for validating Asklepian cult and integrating the new god into Piraeus' religious landscape. The inscription also indicated that Asklepios shared his sanctuary with *synnaoi theoi* like Apollo, his father. Sharing this sanctuary embedded Asklepios in a mytho-historical framework that linked him with well-known gods, but gods known from Asklepios' sanctuary at Epidauros joined him here. For viewers who had seen the large number of relief sculptures from Athens and Epidauros depicting the god alongside a large retinue of associated deities, these shared sanctuaries and repetitive rituals emphasized Asklepios' membership in a divine "family" that helped new worshippers place him in the broader myth-history of Greek religion.[147]

The *synnaoi*, *synbomoi*, and *theoi entemenoi* referenced in Isiac inscriptions may have served a similar function in Thessaloniki's Sarapeum.[148] Several Isiac texts argue for an equivalence between Isis and both Aphrodite and Athena by three methods: ascribing acts and traits of Greek deities to Isis, creating a direct equivalence between Isis and a Greek deity, or creating a new genealogical background for the goddess.[149] In the case of Athena, we can see elements of all three in various parts of Greek literature and epigraphy. Plutarch creates a direct equivalence between the two goddesses in *De Is.* 376a–b, in which he argues that the Egyptians themselves often call Isis Athena because she brought herself into being. At Thessaloniki, a fragmentary inscribed aretalogy grants several of Athena's traditional roles and deeds to Isis. The inscription dates to the 1st–2nd century CE and seems to be a close copy of the Hellenistic Kyme aretalogy.[150] Like the Kyme text, which itself claims to be a copy of a stele set up at the Temple to Hephaistos in Memphis and offers us an archetype for several aretalogies,[151] the Thessaloniki aretalogy includes an account of Isis' powers and great works. The text is broken off before the section where, if the copy is as exact as the existing text would suggest, the author would have revealed Isis' divine powers and roles. In the Kyme text, Isis again is the one who defined Greek and barbarian tongues (line 31: Ἐγὼ διαλέκτους Ἕλλησι καὶ βαβάροις ἔταξα). Similarly, Isis is responsible for human justice, a role usually fulfilled in Greek religion by Athena, in a manner similar to the roles ascribed to her in the Maroneia text, though the wording is different:[152]

> I made good and evil be distinguished by nature. I made nothing more respected than the oath. I delivered the person plotting unjustly against another into the hands of the person plotted against.[153]

In this account, then, Isis is responsible for both the definition of language and the enforcement of justice, human and divine alike, jobs that are traditionally assigned to Athena in Greek religion.

The Thessaloniki aretalogy may have also named Olympian deities as part of Isis' bloodline. For example, in line 5 of the Kyme text, she is described as the oldest daughter of Kronos (Ἐγώ εἰμι Κρόνου θυγάτηρ πρεσβυτάτηι), which would make her Demeter's sister, Athena's aunt, and perhaps even an Olympian deity in her own right. Plutarch gives several conflicting accounts of her parentage, naming Hermes and Prometheus as potential fathers (*De Is.* 352a), though in a later passage Hermes is her grandfather (*De Is.* 355e–356a). In other places, however, Isis is connected back to Egypt. In line 11 of the Kyme aretalogy, Isis (speaking here in the first person) claims that the Egyptian city of Bubastis was built for her (line 11, Ἐμοὶ Βούβαστος πόλις ᾠκοδομήθη); and the text ends with Isis invoking Egypt as the land that raised her (line 57, Χαῖρε, Αἴγυπτε θρέψασά με). Even here, there is distance between Isis and Egypt, since it is not described as her current dwelling place but as her point of origin, an argument made more explicitly in the Maroneia aretalogy discussed in Chapter 3. The Thessaloniki aretalogy, then, represents Isis as a goddess of Egyptian origins who can claim a place among the most important Greek gods.

The Kyme/Thessaloniki aretalogy also defines Isis as the mistress of male–female love and productive sexuality (lines 27, 30), granting her the traditional duties of Aphrodite and Venus that informed that goddess's representation in the Louvre-Naples type displayed in the Thessaloniki sanctuary. Repeated dedications to Aphrodite throughout the sanctuary could have further cemented the connection. In addition to that statue, other, smaller votives were found in the sanctuary. In one mid-2nd-century CE dedication, a priest named Potianos honors Aphrodite Homonoia with an inscribed marble statuette.[154] The statuette depicts the goddess wearing a belted and sleeved chiton with a himation slung low across the waist. In her left hand she holds a cornucopia, and the feet of a small Eros figure are preserved on the right side of the plinth. The inclusion of Eros here, while a normal part of Aphrodite's iconography, would have strengthened the allusion to Isis and her son Harpokrates, another instance of visual equivalence.

By reassigning these powers to Isis, the Kyme aretalogy (and by extension the Thessaloniki aretalogy) takes an expansive view of the goddess that sets her among some of the most prominent female divinities in the Greek pantheon.[155] Within Thessaloniki's Greek sculptural landscape, where Isis appears in Greco-Roman naturalistic style alongside several Greek deities, I argue that viewers could read the statues of Greek goddesses set up in the Sarapeum as avatars of Isis. As the epigraphic evidence indicates, Isis, Sarapis, and Anubis shared their sanctuary with Greek gods, which may have helped Egyptian devotees place the gods within the family of Olympian deities. This connection would have been solidified through the aretalogy, which may have been read as part of the Isiac rituals that were performed in the sanctuary and alongside its statuary.[156]

For devotee viewers, then, their Greek viewing habits would have been altered by their experiences with Isiac texts and rituals and may have led them to find Isis in images of traditional Greek goddesses. Worshippers who had experienced a lifetime's worth of Greek sculpture would have recognized these images as Athenas, Aphrodites, and Demeters. When they reconsidered these statues through the lens of cultic visuality, however, they could have interpreted statues of these same goddesses as a testament to Isis' unifying powers. In this way, devotees experiencing the Greek goddesses within Isis' sanctuary refashioned the already multifaceted visual experience of a sanctuary into a theological exploration of Isiac theology and identity. Having heard this aretalogy, Isiac devotees might see Athena and Aphrodite as aspects of Isis subsumed within Isis' *numen* or as discrete avatars of Isis' universalizing personality, or perhaps even as Isis herself.

If we look back at Isis' main statue types, we can see that religious appropriation also played a role in revisionist visuality. Tran tam Tinh notes that Isis statues often replicate the body types and postures of other Greek goddesses, including Aphrodite, Demeter, Tyche/Fortuna, and Hygeia.[157] Although no Isis statue copies the Aphrodite Louvre-Naples type, similarities in gesture, dress, style, and attributes between Isis and other Aphrodite types would have encouraged devotees to find Isis in textual and artistic depictions of the Greek goddesses and to see Isis as a polysemic and polynymic divine form that could appear as Aphrodite in sculptural form. In the Egyptian cults, where texts primed viewers for epiphanic experiences connected to the sanctuary space, each and every encounter with a divine statue was an encounter with the gods. As a result of these carefully calibrated visual landscapes operating in concert with ritual practices and theological principles, Isiac devotees could see Isis in statues of the Greek gods, and even of goddesses depicted in forms not used for the depiction of Isis. From a cultural perspective, the assimilation of Isis, Demeter, and Aphrodite reinforces Isis' new identity as a Greek goddess.

DIVINITY AND ETHNICITY: THE MATERIALITY OF SCULPTURAL PROGRAMS

> Nor do we think of the gods as different gods among different peoples, nor as barbarian gods and Greek gods, nor as southern and northern gods; but, just as the sun and the moon and the heavens and the earth and the sea are common to all, but are called by different names by different people, so for that one rationality which keeps all these things in order ... there have arisen among different peoples, in accordance with their customs, different honors and appellations.[158]

The statues of Isis, Sarapis, and Harpokrates are examples of just this type of translation. These images embody Egyptian deities in Greek styles, materials, and modes of representation. To create these sculptures, sculptors and patrons borrowed extensively from the types of images used to represent Greek deities who held cognate positions and powers in the Greek pantheon. Plutarch also recognizes the importance of these images in the pursuit of sacred knowledge, arguing that those who use the correct type of sacred symbol "[guide] the intelligence towards the divine" (*De Is.* 378a). Still, the images emphasize the goddess's exoticism through her signature hairstyle and attributes, and in the case of the *Knotenpalla*, through dress. A similar juxtaposition of technical and formal Greekness and Egyptianizing iconography and attributes characterizes other members of Isis' and Sarapis' retinues. In the case of Harpokrates, Isis' son, sculptors use the same types of childlike body and pudgy nudity employed for Aphrodite's son Eros but altered it by adding the Egyptian gesture of touching the finger to the lip.[159] The result is a version of the Egyptian gods that highlighted the gods' transnational and liminal nature and emphasized their exotic origins while embedding them in Greek religious and material worlds.

To conclude, I want to return to the idea of materiality. Curiously, there is no statue of Isis, Sarapis, Anubis, or Harpokrates currently known from Greece that was made from Egyptian stone. Though Egyptian imports are common throughout the empire,[160] and many people of Egyptian descent lived in Greek cities, imported sculptures and sculptures of imported stone are curiously sparse in sanctuaries dedicated to the Egyptian gods – in sharp contrast to other regions, where imports related to Egyptian cults are relatively common. At the other end of the spectrum, the Egyptian sanctuary at Beneventum in Italy contained dozens of Egyptian-style statues imported from Egypt, dozens of Roman-style images carved in imported stone, and even a couple of Egyptian statues recut into Roman portraits.[161] Had they existed, these imports would have been displayed alongside sculptures and objects produced in Greek materials and Greek styles and would have changed viewers' interpretations of these assemblages. While there might be several post-depositional processes contributing to this lacuna,[162] the overwhelming proportion of locally produced statues indicates that Greek devotees had a strong preference for sculpture carved in local materials and styles. In order to explain this phenomenon, I consider here what messages imported statuettes would have conveyed to Greek viewers.

While objects and materials imported from Egypt turn up across the Mediterranean, we have very few examples from Egyptian sanctuary contexts within Greece. Most sanctuaries preserve none at all, and those that do contain one or two small statuettes in dark Egyptian stone.[163] Greeks were highly attuned to materiality. A temple account from Sarapieion C on Delos dating to 156/155 BCE organizes objects first by their locations within the sanctuary, and then by their material.[164] Dedications of gold, silver, bronze, wood, and marble are highlighted, with few other materials even mentioned. The rest of the accounts from the Delian sanctuaries do not use material as an organizing category but still describe the dedication's material clearly. Though the inventories are partial, representing only a few years of the sanctuary's life, they do not mention any basalt or black stone objects, indicating the rarity of such dedications.

Alongside the rest of its sculptural program, the Thessaloniki sanctuary also contained a sphinx statuette imported from Egypt (Figure 32).[165] The object's materiality, with its connections to Egyptian luxury and otherness, could have complicated the cultural narrative of Isis and Sarapis. The sphinx was carved in a highly polished dark basalt stone; only the front half remains. It is depicted in full stride, connecting a smooth lion's body to a badly damaged, beardless face. The sphinx wears a smooth wig that hangs in front of the human shoulders and along the back of the lion's body. There is a dowel hole on the top of the head that would have attached a crown, and over the chest the sphinx wears either a simple apron or a stylized mane that covers the legs. The statue represents the Egyptian god Tutu, also called Τιθοῆς, Τιθόης, and Τοτόης in Greek-language inscriptions.[166] The material, carving style, and subject

32. Black basalt statuette of a sphinx found in the Thessaloniki Sarapeum, late Ptolemaic period. Thessaloniki: Archaeological Museum inv. MΘ 4922. © Hellenic Ministry of Culture & Sports/Archaeological Receipts Fund.

suggest that the Thessaloniki Tutu must have been made in an Egyptian workshop, probably during the Ptolemaic period.[167] The stone's blackness set it apart from the Greek objects carved in white marble. The object's materiality and the material's culturally and temporally situated meaning must have remained important.[168]

Because of its material, which would have been immediately recognizable as an import to the average Greek viewer, the sphinx would necessarily stand apart. Objects like these, whose materiality advertised their foreign origins, functioned as symbols of mobility and cultural encounters with foreigners for their receiving audiences.[169] While not all viewers would have interpreted these objects as elements of Egypt, the majority would have associated them with luxury and excess in a manner that raised their perceived value.[170] More importantly, these statues' materiality acted as a synecdoche for the object's larger biography, a narrative of travel that collapsed distance, time, and space to remind the viewer of the goddess's own journey from Egypt and her current presence in Greece.

Though we cannot fully reconstruct the placement of these objects within the Thessaloniki sanctuary, the sharp contrast in material would have created a division between Egyptian and Greek. As the only known import, the sphinx would have been outnumbered by Greco-Roman and white marble images. The statue's materiality collapsed the viewers' experiences of time and space, bringing an imagined Egyptian past into the Greek present, one in which Egyptian forms and styles take precedent. This need was limited. Instead, through their patterns of sculptural dedications, the devotee community at Thessaloniki wanted to portray a version of the Egyptian gods that had always been part of the Greek pantheon. Even in moments of equivalence, Greek culture needed to be the central feature through which all other cultures could be read, the device through which universalism operated. If, as Pliny the Elder claimed, Rome is the Mediterranean's political and commercial connector, Greece would be its social and religious one.

CHAPTER FIVE

SELF-FASHIONING

Dressing the Devotees of Isis in Athenian Portraits

The Greek vision of Isis examined in text and ideal sculpture also shaped the production of Isiac portraiture.[1] In this chapter, I consider how Isis devotees fashioned themselves after sculpted portraits displayed in the cemeteries of Roman Athens. Perhaps the most famous Isiac sculptures in the ancient Mediterranean, these reliefs were first studied as a corpus by Elizabeth Walters in *Attic Grave Reliefs that Represent Women in the Dress of Isis* (1988). They depict Athenian women of the Roman Empire from the 1st century to 3rd century CE, dressed in the same types of garments used in the goddess's cult images (Figure 33). Though Athens is remarkable for the concentration of this type of funerary sculpture, single examples are known from elsewhere in the Roman Mediterranean – Syros, Tanagra, Phryxou Limen in Bithynia, Apollonia in Illyria, Caesarea in Mauretania, and Rome, as well as two earlier examples from Smyrna. Yet nowhere else was the type used with such frequency.[2] I argue that the images allow devotees to integrate aspects of alterity and foreignness that are embedded by these costumes into normative modes of Greek portraiture. The images thus help to define the subject as one who has undergone the specific identifying processes that transformed the subject into an Isis devotee and, I argue, into a particular kind of Greek.

Consequently, the reliefs participate in an identification process that I call self-fashioning, defined as the process of extending identity through the body to embed oneself in established categories, narratives, and networks as a means of forging or maintaining a group identity.[3] Since this chapter focuses on the role of

33. Grave stele of Sosibia, daughter of Eubios, of the dēme of Kephisia, 160–170 CE. Edward J. and Mary S. Holmes Fund. Boston: Museum of Fine Arts inv. 1971.209.

dress in establishing and expressing membership in a cultic community, the term "self-fashioning" is a bit of a pun, but it also permits us to investigate dress as an agent that helps to construct and define the values, aesthetics, bodies, and other forms of symbolic meaning that provide a sense of commonality to a group.[4]

In a colonial context, self-fashioning is also an aesthetic and cultural response to competing social and cultural needs. Provincial peoples, like the inhabitants of Roman Athens,[5] frequently employed culturally embedded symbols and styles to make seemingly contradictory claims that nuanced their position within the Roman world, to mark themselves as participants in social hierarchies, both locally and Mediterranean-wide.[6] While the pressure to conform to existing visual norms was strong, some chose to express difference through their dress. The association of specific dress and attributes with the human body invests these symbols with the "fact of being a particular body in a particular situation of time and space relative to a particular thing,"[7] a type of embodiment that invites the viewer to engage with the lived experience of its subject, to imagine what it might be like to inhabit a particular body in a specific historical and religious moment. These devotees, then, are choosing to portray themselves as a new type of Greek, one who subscribes to a form of ethnicity inflected with qualities of Egyptianness and difference.

In the context of Isiac cult, I argue, these reliefs relied on a network of symbols and memories to evoke the lived experience of rituals. Tangible elements like dress, hairstyle, and handheld attributes act as signifiers of past events while constructing new ideas and emotions about how those experiences impacted the present. In the Athenian reliefs, devotees are depicted in the same garments and holding the same cult-specific objects as the goddess herself. Wearing this costume, I argue, allowed devotees to employ a costume first used in ideal sculpture and redeployed in rituals to depict themselves in such a way as to signal their membership in this closed part of the cult. Dress and its embodiment, then, played a constructive role in establishing membership within an Athenian Isiac community. These evocations, however, are not always successful, and when viewers cannot recognize them, multiple subjectivities are formed. From an outsider's perspective, these reliefs also construed and represented the community to other Athenians and the world at large in a way that emphasized otherness.[8] Even at a time when the cult was actually increasing in popularity and visibility across the Mediterranean world, this self-fashioning produced a version of the Isiac cult that emphasized its marginality.

Beyond their cultic context, these images are also the product of a Roman province. Though men appear frequently in the cult's epigraphy and held higher-ranking cult offices, only a small handful of portraits depict men in Isiac dress. To explain this gendered dichotomy, I look to provincial portraits from elsewhere in the eastern Mediterranean, particularly the funerary reliefs of Palmyra. Like the Isiac reliefs, these often combine a male figure in Greco-Roman dress and a woman in dress that appears non-normative to the Roman metropolitan eye. When viewed alongside the Palmyrene funerary portraits, Isiac funerary reliefs exemplify a strategy of representation used throughout the empire's provinces: the combination of the tropes of sameness and difference with masculinity and femininity to contextualize new cultural concepts. The Isiac devotees of Roman Athens, then, are participating in broader patterns of provincial portraiture that help them fashion new, more cosmopolitan forms of Greekness.

GENDER AND ETHNICITY IN PROVINCIAL PORTRAITURE

In local and regional case studies of various periods, many scholars have noted the tendency to assert minority forms of identity, particularly local identity,

34. Funerary relief for Maqi, son of M'ani, from Palmyra, ca. 200 CE. Los Angeles: Getty Villa Museum inv. 88.AA.50. Digital image courtesy of the Getty's Open Content Program.

through female portraiture, and in some places even refer to women as the "guardians of ethnicity."[9] Within the corpus of provincial portraits, the funerary reliefs from Palmyra, in the province of Syria, have long held pride of place as a case study for regional ethnicity formation in the face of Hellenistic, Roman, and Parthian imperialism.[10] In this section, I examine how gender informed representations of ethnicity and group membership in funerary portraiture. I argue that there existed an empire-wide pattern of connecting normative Greekness to masculinity and connecting cultural alterity to femininity in funerary portraiture.

More than 3,000 Palmyrene portraits have been preserved. Many of these follow a gendered pattern of dress.[11] Here I focus on the *loculi* reliefs, a set of sculpted funerary reliefs from the 1st century through 3rd century CE that feature bust-length portraits of the deceased. These reliefs normally sealed a burial niche and seem to have portrayed the individuals or small groups

35. Funerary bust for a woman from Palmyra, 3rd century CE. Los Angeles: Los Angeles County Museum of Art inv. M.76.174.249. Gift of Nasli M. Heeramaneck, photo © Museum Associates/LACMA.

interred there.[12] Men frequently wear recognizably Greek forms of dress, particularly the himation, and often carry common Greek male attributes like the book roll, an attribute that indicates his participation in Greek intellectual culture and appears frequently in Hellenistic and Roman portraiture (Figure 34).[13] Women often wear forms of dress assumed to be local, including turbans, veils, diadems, elaborate jewelry, and fringed mantles draped in ways that are not seen in Greco-Roman art (Figure 35).[14] Though the reliefs are carved in a technique and style that are markedly different from those used in either Athens or Rome, they rely, I argue, on the idea that male bodies are best used for establishing belonging within a form of Greekness that was available across wide swaths of the eastern Mediterranean. These types of culturally encoded masculinity, then, have a geographic component that makes an argument of sameness and commonality for men who belonged to discrete

GENDER AND ETHNICITY IN PROVINCIAL PORTRAITURE

and different culture groups. Female bodies, on the other hand, may have been seen as a locus for establishing membership in groups that stood outside the norm, especially groups with a resonance at the local level.

Women and Men in Palmyrene Portraits

Palmyra stood at the intersection of several key trade routes – a cosmopolitan city filled with people from the Asian continent, the Mediterranean, and the Arabian Peninsula. Though the site was inhabited as early as the Neolithic period, Palmyra was probably a city by at least the mid-1st century BCE.[15] From that point through the mid-3rd century CE, the Roman Empire seems to have established some form of administrative control over the city.[16] The city, however, always lay in a borderland, functioning as a point of stability while the Roman and Parthian (and subsequently, Sassanian) empires vied for control over the area. Included in its large and varied corpus of funerary portraits is the relief of Yarkhai, son of Ogga, and his female relative Balya, found in Palmyra and now in the Portland Museum of Art (Figure 36).[17] The two are represented side by side, at bust length, with a *dorsalium* curtain hanging behind the female figure, pinned to the background with large disks

36. Funerary relief of Yarkhai, son of Ogga, and his female relative Balya, mid-2nd century CE. Portland: Museum of Art inv. 54.3. Courtesy Portland Museum of Art.

crowned with palmettes. A dedicatory inscription identifies the pair. The relief's composition and iconography are typical of the gendered forms of representation in use during the mid-2nd century CE.[18] Yarkhai appears in Greco-Roman dress; he poses with his right arm wrapped in his garment and held tightly to his chest, in a format called the arm-sling type. His hair is cut short and arranged in a series of curls brushed forward over the forehead, a coiffure that is recognizable as a contemporary Roman style. His face is largely idealized with portrait features like a furrowed brow, small, wide-set eyes, a small and stern mouth, a circular jutting chin, and large ears that stick out beyond the hair.

His companion Balya, on the other hand, wears a diadem or turban over wavy hair parted in the middle with a lock hanging over the center of the forehead, a style reminiscent of classicizing hairstyles used by Greco-Roman women throughout the empire.[19] Over the diadem is draped an unusual fringed mantle that falls over the shoulders and wraps around the chest,[20] hanging loosely enough to require Balya to grasp it at the nape of the neck, looped over in her left hand. Heyn suggests that this gesture first appears in Palmyrene portraits in 150–200 CE.[21] Like the subjects of many other Palmyrene portraits, Balya wears lots of jewelry: two necklaces, a pair of matching bracelets on each wrist, and a dangling pair of earrings.[22] As Heyn has argued, this jewelry highlights a new role for women in Roman Palmyra: as markers of their family's status within the community.[23] Rather than fashioning themselves as individualized members of a professional group, as most men did, women may have acted as general signifiers of their family's wealth and engagement in the trans-Mediterranean trade of luxury items.[24]

It is tempting to describe Balya's dress as an exemplification of local costume. Yet a lack of early examples makes it difficult to define a Palmyrene style of dress or portraiture that predates the Roman Empire. Because of this gap, Heyn has challenged the reading of female dress as exclusively local.[25] Instead, she argues that we should interpret female portraits and their dynamic iconography as reflections of the subject's value to the family rather than in terms of the individual female subject's biography or self-understanding.[26] This dress, then, probably reflects more accurately how the family wished to be seen by their neighbors: wealthy, powerful, and sophisticated.

The relief, like many other *loculi* reliefs, combines elements of the local and global. As many scholars have noted, the overall composition of these slabs, particularly those that depict pairs or small familial groups,[27] tends to resemble that of freedmen's reliefs from Rome.[28] Though there are some Roman elements, particularly in terms of composition, in these reliefs, they allude more concretely in iconography and style to contemporary norms in Greek portraiture. In the case of Yarkhai, the male figure, the dress and hairstyle have much in common with Greek portraits of the Roman period. Examining the role of cultural identity in male portraiture of the eastern Roman provinces, R. R. R. Smith has highlighted the chiton and himation as legible markers of Greekness that emphasize the subject's local importance and membership in a longstanding tradition of Greek masculinity.[29] Though Yarkhai may not have been a Greek speaker or even identified as a Greek, his dress embeds him in this culturally defined trope of masculinity. Like most male civic portraiture from the region, whether produced by well-connected, Imperial insiders like Herodes Atticus or a wealthy priest from a small town in inner Anatolia, two of the examples of this phenomenon that Smith offers, Yarkhai's portrait prioritizes legibility and connection. His image, then, makes claims that extend outside of Palmyra to the eastern Mediterranean and the Greek-speaking worlds. Balya's dress, on the other hand, makes more specific claims. Some of the garments she wears, including the turban and the fringed mantle wrapped around the chest, are not seen outside the region of Syria, and may represent the day-to-day wear of Palmyrene women. If so, Balya's portrait may be aimed at a primarily local audience familiar with the particular values and subtle meanings attached to specific elements of her dress and jewelry.

Audience and Display

The pairing of these two contrasting figures communicated multiple messages. Yarkhai, through his dress, aimed at a broad audience, not only regional but empire-wide, to claim membership in a high-status group whose powerful members spanned the eastern Mediterranean. Balya's dress, on the other hand, would have been read as unfamiliar and perhaps even as strange to many men who dressed like Yarkhai. The family must have been aware of this dissonance when designing this relief, and the contrast might have been a productive means for claiming membership in both the Palmyrene community and the Greek world more broadly.

Funerary contexts were an especially profitable place to make these types of status claims. De Jong has demonstrated that tombs played an increasingly important role in the day-to-day life of cities in Roman Syria. During the Roman period, tombs became more visible and monumental,[30] serving as a way to promote families to both casual passers-by and neighbors familiar with a family's history and status in the community. At this time, the development of a series of cemeteries to the northwest, southwest, and southeast of the city expanded the Palmyra's available burial space significantly, an indication of the growing importance of funerary culture under the Roman Empire.[31] Tower tombs, hypogea, and mausolea are known from the Roman period, all of which naturally provided opportunities for the display of funerary portraiture.[32] A small number of tower tombs, which comprised several floors of inhumations, were built primarily in an area called the Valley of the Tombs to

37. Tower tombs of Palmyra, 1st century BCE. Photo © Stephen Coyne / Bridgeman Images.

the west and southwest of the city from the 1st century to the 3rd century CE (Figure 37).³³ These niches were covered, after burial, by portrait reliefs depicting prominent members of the clan (Plate 10). In some cases, the reliefs were also displayed decoratively, set into the walls or ceiling without any relation to a specific burial. In around 128 CE, the Palmyrenes largely ceased building tower tombs in favor of hypogea (used from the last quarter of the 1st century CE until about 232 CE) and mausolea (143–232 CE).³⁴ Even in these new architectural contexts the *loculi* reliefs and similar types of funerary portraits remained popular.³⁵

Several changes in artistic and architectural features occurred during the mid-2nd century CE, including sculpted doors and lintels, inscriptions, and plaster and painted decoration in both interiors and exteriors. These changes suggest that engagement with the tomb was seen as an increasingly worthwhile investment.³⁶ Even hypogea often included elaborate aboveground markers to make the tomb more visible. In addition to their proximity to major travel routes and civic buildings, these more visible and monumental features made tombs part of the day-to-day topography of average Palmyrenes.³⁷ Within the tombs, the rise of funerary inscriptions demonstrates an interest in individuating and commemorating specific people within the family, part of the Roman-period "epigraphic habit" observed throughout the provinces.³⁸ The changes reflect a shift toward a funerary culture interested in specific, high-investment commemoration of the deceased individual and their place in a familial and civic context in easily accessible spaces.

Still, the primary audience for these reliefs would have been families and those who participated in familial funerals. As long-lasting representations, the reliefs and the tombs they stood in would have played a key role in reifying cultural memory and defining self and community. Portraits are intended to represent and resemble individuals and to serve as (semi-)permanent fixtures in the landscape, long outliving their subjects. As I have argued here, it seems that Palmyrenes found male bodies most useful for making claims on a cosmopolitan form of Greek identity that resonated on a transregional level. Women's bodies, on the other hand, were used to make claims on more familiar and probably local status-groups. For these viewers, expressions of cultural identity may not have been the most salient aspect of the portrait. But an object may be aimed at multiple audiences and provoke discrepant responses, and I argue that these reliefs also anticipated another, less knowledgeable outside viewer. For the families that used these tombs, the images negotiated competing ethnic and cultural concepts using local styles and iconographies combined with strategies of gendered representation common throughout the Roman provinces. Palmyrenes must have expected that men in Greco-Roman costume would be seen as familiar to outsiders, while the women in these reliefs would have been read as fundamentally othered in some way to those who were not part of the local community. For many provincial peoples of the Roman world, then, alterity was a useful, valuable, and most of all, common strategy for self-representation.

This gendered pattern can also be observed in other corpuses of Imperial-period portraits and ideal sculpture.[39] In painted portraits included with mummy burials from the 2nd century and 3rd century CE, often referred to as the Fayyum portraits, men normally wear Greek or Roman dress or they are represented nude, while women often wear a more local form of dress in order to navigate competing needs for cultural identification (Figure 38).[40] In the northwestern provinces, funerary reliefs regularly depict men in Roman military costume paired with women in local forms of dress, distinct from Roman styles.[41] These types of representations intertwine the concepts of femininity and alterity, employing the female's already marginal status in most ancient societies to map less normative forms of status and identity onto the female body.[42]

ISIAC GRAVE RELIEFS FOR WOMEN

A similar gendered dynamic may be found in 111 grave reliefs recovered from Athens depicting women in the dress of Isis.[43] The reliefs, dating from the Roman period, include images of single women in Isiac dress, women in Isiac

38. Portrait mummy of an adolescent male in Greek clothing from Hawara, 100–120 CE. London: British Museum inv. EA13595. © The Trustees of the British Museum.

dress paired with men in normative Greek dress, and in some cases set within small groups of men and women who wear Greek dress. While some examples of the type appear at other sites around the Mediterranean,[44] no other provincial group seems to have used Isiac costumes in funerary portraiture in such high numbers, indicating that Athenians found the type particularly well suited to their needs. I argue that Greek devotees employed the pattern observed above in order to emphasize their membership in a specific local group of Isis devotees while also embedding themselves in normative forms of Athenian Greekness. The result is a set of reliefs that inflect Greek ethnicity with a sense of alterity, an expression of identity-based difference that relies on concepts of self and other, in which the idea of the other provides an attractive form of marginality that can be used to claim membership in a minority group.[45] In short: alterity announces that the subject has stepped outside the norm.

The grave stele of Sosibia, daughter of Eubios, from the Athenian dēme of Kephissia, pictured at the beginning of this chapter, provides a representative example (Figure 33).[46] The relief depicts a single woman wearing Isis' signature *Knotenpalla* costume, comprising a long-sleeved linen chiton and a fringed mantle knotted in an X-pattern over the chest, which produces a characteristic set of cascading chevron folds over the hips and thighs. In her left hand she holds a *situla* near the left thigh, and in her raised right hand she carries a large *sistrum*. Part of the mantle hangs loose from the body's right side to create a cape-like effect. Her hair is arranged in an adaptation of the Empress Sabina's "Juno" hairstyle, in which loose, curled locks flow down to the shoulder in a manner reminiscent of Isis' corkscrew curls, instead of being tied back into a ponytail.[47] She stands inside an *aedicula*, and across the architrave is written an identifying inscription with the name of her father and dēme.

This costume would have been easily recognizable to even an inattentive viewer as that of Isis. Statues of Isis were displayed in both cultic and non-cultic contexts. For instance, one large statue of Isis *Pelagia* formed part of the decoration of the *scaenae frons* of the theater at Messene (Cover).[48] There is also some evidence to suggest that devotees wore Isiac costumes outside the sanctuary, as in the processions Apuleius describes in *Metamorphoses* 11 (discussed in Chapter 2). In addition, Tacitus recounts an incident in which Domitian dressed up in the linen robes of an Egyptian priest while hiding from his rival Vitellius in the home of a temple attendant near the Capitolium (*Hist.* 3.74.1).[49] The emperor hid among a group of devotees and escaped to the home of Cornelius Primus near the Velabrum. There is no indication of a festival or procession in Tacitus' account, and the story is only believable if devotees (at least sometimes) wore cultic dress in the street. Since the costume also appears frequently in portraiture, which, as we saw above, often features commonly worn clothing, it is not unlikely that these costumes could have been worn in the streets.

Many of these reliefs represent Isiac women alongside other members of their families. One example from the 2nd century CE, now in the National Archaeological Museum in Athens, depicts a couple named Musaios and Amaryllis standing with a second, unnamed woman within a *naiskos* (Figure 39).[50] Amaryllis, in the middle of the three, wears the knotted mantle costume seen in Isiac ideal sculpture and funerary reliefs of Roman Athens; she also carries the *situla* and *sistrum*. Her hair is parted in the middle, and loose, wavy locks flow over her shoulders. Following Greco-Roman portraiture norms, Amaryllis' face, hair, and body are idealized and lack identifying features.

39. Grave stela of Musaios (male), Amaryllis (female, center), and an unnamed woman of Large Herculaneum type (right), Trajanic period. Athens: National Archaeological Museum inv. 1233. Photo: Giovanni Dall'Orto via Creative Commons. © Hellenic Ministry of Culture & Sports/Archaeological Receipts Fund.

On either side stands a figure in normative Greek dress, probably members of Amaryllis' family. Musaios, her male companion, stands to her right and wears his short hair brushed forward. He is dressed in a traditional chiton and himation in the arm-sling posture and carries a book roll. To her left stands a female figure wearing a light chiton under a heavy mantle. She pulls some of the drapery over her left shoulder to produce a series of diagonals characteristic of the Large Herculaneum Woman statue type popular throughout the eastern empire during this period.[51] Like Amaryllis, the unnamed woman has a symmetrical, fleshy face. She wears her hair in a crown of tiny curls typical of Flavian- and early Antonine-period female portraiture.[52] Amaryllis is the central and most important figure in the composition. Her inscribed name is framed by a *tabella ansata*, and she stands between the other two figures, who turn to face her, while

Amaryllis looks directly out to the viewer with her body squared. Though no evidence of paint remains, it is possible that color increased the emphasis further.[53] The costume would have clearly differentiated Amaryllis from her family members.

Amaryllis' alterity would have been established further by her placement in a larger cemetery. Though the majority were found in reuse or modern storage contexts, the few reliefs with archaeological context have been found scattered through the main cemeteries of Roman Athens.[54] Examples have been found in the Kerameikos cemetery, in the area of the Athenian Agora,[55] in cemeteries near modern Stadiou Street, where Sosibia's relief was found,[56] in Herodou Attikou Street,[57] and in the neighborhood surrounding the Temple of Olympian Zeus, which saw significant building activity during the Hadrianic period.[58] It seems that Isiac funerary reliefs appeared in the majority of the active cemeteries known in this period, and there is no evidence that Isiac reliefs were grouped together.[59]

Instead, they probably stood alongside more normative funerary reliefs, a context in which Amaryllis' unusual costume would have been highly visible and easily noticed. A roughly contemporary example found in the area of modern Odos Pireaus/Odos Salaminos in 1915 depicts a male–female pair that is representative of the way in which both genders were commonly depicted in Roman-period funerary reliefs (Figure 40).[60] Like Musaios, the man wears the chiton and himation in the arm-sling style and carries a book roll. The woman wears her chiton and mantle in the Large Herculaneum Woman format; and her hair is arranged in a more classicizing style popular in the second half of the 2nd century CE.[61]

40. Grave stela of a couple from Athens (area of modern Pireaus and Salaminos Streets), late 2nd century CE. Athens: Kerameikos Museum inv. P190. Courtesy Ephorate of Antiquities of the City of Athens, © Hellenic Ministry of Culture & Sports/Archaeological Receipts Fund.

When the two relief types are compared, the difference is immediately clear. If the Musaios and Amaryllis relief were displayed near a funerary relief like the Odos Pireaus example, Musaios and his unnamed female companion would have echoed the figures around them, highlighting Amaryllis' difference even further. Though the Large Herculaneum Woman type's folds are eye-catching, the "X" created by Amaryllis' Isis-knot is even more striking.[62] The attributes she carries, particularly the *sistrum*, also deviate from feminine norms. Athenian women are not depicted often in movement; in fact, their ornate drapery would often preclude it. Amaryllis, on the other hand, raises the rattle in an unusually active gesture intended to suggest the action of shaking. This gesture probably referred to ritual music or to cultic actions Amaryllis performed, characterizing her in a way that runs counter to most female portraiture in Roman Athens. This difference suggests that her participation in these rituals was of particular value to her and her family.[63]

Amaryllis, then, is depicted as an atypical woman, an unusual choice for Roman Athens and indeed the Roman Empire more generally.[64] Female portraiture in this time and place did not often emphasize individuality. Instead, sculptors and patrons relied on established visual norms that set a portrait's subject(s) in positive and recognizable social contexts.[65] Though the garments worn by Isiac women do not flout conservative Greek mores, they still deviate from well-established norms. The majority of Greek men and women chose body types – and for most women, face types – that replicated and referred to existing and easily recognizable models.[66] These visual references gave each portrait meaning and communicated valuable information about the subject to a general audience. Women who used the Large Herculaneum Woman type, for example, might be considered to be ideal matrons: older women who have successfully completed their duties as mothers, daughters, and wives.[67] In deviating from these norms, Isis devotees were making a choice that was not only different: they ran the risk of being misunderstood and negating the purpose of funerary portraiture altogether – to be remembered as part of the local community.

Isiac Funerary Reliefs in an Athenian Context

I argue that there are two distinct but related factors that motivated these extraordinary aesthetic choices. First, there existed a desire to depict these women as initiates into the cults of the Egyptian gods in a manner that would be legible not only to other devotees but to the community at large. Second, as I argue below, these reliefs establish the people depicted on them as part of a bounded group of Isis devotees in Athens that defined Greekness in novel ways and relied on provincial tropes to do so.

In reference to the first factor, these images drew from the lived experience of religious rituals that were, paradoxically, both secret and well known, to construct a recognizable form of Isiac portraiture.[68] These images were recognizable because they depicted a certain type of woman known from cult practice. Scholars have floated several possible interpretations of these figures' identity, including the possibility that these reliefs feature images of Isis herself, but the two most plausible interpretations are that these women either served as priestesses or were initiates.[69] The large number and high concentration of these reliefs within the larger corpus of funerary monuments in Roman Athens make it more likely that they represent initiates.[70] Further, none of the women named in these funerary reliefs appear in other Isiac cult inscriptions from the city, as one might expect had they served as priestesses or other high-level cult functionaries.[71]

For devotees, the reliefs may have referred to a ritual they knew and had personally experienced. In an evocative passage from Apuleius' *Metamorphoses*, the protagonist, Lucius, recently returned to human form, continues his initiation into the cult of Isis.[72] Upon the priest's orders, Lucius stands in front of the cult image on a wooden dais and holds a lit torch. He is then dramatically revealed to a large audience of worshippers. Here, Lucius *stands in* for the cult image.[73] Martzavou has described this ritual as a reproduction of epiphanic experience,[74] but it also serves as an instance of self-fashioning. By placing the god's or goddess's dress upon their bodies, devotees extended themselves into a communion not only with the god but also into a new community with those who had engaged with the divine in the same transcendent way. Apuleius describes this event in greater detail than any other aspect of the initiation, which underscores its affective and ritual significance. Though the passage describes Lucius' transition into a statue of Sol, not Isis, it demonstrates that dress was used in Isiac initiatory rituals as part of a process of transcendence. Such rituals altered the individual participant's subjective experience and must have impacted the devotee in profound ways.[75] Standing in the place of a statue and in close proximity to a cult image of Isis, Lucius becomes part of a sculptural group and "gaze[d] at Isis face to face."[76] The ontological slippage between human, statue, and god here is key to understanding why Isiac dress plays such a key role in these funerary reliefs. By dressing up in this special garment, whose unusual nature requires a lengthy, florid description and a specific name, Lucius is transformed into a new person who in some way embodies the deity through resemblance to the cult image.[77] Engaging with Isis in this boundary-blurring way demanded that the devotee take on a new transcultural identity, requiring the initiate to reconfigure his own understanding of his Greekness.

The Athenian reliefs may have referred to a similar ritual. Scholars have noted that many of the Isiac funerary stelai resemble a fragment of a votive relief depicting Isis *Dikaiosyne* wearing the knotted costume that dates to the early 1st century BCE (Figure 41).[78] These reliefs may have referred to or even reproduced a now-lost image of Isis that belonged to one of the city's Isiac sanctuaries, of which four are known.[79] Though only the bottom of the garment is preserved, there are indications of the characteristic patterns of

41. Votive relief depicting Isis *Dikaiosyne*, early 1st century BCE. Athens: National Epigraphic Museum inv. 8246. Courtesy National Epigraphic Museum, © Hellenic Ministry of Culture & Sports/Archaeological Receipts Fund.

drapery folds and remnants of a fringed cloak known from the funerary reliefs. The resemblance is close enough to suggest that the devotees were attempting to model themselves after a similar image of Isis. Further, Isis *Dikaiosyne*, a version of the goddess dedicated to justice, is known from one inscription in late Hellenistic Athens and another in Hellenistic Delos and seems to represent an instance of colonial cultic practice impacting religious life at Athens.[80] This connection would give the rite a particular local resonance, framing this experience in terms of objects that devotees accessed only through participation in the cult community.

Another 2nd-century BCE votive relief from Thessaloniki depicts a young man standing behind an altar, flanked by his parents who hold Isiac implements (Figure 8).[81] Though Voutiras initially identified the central figure as a statue of Osiris, the fact that his feet do not stand upon the base, as is true for other representations of statues, suggests that this relief depicts something quite different – a devotee. In a later article, he identified the central male figure as an initiate and his parents as part of the viewing crowd.[82] These reliefs could have referred to a similar moment of religious transcendence as the one that Lucius experienced in Apuleius' account, one that involved the initiate embodying Isis by dressing in the goddess's sacred costume and perhaps performing some form of initiatory ritual in front of or near this cult image. Set in their cultic context, these reliefs represent an instance in which devotees and/or their families chose to highlight their commonality with the group over the powerful pressure to conform to contemporary aesthetic values. Rituals like the one that Lucius underwent and, I hypothesize, that the female devotees depicted in the funerary reliefs also experienced, acted as a catalyst in the construction and reification of cultic communities.[83] The knotted dress thus became a way to fashion a form of Isiac cult identity for popular consumption, to mark oneself as part of a particular group who had access to specific cult symbols, objects, and rites not available to the general public.

Within their display context, these reliefs respond to the normativity of Greek portraiture, particularly female portraiture, with a desire to set Isiac women apart. For those who were not familiar with the cult's inner workings, these reliefs and the alterity of their symbolism grouped these women and, as I argue in the section "Looking Outward, Looking Inward," their families, into a defined and bounded community. For those who were initiates, on the other hand, these images established the subject as part of a shared experience.[84] The reliefs and the dress they depict facilitated memory and thus participated in identity building and preservation by enabling the ritual and affective practices that underpinned this group's self-understanding.[85] For initiates, seeing women in the goddess's costume could have prompted a moment of identification by triggering for the initiate his or her own memories of the same experience, thus heightening their sense of belonging in a way that activated their connection to the cultic community.[86]

ISIAC DRESS FOR MEN?

The Amaryllis and Musaios relief (Figure 39) also raises another question: Is Musaios an Isis devotee? Based on the relief's iconography and inscription, there is no reason to suspect he was, but, as I argue in this chapter's concluding section, "Looking Outward, Looking Inward," he might well have been. His clothes, posture, hair, and gestures are all part of the Greek canon of normative masculinity. Indeed, it would be unusual for him to use the same *Knotenpalla* costume as Amaryllis. There are only four or five known examples of funerary reliefs that depict men in Isis' costume.[87] In one Flavian-period grave stele from Piraeus for Sympheron of Miletus and Kallo of Eupuridon, Sympheron wears a *Knotenpalla*, albeit one in which the straps needed to create the X-shape do not all attach properly, while Kallo is shown in the Small Herculaneum Woman format (Figure 42).[88] In his right hand he lifts a *sistrum*, and in his left he holds a rounded object. The arrangement of his mantle, however, follows masculine norms and does not wholly abandon masculine types. His chiton is short and reveals his lower legs, and his mantle creates a

138 SELF-FASHIONING: DRESSING THE DEVOTEES OF ISIS

42. Funerary relief of Kallo of Eupuridon and Synpheron of Miletus (right). Athens: Ephorate of Antiquities of the City of Athens inv. 761. Courtesy Ephorate of Antiquities of the City of Athens, © Hellenic Ministry of Culture & Sports/Archaeological Receipts Fund.

strong diagonal that does not preserve enough drapery for a veil, as a woman would have needed.[89] The relief on the whole is awkward and gives the impression of a failed experiment rather than a well-established type.

The epigraphic record, however, indicates that men participated in the cult in similar, if not greater, numbers in Roman Athens and held most of the priesthoods in the city's Isiac sanctuaries. Heyob determines that about 48 percent of the inscriptions from Athens refer to a woman, which is admittedly higher than the percentages at Rome (37 percent) and Delos (11 percent).[90] Further, there is no evidence of women serving as priestesses of Sarapis or as high priests in charge of a temple, and they seem to have been excluded from many private cult associations.

Even when men used other Isiac attributes, these images were often aimed at other initiates and consequently served a narrower range of social functions. In addition to the few examples of men in the *Knotenpalla* type, there was also a separate priestly costume for men used in freestanding portraiture and painting around the Mediterranean. Across the Mediterranean there existed a costume used for male priests that included a bald or shaved head and a white linen garment (Plate 11).[91] One Hellenistic painted funerary stele from Demetrias in Thessaly depicts its subject, identified through its inscription as both an Egyptian and a priest of Isis, with a shaved or bald head and dressed in a white linen garment.[92] This suggests that this costume was in use in parts of Greece by at least the mid-3rd century BCE and belongs to a widespread and perhaps well-known form of dress used in Isiac cult around the Mediterranean. Sculpted portraits in the round seem largely consistent with this costume type. Two heads, one from Delos and the other from the Athenian Agora, have been identified as Egyptian priests. Both date to the Hellenistic/early Roman period, depicting an older man with a lined, careworn face, a hairless head, and a diadem.[93] Neither was found in context. The identification of these heads as Isiac priests is thus uncertain, since the argument rests primarily on the baldness of the depicted men. Baldness, however, is not uncommon in veristic portraiture, and these heads might represent priests of other deities.[94]

Another type of portrait statue used to depict male devotees of Isis are representations of young boys with Horus-locks. Normally, the hairstyle takes the form of a shaved head or short-cropped hairstyle with a long braid or lock on the right side of the head; it is associated with young boys dedicated to Horus.[95] Christodoulou has recently identified two busts of very young boys as Isis devotees, both of which were recut in the mid-3rd century CE to have long locks of hair at the crown of their heads (Figure 43).[96] Baecke-Dahmen, on the other hand, argues that only locks on the right side of the head can be conclusively linked to Egyptian cults. Two funerary reliefs from Athens suggest that this format, originally used for children, was on occasion applied to adult men as well. In the relief of the son of Soterion from Athens, the woman in Isiac dress in the right is accompanied by a man in a chiton and himation, perhaps her son, who also wears a Horus lock on the right side of his head.[97] A similar fragment from the first half of the 1st century CE depicts a young man in a himation with a lock on the right side and some remnants of a longer lock of hair on the left side, which may indicate a sculptor's error in carving the image.[98] Unlike the Dion busts, these images depict teenage males who have begun to wear adult clothing. This suggests that the lock is motivated by religious participation, likely an early stage of initiation into the cult,[99] more than a desire to indicate youth alone. But again, like the male *Knotenpalla*, these examples are few and far between and must represent a very small number of male Isiac devotees.

43. Portrait bust of a young boy with Isiac tonsure found in the House of Leda at Dion, 2nd century CE and recarved in the 3rd century CE to create the tonsure hairstyle. Dion: Archaeological Museum inv. MΔ 8929. © Hellenic Ministry of Culture & Sports/ Archaeological Receipts Fund.

Male devotees mostly did not use Isiac iconography in portraiture. This choice may have been dictated by context. Unlike the female reliefs, which were displayed to a broad audience in public cemeteries, the few known instances of male portraits that employ Isiac dress may have been aimed at a more limited audience. Swetnam-Burland observed that men in Italy primarily used the Isiac priestly costume in representations displayed in private contexts like homes or sanctuaries,[100] a pattern that may also hold true for Roman-period Greece. A portrait from the Egyptian sanctuary of Marathon, which depicts a man in a fringed himation and long-sleeved linen chiton, was found in the main portion of a private sanctuary that was surrounded by high walls

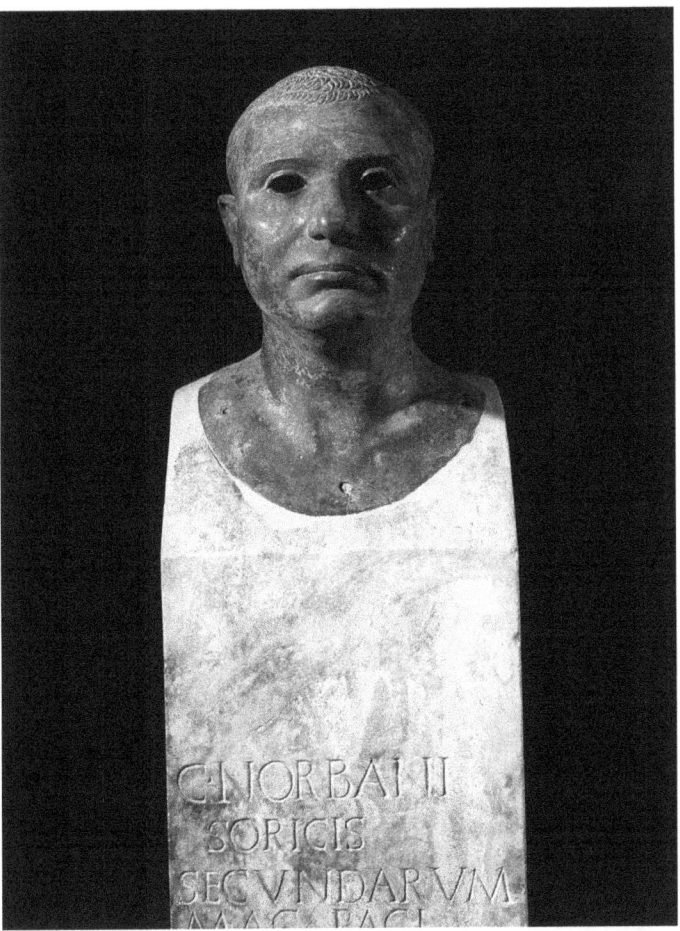

44. Portrait bust of C. Norbanus Sorex from the Pompeii Iseum, mid-1st century CE. Naples: Museo Archeologico Nazionale inv. 4991, CIL X 814. © Scala/ArtResource.

and monumental pylons that could be closed with wooden doors.[101] The bronze portrait bust of the actor century Norbanus Sorex from the northwest corner of the portico of Pompeii's Iseum[102] may underscore this distinction (Figure 44). The bust, dating to the 1st century CE, depicts its subject with a shaved head, and stood inside a sanctuary whose access was similarly controlled by high walls and doors.[103]

Even within sanctuaries, however, it was more common for men to use normative portraiture models. Sarapieion C on Delos, which remained in use through the mid-1st century BCE, preserves the largest number of portraits and inscriptions for portrait statues of any Isiac sanctuary in Greece.[104] In a recent article, Brun-Kyriakidis surveyed the remains of portraiture from this site and found several fragmentary male portraits from the site, including most of a male body draped in normative Greek clothing,[105] a fragment of an idealizing male head with long curly hair and portrait features,[106] an over life-sized head that may depict a Hellenistic prince,[107] and a right-arm fragment from a bronze statue.[108] None of these fragments depict a male subject dressed as an Egyptian priest or devotee, and there is no evidence from a later sanctuary, apart from the Marathon portrait mentioned above, that would suggest a shift in the Roman period.

LOOKING OUTWARD, LOOKING INWARD

As the sculptors and patrons of Isiac funerary reliefs made decisions about how best to represent Isiac women, they relied on extant strategies in use throughout the empire. Women would wear the *Knotenpalla* costume used frequently in statues of Isis around the Mediterranean, while any male figures included in the relief would employ Greek civic attire (Figure 45). This gendered division allowed family members to make claims on normative Greek civic values and embed themselves in Athenian social groups and hierarchies. At the same time, the female body is fashioned to assert membership in a smaller, less normative Isiac cult community. Though Egyptian religion was popular and widely practiced throughout Greece, the cult still relied on a set of symbols that emphasized marginality.[109] Indeed, as I argued in Chapters 3 and 4, this foreignness was part of the cult's appeal. Employing the *Knotenpalla* in funerary portraiture allowed devotees to advertise and contextualize their membership in this community, both to Athenians at large and to other devotees. These reliefs, then, must have played an active role in the construction and definition of the boundaries of Isiac religion.

45. Grave relief of Mousa, daughter of Dionysios, from Halai found in the Herodou Attikou shaft of the Athenian Metro excavations, ca. 150 CE. Athens: Ephorate of Antiquities of the City of Athens inv. M 4609. © Hellenic Ministry of Culture & Sports/ Archaeological Receipts Fund.

If, as I have argued here, the use of cultic dress played an important role in establishing community identity and defining the boundaries of the devotee group, why would men opt out of this process? In order to understand these strategic decisions, it is necessary to set Isiac portraiture from Roman Athens in a broader provincial context. Though Athens did hold a special place in the Roman imagination as the center of Classical learning, its inhabitants still experienced Imperial domination and participated in transcultural artistic and cultural exchanges that occurred throughout the eastern Mediterranean.[110] These reliefs, I argue, are a part of a broader pattern of representing provincial women in dress that highlighted alterity, while provincial men frequently conformed to Greek and Roman norms.[111] By setting Isiac portraiture in its provincial context, I argue, this gendered pattern becomes part of an observable trend of using the female body to negotiate tensions between normative and alternative identity categories in the Roman Empire.

These reliefs might have also used the female body as a locus for making claims about the entire family. In the case of the Palmyrene portraits, viewers were probably meant to understand the paired figures as part of the same family group and to perceive that, altogether, all members of the family engaged in local culture as well as a global Greekness.[112] In these cases, displaying pairs or individual portraits within larger tombs compare and contrast these two cultural concepts to produce new, more nuanced identifications. Similarly, in a study of the early Classical Kerameikos cemetery, Closterman has argued that tomb markers, particularly sculpted grave stelai, highlighted the most important and illustrious members of a family group as a way to establish a familial history and identity for public consumption.[113] Similarly, Isiac reliefs may have acted as long-term claims on membership in this minority group not just for their depicted subject but for the family as a whole. If Athenians are relying on similar representational strategies, group reliefs and the display of several reliefs together may have indicated that a larger familial group also participated in Egyptian religion. Spatial relationships within the cemetery could have enhanced this mechanism even further and allowed stelai that depicted a single devotee to extend their self-fashioning to other members of their family. The choice to use sculpture for these images extended these claims into the future. Placing that alterity on the female body was an especially effective method of negotiating competing cultural needs and identification processes and fashioning a self not only for the deceased but for their families and the generations to come.

This comparative approach helps us better understand what work these portraits do. Within the context of Roman Athens, these reliefs established their subjects as members of a minority community, one that required a significant and sustained effort to join. Participation in initiatory rituals, regular rites, and following cultic regulations structure religious communities,[114] and for members of Athens' Isiac community the reliefs' symbolism, which, I argue, relied on personal memories of ritual experiences, would have been immediately apparent. Devotee viewers who had undergone initiation would remember the experience of the rite and the transformative process of dressing and standing in for the cult image, and perhaps even feel a moment of identifying with the gods again. The affective aspect of this memory cannot be overstated, and these images would have strengthened devotees' feelings of membership and belonging, if only for a second. Portraiture is a way to perform this membership for both insiders and outsiders – to define the self in ways meant to persist.

Alongside these claims, however, the reliefs also embedded Isis devotees and their families in a larger, more transcultural form of Greekness. Through the symbolism of Greek dress, Athenian devotees laid claim to the same types of normative, civic-based masculinity used throughout the eastern empire. Just like their counterparts in Palmyra, Alexandria, or Noricum, Athenians wanted to retain access to prevailing value systems. The chiton and himation offered elites across the east an opportunity to establish their Greekness in a way that was productive under the empire.[115] These funerary portraits, then, became yet another way to embed the more challenging and marginal aspects of Egyptian religion in Greekness – another way to enmesh Isis and her devotees in a contemporary, transcultural, and still normative form of Greekness.

PLATE 1. Mosaic depicting Rome and the personifications of several provinces from the House of Africa in Thysdrus, second half of the 2nd century CE. El Jem, Tunisia: Musée Archéologique. © Gilles Mermet/Art Resource, NY.

PLATE 2. Personification of Egypt from Plate 1. © Gilles Mermet/Art Resource, NY.

PLATE 3. Calendar mosaic from Thysdrus depicting the month of November, 3rd century CE. Sousse: Archaeological Museum. © Vanni Archive/Art Resource, NY.

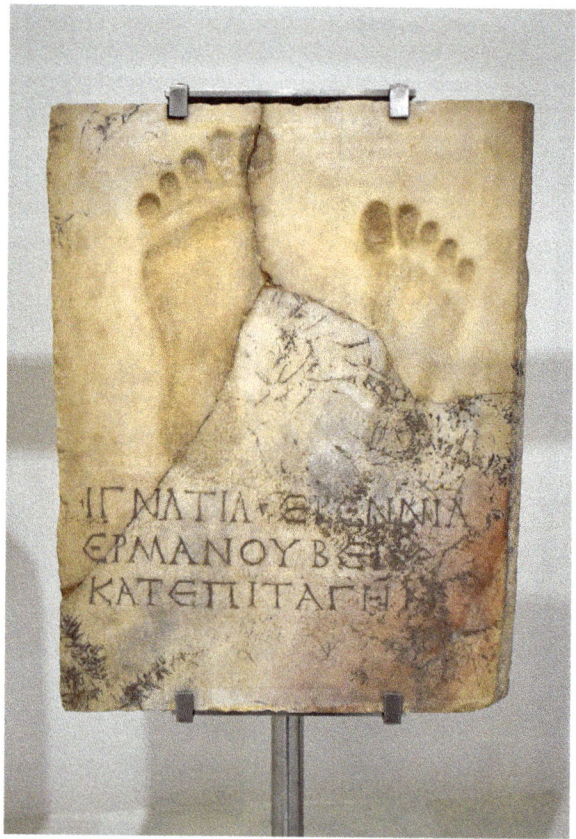

PLATE 4. Votive relief of Ignatia Herennia dedicated to Hermanubis, featuring relief footprints in two different sizes, late 2nd–early 3rd century CE. Dion: Archaeological Museum inv. MΔ 419. © Hellenic Ministry of Culture & Sports/Archaeological Receipts Fund.

PLATE 5. Nilotic wall painting from the Casa del Medico at Pompeii, 1st century CE. Naples: Museo Archeologico Nazionale inv. 113195. © Vanni Archive/Art Resource, NY.

PLATE 6. Group of sculptures depicting Isis, Kerberos, and Sarapis from the Sanctuary of the Egyptian Gods at Gortyna, 3rd century CE. Iraklion: Archaeological Museum. © Hellenic Ministry of Culture & Sports/Archaeological Receipts Fund.

PLATE 7. Statue of Aphrodite of the Louvre-Naples type from the Thessaloniki Sarapeum, 2nd century CE. Thessaloniki: Archaeological Museum inv. MΘ 831. © Hellenic Ministry of Culture & Sports/Archaeological Receipts Fund.

PLATE 8. Head of Isis with corkscrew curls from Thessaloniki, Antonine period. On the left of the head is the cutting for an attached crowning element. Thessaloniki: Archaeological Museum inv. MΘ 2490. © Hellenic Ministry of Culture & Sports/Archaeological Receipts Fund.

PLATE 9. Statuette of Harpokrates from the Thessaloniki Sarapeum, second half of the 2nd century CE. Thessaloniki: Archaeological Museum inv. MΘ 844. © Hellenic Ministry of Culture & Sports/Archaeological Receipts Fund.

PLATE 10. Interior of the Tomb of Iarhai in Palmyra, 2nd century CE. Damascus: Musée National de Damas. Photo: G. Dagli Orti /De Agostini Picture Library / Bridgeman Images.

PLATE 11. Wall painting of an Isiac priest making an offering to a statue of Harpokrates from the portico of Pompeii's Iseum, mid-1st century CE. Naples: Museo Archeologico Nazionale. © Vanni Archive/ Art Resource, NY.

PLATE 12. The Iseum at Dion, 1st century BCE–4th century CE. © Hellenic Ministry of Culture & Sports/Archaeological Receipts Fund.

PLATE 13. Section VI 6 A of the Nilotic panels of colored *sectile* glass from Kenchreai, 4th century CE. Restored to original colors by the Corning Museum of Glass. Isthmia: Archaeological Museum. © Hellenic Ministry of Culture & Sports/ Archaeological Receipts Fund.

PLATE 14. Replica of Isis and Osiris statues displayed in situ at the North Pylon of the Sanctuary of the Egyptian Gods at Marathon. © Hellenic Ministry of Culture & Sports/ Archaeological Receipts Fund.

CHAPTER SIX

SELF-LOCATION
Isiac Sanctuaries and Nilotic Fictions

In this chapter, I want to explore the cults' relationship with Egypt as a concept.[1] In Greece, devotees constructed sanctuaries appropriate to local and regional concepts of Isiac gods. Where exactly Isis lived, however, was a surprisingly difficult question to answer, and Greek Isiac communities often improvised a response. As I have argued, cultic texts and ideal images emphasize the gods' culturally liminal status but ultimately embed the deities, particularly Isis, in Greek paradigms. At the same time, the gods must retain some connection to Egypt to preserve their legitimacy.[2] I argue that devotees negotiated these complex cultic ideas and ethnic stereotypes to materialize three-dimensional landscapes fitting their conceptions of an Egypt appropriate to Isis. These sanctuaries and the activities that occurred within them offered opportunities for imaginative place-making so that Greek devotees might construct their own world within which their reconfigured versions of Isis and her companions lived. As much as these spaces invited devotees to imagine themselves within Egypt, visitors would not forget that they were standing in Greece, often within or just outside city walls and next to sanctuaries of canonical Greek deities. These juxtapositions allowed Greeks to claim Egypt, to possess it in miniature and control its expressions. The result was a space designed to uproot Egypt and replant it on Greek soil.

I argue that the sanctuaries resulted from shifting attitudes toward culture, identity, and memory that inflected life in Roman Greece,[3] as locales that resulted from a long process of negotiation and appropriation between individuals, communities, objects, and rituals.[4] I consider how these sanctuaries came together and developed as part of a process of self-location, a method of identity formation in which individuals and communities consider how close their relationships with other groups are and where they stand in local and global hierarchies.[5] People exist within interconnected webs of material culture, preexisting knowledge and ideas, social hierarchy, and geographic space.[6] Self-location examines these connections by focusing on the cognitive and emotional ways in which human beings situate themselves in the world.[7] My goal is to consider how Isis devotees placed themselves within grids and webs of connections, categories, and affiliations in the ancient world using sanctuary design.

In the case of Isiac devotees in Roman Greece, I argue, experiments with self-location took the form of sanctuaries designed to evoke or reference a sense of being in Egypt, a manipulation of geographic space that both reconfigures Greek myth-history and offers a new fiction of possession and domination (Plate 12). These attempts most often took two forms: allusions to Egyptian architecture and material culture, and references to the landscape of the Nile River. Scholars have referred to these motifs collectively as *Nilotica*, a type of art based on a combination of partial cultural knowledge and persistent stereotypes around Egypt. Several have interpreted this iconography as a venue for participating in imperialism through private and domestic contexts. Within the context of Egyptian cult, then, self-location involves placing Isis and the idea of Egypt in Greece, a form of deterritorialization in which a place is not connected to its own cultural geography.[8] This process results in imagined geographies of Egypt: reproductions of places based on expectations and stereotypes more than on knowledge or experience.[9] Here, Greek communities can reproduce and even own parts of the Egyptian landscape, repurposing distant places for their own ends. These decisions were neither politically nor culturally neutral, and it is important to consider what benefit devotees derived from their encounters with these sacred landscapes, and how existing knowledge, ideas, and memories may have shaped their experiences. Collapsing geographies thus becomes a method for centralizing Greekness, and for granting devotees power and control over other provinces. Rome, however, is always active in the background, and these sanctuaries also offered devotees a means to consider their own power and place in the Roman Mediterranean.

Egyptian sanctuaries are thus constellations of landscape, cult, culture, imagination, style, and politics. Building from this assumption, I argue that Greek features integrated with Egyptian ones, both real and imagined, to produce landscapes that imagined a Greek world that both contains and domesticates Egypt. I begin by defining Nilotica and exploring the prevalence of this iconography in Greece. Then I study the Sanctuary of the Egyptian

Gods at Marathon, which features a central pyramidal structure flanked by Egyptian-style pylons, Egyptianizing statuary, and a riverine setting on the ocean. In the imagined world of this sanctuary, which trades on fantastic imaginings of pharaonic times and places, Egypt was no longer far away and foreign but rather a part of the local and contemporary world that devotees could access regularly through participation in ritual.

The Marathon sanctuary is unusual in many ways, but, as I demonstrate in the next section, aspects of its imaginative self-location appear in the architecture and placement of other Greek sanctuaries. I argue that the sanctuaries in Greece adapted local landscapes and objects to produce a Nilotic aesthetic and atmosphere. In particular, most sanctuaries include a water feature, and some, like the sanctuary at Dion, are set in a riverine environment meant to replicate the Nile's own flora. Others incorporate Nilotic imagery like crocodiles or cattle to create a more conceptual allusion. These sanctuaries granted communities a way to locate themselves within a carefully controlled reconstruction of the Nile, a feature that had cultic uses but also granted Greek devotees a certain power over other parts of the Roman world.

THE NILOTIC AESTHETIC

What version of Egypt did Greek devotees wish to inhabit? Surprisingly, it was not a real or even a realistic rendering of Hellenistic or Roman Egypt. As discussed in Chapter 4, Greek sanctuaries contained few imported objects and served very few Egyptian migrants, if any, after about the 1st century BCE. Instead, Greeks built sanctuaries that were founded on cultural imaginings of the Nile. In his study of Italian material, Versluys defines Nilotic as a form of iconographic representation of the natural world of the Nile in an ideal, abundant way that does not follow directly upon Egyptian antecedents.[10] This term describes imagery and iconography used to depict the Egyptian natural landscape, particularly the Nile River, for Greek and Roman audiences outside of Egypt. These images convey highly stylized and stereotypical visions of the Nile, its banks, and the people and animals imagined to dwell in the landscape in wall paintings, mosaics, and in some cases three-dimensional assemblages in multiple media. The majority of these representations are found in wall paintings and mosaics from houses located in and around Pompeii. But the Nilotic is fundamentally a cultural and geographic fantasy, an imagined landscape that brings far-off Egypt into easily digestible spaces. As argued in previous chapters, Greek ideal and portrait sculpture, as well as the cults' own texts, often construct interdependent cultural relationships between Greekness and Egyptianness. These innovations often involve manipulating mythologies, embedding Egyptian concepts and forms within Greek styles and materials, and equating Greek and Egyptian cultural touchstones.

Representations of the Nile throughout Roman history involved a political dimension. Merrills considers representations of the Nile in text and image as constructors and communicators of geographic knowledge aimed at multiple audiences. In addition to state-produced maps and geographic texts like Strabo's *Geographica*, artworks like the Palestrina mosaic or Pompeiian wall paintings taught local audiences about Egypt, and how to see and think about this exotic place that only a few would visit. In composing these texts and images, authors and artisans employed perspectives that allowed the viewer some remove from the scene. The view from above granted the audience a sense of superiority and control. Rather than engaging directly or even naturalistically with Egypt on the wall, these scenes became a way for people both inside and outside the Imperial administration to engage with the Roman Imperial project. For Merrills, the images represent a moment in which local patrons have appropriated the Imperial geographic iconography of triumphal processions and monuments with the intention of adapting it to claim their own central role in the empire's geographic control.[11]

In a recent study of Nilotica in Pompeiian gardens, Barrett has reconsidered these scenes as eclectic combinations of Roman material culture, Egyptian sources, and the spaces around them.[12] Alongside their political dimensions, these Nilescapes incorporate a partial knowledge of Egyptian cult practices and natural landscapes with Roman ideas to produce "spectacles of otherness."[13] Barrett highlights assemblages in gardens, which combined water features, sculptures, architecture, and paintings, to create a multidimensional Nilotic experience.[14] In her view, the Nilotic effect could be created not just through two-dimensional wall paintings and mosaics but also in three dimensions, through the combination of the sights and sounds of water and the feeling of refreshment – the cool shade and the scented breeze – that these settings provide. Similarly, the sensorial effect of Herodes' sanctuary drew on Nilotic ideas and imagery to transport the viewer and represent colonized lands as a form of "domesticated" empire. The viewer here has power over the content and placement of the image, and by extension a more active role in controlling distant provinces within the Roman world.[15] By bringing the idea of Egypt and its attendant meanings of foreignness into the local and domestic sphere of Greek devotees, Barrett argues, the same feelings of Imperial control described by Merrills were heightened.

Greek Nilotica

Most extant Nilotica comes from Italy, but the region's high concentration is an accident of preservation and excavation. Wall paintings from Vesuvian cities form the majority of this corpus, and Italy's particular climate and soil conditions mean that wall paintings are preserved here in much higher numbers than anywhere else in the Mediterranean. Though most examples of Nilotic iconography were found in domestic contexts, many were found in more public contexts, including baths, tombs, and civic buildings like curiae and basilicae.[16] This pattern suggests that Nilotic iconography was used frequently and in a wide array of settings, both public and private.

Some can be securely connected to a sanctuary or religious context.[17] The sanctuary of Sarapis in Ostia's Regio III included a black-and-white Nilotic mosaic with hippos, crocodiles, a pygmy, and ibises in its central court,[18] and the interior of Pompeii's Iseum contained a wealth of Nilotic imagery, including wall paintings.[19] But the boundaries between the religious and decorative and the domestic and cultic are in fact much more porous than modern scholars have recognized. Religious images could sit in a shrine and simultaneously convey the dedicator's wealth, status, education, and ethnic ties; similarly, images of gods could decorate spaces used for nonreligious purposes.[20] More importantly, ideas generated in one space could inform a viewer's experience of another. Devotees encountered this aesthetic in many places outside the sanctuary and, I argue, brought these ideas to bear on their ritual spaces.

Greece has not traditionally been considered a center for Nilotic imagery, but there is ample evidence to suggest that this iconography was in use throughout the Roman period. The best evidence is a set of Nilotic glass *opus sectile* plaques from 4th-century CE Kenchreai, near Corinth, that feature Nilotic characteristics alongside the iconography of a Roman port.[21] As reconstructed, the panels fit together to create a frieze 33 m in length, roughly organized into three registers.[22] The "pictorial" panels were stacked in an apsidal room in a basement, still packed in shipping crates, and were designed to run as a continuous frieze above a socle. The scenes depict the Nile and other parts of North Africa, particularly the Nile swamp and North African ports.[23] The swamp scenes include several animals and plants common to Nilotic imagery, including crocodiles, lotus plants, flamingos, ducks, the occasional dwarf, and reeds. As recent restorations have demonstrated, the colors would have been highly vibrant, emphasizing the Nile's distinctive flora and fauna (Plate 13). Some panels have particular resonance with Italian wall painting. For example, one of the swamp scenes features a human figure riding a crocodile, set within a marshy landscape dotted with herons and lotus plants.[24] Several wall paintings and mosaics from Italy depict similar scenes of crocodile-riders, often as part of the trope of pygmies and dwarves hunting these animals in the marshes of Egypt. For example, a wall painting from the Casa del Medico in Pompeii features a crocodile-rider in its bottom right corner, which suggests that Greek audiences were familiar with the same types of themes and motifs used in Italian examples (Plate 5).[25]

A similar iconography can be found in earlier domestic and funerary contexts in Greece, which suggests that the Kenchreai panels are not an outlier.[26] The earliest example is a fragment of *opus vermiculatum* mosaic from the first floor of the Maison de Fourni on Delos.[27] Dated to ca. 100 BCE, it depicts a duck among several water plants, including a lotus flower, which may have been part of a larger Nilotic scene decorating the lavish house. Additionally, a wall painting from a corridor of a rock-cut tomb in Corinth, dated to the first half of the 1st century CE, depicts dwarves dancing, feasting, and fishing on papyrus boats in a marshy landscape, presumably on the Nile. The tomb continued to be used into the 3rd century CE, which would have permitted later visitors to view Nilotic imagery whenever they visited the tomb.[28] At Patras, a triclinium floor mosaic in a house found under the modern Odos Kanakari featured a personification of the Nile River as a male figure carrying a cornucopia and a branch as he reclines on a crocodile.[29] Three pygmies appear in the central scene: two of them gesture toward the crocodile from the bottom of the scene while a third stands on the personified river's knee and grasps at his cornucopia. In the border, still other pygmies sail and frolic through a Nilotic environment characterized by large lotus plants. The personification of the Nile is not dissimilar to the statues displayed at Rome, and the frieze of pygmies on boats echo Nilotic iconographies seen in Italy.

These objects indicate that a concept of the Nilotic did exist in Greek art, and that the Greek images follow the tropes and themes observed in Italian art. But the catalogue of Greek Nilotica is slim, and it is reasonable to ask how relevant this iconographic trope was for the Greeks. A numerical perspective, however, provides a context. The five examples discussed above are comparable with the five found in Hispania, the six found in Gaul, and seven from Syria. Because each region has its own local archaeological history, comparing these numbers in absolute terms is not productive, but the proportions indicate that Greece is not lacking in Nilotic material culture.

These images were produced in dialogue with a longstanding Greek interest in the Nile's natural landscape. In Book 2 of Herodotus' *Histories*, we sense that flora, fauna, land, and, most importantly, the Nile River, are vitally important to Herodotus' goal of communicating the marvelous nature of Egypt to his Greek readers. The book begins with a lengthy description of the Nile, and a discussion of its peculiar properties, including its annual flood and its ability to provide Egyptians with crops without much toil (2.11–14, 22–26). References to the natural world recur throughout the narrative, including lengthy discussions of cats, crocodiles, hippopotami, otters, birds, and more marvelous animals like the phoenix and the sacred snake (2.66–76). The ethnographic portion of Book 2 ends with a description of aspects of life on the Nile, including the ways in which marsh-dwellers turned the Nile's plants into food, controlled mosquitos, built boats, and weathered the flood. In 2.93, Herodotus examines the Nile's fish with the same inverted perspective he uses to describe humans: female fish lead the schools homeward and male fish follow. Vasunia has pointed to this passage as an example of othering Egypt's natural environment as a way to construct narratives of alterity,[30] and the rhetoric highlights some common themes in Herodotus' representation of Egypt: inversion, fecundity, marvelousness, and the preserved memory of a very ancient past.

Many late Classical and early Hellenistic authors critiqued Herodotus' representation of the Nile, but the prevalence of these critiques demonstrates that his view of Egypt's landscape persisted after the 5th century BCE.[31] Manolaraki argues that the ability to destabilize perceptions of time and space, to occupy a liminal space between familiar and foreign that "telescopes space and time," is an inherent and persistent feature of the Nile in Greek and Latin literature.[32] Part of this influence can be seen in the continual discussion of the Nile's geography and expeditions to examine Herodotus' claims about the Nile. Though Hecataeus' history seems to have replaced Herodotus' account as the authoritative text on the Egyptian landscape not long after the Nile came under Greek rule,[33] several aspects of Herodotus' version of Egypt, and, more importantly, his deep interest in exploring Egyptian geography, were debated and discussed well into the Hellenistic and Roman period.[34] Throughout late Republican and early Imperial literature, authors like Lucretius, Seneca, Ovid, and Pliny the Elder continued to describe the Nile and its flora and fauna in fantastic terms. Their work frames Egypt as a sublimely timeless, vast space, comparable to the depth and extent of the cosmos itself.[35]

These representations of the Nile would have contributed to the idea that Egypt was timeless. Many Greek viewers would have understood the cyclical nature of Egyptian time, from the annual flooding of the Nile, the cycles of day and night that are tied to the victory of Horus over Seth, and, through that myth, the victory of good over evil.[36] These differences may have given viewers and readers a sense that Egypt existed primarily in the deep past.[37] Of course, the Greeks of the Second Sophistic were constructing a similarly retrospective version of Greekness. Theirs, however, existed in historical time, which was more easily accessed through the well-known texts, inscriptions, and monuments that gave this Greekness a more realistic texture.

In the context of Greek ethnicity, however, the Nilotic aesthetic takes on a territorial meaning. Though Hall defines territory as one of the defining features of Greek ethnicity, Kemezis argues that Second Sophistic Greekness is less invested in the idea of place as a metric of self-definition.[38] For Greek Isis devotees, however, Nilotic images and architectures ground their experiences in a shared territory, even if that territory is largely fictive. By building sanctuaries that would look and feel like what they imagined Egypt to have been, Greeks planted their Egyptian deities into a specific geographic milieu. This territoriality, created through a sense of moving into a new shared place that existed within sanctuary walls, is key to understanding the ethnic nature of Isiac cult in a Greek context. While ethnicity can exist without a geography,[39] a shared sense of place strengthens existing bonds and boundaries that provide critical definition to ethnic groups.[40] These visual and spatial constructs were key to inflecting devotees' Greekness with an Isiac character or flavor.

These accounts, however, often make sense of Egyptian otherness by comparisons with other areas of the Mediterranean, often in ways that deem it inferior. In his sections on plant-based products, Pliny the Elder consistently ranks Egyptian products as inferior to those from elsewhere in the empire.[41] Egypt has the most wheat, but its flour is inferior to that which is milled in Italy (*NH* 18.82); Campanian rose oil is superior to all Egyptian floral oils, even though Egypt produces the largest amount (*NH* 13.26); the Libyan fir is more fragrant than the Egyptian fir (*NH* 12.134); Egyptian linen is the flimsiest for customers, even though it is the most profitable for merchants (*NH* 19.14). Pliny's negative view nevertheless emphasizes the depth of control the Roman consumer (and reader) exerts over Egypt: these items were known and might be compared to other imports, and Roman readers could decide how and when to consume these products.[42]

THE SOPHIST'S NILE AT MARATHON: HERODES ATTICUS' SANCTUARY

The Sanctuary of the Egyptian Gods at Marathon in Attika takes an eclectic architectural and sculptural form meant to reference imagined forms of Egypt and the Nile.[43] In addition to its allusions to Egyptian architecture, sculpture, and natural landscape, the complex also replicated many of the Egyptianizing features of the Emperor Hadrian's Villa in Tivoli. Given Herodes' status as an Imperial official, these references invest the sanctuary and its presentation of the Nile with colonial undertones. Yet Greece itself was a Roman province, and Herodes a provincial subject, albeit a well-connected and wealthy one, who navigated competing claims of Romanness and Greekness throughout his life.[44] The sanctuary thus operates on several intersecting interpretive levels, relying on the viewer's passage through layers of Greek, Roman, and Egyptianizing landscapes – and movement through time – in order to locate the cult in both the Egyptian mythological past and the colonial Greek present.

Born in 101 CE, Herodes Atticus was the scion of a wealthy Athenian family that traced its lineage back to Miltiades, the famous Athenian general who won the Battle of Marathon.[45] His father, Tiberius Claudius Atticus Herodes, was a senator, and his mother, Vibullia Alcia Agrippina, was a wealthy Roman heiress of Greek descent. Herodes Atticus was born at the family villa in Marathon. Tutored by some of the best Greek and Roman philosophical minds of the day, he became a leading intellectual of the mid-2nd century CE.[46] In 140 CE, he was elected archon of Athens. Later that year, the emperor Antoninus Pius brought Herodes to Rome to tutor the future emperors

Marcus Aurelius and Lucius Verus. In the early 140s CE, Herodes was betrothed to a prominent Roman woman named Appia Annia Regilla Atilia Caucidia Tertulla, commonly called Regilla, who was a distant cousin of Empress Faustina the Younger. Thus far, three villas in Greece have been linked to Herodes and his family: Kephissia and Marathon in Attica, and Eva Loukou in the Peloponnese.[47]

Though Herodes' Marathon villa does not appear as frequently in the literary sources as his Kephissia home, there are indications that he frequently brought guests and students there.[48] In a fragment of correspondence, the emperor Marcus Aurelius describes Herodes Atticus as continuing (after 176 CE) to live in his villas at Marathon and Kephissia and to receive throngs of eager young men traveling up from Athens to hear his orations.[49] A similar episode in Philostratus' *Vitae Sophistarum* describes an Egyptian sanctuary that was a prominent feature at the Marathon villa. Herodes promises to meet a new pupil named Agathion at the Temple of Canobus (*VS* 554), which seems to refer to an Egyptian temple in his Marathon villa.[50] Setting the encounter in the Temple of Canobus establishes the complex as part of Herodes' educational process. Admittedly, Philostratus' biographies tend to "fictionalize" for narrative effect, and Strazdins has argued that these works should not be seen as "completely reliable" sources of historical fact.[51] Even if the Agathion encounter is fictionalized, which seems likely,[52] the archaeological evidence described in the section "The Egyptian Sanctuary at Marathon: Date and Use" does indicate that an Egyptianizing building existed on Herodes' land, that it was used by Herodes' favorite companion Polydeukion, and that it served a religious function. As part of Herodes' cherished family estate, the sanctuary was not likely to have been open to the public.[53] Rather, we can assume that only Herodes' pupils and intimate circle visited the Egyptian sanctuary, at least in its initial phases.

The Egyptian Sanctuary at Marathon: Date and Use

The best-preserved area of Herodes' villa lies near the modern village of Nea Makri. It consists of an Egyptianizing complex, a cistern,[54] and a lavish, Imperial-style bath building. The site was popular among 18th- and 19th-century visitors interested in the Battle of Marathon, and in 1843, a large male Egyptianizing statue, now in the National Archaeological Museum in Athens, was found here by Schaubert (Figure 46).[55] In 1968, construction on the neighboring Golden Coast Hotel, located roughly 150 m to the north, revealed another male Egyptianizing statue (Figure 47)[56] and the bottom half of an over life-sized female statue wearing a long Egyptian-style dress (Figure 48).[57] Related rescue excavations found an Egyptianizing pylon and the basic outline of the northern half of the sanctuary.[58] Dekoulakou

46. Statue of Osiris found at the Sanctuary of the Egyptian Gods at Marathon, third quarter of the 2nd century CE. Athens: National Archaeological Museum, Egyptian Collection inv. 1. © Hellenic Ministry of Culture & Sports/Archaeological Receipts Fund.

conducted systematic excavations from 2001 to 2009, and began again in 2014. She uncovered a large complex devoted to the Egyptian gods that was organized into two courtyards. It contained thirteen freestanding statues, about seventy very large terracotta lamps, substantial fragments of Egyptianizing architectural sculpture, and three inscriptions (Figure 49).[59]

Archaeological evidence indicates that the complex was constructed in the mid-2nd century CE. Three marble fragments preserving most of a votive inscription were found inside the sanctuary, providing early evidence of votive dedications. Dekoulakou reconstructs the text to read, "Polydeukion, son of Biboullios, companion of and raised by Herodes, because of his piety" –

47. Statue of Osiris from the North Pylon of the Sanctuary of the Egyptian Gods at Marathon, third quarter of the 2nd century CE. Marathon: Archaeological Museum inv. BE1. © Hellenic Ministry of Culture & Sports/Archaeological Receipts Fund.

evidence that Herodes' favorite foster son, Polydeukion, dedicated at the sanctuary during his lifetime.[60] A bust of Polydeukion (Figure 50), whose archaeological context is described in more detail below, offers further support for this date. Polydeukion probably died in ca. 165 CE.[61] Goette has argued that this particular type of Polydeukion statue was invented in ca. 160 CE and was produced only until Herodes' own death in 177/178.[62] A construction date of ca. 160 CE seems likely.

Earlier studies of the site conducted before Dekoulakou's excavation proposed that the structure might have been a tomb or cenotaph for Polydeukion,[63] but the structure must serve a religious function.[64]

48. Statue of Isis from the North Pylon of the Sanctuary of the Egyptian Gods at Marathon, third quarter of the 2nd century CE. Marathon: Archaeological Museum inv. BE2. © Hellenic Ministry of Culture & Sports/Archaeological Receipts Fund.

Polydeukion could not have participated in his own funerary cult, and the use of the term εὐσεβείας (piety) in the inscription above the statue indicates that his dedicatory action was religious in nature. Another inscription found in the sanctuary includes a (reconstructed) reference to a *xystarch* priest, a priesthood known from Rome that was charged with protecting sacred objects.[65] Further, seventy oversized lamps of multiple types, including seventeen depicting confronting busts of Isis and Sarapis, were found. The lamps have a maximum diameter of 0.40–0.42 m, far too large to serve as day-to-day, functional objects.[66] The depositional context suggests that they were stacked on wooden

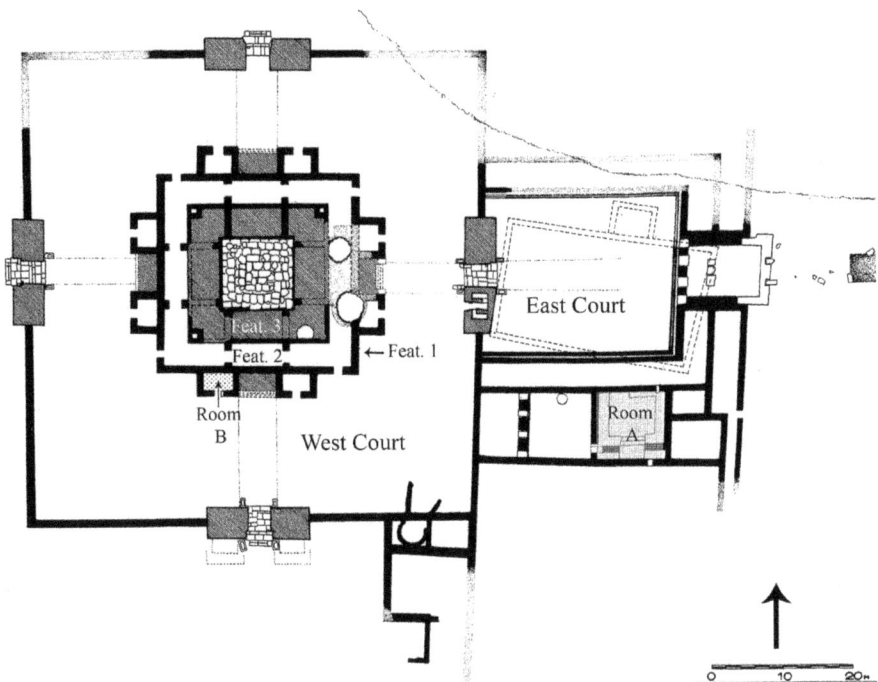

49. Plan of the Sanctuary of the Egyptian Gods at Marathon. Feature 1, the "Terrace" of the pyramidal structure. Feature 2, the cryptoporticus. Feature 3, the central feature. Room A contained a water feature and sculptures, including a bust of Polydeukion. Room B contained seventy lamps with confronting busts of Isis and Sarapis, a sphinx statue, and a life-sized statue of Isis. Modified from Dekoulakou 2011a, pl. 5, courtesy of the *American Journal of Archaeology*.

shelves along the room's western wall: all were found in a large mass of about 2.0 × 2.6 m, and most showed signs of burning on the spout.[67] Fotiadi compares them with other Corinthian lamps found in sacrificial pits at the Palaimonion at Isthmia and deems them part of a special, oversized type used primarily for ritual purposes.[68] Taken together, this evidence strongly suggests the site hosted an active Isiac religious community, at least in its initial phase.

Remarkably, there is no evidence of architectural renovation, sculptural or epigraphic dedications, or perhaps even new lamps after the initial ca. 160 CE phase.[69] The inscriptions and sculpture date to the mid-2nd century CE, which is probably when the sanctuary was constructed. Their technical and stylistic similarities suggest that these elements were planned as a cohesive group and executed by a single group of sculptors. But the sanctuary may not have been abandoned. Recent excavations to the south of the sanctuary and in a destruction layer in the south tower of the East Pylon have uncovered pottery and coin evidence in a series of rooms to the south of the sanctuary, suggesting

50. Portrait bust of Polydeukion found in Room A of the Sanctuary of the Egyptian Gods' East Court, ca. 160 CE. Marathon: Archaeological Museum. © Hellenic Ministry of Culture & Sports/Archaeological Receipts Fund.

continued use until at least the early 4th century CE.[70] It is unclear who owned and used the villa and sanctuary site after the mid-2nd century or if the later use was primarily religious in nature.

Architecture

Most devotees would have entered the sanctuary from the east through a large Greek-style propylon.[71] Visitors first entered the rectilinear East Court, which measures 22 × 26 m. Much of the northern side of the East Court was destroyed by erosion and modern construction, but the southern side of the court is largely preserved. The central room (Figure 49, Room A), which devotees entered through the courtyard's southern side, probably served as a ritual meeting and dining space. The room contained stone benches along two sides and a raised platform, flanked by two connected pits, approximately 1 m deep and lined with waterproof cement, along the south side. The rest of the rooms were used for storage. A large wine *pithos* was found in situ in the room just to the west of Room A, and large fragments of other *pithoi* were found in the area, indicating that large amounts of wine and perhaps other foodstuffs were stored here.

After passing through this courtyard, the devotee would proceed through to the West Court. The West Court is enclosed by a roughly square peribolos wall (whose sides range in length from 60.5 to 64.6 m) and has a large central pyramidal structure at its center.[72] Pylons in the middle of the peribolos wall on each side closely follow the style used in New Kingdom, Ptolemaic, and Roman sanctuaries across Egypt (Figures 51 and 52).[73] Each pylon corresponds to one of the four cardinal directions and consists of two rectangular towers made of rough stone and bricks veneered with finer stones.[74] The towers are solid constructions, with the exception of the south tower of the East Pylon, which contained two rooms and a corridor at ground level and two staircases leading to a now-lost upper level. The only full-length portrait from the sanctuary, a now-headless depiction of a bare-footed man in a short, fringed *himation*, was found in the area of the East Pylon,[75] which may suggest that this doorway held special prominence. Architectural calculations indicate that the doorways were 5 m high, and that the towers were even taller.[76] One lintel in

51. The South Pylon of the West Court, viewed from the south. The constructions flanking the doorway would have reached over 5 m in height and were revetted in marble. © Hellenic Ministry of Culture & Sports/Archaeological Receipts Fund.

52. The First Pylon of the temple complex at Philae in Egypt. Photo: Marc Ryckaert via Creative Commons.

Egyptianizing style, featuring cavetto cornices and a solar disc flanked by two hooded cobras – a reference to the Egyptian *uraeus* – was found in the ravine near the site in 1968, and two fragments of a second lintel were found inside the East Court outside the East Pylon in the 2011 excavations.[77] Dekoulakou suggests that each pylon would have had a similar Egyptianizing lintel at the top of the doorway. When paired with the Egyptian-style pylons, the full effect would have clearly alluded to Egyptian precedents in a way that Herodes' elite and well-traveled audience would have recognized.

The central architectural feature was a stepped pyramid-like structure set in the center of the main sanctuary square (Figure 53, marked on Figure 49). Though the ancient viewer probably experienced the entire pyramidal structure as a single architectural feature, it consists of three separate constructions: an exterior terrace, a covered cryptoporticus, and the stepped pyramidal structure built of limestone conglomerate. Following paved walkways from the pylons, devotees first encountered the terrace, a 0.65 m thick wall made of *opus caementicium* that encircled the cryptoporticus and the pyramidal construction (Figure 49, Feat. 1). An Ionic colonnade ran around the edges of the terrace, and several of the fallen white marble columns, bases, and capitals were found inside the collapsed cryptoporticus. At each corner of the terrace was a small water basin made of bricks lined with waterproof plaster. The basin at the southwest corner preserves a terracotta pipe that may have fed the reservoir, but no remains of pipes have been found for the other three. Four small

53. View of central pyramidal feature of the West Court from the east. © Hellenic Ministry of Culture & Sports/Archaeological Receipts Fund.

staircases, each in line with one of the pylons, led the devotee across the terrace and a covered cryptoporticus toward the top of the pyramidal feature. Fragments of roof tiles and red-painted fresco walls have been found inside the cryptoporticus, suggesting that the corridor was roofed and plastered. No figural frescoes have been found. Because the cryptoporticus' roof has not been preserved, we cannot be sure whether the walkway continued to the top of the pyramid. Flanking each staircase was a pair of small rooms, which are discussed in more detail below.[78]

Reconstructing this feature's original shape and appearance is difficult. Though there were several pyramid tombs in Rome, there are no close comparanda for a feature like this one.[79] As preserved, the pyramidal structure's core seems to indicate a stepped shape, though traces of mortar suggest that architectural elements may have been attached to the core, changing the monument's profile. A rectangular gap in the masonry at the top (1×1.4 m, with a depth of 0.5 m) probably held a crowning feature or structure – perhaps another course of conglomerate masonry or even an obelisk. Obelisks are a more common feature of Nilotic wall paintings and mosaics than pyramids, and the Fifth Dynasty solar temple of Userkaf in Abusir in Egypt used a pyramidal base to support an obelisk.[80] In my view, the structure was most likely intended to reference Egyptian pyramids, some of the best known and most iconic buildings in Egypt, or another characteristically Egyptian building type.

The sanctuary's sculptural program would have further contributed to the sense of relocation. In a room to the west of the south staircase (Figure 49, Room B), Dekoulakou discovered an assemblage that suggests either purposeful deposition or an attempt at preserving the cult in its late stages. In the room's northeast corner, Dekoulakou found an Egyptianizing sphinx statue wearing a *uraeus* and *nemes* headdress stored next to the cluster of oversized lamps discussed above (Figures 54 and 55).[81] At the time of deposition, the statue was cemented in place with its face against the north wall.[82] Lying on the floor near the sphinx a fourth female statue was found, wearing Isis' knotted costume (Figure 56).[83] It is similar in style and composition to three other Isis statues found at the site, discussed in the section "Time and Style in

54. Statue of a sphinx from the Sanctuary of the Egyptian Gods at Marathon, third quarter of the 2nd century CE. Marathon: Archaeological Museum inv. Λ437. © Hellenic Ministry of Culture & Sports/Archaeological Receipts Fund.

55. Excavation photo showing the findspots of the sphinx, a statue of Isis tentatively associated with the East Pylon, and seventy oversized lamps in Room B. Reproduced from Dekoulakou 2011a, fig. 6. © Hellenic Ministry of Culture & Sports/Archaeological Receipts Fund.

Ideal Sculpture." Isis here stands in a frontal posture, wearing a thin, short-sleeved tunic under a heavy mantle, knotted at the breast, that forms the *Knotenpalla*'s characteristic "X" shape and produces a cascading set of drapery folds over the hips and thighs.[84] Posed in a stiff, archaizing posture, she holds a hook close to the right thigh, probably an adaptation of the crooks seen frequently in New Kingdom and later Egyptian funerary art (Figure 57).[85] Much like the sheaves of wheat and roses held by the other Isis statues, this crook would have been visible only to the most observant viewers. Over a corkscrew-curl hairstyle, Isis wears a cap with a hooded cobra *uraeus*, continuing the eclectic use of Egyptian symbols seen in the sanctuary's architecture.

Looking at these sculptures together with the architecture, it is clear how much effort was expended by Herodes and his artisans to create for the sanctuary's visitors a sense of being in Egypt. In terms of architecture, the massive pylons and the architectural sculpture would have been recognizable as Egyptian, based on the fragments that remain. Many elite Romans visited Egypt and saw temples and pyramids; they also encountered Egyptians through commercial transactions or artistic commissions.[86] Throughout the whole sanctuary, viewers' previous experiences with Egypt would have made these references easier to spot, and perhaps even enhanced the cultural meanings attached to these architectural features. When viewed in concert with the

56. Statue of Isis *unica*, tentatively associated with the East Pylon of the Sanctuary of the Egyptian Gods at Marathon, third quarter of the 2nd century CE. Marathon: Archaeological Museum inv. 438. © Hellenic Ministry of Culture & Sports/Archaeological Receipts Fund.

57. Detail of Marathon Archaeological Museum inv. 438 showing the Egyptianizing crook implement held in the right hand. © Hellenic Ministry of Culture & Sports/Archaeological Receipts Fund.

other elements of the sanctuary's architecture, then, the pyramid contributes to a sense of being in Egypt, of having left the Greek world outside the sanctuary gates on a journey to a new and foreign place.

Time and Style in the Ideal Sculpture

Along with the invocation of place, much of the sanctuary's ideal sculpture experiments with the viewer's sense of time by imitating or alluding to the pharaonic Egyptian past. Dekoulakou reconstructs two pairs of Egyptianizing statues flanking each pylon – one pair on the outside of each pylon and another pair inside – for a total of eight pairs in all. Each pair consisted of a male and a female statue carved in a markedly Egyptianizing style and dressed in Egyptianizing costumes (Plate 14). Of the sixteen original statues, eight have been found: four male statues and four female statues. Fragments belonging to a fifth male statue carved on a larger scale were found outside the South Pylon in 2001, which may indicate that the pairs on the court's exterior were larger.[87] Apart from the female statue from the North Pylon, whose top half is missing, the rest are almost fully preserved.

Four female figures carved in a blocky, Egyptianizing style depict the goddess Isis. One has been discussed in the section "Architecture," and the remaining three should be treated as a group. These were found near their original bases at the South, West, and North Pylons. The examples from the South (Figure 58) and West Pylons (Figure 59) are almost completely preserved, with only minor chipping.[88] They were found tipped off of their bases (Figure 60). The fourth Isis statue, discussed in the section "Architecture," is carved at a similar scale and may have stood at the interior of the East Pylon of the West Court.[89] The North Pylon statue was found in a ravine to the north of the sanctuary and is preserved only from the waist down (Figure 48). These over life-sized images depict Isis wearing a clingy, long-sleeved shift-dress over a thin, delicate dress that hangs down to the plinth.[90] The hair is arranged in the goddess's traditional corkscrew curls,[91] divided into sausage locks that hang down over the shoulders. Like their male counterparts, these statues also use back pillars and Egyptian frontality, perhaps to impart a sense of divinity to the image.

Each Isis statue holds a different set of attributes that identifies her with one of the several syncretized versions of the goddess popular throughout the Mediterranean.[92] The Isis of the South Pylon has sheaves of wheat, alluding to Isis-Demeter; the Isis of the West Pylon holds roses to represent Isis-Aphrodite. The North Pylon Isis holds small rolls of papyrus or cloth, a common feature of Egyptian statuary referring to an Egyptian version of Isis. These attributes are very small and, again, would be noticed only by more perceptive viewers. The prominent Egyptianizing headdresses, a tall *polos* for Isis-Aphrodite (headdress height, 0.29 m) and an ovular Isiac solar disc set in cow horns for Isis-Demeter (headdress height, 0.29 m),[93] would have reinforced the statues' distinct identities more clearly. Like the statues discussed in Chapter 4, these images were designed to provoke a polysemic viewing experience. For example, Isis-Aphrodite's thin, close-fitting garments reveal her navel in much the same way that many Aphrodite statues depict the body. This eclectic combination of Egyptianizing and Greek iconographies connects the image to both deities and clarifies that aspect of Aphrodite (namely, her sexuality) which must be considered as viewers interpret this novel image. In this way, these three images of Isis exploit their similarities and combine Greek and Egyptian precedents to reinforce the idea that they are aspects of the same Egyptian goddess.

58. Statue of Isis-Demeter from the South Pylon of the Sanctuary of the Egyptian Gods at Marathon, third quarter of the 2nd century CE. Marathon: Archaeological Museum inv. 414. © Hellenic Ministry of Culture & Sports/Archaeological Receipts Fund.

59. Statue of Isis-Aphrodite from the West Pylon of the Sanctuary of the Egyptian Gods, third quarter of the 2nd century CE. Marathon: Archaeological Museum inv. 545. © Hellenic Ministry of Culture & Sports/Archaeological Receipts Fund.

60. Excavation photograph depicting the statue of Isis-Demeter tipped off of its base. Reproduced from Dekoulakou 2011a, fig. 20. © Hellenic Ministry of Culture & Sports/ Archaeological Receipts Fund.

The statues are carved in an archaizing style, so that they appear to date from an age long before the mid-2nd century CE. Several scholars have studied archaism in Greek and Roman sculpture, in which sculptures produced in later periods (usually the Julio-Claudian period) reproduce aspects of Archaic Greek art, particularly drapery, hairstyles, and facial features.[94] But the Marathon statues look beyond the Greek past. With their stiff, upright postures, back pillars, and Egyptian-style garments, these objects follow earlier Egyptian aesthetic norms. The images do not reference Hellenistic or Roman Egypt but pharaonic Egypt, and also suggest that Herodes is here displaying a knowledge of what "real" Egyptian sculpture looked like. Because of its particular meanings for ideal sculpture, archaism would have been especially useful for representing Egyptian deities. It offers legitimacy to new cults, recalls lost or supposedly lost objects, and renders images otherworldly.[95] It gestures toward key ontological differences between mortality and divinity, separates the object from the world it inhabits, and most of all, grants it divine potency.[96] Most importantly, by manipulating the viewer's sense of the age of the object, the object become timeless, a part of myth-time rather than historical or even human time.

The timelessness of these images intersects with their Egyptianness. Barrett has coined the term *pharaonizing* to refer to this stylistic trope, which can be found at several other Isiac sanctuaries and as a garden decoration at Pompeii.[97]

Pharaonizing sculpture emulates attributes, iconographies, conventions, proportions, and postures found in Egyptian art of the Pharaonic period.[98] This style seems to have been especially appropriate for sculpture, which could borrow earlier Egyptian styles and formats from statuettes that circulated widely and easily along Mediterranean trade routes.[99]

The allusions in the examples studied here are not necessarily grounded in a specific dynasty or period but rather in a generalized, almost mythological sense of "Egypt before." As I argued in Chapter 3, a sense of timelessness was one of the prevailing stereotypes about Egypt in Greco-Roman literature. Egypt functioned on a nearly cosmic timescale, unlike the shorter rhythms of historical time that often characterized ideas of Greek history.[100]

This lack of historical context and specificity reduces the gods to well-known essentialist tropes and in many cases erases the specific meanings of these features in Egyptian art and religion. For example, the statue of Isis in the *Knotenpalla* carries a loop in her right hand (Figure 56). Though Dekoulakou identifies this attribute as a loose adaptation of a little-known Sixth Dynasty symbol, it is much more likely that the symbol approximates and misuses Osiris' crook and flail, which are associated with kingship, to give the statue a greater sense of Egyptianness.[101] In the case of the Marathon sanctuary, archaism alludes to a distant but unspecified past that is similar to the deep mythological time referenced in the cults' texts. No specific pharaoh, dynasty, or even time period can be connected to these objects – just a vague sense of long ago. As with their Greek counterparts, this connection would have imbued these images with a sense of sacrality and permanence. The materiality of the site, which was constructed out of local material and sculpted with local techniques, would have complicated this effect. The Pentelic marble grounds Isis and other iconic Egyptian motifs within the Greek world. The recognizable sculptural techniques and proportions familiarize these objects, fashioning their Egyptian subjects to look as though they were part of a longer and familiar tradition, even though the memories they sought to evoke never existed in fact.[102]

The ethnic narrative presented here is messy and complex, which may suggest that the artisans and their patron were experimenting with a three-dimensional version of a new message: that Egypt's past is connected to or even part of Greece's present. As we saw in the epigraphic and literary sources discussed in Chapter 3, time and time again, Greek devotees manipulated myth-histories of the goddess to include her in the Greek pantheon. The landscape here is part of a new mythological timeline in which Isis may be embodied in Greek materials and grounded in Greek pantheons, or she may be the daughter of Hermes or Prometheus (Plut., *De Is.* 352a–b) or Kronos (*I.Kyme* 41, line 5), or she may be born from the earth itself (Maroneia, *SEG* 26 821, lines 15–16). Even still, the style highlights its otherness. These images, which diverge widely from other representations of Egyptian deities and from the normative style used throughout the region, emphasize Isis' continued connections with Greek traditions and the world of the Nile. The program's ultimate goal was to shift the viewers' perception of Greece, granting it an increasingly central role in that deep past.

Gods, Portraits, and Roman Imperial Networks

The sanctuary also makes claims on Roman power that serve Herodes' more contemporary political and intellectual interests. The four male statues that stood alongside the Isis statues wear Egyptianizing costumes and are carved in pharaonizing formats and styles (Figures 47 and 61).[103] With arms held close to

61. Statue of Osiris from the South Pylon of the Sanctuary of the Egyptian Gods, third quarter of the 2nd century CE. Marathon: Archaeological Museum inv. 415. © Hellenic Ministry of Culture & Sports/Archaeological Receipts Fund.

the sides, they grasp small cylindrical objects with rounded edges, a common feature of Egyptian statues.[104] Each male wears a belted Egyptian *shendyt* kilt with a codpiece. They have soft, oval faces with heavily lidded eyes, broad noses, round chins, and strong naso-labial folds. The sculptural style combines Roman-era techniques and earlier traditions of Greek and Egyptian art.[105] The North Pylon statue preserves a *kalathos* that stood on top of the *nemes* wig.[106] The other examples preserve a similar cutting at the top of the head, which indicates that all four of the male statues inside the pylons wore the same headgear.

Though this form usually represents a pharaoh in Egyptian art, the Marathon statues most likely represent the Egyptian god Osiris. These statues diverge from the more popular of the Sarapis types. The contrast suggests that the Marathon statues depict not Sarapis but rather another Egyptian god whose sculptural types are not well defined in Greco-Roman art. Osiris is the most likely candidate. Osiris received veneration at several Greek sanctuaries, including Thessaloniki, Gomphoi, and Delos.[107] Though normally depicted as a mummy or sarcophagus in EgyptIan art, he often takes anthropomorphic form in Roman art.[108]

There are also historical and philosophical reasons to suggest that Herodes intended these statues to represent Osiris. As a central figure in Athenian Middle Platonism, Herodes would have read much of Plutarch's work, including *De Iside*, considered to be among the most mature of Plutarch's treatises on the key Platonic question: the nature of the gods and their presence on earth.[109] Calvenus Taurus, his teacher on Plato, may have been a student of Plutarch and perhaps even introduced Herodes to him.[110] As I have argued, the sanctuary probably served a philosophical as well as a religious function, and statues of Osiris would have been especially useful for an audience who used the sanctuary for intellectual discourse and teaching alongside its religious functions.[111]

The identification as Osiris is also appealing because of the similarities between these statues and the images of Osiris-Antinoos from Hadrian's Villa at Tivoli (Figure 62).[112] The Marathon and Tivoli Osirises wear the same kilt and carry the same rounded objects; they have a similar headdress and their bodies are posed in the same way.[113] The Marathon statue, however, should not be considered a copy.[114] The difference in style would have produced two unique viewing experiences. The Tivoli Osiris is carved in a contemporary style and lacks a back pillar, which produces a lighter, more energetic, and more contemporary figure. Though the statue lacks clear portrait features, a mid-2nd century CE viewer would still be able to infer from context that the image stands somewhere between divinity and portrait. The pharaonizing style of the Marathon example, on the other hand, argues for its antiquity and sacrality. The stiffness in the posture, heaviness of the body and carving, and

62. Statue of Osiris-Antinoos from Hadrian's Villa at Tivoli, Hadrianic period. Rome: Vatican Museums-Gregorian Egyptian Museum inv. 22795. © Album / Art Resource, NY.

the lack of a clear reference to a living person would have made the Marathon statue seem much older, even though it was probably produced shortly after the Tivoli Osiris. It is hard to argue that Herodes and his sculptors were not inspired at least in part by the Tivoli statue,[115] but the Marathon example is better understood as an adaptation of an iconographic type to suit Herodes' need for a more archaizing image.

In the rooms flanking the staircases were also found three marble statues of Horus-falcons wearing the double crown of Egypt – two from the room to the south of the west staircase and another from the room to the east of the north staircase (Figure 63) – that may have been further examples of free copies from Tivoli.[116] Horus is the son of Osiris and Isis in Egyptian mythology; he is frequently depicted in Egyptian art as a falcon, as in the Ptolemaic statues that flanked the entrances of the temple gate and first courtyard of the god's temple

63. Statuette of Horus in falcon form from the Sanctuary of the Egyptian Gods at Marathon, third quarter of the 2nd century CE. Marathon: Archaeological Museum inv. Λ653. © Hellenic Ministry of Culture & Sports/Archaeological Receipts Fund.

at Edfu.[117] The Marathon examples, however, are locally made products. The toolwork and style are recognizably Athenian and are consistent with the rest of the sanctuary's sculpture. During the 2nd century CE, Greek sculptors normally represented Horus as Harpokrates, whose anthropomorphic form closely resembles that of Eros.[118] Herodes may have chosen a falcon-headed

Horus to heighten the sense of Egyptianness within the sanctuary. But this choice echoes a similar one at Hadrian's Villa. A similar Horus falcon wearing the double crown of Egypt was found in the Tivoli villa's Palestra among other Egyptianizing sculpture.[119] The two are not direct copies – there are several small differences, including the arrangement of the feathers in the wings and the relative size of the crown. Still, the unusual choice to represent Horus as a falcon underscores further the links between these two sites.

Though Tivoli was not the only model for incorporating Egyptianizing iconography into domestic contexts, buildings like those at Tivoli that included Egyptian themes, including the Canopeum, the "Antinoeion," and the Palestra formed a significant part of Herodes' inspiration.[120] Both the Tivoli and Marathon villas imagine fantastic versions of Egypt that are simultaneously domesticated, ordered, and contained within the Roman world. These sites create for visitors a sense of control and perhaps even domination over foreignness and foreigners. According to a passage in the *Historia Augusta*, from which the popular modern name *Canopeum* is derived, this building was one of many within the villa named for important places in the eastern Roman Empire, including sites named for famous places in Greece like the Lyceum, Academia, Prytaneum, and Tempe.[121] Viewed in this light, the Tivoli villa becomes a geographic metaphor, a site designed to present an easily digestible representation of empire through Greek and "Greek-looking" material culture.[122] Though there is no specific evidence that Herodes visited Hadrian's Villa at Tivoli, the social and political context suggests that such a visit could have occurred. Herodes served as a provincial governor in Hadrian's administration (*V S* 548), and the two moved in similar circles and knew many of the same people. It is plausible that Herodes visited the villa at Tivoli in his youth when Hadrian was still emperor, but even if not then, archaeological evidence suggests that the villa remained in use under Marcus Aurelius, whose close personal and intellectual relationship with Herodes is well established.[123] Herodes may have seen an Egyptian sanctuary within the confines of a large, luxurious villa as a desirable allusion that would have appealed to the other high-level members of his social circles.

Underlying that access, however, is a shared interest in the foreign, in the practice of embedding an exoticized version of Egypt into a villa's life of religious practice and *otium*. As Barrett has argued, the version of Egypt presented at Tivoli is one of productive and peaceful partnership, where Hadrian seeks to represent himself as the founder of a peaceful, new Golden Age in Rome achieved through a partnership forged between the colonizer and the colonized.[124] This method of representation was a technique that turned architectural place-making into a metaphor of Roman imperialism. This convenient fiction, which overlooks ongoing strife in the empire's borderlands and its rebellions within, could also have underpinned Herodes' own rosy version of Roman imperialism, with which he was personally involved. The artistic references to similar images at the Imperial villa may have cast Herodes as a participant in the new Antonine Golden Age, as someone who, like the emperors, could domesticate the foreign and enjoy leisure activities while surrounded by the exotic.

These allusions would have been strengthened by the display of Imperial portraits within the sanctuary. Inside Room A of the East Court was found a portrait bust of Polydeukion, Herodes' foster son and student (Figure 50).[125] The Polydeukion bust, which was discovered at the bottom of the two stairs leading up to the platform at the room's southern edge, has several formal and stylistic parallels with the busts of Herodes, Marcus Aurelius, and Lucius Verus found nearby (Figures 64 and 65).[126] Fauvel in 1788–1789 excavated busts of Herodes Atticus, Marcus Aurelius, and Lucius Verus, now in the Louvre and Ashmolean Museums, in a marshy area near ruins he identified as the tomb of the Athenians.[127] The holes from his excavation are still visible on the site directly south of Room A.[128] Based on the "palm-like" supports that fanned

64. Bust of Herodes Atticus, thought to be from Marathon, third quarter of the 2nd century CE. Paris: Louvre inv. MA1161. Photo: Thierry Ollivier. © ArtResource.

65. Bust of emperor Marcus Aurelius in cuirass, thought to be from Marathon, mid-2nd century CE. Paris: Louvre inv. MA1161. Photo: Hervé Lewandowski. © ArtResource.

up the back of the busts, Fittschen has argued convincingly that these three would have been displayed together as part of a portrait gallery.[129] The busts are all about 60 cm tall; they use the same palm-like support that Fittschen identifies with a single Attic sculptural workshop;[130] and they wear costumes that mirror each other closely. If we include the Polydeukion bust, we can reconstruct a symmetrical set of pairs focused on Herodes and his pupils: Herodes and Polydeukion in the Greek himation, Lucius Verus and Marcus Aurelius in the Roman military costume. These technical, formal, and stylistic resonances would have been best appreciated if the busts were displayed together. The Polydeukion statue's findspot leads Dekoulakou to argue that it probably stood on the platform at the south side of Room A. If the four busts of Polydeukion, Herodes Atticus, Marcus Aurelius, and Lucius Verus were displayed together, all four could have shared this platform or stood elsewhere in the immediate vicinity of Room A.

Herodes included these portraits in the sanctuary to highlight his complementary roles of Greek philosopher and Roman political official. First, the busts promote Herodes' identity as an intellectual, connecting him with a long tradition of philosopher portraits in the Greek East.[131] As the former tutor of Marcus Aurelius and Lucius Verus, as well as a major patron of the Middle Platonists, Herodes had a prominent role in the Athenian and Imperial philosophical community that granted him a high status among the intellectuals who would have visited this sanctuary. These images, however, also draw attention to another aspect of Herodes' biography: his participation in the Imperial and provincial governments of the Roman Empire. Herodes served as archon at Athens, as senator at Rome, and as prefect of Asia. Including military rather than intellectual portraits of the emperors may have alluded to this aspect of his life and underscored his political power alongside his intellectual prominence.

Viewed in a provincial context, these connections may have provided a way for Greek elites to ascribe to Romanness. Individuals in the Roman provinces, particularly in the Greek-speaking provinces, often dedicated monuments and objects that depicted victory over foreign lands, to assert their power by association with Rome.[132] Including Polydeukion in this group sets Lucius Verus and Marcus Aurelius among Herodes' pupils and places Herodes in a position of power. The portraits may even have positioned him as an emperor-equivalent.[133] Just like the emperor, Herodes here has tamed Egypt and improved it, and in doing so has erased the complex and restive world of 2nd-century CE Egypt. Placed in a domestic sphere, Egypt is now an idyllic sacred space inhabited by the wondrous and exotic Egyptians of the deep past. The Greek provincial viewer becomes the agent of control rather than its victim. The site, then, becomes a way for Herodes and his family and friends to position themselves alongside the emperors, to grant themselves a higher and more central position in the Roman world.

SENSORY REPRODUCTIONS: WATER FEATURES AS NILES IN GREEK SANCTUARIES

Herodes' sanctuary draws on an Egyptianizing aesthetic used throughout the Mediterranean world that scholars have called "Nilotic." Bioarchaeological studies have not been conducted at Marathon, but other lavish sanctuaries to the Egyptian gods, such as the Iseum Campanese at Rome, were thought to contain imported animals and plants to enhance a Nilotic atmosphere.[134] In order to understand these connections more fully, another aspect of Herodes' sanctuary must be considered: the landscape. The site selected is marshy and filled with water plants and animals.[135] Immediately to the north of the sanctuary was an artificial canal dating to the Roman period that directed much of the water emitted from the spring at the foot of Mt. Angeliki into the sea.[136] This is not happenstance. The canal would have bestowed the area, already closely associated with the sea, with a riverine aspect that alluded to the Nile Delta.

The Marathon sanctuary, however, is extraordinary, both in terms of its décor and its preservation. Did other Isis devotees in Greece use Egyptianizing and Nilotic aesthetics as part of their worship? If we consider how Nilotic landscapes could be constructed in three dimensions and through combinations of sensory experiences, the references become clearer. The most obvious Nile signifiers are water features. Nearly every Egyptian sanctuary in Greece had a structure to hold water for ritual purposes.[137] In her catalogue of the main cult sanctuaries in Greece, Kleibl identifies architectural structures for water storage at the Egyptian sanctuaries on Delos (Sarapieions A and C, and B had a small tank), Philippi, Eretria, Thessaloniki, and Gortyna.[138] More recent work identified water crypts at Messene and Rhodes and confirmed the presence of a water feature at Argos.[139] Even the Marathon sanctuary, which had an artificial creek flowing just outside its North Pylon, had four small water basins fed by a pipe. Only the sanctuary at Thera, which is very poorly preserved, and the temple on the South Slope of the Athenian Akropolis, lack evidence for a water feature within the sanctuary.[140]

Water facilities took several different forms, many of which draw on Egyptian precedents to make the Nile references more explicit. Some, such as the crypts at Sarapieion B on Delos, Thessaloniki, Gortyna, and Rhodes, involve descending a staircase into a cistern, spring, or water basin, which references Egyptian structures related to the Nile like the Nilometer (Figure 66).[141] Nilometers were structures used to measure the Nile's rise during the annual inundation that marked the beginning of the Egyptian

66. Water crypt in the Sanctuary of the Egyptian Gods at Gortyna. © Hellenic Ministry of Culture & Sports/Archaeological Receipts Fund.

agricultural season and was celebrated with feasting and festivals. In the Ptolemaic and Roman periods, these structures normally took the form of long staircases leading underground to a chamber or basin within a temple. Many contained markings to help priests measure water levels, though measurement does not seem to have been part of the Greco-Roman cult practice. The iconography of these celebrations made its way into many Nilotic paintings, mosaics, and figurines in adapted form.[142] The water itself, like the Nile, is identified with Osiris and eternal life, and, based on the presence of joint epigraphic venerations of Osiris and *hydreios* at several sanctuaries,[143] this meaning likely persisted in Greece. The act of walking down the staircase would have produced a change in temperature and brought the devotee out of the light and into the damp darkness, contrasts that would have heightened the affective experience of any ritual activity that took place there.

Other sanctuaries attempted to recreate the experience of being in the Nile itself. The Iseum at Dion sits alongside the Vaphyras River, and several natural springs fed the pools in two of the *naiskoi* temples. Like the sanctuary at Marathon, the Dion sanctuary was filled with water features, including flowing water from natural springs and occasional floods, which recall the Nile's marshes. The sanctuary also had architectural features and sculptural décor that referenced the Nile. A pair of parallel balustrade walls punctuated by regularly spaced rectilinear piers is reconstructed as a water basin (Figure 67, approximately 1 m wide). The basin runs east–west across the sanctuary and divides the area in half. The basin may have been fed by the sanctuary's natural springs, which also filled other water features.[144] Several scholars have identified this feature as a reproduction of the Nile, which would have centered much of the visitor's attention on the river as he or she performed tasks and devotional rites in the sanctuary.[145] The Nile basin was the focal point of the sanctuary: it divided the sanctuary's main open courtyard space in half, and devotees using the sanctuary would have had to walk around it to get from one side of the sanctuary to the other. Those visiting the sanctuary and performing everyday rites would have had to adapt their movements to account for the Nile in their midst.

The references to the Nile could be reinforced further through sculpture. At Dion, the water basin's balustrades held small dedications and votive sculptures. Near the western end of the basin, which terminates in the sanctuary's main altar, were two marble statuettes of bulls and a statue of Aphrodite.[146] One of the bull statuettes sat on a small marble pedestal on the eastern side of the altar, directly next to the western terminus of the water feature, and its mate probably stood on one of the other marble pedestals on the other sides of the altar (Figure 9). These bulls, which represent the Egyptian bull god Apis, would have strengthened the feature's allusions to the Nile River. As early as the New Kingdom, Apis was identified with Osiris and was considered to be a fertility deity connected with the Nile. Bulls representing Apis were buried in

67. Central water feature within the Iseum at Dion. © Hellenic Ministry of Culture & Sports/ Archaeological Receipts Fund.

underground chambers, and the god is sometimes included in Isiac dedications in Greece.[147] Similar statuettes were found in the Egyptian sanctuary's water crypt at Rhodes,[148] and a set of bovine figures was found in the crypt at Gortyna on Crete.[149] The excavator, Oliveri, identified them as *bovetti*, which Salditt-Trappman linked with the Apis bull. Though Wild argues that the Gortyna examples are not Apis because the reclining bovine more normally refers to a cow rather than a bull in Egyptian art, the repetition of the iconography suggests that there may have been a connection between cattle and the Nile for several Isiac communities. He also suggests that the Gortyna images represent Isis and links them specifically to a rite described in Plutarch's *De Iside*, in which a cow is led seven times around the temple of Helios in a ritual called the Search for Osiris.[150] The bovine images could also have been brought into the water crypt as part of the *inventio Osiris* ritual, where devotees found the god personified in the water itself.[151] Even at sites without a water feature, then, a Nilotic landscape might have been constructed through other methods. But the persistence of this allusion suggests that domesticating the Nile, bringing this vital part of the Egyptian landscape into the sanctuary space, was an important aspect of constructing a space ideal for Isiac worship.

Other animals from the Nile made appearances in Isiac sanctuary decoration. Di Vita identifies a building near Gortyna's praetorium as a 4th-century CE sanctuary to the Egyptian gods and links with it an unusual limestone *sima* with a highly detailed crocodile waterspout (Figure 68). The *sima*, now in the Aghii Deka Apotheke, was found 3.2 m from the front of the *cella* and details the crocodile's head, including its long and scaly snout, triangular teeth,

68. Sima with crocodile spouts from the Praetorium at Gortyna, 4th century CE. Aghii Deka: Apotheke, Italian School of Archaeology at Athens. Photo: Italian School of Archaeology Photo Archive neg. B/27002.

forward-looking eyes with incised irises, and beard along both sides of the face.[152] There are no comparanda for this object, which suggests it may have been commissioned and imported from Egypt especially for this monument. Within Nilotic wall painting, crocodiles are prevalent, and this idiosyncratic piece of Egyptianizing architectural sculpture would have emphasized a connection with the Nile even to casual passers-by. The identification as an Egyptian sanctuary, however, is somewhat tenuous. Based on epigraphic and historical evidence, Di Vita argues that this phase of the sanctuary must date to the 4th century, and that the *sima* may have been imported through its dedicator's ancestral connections with the Roman rule of Egypt.[153] But the *cella* temple has a 2nd-century CE phase, and based on the lack of significant 4th-century CE renovations that could be called an *oikos* within Gortyna's Egyptian sanctuary, Di Vita argues that this temple should be identified as a renovation of Flavia Philyra's late 1st-century to early 2nd-century CE *oikos* for the Egyptian gods.[154] If his identification is correct, this *sima* would be the most explicit piece of Nilotic sculpture found in an Egyptian sanctuary outside of Marathon.

Set alongside these Nilometers, Egyptianizing animals, and water basins, Herodes' sanctuary can be reevaluated as a logical extreme of an otherwise common pattern. Several features like water basins, bull statuettes, pharaonizing style, subterranean chambers, and a marshy landscape could combine in various forms to produce a Nilotic effect.[155] These allusions would set the entire sanctuary in the same mytho-historical, deep time place where Isiac aretalogies rewrote Isis' history. But Marathon's devotees did not forget that they stood on a beach in eastern Attica. This version of Egypt was manageable and contained. It was an Egypt inhabited by Roman emperors and Athenian intellectuals, made out of local materials by Athenian artisans. Like other forms of Nilotic images and three-dimensional places, it was a space of domestication that linked the foreign with the familiar. A connection with Rome was necessary, however, to locate the viewer at the top of Mediterranean social hierarchies. To this end, Herodes employed references to the Imperial family and their Tivoli villa, both through portraiture and through an eclectic, innovative pharaonizing style, to elevate his and his viewers' social status.

PROVINCIALIZING THE NILE

The sanctuary at Marathon demonstrates the ways in which a Nilotic landscape in a Greek sanctuary could be exploited to centralize Greek culture within the Roman Empire's cultural hierarchies. At Marathon, the Egyptianizing architecture worked with the Egyptianizing sculpture and the natural landscape to transport the viewer into an imagined Egyptian past, one that was familiar and easily controlled. In addition to creating an environment that supported the cult's ritual and ideological goals, I argue, these sanctuaries reclaimed the Mediterranean world for Greek culture and Greek devotees. Underlying this experience was a background of Roman imperialism, heightened by a pair of Imperial portraits set up inside the sanctuary. Through its allusions to the Canopeum at the Tivoli villa, the sanctuary reminded viewers of Herodes', and perhaps their own, involvement in the expansion of Imperial power over the eastern Mediterranean. Greek culture, however, underpinned these connections. Egyptian subjects were rendered in Greek archaistic styles and materials, which sets up Greek art, culture, and religion as the central mediating factors in a diverse Mediterranean world. Here, devotees could access Egypt in a way that felt powerful and could control and calibrate their representations of Egypt to emphasize their own importance as a dominant cultural force.

The same types of aesthetic strategies we have seen throughout our study of Isiac cults in Greece appear in these sanctuaries, including the manipulation of deep time, the construction of new relationships with the Greek pantheon, and collapsing the distance between Greece and Egypt through the materiality of the objects that embodied Isis. Here, through a creative act of place-making, Herodes' audience can experience these new narratives in three dimensions. While Herodes' sanctuary is unusual in many ways, I have argued here that aspects of his sanctuaries can be connected to common themes in sanctuaries throughout Greece, particularly the desire to replicate the Nile and the use of Greek materials for Isiac sculptures and sanctuaries. Set in provincial Greece, the Nilotic aesthetic takes on a new meaning. In her book on the gardens at the Palace of Versailles, Mukerji argued that Louis XIV's gardens at Versailles (and 17th-century French gardens on the whole) reflected French political concerns, particularly France's territorial policies across its empire.[156] She argues that the carefully ordered plant-beds, which contained specimens from disparate parts of France's empire, ordered by dramatic architectural and sculptural features, articulated Louis XIV's desire to develop new spheres of French control through control of natural landscapes.

I argue that Herodes' shrine has similar intentions. As an active member of the Roman Imperial administration, Herodes' work brought him into contact with the far-flung peoples that Rome sought to control. By deterritorializing Egypt and setting it within his Greek villa, his sanctuary glosses over the violence inherent in Imperial control, and instead follows the Imperial norm of presenting a diverse empire in harmony, a most convenient fiction. The aesthetic's main purpose, then, was to grant its viewers a sense of control over distant places. While the Marathon sanctuary has many unusual features, including its pharaonizing style and excellent preservation, it draws from a set of features and concepts available throughout the Mediterranean. Several scattered examples of Nilotic scenes, most of them from domestic contexts, indicate that the exoticized and timeless view of the Egyptian natural landscape was not exclusively an Italian concept but one that was available to and employed by Greeks and other provincial peoples. Looking at the frequent presence of water features and representations of particular animals at other sites in Greece suggests that many communities chose to include allusions to the river, its water, and the divinities embodied by it in their sacred architecture. Though there is not currently any archaeobotanical evidence to prove that Egyptian plants and animals were imported and used within these sanctuaries, we should not overlook the possibility that some communities may have done so. Like the Pompeiian gardens, these architectural allusions and natural landscapes combined with sanctuaries' sculptures and rituals to construct multidimensional and sensory experiences of Egypt for devotees, right in their own hometowns. These sanctuaries thus locate Greek culture and the Greeks that practiced it at the very center of Roman control.

CHAPTER SEVEN

CONCLUSION
Graecia Capta, Aegypta Capta

MEDIATING A NEW GREEKNESS: ISIS, EGYPT, AND FASHIONING A GREEK IDENTITY

Throughout this book I have argued for a new, more precise set of heuristics to study the processes that construct ethnicity in a global Roman Empire. I have applied concepts of groupness, self-understanding, self-fashioning, and self-location to help define how Isiac communities redefined Greek ethnicity for themselves. In order to write histories that avoid essentialist renderings of Greekness, Romanness, and Egyptianness, we must think of ethnic identity as the product of what individuals and communities chose to do in moments when different groups collided. At the same time, however, we must recognize that this is not necessarily how ancient peoples would have understood ethnic identity. Still, a modern, etic perspective on these questions is useful, especially when contrasted with ancient, emic perceptions. Ethnicity often seems clearly defined to those who live with it, but with the benefit of hindsight, scholars can see the fluidity of ethnic categories.

The complex processes of identity formation discussed in this book overlap, interact, and intertwine with one another to produce ethnic ideas, but more importantly, they can fail and fall apart. It is just this contingency that permits the development of new forms of ethnicity like the one I have described here. What this method ultimately offers is more precision: the ability to pick out minority and intersectional perspectives and reconstruct their ideas, values, and meanings in discussion with more normative ideas of self and community.

A careful, dynamic study of material culture has much to add to this conversation. Art and other objects played an active and constitutive role in the production and maintenance of ethnic ideals. Elements like material, technique, style, and display make implicit arguments about foreign versus local origins and participation versus nonparticipation in normative culture. Sharing ideas, practices, and images across the region produced a sense of groupness, and, through the creation of imagined geographies discussed in Chapter 6, even offered these devotees an imagined shared territory. By reading Isiac sculpture and architecture alongside literary and epigraphic evidence, we can see that these meanings arise from an Isiac cultic context. These objects defined, displayed, and engaged devotees in a specific and shared version of Egyptian cult: Isis is universal, but that universality is mediated through Greek culture and materials; Isis is Egyptian, but her Egyptianness is represented through Greek style.

In order to show that Isis devotees had their own perspective on Greekness, it is first necessary to demonstrate that an Isiac community existed and had some impact on the ways that devotees saw themselves. I have argued that these features encouraged devotees to believe that Isiac communities had groupness: the idea that a bounded and definable community existed in a given time and place. In the context of modern scholarship, this point has major implications for how we study Isiac cults. Cumont's decision to group Egyptian religion with the worship of Cybele and Mithras produced a reified scholarly category. But some have questioned whether this grouping actually reflects ancient ideas – concluding instead that this classification obscures critical differences.[1] If devotees of Mithras and Cybele identified themselves with the cults in the ways that Greece's Isiac devotees could, as I have argued here, the similarities would recommend preserving Cumont's "oriental" religions category.[2] But if not, the differences could reveal meaningful information about ancient cult practice and experience. Some epigraphic dedications indicate that a few Isis devotees came to identify themselves closely with the gods themselves, and that they devoted themselves to the cults' service throughout their lives. It is impossible to determine how often this event happened. But epigraphic evidence from around the region indicates that many communities offered opportunities for devotees to engage deeply with the cults, integrating Isiac religion with other meaningful forms of identification, including family membership. More regional studies could also produce useful comparisons to understand to what extent local communities might adapt the cults, and what had to stay the same to produce a sense of regional and global belonging.

Devotee communities needed a shared set of symbolic meanings to retain their sense of connection. I have described three different methods of creating this meaning. To begin with, I suggested that Isiac aretalogies and sculptural types, shared throughout the region and in some cases replicated quite closely, combined to create a defined sense of shared self-understanding. These gods came from Egypt, but they had been closely connected to Greece and Greek culture for a long time. Funerary portraiture, at least in Athens, suggested that devotees identified with this representation of the gods, and that the cults placed a special emphasis on devotees' ability to embody these deities. Viewed in this light, the images that the Greeks produced of Isis and Sarapis and their companions represent attempts to construct a deity that devotees would come to see as part of themselves. Imported materials and objects were less useful in this context than statues that were familiar and referenced well-known deities and myths. Though Isis and Sarapis must retain their connections with Egypt, these images, when viewed alongside the aretalogies that reframed the gods as part of Greek myth-history, allowed devotees to visualize themselves as one with the gods without surrendering their claims on more normative forms of Greekness.

At the same time, these images still diverged noticeably from other forms of ideal sculpture. When their dress and attributes were placed on mortal bodies, they offered their devotees an opportunity to fashion a new form of self that wove together messages of alterity and normativity. Worshippers in this dress distinguished themselves from the rest of Athenian society and reinforced their participation in the cults' groupness. The vast majority of those who incorporated Isiac costumes into their portraiture were women, which suggests that this form of alterity was layered onto gender. I have observed similar patterns of contrasting self-representations throughout the Roman world. Set in a provincial context, Isiac portrait types overemphasized the marginality of Isiac cult and allowed their subjects to claim membership in both local and global forms of Greekness. Here it is clear that the Isiac communities are looking out into the rest of the Mediterranean to determine the best ways to express a nuanced form of Greekness, one that emphasizes alterity while also participating in the global Roman Empire.

The final process I have discussed here is self-location. The sanctuaries that were built by devotees create three-dimensional assemblages that attempt to recreate sensory and natural aspects of the Nile Valley. In some places, like the Philae-style pylons at Marathon or the *sphinxallée* of Sarapieion C on Delos, the allusions are monumental and easy for a modern viewer to perceive. Other sites, like Sarapieion A on Delos and the Iseion at Dion, were constructed in marshy areas with access to fresh water – a setting that would recall the Nile's own landscape. Eretria and Athens had fountains that provided a fresh flow of water.[3] Some, like the Sanctuary of the Egyptian Gods at Gortyna, created artificial areas that recreated Nilotic experiences. These efforts including piping in water to water crypts with steps that led the devotee into a lowered basin that alluded to Nilometers: ritual buildings that measured the Nile flood. Even unimposing sanctuaries like Sarapieion B on Delos and at Philippi contained artificial basins to hold water. To varying degrees, these Greek sanctuaries thus became three-dimensional, imagined geographies of the Nile that could be contained in situ. Barrett has recently highlighted the role that domestication and miniaturization plays in local experiences of Imperial power and suggested that Nilotic wall paintings offered Pompeiians a way to see themselves as participants in Roman imperialism.[4] Similarly, these built environments gave Greek communities a central role in the exertion of Imperial control over other provinces. By building the Nile in miniature and on Greek soil, devotees deterritorialized Egypt and granted themselves the power to determine its future. The Nile could run through Greece, and Greek devotees could control how it moved and where it ran. As a result, they felt as if controlled the gods and the mythology that reconfigured Isis and Sarapis as migrants to Greece.

For Isiac communities in Greece, then, Greekness meant something different. The Second Sophistic Greekness that occupies a central place in the study of Greek ethnicity under the Roman Empire offers a useful metric by which to define this minority perspective. As discussed in Chapter 1, elite male Second Sophistic writers like Pausanias, Plutarch, and Aelius Aristides put forth a Greekness that reproduced favored aspects of 5th-century BCE Greek (particularly Athenian) culture. These desires were expressed through several means, such as the revival of an archaizing Attic dialect, the continued emphasis on genealogy and purity, and the implication that the excellence of these earlier Greeks lived on. This version of Greekness certainly responded to Roman Imperial pressures and preferences but gave the illusion that Greece remained free, prosperous, civilized, and pure.[5] Put simply, Second Sophistic Greekness reached into the historical past to recreate an idealized version of a society that had existed in a specific and definable place and time. This past could be mapped onto Greece's Roman-period landscape and culture; it could be rewritten to respond to contemporary needs, but it was in some way knowable.

Isiac Greekness, on the other hand, relied on a different set of temporal and geographic references that produced a minority form of Greek ethnicity with a distinct texture and orientation. In terms of time, Isiac texts operate on a mythical scale. Though the Chronicle of Sarapieion A places the arrival of Egyptian deities in the recent past, most other aretalogies focus on the gods' origins, staking Isis' claim to a familial relationship with the Titans and the Olympian deities. Isis thus becomes part of the Homeric world as well as the historical one. This archaizing temporality serves a similarly justifying function to the Second Sophistic's classicizing temporality, but it must tread further into the past to justify Isis' status as a Greek deity. There are similarities here between the renegotiation of Isis' genealogy through mythical manipulation and the way in which cities around the Mediterranean argued their way into the Panhellenion's version of Greekness. Her universality serves as a metaphor for globalization, unifying a wide array of cultures and pantheons under a god who, though she is from Egypt, is in some way fundamentally Greek. But Isis' claims are neither political nor pragmatic. Rather, I argue, they are ethnic, a way for Greek communities to claim Isis as one of their own culture group and rewrite her as an actor in the most vaunted parts of Greece's primordial past.

In terms of landscape, Isiac Greekness consumes the far-off, reproducing it in local places and forms. The version of Egypt they have appropriated for their own use is based in imagination more than experience. Emblematic objects and places like sphinxes, pyramids, pylons, and the Nile occupy a central place in Greek sanctuaries, but certainly there were more common Egyptian imports like pottery, textiles, or grain. Greek texts alluded to Isis' new home in Greece and her special attachment to Greek people and places, whether mythological or real. In order to translate Isis into a version suited to Greek ethnic ideals, devotees deterritorialized Egypt, reconsidering and representing it on a small scale inside Greek sanctuaries and homes. This impulse should be interpreted as a response to Roman imperialism. The cults and their attendant references to exoticism, transculturality, migration, and translation provided a space in which to see Greekness as the fundamental connector throughout time and space. Devotees constructed Egyptian cults that gave them and their culture a heightened agency in the construction of transcultural power and imperialism. They could take distant Egypt and appropriate it for their own use, much as their own culture was appropriated by Roman elites. Rather than suffering themselves to be identified as the colonized, they used Isiac cults to grant themselves the power and space to colonize others.

Isiac Greekness, then, is different primarily in the methods and materials it uses to define its community. By focusing on process and parsing out the specific actions that produce identities and identification, we can describe with more precision what ethnicity is and what it does. Ethnicity here functions as a type of shared commonality motivating a narrow sphere of interpretive actions that can, in turn, produce symbolic meaning that impacts ideas of self. For devotee communities, I argue, Isiac cults offered a place to explore and experiment, to see where they belonged in the Mediterranean's hierarchies of power, culture, and ethnicity. These shifts occur against the backdrop of a globalizing Roman Empire. As Roman imperialism tightened the web of Mediterranean connectivity, provincial communities reacted with a set of globalizing strategies. As I have argued here, Isiac Greeks used many of the same strategies, including time-space compression, standardization across multiple communities, and the deterritorialization of Egyptian gods.[6] Though Rome did not necessarily promote Egyptian religion, the cult benefited from the changes brought about by the empire and gave local communities a method of response that strengthened their own agency.

More importantly, Isiac cults testify to the role that religion, along with concepts like gender, social and legal status, and economic resources, can play in fragmenting ethnic ideas. This intersectional approach could be taken much further. Different intersectional lenses could be applied to Greekness and other forms of ancient ethnicity. Ethnicities also have historicity, and it would be ideal to trace out how this one changes over time. I am not certain exactly when Isiac Greekness ends, and how it intensifies, weakens, contracts, and fails over time. The idea of Isiac Greeks must have developed at some time after the 3rd century BCE, and Moyer's observation that the aretalogies become standard sometime around the 1st century BCE might be a valid beginning point. Many sculptures are produced, and sanctuaries founded and renovated, in the mid-2nd century CE, which might mark an apogee. Little is produced after the late 3rd century CE, which may have been a time in which Isiac cults and ethnic ideals lost their appeal. This moment could be seen as a failure of Isiac Greekness, the moment in which the community fractures and falls apart. But these are only broad strokes and do not account for the microhistories of local communities and more specific responses to historical events and changes over shorter spans of time. The Isiac Greekness I have described here likely changed over time and had particular local resonances and textures, and this book, with its long time span and regional focus, has not accounted for these.[7] It is easier to find evidence of an ancient phenomenon as it succeeds, and I have accounted very little for the history of Isiac cults' decline and failure. I leave this work to future scholars.

Most of all, my work here suggests that certain types of religious actions can inflect and divide larger ethnic groupings in colonial settings. That is, joining some cults produced new forms of ethnic identification.[8] Modern readers can see the connections between ethnic and religious divisions in the modern world in bloody conflicts, such as the Irish Troubles and the Kosovo War of the 1990s. Nothing similarly violent arises in our ancient sources, and we should not assume that devotees rejected other forms of Greek ethnicity. Worshippers continued to engage with their birth families and to hold civic office and in some cases priesthoods in other cults. I argue, however, that Isiac Greekness suggests that cults could shift ethnic definitions and ideals and create soft but meaningful boundaries. As it made space for itself in Roman Greece, Isiac Greekness offered devotees a more central and outward-looking position in the cosmopolitan Roman Mediterranean, allowing these provincial peoples more agency in their experiences of Roman colonial power. In constructing new mythologies of Isis and Sarapis that located the gods in Greece's deep history, they constructed a world in which Greekness was the key mediator for mobility, both human and divine, and transcultural exchange. Egypt became something that Greeks could consume, domesticate, and reproduce in their own lands and on their own terms.

CONCLUSION: GRAECIA CAPTA, AEGYPTA CAPTA

LUCIUS AND THE STATUE, REVISITED

In this book I have argued that the Egyptian cults, through their texts, objects, and built environments, produced a form of Greekness distinct from others practiced throughout the region. I have referred many times to the scene in *Met.* 11.24 in which Lucius stands on the dais, dressed like a statue, and receives veneration in place of the cult image as part of his initiation. This passage has run through my head as I wrote this book, and I have considered it in several places from religious and artistic angles. Even if, as some would argue, Apuleius' portrayal is wrong in the details, there is something about his account that is representative of the responses that Isiac cult must have evoked in its devotees. To conclude, I want to return to the key question of what it meant for a Greek person living under the Roman Empire to join the Isiac cults. Apuleius' depiction of Lucius' initiation, though fictional, prompts several questions that frame my answers here.

Did Lucius' initiation lessen his Greekness? I have argued that Isiac cults reoriented rather than replaced normative Greek ethnic identities. Isiac Greekness, as I have reconstructed it, is distinct but not discrete from more normative forms of Greek identity. In a period where the boundaries of Greekness were highly contested and vigorously policed, the Egyptian cults could not have been an ethnically neutral concept. Isiac cults were closely associated with the people and places of Egypt itself, and Greco-Roman literary and artistic media portrayed the Nile as a space of otherness, experimentation, unknowability, the reconciliation of opposing concepts, and translation. By the Antonine period, Egypt could be separated from its geographic locale and reconstructed in new places. Greek devotees relied on this imagined geography of Egypt and Egyptian deities to construct their own version of Isiac worship. These tendencies allowed Greek devotee communities to reimagine Egypt and its cultural ideals as a fundamental part of Greece. But Lucius' initiation did not involve a repudiation of all he was before. Rather, membership in an Isiac community intersected with Greekness to produce a new form of ethnic-religious identification. Lucius and those who joined the cults became a new kind of Greek, one that inflected more normative forms of Greek ethnicity with an outward-looking perspective on the Mediterranean world.

How does material culture affect the devotee's idea of himself? In *Met.* 11.24, Lucius stands upon a dais in front of a cult image of Isis and receives veneration from other devotees while dressed as Sol. Scattered pieces of evidence indicate that similar rites occurred in a few places and times. A sculptural representation of an initiate atop a statue base is known from 2nd-century BCE Thessaloniki (Figure 8), and, as argued in Chapter 5, the funerary reliefs from Roman Athens depicting women dressed as Isis reference a similar initiatory rite practiced there. Costume was a common part of Egyptian cults and, in turn, part of local sculptural repertoires in many parts of Greece. But ultimately this passage is a moment of embodiment, in which the initiate becomes part of the cultic community's inner circle by standing in for the god. Dedicators defined these gods through sculpture, and in this moment, Lucius becomes an alternative personification of a deity. Telescoping outward, Lucius stands among other statues and objects that decorated the Kenchreai sanctuary. Most of these represented Egyptian places and deities in Greek materials and styles. At the same time, their dress incorporated attributes and patterns that marked out the gods as different from their Greek counterparts. These images helped to define who the Egyptian gods were to their devotees – foreign, yet familiar. But the materiality of these objects was deeply Greek, and Lucius' status as a Greek-speaking citizen of Corinth echoes the materiality of the cult object, for his body is Greek as well. Made from Greek materials and by Greek workshops, these statues announced their origins from Greece's soil to the viewer and embodied the gods within a familiar visual landscape.

Still, the costume retains its connotations of alterity and difference, which may indicate a desire for oppositions and dichotomies between whose poles the cults thrived. Much of the cults' material culture constructed this alterity. Lucius' garment is multicolored and intricate, featuring floral patterns, intricate animal designs, and luxurious fabrics. In addition to the vestment and chlamys, Lucius carries the goddess's lighted torch, which is seen in some sculptural examples that depict Isis-Demeter[9] and a crown made from palm fronds.[10] Once dressed in this outfit, Lucius stands on the tribunal and is revealed to a *populus* who have come to behold him. Apuleius is careful to highlight the dramatic nature of this encounter by highlighting the role of the curtains (*repente velis reductis, in aspectum populus errabat, Met.* 11.24). This passage suggests a group of devotees awaiting the revelation of the divine image, hidden behind a curtain, who instead come upon Lucius in the guise of the goddess. In this moment, Lucius has become one with the image and with the goddess, achieving the ideal moment of transcendence.

Lucius' moment on the platform serves as an epiphany, bringing the goddess to devotees in a way that suggests that these viewers had a common set of values that informed their experiences.[11] These epiphanic moments are part of Isis' and Sarapis' separation from Egypt. Greek devotees were primed to expect the gods to appear to them, whether in dreams or in the sanctuary. Much like the statues studied here, Lucius' viewers would have seen him as caught between their stereotypes of Egypt and iconography and his everyday life as a Greek inhabiting the Roman Empire. His humanity rewards their expectations, providing a statue in the present that embodies the goddess and has the potential to directly intervene in the viewers' lives.

Through these media, Egyptian cults and their gods offered a globalizing road map across the geographic, conceptual, and cultural boundaries that defined the Roman Mediterranean. In this moment, Lucius stands at the intersection of Greekness, Egyptianness, and Romanness. The statue he represents is Greek in material and style, much as he is of illustrious Greek ancestry and navigates Apuleius' representation of 2nd-century CE Greece, even in the form of an ass, with the ease of a native. But as a Corinthian with a Latinate name and a fluent command of Latin, Lucius may have connections to Rome's colonial rule and some claim on Roman status.[12] In some ways, he is emblematic of the complex cultural webs that Roman imperialism wove in Greece. Adding in their version of the Egyptian cults, in which Isis and Sarapis have deep roots in both Greece and Egypt, introduced a new element that broadened the dialectic beyond the Greco-Roman world and at the same time made Greece and Greek culture its center.

APPENDIX

Catalogue of Sculpture Associated with the Thessaloniki Sarapeum in the Thessaloniki Archaeological Museum

Museum inventory number	Publication/*RICIS* citation	Item description	Date	Findspot according to museum records
228	Despinis et al. 1997–2020, vol. 1, cat. 44	Three-sided Hekataion with dog	1st century BCE	Found near the Sarapeum, beginning of 1939
827	Despinis et al. 1997–2020, vol. 1, cat. 49	Votive plaque with two ears, dedicated by Avia Polla to Isis *epikoos*	Second half of the 1st century BCE	Found in the Sarapeum
828	Despinis et al. 1997–2020, vol. 1, cat. 50	Votive relief with three ears	?	Found in the Sarapeum
831	Despinis et al. 1997–2020, vol. 1, cat. 75	Statue of Aphrodite in the Louvre-Naples or Fréjus type	1st century BCE to first half of the 2nd century CE	From the Sarapeum
832	Despinis et al. 1997–2020, vol. 1, cat. 76	Statue of a female divinity, possibly Artemis, Athena, or Demeter	2nd century CE	Found in the Sarapeum
833	Despinis et al. 1997–2020, vol. 1, cat. 77	Classicizing statuette of Artemis or Athena wearing a peplos	2nd century CE	From the Sarapeum
834	Despinis et al. 1997–2020, vol. 2, cat. 190	Statuette of Pan with cape and goat legs	End of the 2nd century CE	Found in the Sarapeum
835	Despinis et al. 1997–2020, vol. 2, cat. 161	Torso of a male statue, possibly Anubis/Hermanubis. Wears a short chiton and *chlamys*	1st century CE	Found in the Sarapeum
836	Despinis et al. 1997–2020, vol. 4, cat. 784	Portrait statuette of a young male wrapped in a himation	Hellenistic period?	From the Sarapeum
837	Despinis et al. 1997–2020, vol. 4, cat. 677	Statuette of Sarapis *débout*	1st century BCE	From the Sarapeum
838	Despinis et al. 1997–2020, vol. 3, cat. 377	Relief with a woman and child or slave	Second half of the 1st century CE	Found near the Sarapeum
839	Despinis et al. 1997–2020, vol. 2, cat. 159	Female head; several possible identifications including a Muse, Artemis, or a Ptolemaic queen	1st century CE	Found near the Sarapeum

840	Despinis et al. 1997–2020, vol. 3, cat. 383	Head of a young man; resembles Hermes Richelieu type	1st century CE	Found in the Sarapeum
841	Despinis et al. 1997–2020, vol. 1, cat. 48	Votive plaque with footprints dedicated by Caecilia Polla	?	Found in the Sarapeum
842	Despinis et al. 1997–2020, vol. 2, cat. 336, *RICIS* 113/0568	Votive footprint relief with dedication to Isis Nymphe by Aemilius Eutychos	First half of the 3rd century CE	Found in the Sarapeum
843	Despinis et al. 1997–2020, vol. 1, cat. 87	Statue of Isis or a priestess of Isis in dark marble wearing the *diplax*	Mid–2nd century CE	From the Sarapeum
844	Despinis et al. 1997–2020, vol. 1, cat. 86	Statuette of Harpokrates	2nd century CE	Referenced as part of the Sarapeum
845	Despinis et al. 1997–2020, vol. 2, cat. 207	Torso of Harpokrates preserving thighs and part of arm reaching up to mouth	Second half of the 2nd century CE	Found in the Sarapeum
846	Despinis et al. 1997–2020, vol. 1, cat. 104	Table support with Herakles resting and *erotes*	2nd quarter of the 3rd century CE	From near the Sarapeum
849	Despinis et al. 1997–2020, vol. 3, cat. 490	Portrait statue of a man in himation	First half of the 2nd century CE	Found in the Sarapeum
851	Despinis et al. 1997–2020, vol. 4, cat. 818	Veiled female portrait statue of a woman, arm-sling type	Mid–1st century CE	From the Sarapeum
852	Despinis et al. 1997–2020, vol. 3, cat. 630	Fragment of an Attic sarcophagus with a male head	Last quarter of the 2nd century CE to 2nd quarter of the 3rd century CE	Found in the Sarapeum
855	Despinis et al. 1997–2020, vol. 2, cat. 294	Male portrait head; youth with long sideburns, incised irises and pupils	Ca. 220 CE	Found in the area of the Sarapeum
856	Despinis et al. 1997–2020, vol. 3, cat. 477	Female head, veiled, perhaps of the Pudicitia type	?	Found in the area of the Sarapeum
868+2596	Despinis et al. 1997–2020, vol. 4, cat. 899, Stefanidou-Tiveriou 2018	Large-scale fragmentary relief depicting a young man in Macedonian dress carrying an animal	End of the 1st century BCE–early 1st century CE	Found in the Sarapeum

(continued)

(continued)

Museum inventory number	Publication/*RICIS* citation	Item description	Date	Findspot according to museum records
875	Despinis et al. 1997–2020, vol. 4, cat. 693	Nude torso of a male youth, possibly Ganymede	Middle of the 2nd century CE	From the Sarapeum
897	Despinis et al. 1997–2020, vol. 1, cat. 84	Head of a statue of Sarapis	Early to mid-Antonine period	To the east of the house owned by Mr. Varelas on Olympou Street; probably from a different Egyptian sanctuary
973	Despinis et al. 1997–2020, vol. 2, cat. 333, *RICIS* 113/0565	Votive footprint relief with two feet of same size	2nd century CE	Found in the Sarapeum
976	Despinis et al. 1997–2020, vol. 2, 335, *RICIS* 113/0567	Votive footprint relief with *kat' epitagen* inscription	Second half of the 2nd century CE	Found in the Sarapeum
981	Despinis et al. 1997–2020, vol. 2, cat. 334, *RICIS* 113/0547	Votive footprint relief with one large foot and indications of a second smaller foot	Second half of the 2nd century CE	From the Sarapeum
986	Despinis et al. 1997–2020, vol. 1, cat. 47	Cylindrical altar with garlands dedicated to Isis Orgia by Gaius Folunius Verus	Second half of the 1st century BCE, with a second inscription in the 2nd century CE (reused as a water basin)	Found in the Sarapeum in 1939
995	Despinis et al. 1997–2020, vol. 1, cat. 51	Votive relief with two ears dedicated by Phoukia	End of the 1st century BCE to 1st century CE	Found in the Sarapeum

996	Despinis et al. 1997–2020, vol. 1, cat. 88	Statuette of Aphrodite Homonoia	Mid-2nd century CE or later	From the Sarapeum or the Vasiloglou plot?
997	Despinis et al. 1997–2020, vol. 1, cat. 67	Votive relief dedicated to Osiris *mystes* depicting two priests and an initiate	Late 3rd to mid-2nd century BCE	Found in the Sarapeum
998	Despinis et al. 1997–2020, vol. 2, cat. 177; *RICIS* 113/0529	Votive plaque with ear; epigraphic dedication by Markos Agelleius to Isis *epikoos*	1st century CE	From the Sarapeum; 1939 excavations
1011	Despinis et al. 1997–2020, vol. 1, cat. 27	Female head, likely Isis	3rd century BCE	From the Vasiloglou plot near the Diikitirion, 1938
1017	Despinis et al. 1997–2020, vol. 1, cat. 80	Head of a bearded god, possibly Sarapis or Zeus	2nd century CE	From the Vasiloglou plot (near the Sarapeum), 1938
1640	Despinis et al. 1997–2020, vol. 3, cat. 529	Votive relief with ears and grape vines dedicated to Dionysos *kat'euxen*	2nd century CE, after the reign of Hadrian	From the sanctuary of Sarapis
1955	Despinis et al. 1997–2020, vol. 2, cat. 332, *RICIS* 113/0566	Votive footprint relief to Isis Tyche with *kat'epitagen* inscription and two feet of different sizes	First half of the 2nd century CE	Found near Odos Diokitirios and Odos Eleni Svoronou
1977	Despinis et al. 1997–2020, vol. 4, cat. 865	Right foot of a female statue	2nd century CE	On an excavated plot on Odos Diokitirios and Odos Eleni Svoronou
1132+1150	Despinis et al. 1997–2020, vol. 2, cat. 162	Hermaic stele of Priapus; inscription includes the name ΦΙΛΑΡΓΥΡΟΣ at base	1st century CE	Found in the area of the Sarapeum at the beginning of 1939
2490	Despinis et al. 1997–2020, vol. 1, cat. 85	Head of Isis with thick corkscrew curls	Early Antonine period	Thessaloniki, 5 Eleni Svoronou Street, October 1960
2610 A+B	Despinis et al. 1997–2020, vol. 2, cat. 237	Fragments of a female portrait preserving a hand resting on some drapery; identified as a *lekanephoros*	Second half of the 2nd century CE or beginning of the 3rd century CE	Found in the Sarapeum

(continued)

(continued)

Museum inventory number	Publication/*RICIS* citation	Item description	Date	Findspot according to museum records
4922	Despinis et al. 1997–2020, vol. 1, cat. 46	Basalt sphinx representing the god Tutu; from Egypt	Late Ptolemaic Egypt, perhaps beginning of the 1st century BCE	Found in the Sarapeum
10844	Despinis et al. 1997–2020, vol. 2, cat. 262, *RICIS* Suppl. 113/0579	Portrait bust of the priest L. Titonius Primus	Dated to the Trajanic period but must have a 3rd century to 4th century CE reuse period (LAM)	Found near Odos Skra, associated later with the Iseo (?) Catalogue doubts any connection with the sanctuary

NOTES

CHAPTER 1

1. 2nd century to early 3rd century CE. Slim 1996, 25, 32, figs. 6, 9; Slim and Slim 1996, 15, fig. 2; Huskinson 2000, 3–20, fig. 1.1–3.
2. SHA *Hadr.* 5, 27. On the architecture, see: Claridge 1999. Palazzo Massino alle Terme inv. 428497; found between 1655 and 1667 during the demolition of the Church of Santo Stefano del Trullo. A drawing (Biblioteca Apostolica Vaticana, *Cod. Barb. Lat.* 4333) indicates that the hands, which hold a bouquet of greenery and a pomegranate, are modern reconstructions: Sapelli 1999, 52–55, cat. 10. Simon initially identified the figure as Egypt, and the piece is illustrated in the *LIMC* catalogue entry for *Aegyptos*: Helbig 1963, vol. 2, 245, cat. 1437 (Simon); Jentel 1981, vol. 1, 380, no. 8. Sapelli agrees with this identification and notes that it is widely accepted. Though this type of hairstyle, with its deeply drilled rows of curls, might normally be considered yet another feature of Isiac iconography, the same style appears on other *provincia* reliefs in the sequence and is more likely a workshop style.
3. *SEG* 47 (1985), 35; R. R. R. Smith 1988, 55; plate 10.1, 2013, cat. B-Base 25. Found in the South Parodos of the Theater. The relief is unusual because it is made of a single piece of marble; the rest of the *ethne* from the Sebasteion are made of two. Smith notes the pattern of drapery but does not connect the relief with images of Isis and her priestesses. A relief from the "Parthian Monument" at Ephesus also features a female figure dressed in Isiac costume and wearing her hair in heavy "Libyan" locks that may depict Egypt: Vienna, Kunsthistorisches Museum inv. I, 1654a–c; Landskron 2006, 102–103, abb. 1.
4. Though none of these images was found in the provinces of Achaia or Macedonia, there may have been a freestanding version of an *ethne* gallery in the heart of 2nd-century CE Athens. Pausanias mentions a series of bronze statues representing the "colonies" of Athens in the Hadrianic Temple of Olympian Zeus, which Smith connects with sculpted *ethne* galleries: Paus. I.18.6; R. R. R. Smith 1988, 71n47; Camia and Corcella 2018.
5. I have studied a small group of these Egyptian migrants in: Mazurek 2016.
6. The Second Sophistic refers to literary and philosophical works produced by elite Greek pagans in ca. 50–250 CE. The majority of these works were performed orations, many of them on philosophical topics, that allowed the speaker to demonstrate his deep command of Greek literature, philosophy, and language. See further: Whitmarsh 2001, 2015; Eshleman 2012.
7. Most notably: Bowie 1970; Swain 1996; Whitmarsh 2001. More recently, Strazdins (2022) suggests that this retrospective attitude also represents a concern with the future, while still emphasizing the key role of temporality in defining Greek culture.
8. Greece's cultural system was never closed, and many social institutions considered key to Greek culture, including the symposium (Topper 2012), had their roots in foreign cultures. Nevertheless, as I will demonstrate, many early formulations of Greekness relied on the fiction that Greek identity and culture came from Greece itself.
9. Some early scholars have called this an *interpretatio graeca* of Isis (Vandebeek 1946), but my approach here is to consider these changes more dynamically and fluidly. For more recent approaches that nuance the *interpretatio* model, see: Ando 2005; von Lieven 2016. My work only begins to explore the intersectionality of Greek identity, and here I focus on a dissonant

10 See the examples in: von Moock 1998; Walters 1988.
11 Mattingly (2004, 2014) proposed discrepant experience as a model for assessing the differing impacts of Roman imperialism on smaller subgroups within imperial contexts. In the modern context, the key work on intersectionality is: Crenshaw 1991. See further discussion in the section "Viewership, Objects and the Search for Ethnicity."
12 The precise terminology for objects made in the northern Mediterranean that depict Egyptian subjects is hotly debated. See the discussion in: Barrett 2017a; Malaise 2005, 201–220; Mol 2015a; Swetnam-Burland 2015, 12; van Aerde 2015, 32–33, 61, 292. Like Barrett, I use the term "Egyptianizing" because it is useful for us as modern scholars to distinguish imported objects from local imitations and adaptations, even if ancient viewers may not have placed the same value on an object's origins.
13 Barrett 2019; Bricault and Versluys 2012, 2014a; Mol 2012; Versluys 2015, 2016.
14 Bricault and Veymiers (2011) have published a wealth of material that permits new inquiry into the sanctuaries at Marathon, Argos, Rhodes, Messene, and Dion.
15 For a discussion of materially-oriented methodologies of Roman history, see: Mol 2017; R. R. R. Smith 2006; van Oyen 2017.
16 Among the many studies that have dealt with the difficulties of the archaeology of religion, see: Raja and Rüpke 2015; Elsner 2012; Kyriakidis 2007.
17 Swetnam-Burland 2015; Mol 2015a; Pearson 2015.
18 Barrett (2019, 312–314) espouses a similar view, arguing that the categories of "decorative" and "religious" are modern ideas. The images of Egyptian deities and landscapes in Pompeiian wall paintings, small finds, and furniture reflect an understanding of their religious significance and are deployed in ways that are suitable to their display contexts within the Roman home.
19 Transculturality describes the human phenomenon of constant motion. It refers to those people, things, and ideas residing in the liminal spaces between cultures, across boundaries, and in the middle ground that are most fertile for the production of new cultural forms that incorporate elements from multiple existing traditions. See further: Flüchter and Schöttli 2015; Pangiatopoulos 2011.
20 My model of Greekness, which is based on process, is fundamentally anti-essentialist. These people that I have called Greeks probably ascribed to several different types of overlapping identities at the same time, and Greekness may not have been the most important or valuable of these identities at a given moment. See further: Concannon 2014, 14–17; C. P. Jones 2008.
21 With the notable exception of Alcock (1995) and Woolf (1994), scholars have not included Greece in the growing field of Roman provincial history and archaeology. See: Papaioannou 2016.
22 Most notably, Gruen's (1986) account of an accidental and ad hoc Roman conquest portrays Romans as reluctant imperialists with little interest in involving themselves in local affairs until forced to do so. While I am generally in sympathy with Gruen's arguments about international diplomacy, this perspective minimizes the military violence that Greeks experienced. Even if the Romans did not see these wars as wars of conquest, it is hard to imagine that the Greeks who lived through them held the same opinion. There are other military histories that focus on 3rd- and 2nd-century BCE wars in their Greek contexts (e.g., Waterfield 2014), but here again the lived experience of these wars and their impact on Greek communities is very much in the background. See also Alcock (1995, 1–32) for a more nuanced view.
23 Engels (1990, 14–15) offers an alternate account. After the Roman victory at Cynoscephalae in 197 BCE, Corinth joined the Achaian League, effectively coming under Roman control. In 147, due to Roman threats to detach Corinth from the Achaian League and thus to reduce its power, Corinth dismissed its Roman ambassadors. In the meeting of the following year, Rome's ambassadors were shouted down. Either way, Mummius' sack of the city is explained as vengeance for a slight against Roman honor.
24 Strabo 7.23; Fowler and Stillwell 1932, 27.
25 Strabo 8.22.6, 8.6.23. Similarly, Paus. 7.16.8. Polybius (39.3) records the looting and

describes the callousness of the Roman soldiers, who played dice on the works they seized: Walbank 1997, 95; Romano 2003, 279.

26 *Tusc.* 2.33.53. Similarly, Servius Sulpicius Rufus (*Fam.* 4.5.4) described Corinth as a city in ruins in 45 BCE. James (2014, 21–25) rightly points out that the Latin terminology of *diruere* and *delere* can also be used to identify conquered cities more generally.

27 James 2014.

28 Hoff 1989, 271–272; Thakur 2007, 107–109.

29 Waterfield 2014, 216–220. An inscription dated shortly after 168 BCE from Demetrias in Thessaly (SEG 56.626) outlines the redistribution of land previously owned by the Macedonian kings and tax exemptions for the Magnesians, who had supported the Romans in the Third Macedonian War: Kravaritou 2016, 145–146. On Delos, a *senatus consultum* dated to ca. 166–164 BCE (*ID* 1510) indicates that a Delian (Demetrios of Rheneia) successfully petitioned the Roman Senate to overturn the Athenian colonial government's decision to shut down a Sarapieion: Bricault 2005, 227–228, cat. 202/0195, plate 48; Roussel 1913.

30 Habicht 1997, 351–369; Waterfield 2014. Earlier, Rutilius Rufus and Marcus Marcellus had fled Rome to safety in Mytilene, and T. Pomponius Atticus escaped from Cinna in Athens (Dio, *frag.* 97.2; Cic., *Brut.* 250; Sen., *Helv.* 9.4, Nep., *Att.* 2–4).

31 On the Legio IV Macedonia, see: Syme 1933. Syme's study of the Roman legions after the Pannonian War suggests that many Macedonians joined the army, though he does not explain how he determined the origin of these soldiers, and that at least two more legions were given the name Macedonia in the early 1st century CE. Philippi became a colony for Antony's veterans, and Dion, Stobi, Patras, and Heraclea became colonies for veterans of the Roman army. Corinth was an unusual colony in that it settled *negotiatores* (merchants) and freedmen rather than veterans.

32 *CIL* XIV, 67; Sherk 1957, 53–55.

33 Sherk 1957, 60–62.

34 Paus. 10.8.2; Hall 2002, 136–142; Romeo 2002, 24.

35 Joseph., *AJ* 19.7–10; Dio Cass. 59.28.3–4; Suet., *Calig.* 57.1.

36 Spawforth 2011, 236–237; Kennell 1988, 245–251.

37 Karivieri 2018, 283–285; Preston 2001, 86–88; Swain 1996, 1–10.

38 *IG* 7, 428/429, rededicated as Appius Claudius Pulcher; *IG* 7, 349/350, rededicated as Marcus Agrippa: Platt 2007, 254. Plutarch (*Ant.* 60.4) also tells us that the Athenians reinscribed two colossal portraits of Eumenes and Attalos for Marc Antony, which Shear (2007, 244) suggests stood on the Akropolis near pillar monuments on the site of the later Monument of Agrippa.

39 Shear 2007. Dio Chrys. (*Or.* 71–72) condemns this practice, which suggests that it continued into the 2nd century CE.

40 *IG* I 3, 850+ *IG* 2 2, 4168 (signature of Kritios and Nesiotes and dedication of Hegelochos), *IG* 2 2, 3882+4117 (signature of Praxiteles). See: Shear 2007, 242–246.

41 Alcock 1995; Borg 2011, 218–228.

42 Spawforth 2011, 59–86; Alcock 1995, 93–128; Shear 1981. Borg (2011) reassesses the archaeological evidence for the "infilling" phenomenon and argues that most new temples were dedicated to gods already worshipped in Athens, if not on the precise spot where the Roman temples stood. Though she emphasizes that most of the Augustan-period changes were continuations of Hellenistic-period dedicatory practices in the Agora, she does note the major impact of these new monuments on Attica's architectural landscape.

43 *IG* 2 2, 3173. Pammenes, the dedicator, is identified here as the priest of Roma and Augustus Soter. See further: Hoff 1992. On the building's architecture see: Thakur 2007; Binder 1969.

44 On the delicate political situation in early Augustan Athens: Hoff 1989.

45 Contra: Thakur 2007, 115, see Rose 2005, 51–52; Baldassarri 1995.

46 Borg 2011, 21–28; Geagan 1997; Hoff 1989; Whitmarsh 2015, 11–12.

47 Hoff 1989; Thakur 2007, 121–122.

48 Hoff 1989, 268–269. Another rebellion in 13 CE is mentioned in later 3rd-century CE sources, including: Euseb., *Chron.* 197.4; Oros. 6.22.2. See further: Syme 1979, 198–204.

49 Hoff 1989, 269–274. On active statues in Greek literature and history, see: Platt 2011, 77–169.

50 Adams 1989; Gleason 2010, 127–130; Boatwright 2000, 145–146. Hadrian visited

Athens in 124/125, 128/129, and 131/132, and became one of the city's eponymous heroes.
51 *IG* 2 2, 5185, *SEG* 29, 198. There is some debate about whether the first line of the inscription, αἵδ' εἴσ' Ἀθῆναι Θησέως ἡ πρὶν πόλις, should be understood as "formerly that of Theseus" or "the ancient city of Theseus": Adams 1989, 11–12.
52 Daly 1950; Woolf 1994, 133–134.
53 Romeo (2002, 25) argues that the Panhellenion was modeled on the Delphic Amphictyony in its original organizational structure. In their analysis of fifty-four inscriptions related to the Panhellenion, Spawforth and Walker (1985) note that most of them make claims for membership based on Greek ancestry, a history of good relations with Rome, and previous benefactions from Hadrian. This new association resulted in several new Imperial dedications in Athens, including the Panhellenia games (Cass. Dio 69.16.2), a temple of Hera and Zeus Panhellenios (Paus. 1.18.9; Cass. Dio 69.16.2), a Pantheon (Paus. 1.18.9, 1.5.5), and a library (Paus. 1.18.9). Hadrian also endowed the city's grain supply (Cass. Dio 69.16.1) and began construction on an aqueduct and terminating reservoir (completed by Antoninus Pius, *CIL* 3 540 = *ILS* 337). See: Boatwright 2000, 145.
54 C. P. Jones 1999, 112–121. It is worth noting that Jones believes that kinship-based diplomacy between cities generally declined during the Roman Empire, except in this case.
55 Romeo 2002, 21–31.
56 Paus. 8.4.3. These familial ties could be proved through many methods (S. Saïd 2001, 288–289; Woolf 1994, 129–130), including mythological manipulation. Romeo (2002, 29) suggests that arguments based on *genos* were easier and more effective than those based entirely on mythology.
57 Hall 2002, 30–55.
58 Whitmarsh 2013, 62–65. Whitmarsh's idea of resistance encompasses both rebellion and more subtle processes of subversion, sabotage, localism, and other improvised strategies that do not rise to the level of violence; contra: Ando 2000, 49–70.
59 Elsner 2001.
60 Kemezis 2014, 393–394.
61 Versluys 2010, 11; 2015, 146.
62 Martin 2017.
63 Hall 2002, 11. Gruen (2013) insists that Greek and Roman culture had no term for ethnicity and denies that racialized thinking was a major concern, but still considers the modern concept a useful heuristic.
64 Vlassopoulos 2015, 1–10.
65 Morgan 1991, 133; 2003, 10–17.
66 In a similar vein, McCoskey (2012, 2–3) defines race as a social construct imposed upon the human body that ascribes predictive characteristics to members of a group. This focus on bodily features and genetic relationships does not map well onto the evidence discussed in this book, and I have chosen to use the term ethnicity instead.
67 Many archaeological studies of race and ethnicity, particularly in the 18th century through the early 20th century, produced racist and erroneous interpretations. Hall (1997, 111–114) and S. Jones (1997, 1–12) gather several relevant examples.
68 Versluys 2017, 24–27.
69 Hall 1997, 111–142.
70 The theory of object agency is outlined clearly in: Gell 1998. Some recent applications in Roman contexts include: van Eck and Versluys 2015; Mol 2017; Versluys 2016. Bordieu's theory of *habitus* provided the groundwork for earlier studies that emphasized the active role that objects play in the creation of culture, including ethnic consciousness. See: Bell 1992; Bordieu 1990; S. Jones 1997.
71 Hall 1997, 137–141.
72 Latour 2005.
73 Antonaccio 2003, 2004; Gruen 2011, 2013a, 2013b.
74 Brubaker 2004, 4–5.
75 Antonaccio 2005, 97–100.
76 Antonaccio 2003, 59–61; 2005, 100–101. Hybridity in this context refers to those moments when the colonizing group's culture and identity change in response to contact with new groups, particularly in moments of creative adaptation and misunderstanding: Antonaccio 2003, 59–61; 2013. See also: Malkin 1998, 2011.
77 S. Jones 1997, 96. See also: Barth 1969, 9–10. Similarly, Crenshaw (1988, 1369–1381) argues that these racial divisions have cultural values that create and underpin systems of domination.
78 The approach became popular in the mid-1990s and continues as a major line of

79 Pitts 2007, 494–495. See also: Hölscher 2008. Pitt's critiques apply to most work prior to 2013. Even the best of these pre-2007 studies dealt with the concept of identity in a problematic way: Malmberg 2011.
80 Revell 2005, 1–9.
81 For example, Andrade focuses on the intersection of local idioms in Syria with Second Sophistic Greekness; Stone has looked at Apuleius's portrayal of characters' actions to assert different types of ethnic identities; and Rebillard has argued for more situational forms of Christian identities that are activated by particular contexts: Barrett 2019; Stone 2014; Mattingly 2014; Andrade 2013, 1–8; Rebillard 2012, 1–7; Geary 2002. Whitmarsh (2001, 90–103) does not draw on Brubaker directly, but uses a similar concept of "self-making" to discuss *paideia*, *mimēsis*, and other identity-building practices in Greek literature.
82 Crenshaw 1988, 149–152.
83 Crenshaw 1991. See further: Cho et al. 2013; Chang 2002.
84 Crenshaw 1991, 1242.
85 Pitts and Versluys 2015a; Hodos 2017.
86 Jennings 2011, 21–31, 129–141. Jennings insists that each period has its own experience of globalizations and prefers to speak of globalizations rather than a single process.
87 Luraghi 2014, 217.
88 Elsner 1995, 2007, 2012; Platt 2011; Squire 2009, 2011.
89 As suggested for the Second Sophistic context by Dench (2017). Chang (2002) notes a similar conflict in the definition of race in the American context.
90 Vlassopoulos 2015, 5–8.
91 S. Saïd 2001, 294–295.
92 For a more detailed chronological exploration of Greekness, with criticisms of the chronological approach, see: Vlassopoulos 2013, 7–11. Vlassopoulos proposes instead a Hellenization-focused approach that looks at the spread of Greek identity and culture across the Mediterranean, which is more appropriate to the study of other regions.
93 Gruen 2013, 1–3; Hall 2002, 31–55; Morgan 2003, 4–16; McCoskey 2012, 49–56.
94 See Hall (2002, 173–175), with accompanying references. Hall's argument reflects a broader consensus, as reflected in: McCoskey 2012, 56–58.
95 Flowers 2000, 65–66; Hall 1989; 2002, 175–189.
96 Hall 2001; Engels 2010.
97 Hdt. 5.22.1–2; Hall 2002, 154–157.
98 Isoc., *Paneg.* 50.
99 Hall 2002, 209–210; Burstein 2008, 76–77; S. Saïd 2001, 282; McCoskey 2012, 63. Hall specifically refers to this as a transition from ethnicity to culture, but according to Brubaker's definitions, these changes are best understood as a different method of defining the ethnic group.
100 Hall 2002, 210.
101 Flowers 2000, 65–66.
102 S. Saïd 2001, 278. Saïd also notes the importance of religion in the reckoning of Greekness by Isocrates and Demosthenes, which plays an important role also in Mackil's (2012) arguments about the formation of *koinōnia* in Archaic Greece.
103 Luraghi 2008.
104 Walbank 1981, 46–59; McCoskey 2012, 53–58; Fischer-Bovet 2015, 9–13.
105 Bingen 2007, 244–245.
106 Riggs (2005, 19–20) argues that the distinction is based on language and not on a legal category, but the papyrological evidence given in historical studies like Bagnall and Frier (1994) and Rowlandson (2013) demonstrates convincingly that these were legal categories as well as ethnic descriptors.
107 Jördens 2012, 247–248; Riggs 2005, 19–21. Several of these social norms, particularly access to the *gymnasium*, were codified into law under Roman rule.
108 Vandorpe 2012, 262–263.
109 Burstein 2008, 61–66.
110 Rowlandson (2013, 219) notes that several people of Egyptian descent received the status of Macedonian *katoikoi* even though they were not considered to be descendants of Greek settlers. Fischer-Bovet (2015, 35) notes that there is evidence that Macedonian soldiers married local women of the priestly class in the early Ptolemaic period, and that some of their descendants seem to have used both Egyptian and Greek names and held high-

level administrative positions, including the office of *dioikētēs* (finance minister) under Ptolemy II.
111 These individuals retained citizenship in their ancestral Greek *poleis*, which they used in legal documents: Burstein 2008, 72–73.
112 Fischer-Bovet 2015, 41–44.
113 Fischer-Bovet 2015; Rowlandson 2013, 217–219; Vandorpe 2012, 263–264.
114 Rowlandson 2013, 219–220; Jördens 2012, 249–253. Egypt's large Jewish population had an ambiguous legal status.
115 Rowlandson 2013, 222–223; Jördens 2012, 252–253. It is not clear what power these citizens had over the *chora*.
116 Riggs 2005, 20–21; Vandorpe 2012, 268–269.
117 SB 12.11012 = Canducci 1990, 1991; Montevecchi 1970; Rowlandson 2013, 225.
118 Bagnall 1997.
119 Rowlandson 2013, 225–226.
120 Rowlandson 2013, 226; Jördens 2012, 253–254.
121 See also: Barth 1969.
122 Bowie 1970; Swain 1996; Whitmarsh 2001.
123 Aristid., *Or.* 1.16.
124 Kemezis 2014, 391.
125 S. Saïd 2001, 290.
126 Whitmarsh 2001, 90–130; 2015, 14. See similar examples at *VS* 531, 564, 567, 571, 574, 588–591, 600, 605, 609, 613, 616, 617, 627. See further: Anderson 1993, 119; Flinterman 1995, 51.
127 Whitmarsh 2001, 94–96.
128 Eshleman 2012, 2.
129 Whitmarsh (2001, 90–91), in reference to the use of the verb *diapherein* in Iambl., *VP* 44.
130 Eshleman 2012, 1–15; Too 2001, 357–458; Whitmarsh 2001, 7–8, 90–130; 2015, 13–15.
131 Richter 2011, 7–8; Preston 2001, 87–90.
132 *Education* 4a.
133 Whitmarsh 2001, 116–117.
134 Barth 1969, 15.
135 Connelly 2001; Whitmarsh 2001; Eshleman 2012, 1–20; Strazdins 2022.
136 Dio Chrys., *Or.* 37.25–27. See further: Kemezis 2014, 401; König 2001; Beall 2001, 92–95; S. Saïd 2001, 292; Swain 1996, 43–51.
137 Ἕλλησι μέν, ἵνα ἔχωσιν οἱ ἐπιχώριοι τῆς Ἑλλάδος παράδειγμα ὡς οὐδὲν τὸ παιδευθῆναι τοῦ φῦναι πρὸς τὸ δοκεῖν διαφέρει. Though τὸ δοκεῖν could be translated as "renown," the context connects renown with Greekness, specifically the Greek culture obtainable through *paideia*. Concannon (2014, 39–44) has argued that Favorinus' arguments about his statue cast him as the ideal Greek and aligns the Corinthians, who descended largely from Italian *negotiatores* and freedmen, with the brutish Romans that, like Mummius, could not appreciate true Greekness.
138 R. R. R. Smith (1998, 63–66) outlines dress options for male portraits: equestrian and cuirassed (neither of which would make sense for Favorinus' status as an intellectual), some version of the Greek chiton and himation, or, rarely in the 2nd century CE, a toga. Literary attestations of Favorinus repeatedly emphasize his choice to define himself as a Greek (König 2001), and a portrait in a chiton and himation seems most appropriate. See further: Philostr., *VS* 489; Gleason 1995, 3–20.
139 Cass. Dio 21.15–16, 31.162–163, 39.3, 48.8.
140 R. R. R. Smith 1998; 2006, 65–71; P. Stewart 2008, 79–80. On the location of the statue, see: Concannon 2021; White 2005, 67–73.
141 Kemezis 2014, 394–395; S. Saïd 2001; Swain 1996, 42–63.
142 Kemezis 2014, 391.
143 Eshleman 2008, 2012.
144 Most notably, Swain (1996, 67–94) and Woolf (1994) have argued that Greeks viewed Romanness as a primarily political form of identity. Gruen (2013) and McCoskey (2012, 75–76) has argued that the Roman world did not operate within an ethnic hierarchy and were not particularly anxious about identity. More recent work has taken a more nuanced perspective that integrates material evidence and argues for models based on coexistence, mutual competition, and dialectic formation: Kemezis 2014, 389–400; Papaioannou 2016, 37–40.
145 Brubaker 2004, 9–18; Calhoun 2003; Lichterman et al. 2017.
146 Díaz-Andreu and Lucy 2005, 1–2.

CHAPTER 2

1 Giridharadas 2018.
2 *IG* 5 2, 472; Dunand 1967, Bricault 2005 43, cat. 102/1702; Veymiers 2014, 144; Martzavou 2018, 147. The inscription has been dated generally to the 2nd–3rd century CE; it is now lost. The translation is my own, with thanks to Bill Beck for his advice.

3   Martzavou 2018, 147.
4   Brubaker 2004, 13. See further: Calhoun 2003; Yans 2006; Brubaker 2009. On the other hand, Barrett (2019, 33–34) rightly argues that we should not simply assume groupness for Isiac cults.
5   Brubaker 2004, 9–19.
6   Often described through the concept of glocalization: Hodos 2009, 21–25; 2017, 10–12; Pitts and Versluys 2015b, 14–17 or of discrepant experience: Mattingly 2014.
7   For example: Sfameni Gasparro 2016.
8   Muniz Grijalvo 2009; Matricon-Thomas 2012.
9   Veymiers 2018, 1. See also: Pachis 2003, 104.
10 On the "identité religieuse" in Isiac cult, see: Sfameni Gasparro 2018.
11 As argued by Rüpke, Isiac cult "is not held together by some metaphysical instance called Isis, but by communication of individuals who decide to frame their religious action as communication with such a goddess, and who thus gain agency and collective identity in ever more specific forms" (Rüpke 2018, 72).
12 Smart 1983, 2–3.
13 Rüpke 2014, 5.
14 See for example: King 2003, 297–301.
15 Rüpke 2016, 2–4. See also: Woolf 2007, 130; Chaniotis 2013, 172–173.
16 Barrett 2019, 302–303. While the latter two categories are critical for Barrett's study of Pompeiian wall paintings, they are less important to my study of religious practice.
17 *Met.* 11.13, 15, 16; de Souza 2003, para. 8. In some cases, the term is contrasted with terms like *profani* or used in discussions of rites and thus seems to refer to initiates. Though there is no cognate term in Greek epigraphy, Plutarch refers to devotees as *Isiakos*, a term that reconciles well with the names of the cultic associations discussed in the section "Cult Associations as Social Groups."
18 Feil 1992, 32–33; J. Z. Smith 1998, 269–270.
19 For a deeper discussion of the scholarship on this problem, see: Egelhaaf-Gaiser 2000, 31–38.
20 Tilg 2014, 84–130.
21 Winkler 1985, 123–132, 219–227. Similarly, Libby (2011) argues that the moon and mirror imagery in Book 11 is meant to suggest that Isis is a fraudulent deity.
22 Méthy 1996, 1999a, 1999b, 1999c; Méthy, however, notes the differences between Apuleius' Platonic characterization of Isis and the Isis depicted in other cultic media. See further: Gasparini 2011; Mazurek 2018, 633–638.
23 Finkelpearl 1998, 183–213. Her argument builds on those put forth in: Merkelbach 1962. See also: Egelhaaf-Gaiser 2000, 32–33.
24 Harrison 2004, 238.
25 Millar 1981; Egelhaaf-Gaiser 2000, 29–103; Rife 2010, 409–410.
26 Egelhaaf-Gaiser 2000, 103–104. See also: Harrisson 2012, 223.
27 Gasparini 2011, 699–701.
28 Moormann 2018; Pfeiffer 2018.
29 Griffiths 1975, 1–6; Millar 1981, 63–66; Martzavou 2012a, 271–274. Even those who are highly skeptical of Apuleius' account still use him in their reconstructions of Egyptian cult, including: Bricault 2013, 433–437; Veymiers 2018, 47–50.
30 Finkelpearl 1998, 184–213. See also: Keulen 2015. Too (1996, 150–151) argues against reading Apuleius' works as truly autobiographical, particularly the *Apologia*, because she believes the author's desire to represent his poetic and philosophical interest in the impossibility of accurate representation overrides any impulse to accurately represent himself.
31 Merkelbach 1962.
32 Gordon 2016.
33 This includes: Bricault 2013, 428–434; Martzavou 2012a, 273–275; Veymiers 2018, 48–49; Malaise and Veymiers 2018, 504–505. See further: Pfeiffer 2018.
34 Dunand 1973b, 153–154.
35 Relying on the Calendar of 354 and John the Lydian; Bricault 2006a, 134–146.
36 Isiac rites were also integrated into other cultic calendars. An inscription from late 1st- to early 2nd-century CE Athens requires a sacrifice of a cock, several fruits, wheat, and barley while making a *melikraton* libation for Nepthys and Osiris on the thirteenth day of the month Boedromion. This act is part of a larger calendar that belonged to a group of people (perhaps a family or private association) devoted to the Eleusinian cults, and including Osiris and Isis here may indicate that the group equated them with Hades and Persephone. *IG* 3 77 = *IG* 2/3 2, 1367; Dow 1937, 224–225; Dunand 1973a, 139–139; Bricault 2005, 18–19, cat. 101/0225; 2013, 353–355.
37 Firm. Mat., *Err. Prof. rel.* 2.6. Alvar notes similarities here with other classical writers,

38 El Jem, Archaeological Museum, 3rd century CE; Stern 1965, fig. 3.
39 Grand-Clément 2018, 349–350; Sfameni Gasparro 2018, 91.
40 Alvar 2008, 301–302.
41 IG 10 2, 108 II.3; Merkelbach 1973, 45–49; Bricault 2005, 139, cat. 113/0506.
42 Plut., De Is. 366f; Alvar 2008, 302n380. Alvar believes that Plutarch is referencing a rite specific to Egypt, most likely to Dendera, Alexandria, Canopos, or another Delta site.
43 Veymiers 2018, 57; Pfeiffer 2018.
44 Grand-Clément 2018, 341–347. A fresco from Stabiae (cubiculum W25, Villa of Varano, Naples, Museo Archeologico Nazionale inv. 8972; De Caro 1996, cat. 3.52) depicts the beginning of an Isiac procession with a similarly rigid delineation of ritual personnel, but Moormann (2018) has pointed out that it comes from a domestic context and may not depict a specific rite.
45 Mol and Versluys 2015, 455–456; Veymiers 2018, 56–57.
46 Mol and Versluys 2015, 459.
47 Kindt 2012, 66–70; with further bibliography at 67n76.
48 Dunand 1973b, 138–144; Bricault 2013, 265–278; Martzavou 2012a, 2018.
49 On these gradations of religious actors and agents in the cults, see: Martzavou 2012b, 64–68.
50 Arnaoutoglou 2018, 268–269. The associations followed local civic norms for terminology, hierarchy, and regulation, which suggests that they did not operate wholly outside of civic control.
51 The associations were organized around the numbers nine and ten, but the principles of organization are unclear, that is, whether they met on the ninth day of the month (or every ninth day) and whether they donated one-ninth of their income to the sanctuary. Dunand (1973b, 174) associates the associations with initiation and thinks that membership must have required supplemental rituals; Bricault 2013, 293. Arnaoutoglou (2018, 256–257) seems to associate these groups with those who celebrate a monthly festival on the ninth or tenth day of the month. On associations at Dion and Delos, see: Hudson McLean 1996; Nigdelis 2010.
52 Dunand 1973b, 182–183; Alvar 2008, 227–230; Bricault 2013, 288. In some places the priest also headed associations that operated within his sanctuary, as in the case of Mennas, who served as priest in Sarapieion C in 156 BCE and as *synagogos* of the Sarapiasts, an association focused on Sarapis: Delos, Archaeological Museum inv. G 588a–g; IG 10 4, 1307; Bricault 2005, 225–226, cat. 202/0191.
53 Arnaoutoglou 2018, 268.
54 It is also possible that the *hypostoliasts* were named for a costume that they wore in particular rites. On the *stoliasts*, see: Dunand 1973b, 145, 153–154. Examples of *stoliasts*: Berlin, Antikensammlung inv. Sk 706; IG 3 140; IG 2/3 2, 4818; Bricault 2005, 20, cat. 101/0229, 2nd–3rd century CE. Martzavou (2018, 147) also points out that the language of the funerary inscription of Dionysia of Megalopolis, discussed at the beginning of this chapter, may describe someone who performed a similar function. *Hypostoliasts* from Eretria: IG 12 Suppl., 571; Bruneau 1975, 73–75, nos. 3, 112–114, plate 30; Bricault 2005, 46, cat. 104/0103. Found in the Iseion, dates to the beginning of the 2nd century BCE. Hypostoliasts from Demetrias: IG 9 2, 1107; Fraser 1960, 44, 54, no. 13; Dunand 1973b, 47–48; Bricault 2005, 126–127, cat. 112/0703. The Demetrias texts date to ca. 117 BCE and were found reused in the Church of the Panagia in Makrynitsa. *Hypostoliasts* from Amphipolis: Veligianni 1986; Bricault 2005, 169, cat. 113/0908; Veymiers 2009, 485–489. On the *hypostoloi* more generally, see: Malaise 2007. Even in this case, the costume seems to have been connected to the performance of a specific ritual action or priestly status, and recent work by Albersmeier (2018) does not identify this costume as characteristic of a particular subset of devotees; Malaise 2007, 309–319.
55 IG 4 2, 742; Bricault 2005, 37–38, cat. 102/0405. Similarly, in the Chronicle of Sarapieion A (IG 11 4, 1299, lines 47–49), the priest sings to the god daily.
56 Arnaoutoglou 2003, 271–272, App. II.
57 Arnaoutoglou 2018, 269–270, App. I. The attestations from Rhodes include IG 12 1, 165 (Rhodes Town, 2nd century BCE); IG 12 1, 157 (Rhodes Town, 1st century BCE); IG 12 4, 1027 (Kos, 1st century BCE); *NSill*

58. 493 = Bricault 2005, 409, cat. 204/1008 (Kos, Roman period); *SEG* 55, 1122*bis* (Knidos, 1st century BCE–1st century CE); *I.Lindos* 2, 391 (Lindos on Rhodes, 10 CE); *I.Lindos* 2, 392a (Lindos on Rhodes, 10 CE); *I.Lindos* 2, 392b (Lindos on Rhodes, 10 CE); Bricault 2014, cat. 201/0105.

58. Isiasts: Bricault 2005, 409, cat. 204/1008. Anoubiasts: *IG* 13 4, 2781; Bricault 2008, 301, cat. 204/1013; 1st century BCE, contra, Carbon 2016, 201. See: Veymiers 2018, 34. Rebillard (2010, 14–18) has argued that Oriental/mystery cults did not bury collectively in order to avoid conflict with the strong norm of burial with the familial group. As I argue in the section "Practicing Family and Community at Roman Dion" and in Chapter 5, however, there is evidence to suggest that, in many cases, familial identity and cultic identification were not in conflict, because whole families joined the cult or saw cultic identity as compatible with familial expressions of status. See also: Alvar 2018, 242–244. Rebillard's survey lumps Isiac cults in with Mithras and Cybele cult groups and does not directly address any Isiac evidence, including the two inscriptions I have highlighted here, or any inscriptions with similar phrasing (*horos thēkaiōn*) that clearly indicates a bounded area for burials assigned to an association. In the case of the Anubiasts, the burial area was overseen by a specific, named priest, Apollonios, son of Asklepiodoros – a requirement Rebillard applies to his analysis of Christian burials.

59. Bricault has collated the archaeological, epigraphic, and iconographic evidence for this ritual, including an Egyptian Anubis mask with eyeholes: Hildesheim, Pelizaeus-Museum inv. 1585. See: Bricault 2001a; Sfameni Gasparro 2018, 88–104. The idea that the Anubophores were actors hired to play the part cannot be discounted, though it seems unlikely.

60. *CIL* 12 1919 (destroyed); text dated to the first half of the 3rd century CE.

61. Voutiras 2005, 286; Nigdelis 2010, 17.

62. *SEG* 32, 167; Bricault 2005, 30, cat. 101/0402.

63. Apul., *Met.* 11.11: *cum dei dignati pedibus humanis incedere.*

64. *IG* 11 4, 1300 = Roussel 1915/1916, 50b; Bricault 2005, 220, cat. 202/0175. The plaque joins with *IG* 11 4, 1234 = *CE* 50a; Bricault 2005, 220, cat. 202/0173. The decree is an order of Osiris, dedicated to Zeus and Magna Mater, and put forth by Aristokydes, son of Demertos, and Artemon, son of Pytheas. Aristokydes is known elsewhere as an *oneirokritos* (dream-interpreter): Roussel 1915/1916, 74; *ID* 2041; Bricault 2005, 246, cat. 202/0218. Albersmeier (2018, 452–454) notes that most painted representations of devotees within sanctuaries show them in white clothing.

65. *ID* 2180; Roussel 1915/1916, cat. 16; Bricault 2005, 230, cat. 202/0199. Bricault favors a mid-2nd-century BCE date for this regulation because he interprets it as a response to a *senatus consultum* of 164 BCE (*ID* 1510). Chuvin and Yoyotte (1986, 59n77), on the other hand, date it to the beginning of the 1st century BCE based on prosopographical evidence. I disagree with Bricault's argument that women were excluded entirely from Sarapieion A after the *senatus consultum* as a way to heighten the sanctuary's prestige. Women appear as members of associations and as dedicators in mid-2nd-century to early 1st-century BCE inscriptions from Sarapieion A, including Nikaso, daughter of Hippokrates (*ID* 2116; Bricault 2005, 229–230, cat. 202/0197), and thus could not have been wholly excluded from the sanctuary. Nikaso's dedication mentions the same priest, Horos, son of Horos from Mount Casion, who is mentioned in *ID* 1510. Further, the fact that the text was inscribed on two separate plaques would suggest that together they marked out a particular space rather than the whole sanctuary, which had only one entrance.

66. *SEG* 28, 421; Bricault 2005, 42–43, cat. 102/1701. See also: Te Riele 1978; Lupu 2004, 205–213. Another inscription from 2nd-century BCE Priene states that the sanctuary must be purified, as a matter of routine, with the blood of a chicken. *I.Priene* no. 195; *SEG* 15, 688; Bricault 2005, 440–442, cat. 304/0802.

67. Lupu 2004, 212. See further: Alvar 2008, 177–192. Chaeremon describes a comparable rule on abstinence from sex and certain foods before certain festivals (Porph., *Abst.* 4.7), and temple personnel were similarly abstinent for up to nine days before certain rites (Sauneron 1962, 340–349).

68. *SEG* 22, 114; Oliver 1965; Bricault 2005, 29–30, cat. 101/0401.

69 Bøgh (2015, 278) argues that only initiates could enter, but such a law would be highly unusual.
70 See, for example, the many regulations on dress in the sacred law at Adania: Gawlinski 2011.
71 We might compare these regulations with the rules of the fasts traditionally observed during Ramadan and Lent in preparation for Eid al-Fatr and Easter.
72 Hudson McLean 1996, 186–194.
73 Bell 1992, 69–142; Alvar 2008, 216–221.
74 The following description is based on Apul., *Met.* 11.21–30 and relies in particular on the analyses of: Griffiths 1975; Alvar 2008, 336–343.
75 Bøgh 2015, 278–279. This calling seems to have driven Lucius to impatience: Keulen 2015.
76 Dunand 1973a, 57–58; Alvar 2008, 340–341. Alvar argues that a larnax dedicated to Osiris from the Thessaloniki Sarapeum (Thessaloniki, Archaeological Museum inv. MΘ 979, *IG* 10 2, 108, Bricault 2005, 139, cat. 113/0506) served as a ritual barque in a festival celebrating the reassembly of Osiris. Though Dunand does not connect this object with initiation rites, this object should probably be considered a cultic implement for the reenactment portion of the initiation rites, perhaps among others. On Osiris as a cosmic and solar deity, particularly in the New Kingdom, see among many others: Darnell 2004, 374–425; Spalinger 2008; Assmann 2009, 28, 61–62; Barrett 2011, 133–134; M. Smith 2017, 271–355.
77 Griffiths 1970; Heyob 1975, 57–59; Nielson 2002, 212–236.
78 Gasparini 2018, 716–722. Gasparini also notes that several Isiac sanctuaries throughout the Mediterranean are located near theaters, including the sanctuaries at Pompeii and Messene.
79 Alvar 2008, 341. The author argues that this section of the text relies on the oft-employed pun between *theos* and *thauma*: Elsner 2007, 289–300.
80 Dunand 1973b, 174–175.
81 Bremmer 2014, 113–114. Bremmer argues that there is no evidence of mystery rites prior to the 2nd century CE, but the literary and sculptural evidence surveyed here suggests otherwise. There may be some Egyptian precedent for the "mystery" aspect of Isiac cults. See Hornung 1994; Burkert 2002; Moyer 2011, 258–260; Barrett 2019, 309n243, 312n263.
82 Bithynia: *SEG* 28, 1585; Bricault 2005, 473, cat. 308/1201; Tralles: *I.Tralles* 86; Bricault 2005, 428, cat. 303/1301.
83 Rome: *CIL* 6 2244; Bricault 2005, 545, cat. 501/0165. Naples: *CIG* 3, 5793; Bricault 2005, 608–609, cat. 505/0165. Forum Popilii: *CIL* 11, 574; Bricault 2005, 636, cat. 512/0201.
84 Plut., *De Is.* 352c, ἀλλ' Ἰσιακός ἐστιν ὡς ἀληθῶς ὁ τὰ δεικνύμενα καὶ δρώμενα περὶ τοὺς θεοὺς τούτους, ὅταν νόμῳ παραλάβῃ, λόγῳ ζητῶν καὶ φιλοσοφῶν περὶ τῆς ἐν αὐτοῖς ἀληθείας.
85 Malaise and Veymiers 2018, 500. These include vv. 22–23 of the Maroneia hymn, or aretalogy: *SEG* 26, 821; Grandjean 1975, 17–21; Bricault 2005, 177–178, cat. 114/0202; vv. 10–12 of the Andros aretalogy: *IG* 12 5, 739; Bricault 2005, 362–368, cat. 202/1801; v. 22 of the Kyme aretalogy, a copy of which was found in the Thessaloniki Sarapeum: *I.Kyme* 41; Bricault 2005, 423–425, cat. 302/0204. A litany preserved in *P.Oxy.* 11, 1380 also uses the term *mystes*. These hymns are discussed at length in Chapter 3.
86 *IG* 10 2, 107, Bricault 2005, 138, cat. 113/0505, Thessaloniki, Archaeological Museum inv. MΘ 997; Despinis et al. 1997, vol. 1, 91–93, cat. 67; Bricault 2013, 429–431.
87 Voutiras 2005, 283–285; Malaise and Veymiers 2018, 504–505.
88 *IG* 10 2, 103, Bricault 2005, 156, cat. 113/0552. The base was originally an altar (Thessaloniki, Archaeological Museum inv. MΘ 986, first used about 35 BCE) and then rededicated in the 2nd century CE as a statue base dedicated by Folounios Oueros to Isis Orgia: Dunand 1973b, 174–175; Steimle 2004, 302–304; Steimle 2008, 103–106; Bricault 2013, 429–431.
89 See: Alvar 2008, 337–341.
90 Apuleius *Met.* 11.23, trans. Griffiths 1975. *Igitur audi, sed crede, quae vera sunt. Accessi confinium mortis et calcato Proserpinae limine per omnia vectus elementa remeavi, nocte media vidi solem candido coruscantem lumine; deos inferos et deos superos accessi coram et adoravi de proximo.* Variations of this story extend throughout Egyptian religious history, with the gods' names and functions changing according to the location and time period. In one strain of Egyptian belief,

the sun journeys across the sky during the day and is swallowed by the snake Apophis at night, thus arriving in the realm of the underworld. Either Osiris or Horus battles the snake, and their victory ensures the return of the sun at dawn. For a historical account of Egyptian solar religion during the New Kingdom, see: Assmann 2009.

91 On solarity in Egyptian religion and the adaptation of these concepts into Greek media, see: Corcoran 1995, 49–57; Dunand and Zivie-Coche 2004; Barrett 2011, 119–250.

92 Platt 2011, 13–14. Platt notes several instances in which human beings are either mistaken for or represented as epiphanies of the Greek gods. The situation here is much more complex, but we might note briefly the Platonic analogy between Isis and her role as a seeker of truth in Plutarch and the comparable role portrayed by Lucius in the *Metamorphoses*. See: Brenk 1999, 2005; Griffiths 1970, 70–74; Hani 1976.

93 Keulen 2015.

94 Bordieu 1977; Tweed 2008, 136–143.

95 Tweed 2008, 136–163.

96 Pandermalis 1982a, 729; 2016, 22.

97 The identification of the earlier temple is based on an archaicizing statue of Artemis Eilytheia that was discovered in the courtyard to the east of the altar, and an inscribed base dedicated to her (Dion, Archaeological Museum ΜΔ 427; inscription may read ΑΡΙΣΤΙΩ ΜΕΝΤΟΡΟΣ / ΑΡΤΕΜΙΔΙ ΕΙΛΕΙΘΥΙΑΙ. See: *SEG* 34, 629; Giuman 1999, 430; Bricault 2005, 133, cat. 113/0215; Pandermalis 1982a, 731; 2016, 112, cat. 28).

98 Pandermalis' excavations began in 1978 and concluded in 1984. Regarding the site's excavation history, see, with accompanying bibliography and abundant illustrations: Pandermalis 1982a; 1997, 24–29; 2000, 88–90; 2016, 22–24. He cites the presence of neat stacks of architectural elements under a stratum of mud approximately 30–40 cm deep as evidence for the community's attempts to repair the sanctuary between the earthquake and flood. My summary here relies both on Pandermalis' reports and my own visits in 2012, 2014, and 2019.

99 The family is quite large. They are attested at many sites throughout Greece, usually in small numbers, at Dion, Beroia, Thessaloniki, Herakleia Lyncestis, Styberra, Delos, Corinth, Lakonia, the Argolid, Arcadia, and Eleia. There are 164 mentions of the Anthestii at Rome, and 29 mentions in southern Italy, for a total of more than 240 mentions around the Mediterranean. For these references, see: Demaille 2008, 193–198. Other Italian families like the Salarii and the Herennii (discussed in the section "The Herennii") also moved from Delos to Macedonia, some with intermediate stops in Eretria: Martzavou 2010, 191–193.

100 Rizakis 2002, 110–114. Italian communities appear earlier in Thessaly and Epiros.

101 Rizakis 2002, 109–112.

102 Le Dinahet-Couilloud 1974, 86–87, no. 64.

103 Amphipolis, Archaeological Museum inv. L 1165; Veymiers 2009, 485–487, fig. 8. Rizakis (2003, 120n44) has argued that the Anthestii of Dion were descendants of Italian merchants who settled in the region during the Republican era, and it is possible their relatives included Anthestii at other Macedonian cities: Bricault and Versluys 2014b, 20–21.

104 *AE* 1998, 1209; *SEG* 34, 630–632; Bricault 2005, 131–133, cat. 113/0207–0212; Demaille 2008, 198–201. The dating of these inscriptions, particularly those in the Iseum, is problematic. Based on the archaeology of the site, it seems most likely that they would have been inscribed after the sanctuary's renovation in the Severan period. Others have argued for a 1st-century BCE to 1st-century CE date for these inscriptions (Rizakis 1998, 604; Brélaz and Demaille 2017, 127–128) because Amphio should have been precluded from holding local office due to the Lex Visellia of 24 CE. This earlier date would support a stronger link with the movement of *negotiatores* from Delos into Macedonia during the 1st century BCE, but Coles (2017) has pointed out that this law was not enforced uniformly throughout the empire. An earlier date would also mean that all of the inscriptions were moved from their original display locations. In my opinion, the placement of the Aphrodite Hypolympidia statue and its base, which I discuss later in this section, makes a 1st-century BCE or CE date less likely.

105 *AE* 1998, 1209; Pandermalis 1984, 276; Bricault 2005, 131, cat. 113/0207. Publius Anthestius Amphio held the offices of aedile, duumvir quinquennial, and augur: Bricault

2013, 187. Two other inscriptions naming the pair as dedicators were found outside the sanctuary. The first records the dedication of a shrine for Liber and the *colonia* by the couple: *AE* 1950, 20; *CIL* 3 2, 180; Makaronas 1937, 528, plate 1. The inscription was found about 100 m to the east of the theater in the excavations of the Temple of Zeus, along with a second that records a dedication of M. Pontius Iucundus to Liber Pater: *AE* 1950, 20; Makaronas 1937, 529–533, plate 2; Demaille 2008, 201n1. The second records Anthestia Iucunda's dedication of an altar to Diana and the *colonia*: *CIL* 3 2, 181; Pandermalis 1971, 402, pl. 197; Aupert 1976, 662; Demaille 2008, 202n7. The inscription was found reused in a tomb to the east of the theater.

106 Bricault separates the two texts in his corpus – the Greek: Bricault 2005, 132, cat. 113/0208; and the Latin: Bricault 2005, 132, cat. 113/0209. Others have published the two texts together: *SEG* 34, 630; *AE* 1998, 1207; Pandermalis 1984, 275–276.

107 Dion, Archaeological Museum inv. MΔ 4 +383; Pandermalis 2016, 112, cat. 29. See further: Pandermalis 1982a, 733–735; 1984, 275–276; 2000, 104–109; Pingiatolglu 2010, 189, fig. 5. The statue is a copy of the Tiepolo Aphrodite type discussed in: A. Stewart 2012, 288–298.

108 Pandermalis 2016, 112.

109 This cult is attested in a 3rd-century BCE statue base inscription that was found in the sanctuary of Isis-Tyche (constructed in the 3rd century CE), which may have been reused: *SEG* 34, 629; Pandermalis 1984, 275, fig. 2; Bricault 2005, 133, cat. 113/0215, plate 19; Pandermalis 1982a, 782.

110 *SEG* 34, 631; *AE* 1998, 675; Pandermalis 1984, 277; Bricault 2005, 132, cat. 113/0210.

111 *SEG* 34, 633; *AE* 1998, 1212; Pandermalis 1984, 277; Bricault 2005, 133, cat. 113/0213.

112 The statue is unpublished, but it is on display in the Dion Archaeological Museum, and photographs of the statue appear in: Pandermalis 1997, 77. A replica stands on the site where the original was found.

113 Van Bremen 2003, 313; Dillon 2010, 38–51.

114 Dillon (2010, 38–41) finds examples of this phenomenon dating back as early as the 4th century BCE in Athens. Most of these seem to honor priestesses or women who made other significant religious or financial contributions to the city.

115 Dillon 2010, 47–51.

116 Hatzfeld 1975, 41n2; Rizakis 2002, 125.

117 *IG* 10 2, 124; Bricault 2005, 143, cat. 113/0519. The inscription is in Greek and is dated to the reign of Marc Antony. Though the fragmentary nature of the inscription makes it impossible to determine its precise meaning, there is mention of a propylon (though it is unlikely, based on line breaks, that Marcus Herennius dedicated it), and several Greek male names with filiations are included in the list.

118 *IG* 10 2, 113; Bricault 2005, 145, cat. 113/0524. The inscription is in Greek.

119 See, with accompanying bibliography: Rizakis 2002, 125–126; 2003, 121–123.

120 *SEG* 34, 623; *AE* 1998, 1202; Pandermalis 1984, 273–274; Bricault 2005, 130–131, cat. 113/0204. Rizakis (2002, 125n79) identifies her as a relative of the Herennii and as the possible daughter of a *duumvir*. Rizakis also believes many of the inscriptions of the Anthestii and Herennii in the Iseum at Dion predate the renovations and were consequently rededicated.

121 Published and discussed in: Christodoulou 2011.

122 Revell (2016) has pointed to the tremendous variety in the style and form of these reliefs and argues that each cultic community may have used them in a manner more consistent with local cult practices than a universal Isiac cult. The precise meaning of the footprints is contested, and I deal more with this issue in Chapter 3.

123 *SEG* 34, 623; *AE* 1998, 1203; Pandermalis 1984, 273–274; Bricault 2005, 130, cat. 113/0203. The formula κατ'ἐπιταγήν appears in footprint reliefs from Beroia, Thessaloniki, and Maroneia, as well as another dedicated by Ignatia Herennia, a likely member of the Herenii. Beroia (1st century BCE): Bricault 2005, 135, cat. 113/0303. Thessaloniki: (1st century BCE–2nd century CE [?]) *IG* 10 2, 89; (2nd–3rd century CE) *IG* 10 2, 104; *IG* 10 2, 120. Maroneia (end of the 2nd century to the beginning of the 3rd century CE): *SEG* 48, 903.

124 *AE* 1998, 1205; Pandermalis 1984, 274; Bricault 2005, 131, cat. 113/0206. The inscription is in Greek. Hermanubis is attested in Thessaloniki and Delos. Thessaloniki (3rd

125 century CE): *IG* 10 2, 220. Delos: (103/2 BCE) dedication to Hermanubis Nikephoros, *ID* 2156; (93/2 BCE) text reconstructed as "Hermes-Anubis," *ID* 2162.

125 I count Ioulia Phrougiane Alexandra, whose portrait was displayed directly next to those of two Anthestiae and Gaios Hostios Philon, whose footprint relief was displayed atop a base dedicated by Herennia Pagilla, as proximal relations.

126 Dedications: *SEG* 34, 622, 626, 627; Pandermalis 1984, 273–274; Bricault 2005, 130–132, cat. 113/0201, 113/0202, 113/0218. On the epithet, see: Bommas 2002; Malaise 2005, 84–94, 150–151; Steimle 2008, 119–120.

127 *SEG* 34, 624; Bricault 2005, 133, cat. 112/0217.

128 Bricault 2008, 299, cat. 114/0210, col. II. 6–8 (siblings), 51–52 (father and son).

129 *I.Cos* EV 375; Bricault 2005, 406, cat. 204/1001.

130 *I.Cos* EV 278; Bricault 2005, 407, cat. 204/1003.

131 *CIG* 2, 1800; Bricault 2005, 120, cat. 111/0102.

132 Moyer 2011, 195–197; Mazurek 2016. The 4th-century date omits earlier instances of sanctuaries used by resident communities of Egyptian migrants, including the well-known mention of a 5th-century group discussed in: *IG* 2, 168; Bricault 2005, 3–4, cat. 101/0101. At Kamiros on Rhodes (ca. 249 BCE), the priest of Sarapis is listed sixth among the city's most powerful priesthoods: Bricault 2005, 381, cat. 204/0201; 2013, 141.

133 As recorded in an inscription of the end of the 3rd century BCE from Sarapieion A at Delos: *IG* 11 4, 1299; Bricault 2005, 195–198, cat. 202/0101. See: Bruneau 1973, 130–136; 1975, 280–283.

134 *IG* 12, Suppl., 562; Bruneau 1975, 72–73, no. 1; Bricault 2005, 46, cat. 104/0101. The sanctuary's first architectural phase dates to ca. 300 BCE.

135 Kavala, Archaeological Museum inv. Λ770, *Bull.* 1972, 265; Bricault 2005, 167–168, cat. 113/0901. Veymiers (2009, 476–478, figs. 4–5; 512, App. 1) argues that the letter forms suggest the inscription should not predate the second quarter of the 3rd century, a date that Bricault (2014) accepts.

136 Argos, Archaeological Museum inv. E 221; Bricault 2005, 39, cat. 102/0801; Veymiers 2011, 113–115, fig. 3.

137 Swetnam-Burland 2011; Albersmeier 2018, 449–458.

138 Stamatopoulou 2008.

139 *IG* 2, 168; *IG* 2/3 2, 337; Bricault 2005, 3–4, cat. 101/0101.

140 Mazurek 2016, 58–61.

141 Not all of these new foundations should be tied to the Delian diaspora. Sanctuaries at several sites have foundation dates in the 2nd century BCE, including Daulia and Tithorea in Phocis, Naupactus in Aetolia, Larissa in Thessaly, Thasos in Macedonia, Gortyna on Crete, as well as several shrines dedicated in Athens. On these sites, see the relevant sections in: Dunand 1973b. On this migration more specifically, see: Martzavou 2010; Gettel 2018.

142 Thessaloniki's sanctuary, for example, dates back to the 3rd century BCE, not long after the city's original foundation: Dunand 1973b, 54; Bommas 2002. Dunand also references a man named Phylakides, who is known from other dedications to Osiris, dedicating a ritual barque. Ritual barques are well known in Egyptian religion, which may suggest that Thessaloniki also had an Egyptian founding priest. Dunand, however, doubts the presence of an Egyptian founder because all of the earliest inscriptions for the cult are in Greek and feature Macedonian names.

143 Martzavou 2010, 187–189, figs. 1, 2.

144 *IG* 12 5, 912; Bricault 2005, 348, cat. 202/0604, after the 1st century BCE (?).

145 List of *navarchs*: *Bull.* 1969, 449; Bruneau 1975, 94–95, no. 15, plate 35.1; Bricault 2005, 54–55, cat. 104/0204.

146 A series of stelai listing the *navarchs*: *IG* 12 Suppl., 557, 1st century BCE; *IG* 12 Suppl., 558, 1st century BCE. A votive stele naming a *navarch*: *IG* 12 Suppl., 565, 1st century BCE.

147 A *trierarchos* named Aulos Anthestios was honored by another Isiac association for his excellence: Veligianni 1986; Bricault 2005, 169, cat. 113/0908.

148 *IG* 10 2, 83; Bricault 2005, 144, cat. 113/0521; Martzavou 2010, 191. On the Salarii, see: Martzavou 2010, 193; Bricault 2013, 150–151. On the *hydreion* of Sarapeion C of Delos, see: Siard 2007.

149 *IG* 10 2, 255; Bricault 2005, 150, cat. 113/0536. On the role of dream oracles in Isiac cults in Greece and Italy: Alvar 2008, 333–335; Renberg 2017, 330–392.

150 Bricault and Versluys 2014b, 23–25.
151 Moyer 2017, 321–324.
152 *IG* 10 2, 254 (Thessaloniki); *I.Kyme* 41 (Kyme); *IG* 12 5, 14 (Ios); Bricault 2005, 463, cat. 306/0201 (Telmessos, notice only); *SEG* 26 [1976], 821 (Maroneia); *IG* 12 5, 739 (Andros); Bricault 2008, cat. 113/1201 (Kassandreia). Many scholars include in the corpus the 1st-century CE account of Diodorus Siculus 1.27.3–4, which claims to be a translation of the original aretalogy from the Temple of Ptah at Memphis in the aretalogical canon as well: Žabkar 1988, 143–145. Isiac aretalogies are also known from the Temple of Isis, built by Ptolemy II at Philae, and the hymns of Isidorus from the temple of Renenutet at Narmouthis (modern Medinet Madi), sites in Egypt closely associated with Ptolemaic and Roman Imperial patronage: Vanderlip 1972; Žabkar 1988; Moyer 2016, 216–219.
153 *IG* 11 4, 1299; Bricault 2005, 191–192, cat. 202/0101 (Delos, to Sarapis); *IG* 12 5, 14; Bricault 2005, 59–60, cat. 104/0206 (Chalkis, to Harpokrates); and *CIG* 2, 3724; Bricault 2005, 470, cat. 308/0302 (Kios in Bithynia, to Anubis).
154 Pachis 2003, 105–110; Bricault 2013, 75–80; Moyer 2017, 320; Veymiers 2018, 29–31.
155 Martzavou 2012a, 267–269.
156 Moyer 2017. The Andros aretalogy also displays similarities in organization and punctuation but has been rendered in hexameters that necessitated some adaptations. Moyer argues that these six aretalogies all derive from a single Memphite text similar to the one described in Diodorus Siculus. The interest in punctuation may indicate a growing familiarity with Roman epigraphic norms.
157 Moyer 2017, 335–338.
158 Moyer 2011, 42–51. Gasparini and Gordon (2018) argue that there are nine distinct phases of "Egyptianisms" linked to particular historical contexts. By sketching the history of this trope, I attempt to give some chronological texture to the concept.
159 Barrett 2019, 302–315; Gasparini and Gordon 2018.
160 Sfameni Gasparro 2018. These modern definitions do not correspond with the Classical Latin *religio*, which focuses on repeated actions and efforts to serve or communicate with a god. Modern concerns about religion (as in "the sole true religion" or religious exceptionalism) and religions (the idea that there exist several religious traditions that are distinct from each other) do not apply here either, since Isiac devotees frequently participated in other normative forms of cult. See: J. Z. Smith 1998; Feil 1992.
161 Barrett 2019, 305–315. The evidence from other provinces has not yet been sufficiently studied to determine if these two regions are representative or if they reflect the two extremes of a spectrum.

CHAPTER 3

1 Moyer 2017.
2 Squire 2009, 2011; Platt 2011.
3 In order to reconstruct a cultic mode of viewing, I take a synchronic approach that prioritizes the Egyptian cults' consistency through time. I do not argue that the cult remained completely consistent across time and space, but that many of the same religious concepts remained relevant to Isiac devotees and continued to be replicated and reinterpreted by local communities from their beginnings well into the 3rd century CE. For the historical contingencies of Egyptianisms in these periods that may have mediated Greek perceptions of Egypt, see: Manolaraki 2013; Gasparini and Gordon 2018.
4 For example, on the role of epiphany in Greek and Roman experiences of cult images, see: Bremmer and Erskine 2010; Platt 2011, 256–287; Bussels 2012, 9–20.
5 Jennings 2011, 129–141; Pitts and Versluys 2015b, 14–17.
6 Versluys 2015, 155–158.
7 Swetnam-Burland 2015, 143.
8 Gruen (2011, 76–79) particularly highlights this aspect of Herodotus' account.
9 Vasunia 2001, 210–215. These sections provide Vasunia with the best fodder for constructing his postcolonial readings of Classical Greek texts.
10 Vasunia 2001, 240–247. Vasunia builds on the discussion in: Froidefond 1971, 337.
11 Hartog 1988, 212–259.
12 Vasunia 2001, 75–135.
13 On the concept of cultural ambivalence, see: Gruen 2011.
14 Moyer 2011, 42–83.

15 Vasunia 2001, 92–100.
16 τοῦτο δὲ ποιεῦσι οὕτω τοῦδε εἵνεκεν, ἵνα μὴ σφι οἱ ταριχευταὶ μίσγωνται τῇσι γυναιξί.
17 Lateiner 1989, 135–137.
18 Similarly, Herodotus assumes a disapproving tone when describing how Egyptian women bare their breasts during mourning (2.85.1). Lateiner 1989, 138.
19 Vasunia 2001, 95. See also: Hartog 1988, 212–214.
20 ὅτι πλεῖστα θωμάσια ἔχει ἢ ἡ ἄλλη πᾶσα χώρη καὶ ἔργα λόγου μέζω παρέχεται πρὸς πᾶσαν χώρην (Hdt. 2.35).
21 Diod. Sic. 1.23.2, 1.61.3, 1.69.4, 1.77.5, 1.79.4, 1.92.3, 1.96.1–4, 1.97.4–1.98.6.
22 This happens particularly frequently between Osiris and Dionysus, Isis and Demeter, and Zeus and Ammon (Diod. Sic. 1.11.3–4, 1.12.2, 1.12.3–4, 1.12.7, 1.13.3, 1.13.4, 1.14.3–4, 1.15.3, 1.15.6–7, 1.15.9, 1.96.4–5). See: Gruen 2011, 95.
23 Sfameni Gasparro 2018, 78–79.
24 Diodorus seems to have obtained the tale from the work of a certain Agroitas (Schol. Ap. Rhod. 1248). See: Burton 1972, 11–12. The episode is followed by a reference to Herakles' rescue of Prometheus, further embedding the narrative in the Greek mythological canon. See: Gruen 2011, 96.
25 Gruen 2011, 97–99.
26 Murray 1970, 150; Froidefond 1971, 231–353; Vasunia 2001, 183–246.
27 Muntz 2017, 197–205.
28 Muntz 2017, 200.
29 Muntz 2017, 204. This focus on legal institutions probably reflects Diodorus' own interest in the foundations of cities, laws, and great discoveries in the arts and sciences (as stated in 1.2.1).
30 Manolaraki 2013, 6.
31 Manolaraki 2013, 223–225.
32 Dio Cass. 51.16.5.
33 Strabo 17.1.10; Manolaraki 2013, 29–33.
34 Tib. 1.7.23–28; Bowditch 2011. We might add here Juv. 15, discussed in: Alston 1996, 100–103; Swetnam-Burland 2015, 167–181.
35 Swetnam-Burland 2010; 2015, 65–104; Mol 2017, 172–175; Versluys 2010. The importance of Egyptian imports is explored in: Pearson 2021.
36 Swetnam-Burland 2015, 63–104; van Aerde 2015, 63–183.
37 Van Aerde 2015, 284–296.
38 Manolaraki 2013, 121–132; Versluys 2013, 256; Barrett 2019, 25–28.
39 Tac., *Hist.* 4.82, Suet., *Vesp.* 7.1. On the sanctuary at Benevento, see: Müller 1969; Pirelli 2006; Clausen 2013. Regarding the Iseum Campanese, see Lembke 1994; Versluys 2002, 353–355; Brenk 2007a, 2007b; Bommas 2012; Petersen 2016.
40 The most notable exceptions are the wall paintings in Pompeii's Iseum. I discuss the concept of the Nilotic more thoroughly in Chapter 6. See further: Versluys 2002, 261–303; Merrills 2017, 106–149; Barrett 2019, 51–96.
41 Versluys 2002, 217–223.
42 Barrett (2019, 51–53) comments on the physiognomy and representation of these figures in greater detail.
43 Naples, Museo Archeologico Nazionale inv. 113195. See the discussion of the frescoes from this house in: Barrett 2019, 182–222.
44 Naples, Museo Archeologico Nazionale inv. 113196. It is worth noting that these scenes depict Egyptians in a more negative light than most other Nilotic frescoes do. Some examples, including the Nilotic border of the Alexander Mosaic in the Casa del Fauno, depict the Nile as an idyllic scene filled with plants and animals and empty of people: Merrills 2017, 52, 118, 131; Barrett 2019, 223–249.
45 Barrett 2019, 339–349.
46 Manolaraki 2013, 225–226. On Hadrian's connections with the Nile, especially as mediated through his relationship with Antinoos, see: Birley 1997, 235–258; Boatwright 2000, 190–203. On the Canopeum, see: Grenier 1989, 1999, 2008; Pensabene 2009; MacDonald and Pinto 1995, 107–116. On the Antinoeion, see: Mari 2004; Mari and Sgalambro 2007; Renberg 2010.
47 On the Platonic issues in the *De Iside et Osiride*, see: Froidefond 1987; Opsomer 1998, 2005; Brenk 1999, 2005; Richter 2001.
48 Griffiths 1970, 57–58.
49 Appadurai 1990; Versluys 2015, 153–158; Jennings 2017.
50 This chapter focuses on Isis' deterritorialization. The deterritorialization of Egypt is discussed in much more detail in Chapter 6.
51 Richter 2011, 209–215; Manolaraki 2013, 254–257.
52 On this dispute, see: Fraser 1960; Welles 1962. For a more recent bibliography, see: Bricault

53 and Versluys 2014b, 8–14; Malaise 2005, 127–138; Milleker 1985, 121–124.

53 Moyer questions Roussel's early 3rd-century BCE date for the inscription, arguing that Roussel's argument is based on now-overturned ideas about the accuracy of dating by letter form. He believes that the inscription's connection with a similar inscription dedicated to Nike should date the inscription more broadly to the end of the 3rd century through the first part of the 2nd century BCE, following Fraser, Engelmann, and Reger's broader picture of a 3rd-century Cyclades largely free of imperial hegemony. Roussel 1915/1916, no. 1, 71–78; Moyer 2011, 156–157; 2008, 101–103.

54 The Apollonios narrative is found at lines 1–28, and the Maiistas narrative at lines 29–94.

55 There are some examples of Greek priesthoods passed down along family or clan lines, such as the priesthoods controlled by the Eteoboutadai, the Praxiergidai, the Eumolpidai, and the Kerykes clans. Bubelis has argued that in some instances the Eumolpidai passed priesthoods through an *oikos*, but even in that case the priesthood seems to have followed from the oldest male relative in the *oikos* to the next oldest male relative rather than directly from father to son, much like the priesthood of Poseidon Isthmios at Halikarnassos (*SIG* 1020, ca. 240–140 BCE). See: Broadbent 1968, 23–27; Bubelis 2012.

56 Vallois 1944, 85, 93–95, 110; Dunand 1973b, 87–89; Moyer 2011, 195–200.

57 A similar or perhaps the same conflict is mentioned in a *senatus consultum* from 164 BCE (*ID* 1510, Roussel 1915/1916, cat. 14; Bricault 2005, 227–228, cat. 202/0195). According to this inscription, a Delian priest of Sarapis named Demetrios appealed to the Roman Senate after the Athenian government shut down his cult. The Roman Senate ruled in favor of the priest, commanding the Athenians to reinstate the cult. As Huzar (1961–1962) notes, this inscription marks an unusual instance of Roman intervention into the local administration of cults. See also Roussel 1915/1916, 310; 1913.

58 The exact nature of the dispute is unclear. Engelmann (1975, 24, 44) interprets the incident as an allegory for the battle between Seth and Osiris, which may underlie the presentation of the event. However, the fact that a *senatus consultum* was issued on the matter (see n. 57) argues for its primary purpose as a historical document. Other scholars have argued that the Sarapiastes did not legally buy the land: Vial 1984, 156. Perhaps the Sarapiastes failed to get permission to build a foreign sanctuary: Roussel 1915/1916, 251; Engelmann 1975, 44–45; Bruneau 1990, 562; Vial 1984, 156. Perhaps they encroached on a neighboring plot (Engelmann 1975, 45, 52) or evaded their taxes (Baslez 1977, 47–48).

59 Roussel 1915/1916, 19–23; Bruneau 1970, 457–466; 1973; Wild 1981, 34–36; Siard 1998; Kleibl 2007, 3–4; Barrett 2011, 131–134.

60 Moyer 2011, 195–197; Mazurek 2016.

61 On Amphipolis: *Bull.* 1972, 265; Bricault 2005, 167, cat. 113/0901; Kavala, Archaeological Museum inv. Λ770. On Demetrias: Volos, Archaeological Museum inv. Λ52, Stamatopoulou 2008. On Argos: Argos, Archaeological Museum inv. E 221; Bricault 2005, 39, cat. 102/0801; Veymiers 2011, 113–114.

62 Heynen 2006, 287–289; S. Jones 2010, 183–184.

63 S. Jones 2010, 181–182.

64 Heynen 2006, 289–290; Lowenthal 2013, 96–99, 117–122.

65 Lowenthal 1992, 187.

66 *IG* II 4 1299, lines 29–94; Bricault 2005, 195–198, cat. 202/0101.

67 A hymn for Anubis is known from Chios (Totti 1985, cat. 5), and a first-person aretalogy of Harpokrates is known from Chalkis (Totti 1985, cat. 6). There is also an iambic praise hymn for Isis known from Kyrene, but Moyer (2017, 318n1) has determined that the text is unrelated to the Greek examples.

68 Telmessos: unpublished, late Hellenistic period, notice in: Bricault 2005, 463, cat. 306/0201. Maroneia: end of the 2nd century BCE, *SEG* 26 (1976), 821; Grandjean 1975, 17–21. Andros: 1st century BCE–1st century CE, *IG* 12 5 739. Kyme: 1st century BCE–1st century CE, *I.Kyme* 41. Thessaloniki: 1st–2nd century CE, *IG* 10 2, 254. Kassandreia: 2nd century CE, Bricault 2008, 105–107, cat. 113/1201. Ios: 3rd century CE, *IG* 12 5, 14. *P.Oxy.* 1380 (98–136 CE) has also been identified as part of this corpus.

69 On the two types, see: Fowden 1986, 47–49; Papanikolaou 2009; Martzavou 2012a, 270–281.

70 Diod. Sic. 1.27.3–5, ca. 60–30 BCE. See further: Grandjean 1975, 10–15; Fowden 1986, 47–48.
71 Žabkar 1988.
72 Martzavou 2012a, 276–277.
73 Alvar 2008, 188–189; Martzavou 2012a, 276; Moyer 2017.
74 Platt 2011, 62–63, 72–76.
75 Festugière 1949.
76 On the spatial arrangement of these texts, see: Moyer 2016.
77 Isidorus, *Hymn* I.11–13, trans. Žabkar 1988, 137–138. ὅσσοι δὲ ζώουσι βροτοὶ ἐπ' ἀπείρονι γαίηι./ Θρᾶικες καὶ Ἕλληνες, καὶ ὅσσοι βάρβαροι εἰσι, / οὔνομά σου τὸ καλόν, πολυτίμητον παρὰ πᾶσι, / φωναῖσι φράζουσ' ἰδίαις, ἰδίαι ἐνὶ πάτρηι. / Ἀστάρτην Ἄρτεμίν σε Σύροι κλήζουσι Ναναίαν / καὶ Λυκίων ἔθνη {η} Λετοῦν καλέουσιν ἄνασ[σαν / Μητέρα δὴ κλήιζουσι θεῶν καὶ Θρήικες ἄνδρες, / Ἕλληνες δ' Ἥρην / μεγαλόθρονον ἠδ' Ἀφροδίτη[ν / καὶ Ἑστίαν ἀγαθήν, καὶ Ῥεῖαν, καὶ Δήμητρα, / Αἰγύπτιοι δὲ Θιοῦιν, ὅτι μούνη εἶ σὺ ἅπασα[ι / αἱ ὑπὸ τῶν ἐθνῶν ὀνομαζόμεναι θεαὶ ἄλλαι. Isidorus wrote his texts for a Greek audience and exhibits a wide knowledge of the Greek literary tradition. It is therefore appropriate to consider him part of the Greek canon of aretalogies: Fantuzzi 2004, 350–353, 360–363; Fowden 1986, 50; Sfameni Gasparro 2007, 51; Moyer and Dieleman 2010.
78 Richards 1999, 93–95. On immanence in Egyptian religion, see: Frankfort 1948, 23–29; Assmann 1997, I, 13–18. Though gods were not strongly connected to specific places in earlier periods, by the Late Period (712–323 BCE), most deities had a "home" temple(s) and were located more securely in Egyptian landscapes: Hornung 1982, 223–228.
79 Meskell 2003, 49–52.
80 Moyer 2016, 219. On Isis and the Egyptian landscape, see: Richards 1999; Assmann 2001; Meskell 2004, 90–92.
81 Versnel 1990, 35.
82 Alvar 2008, 161.
83 Versnel 1990, 1–38.
84 Albersmaier 2005, 310–311; Sfameni Gasparro 2007, 70–71; Heyob 1975, 39–51; Žabkar 1988, 46, 129–132.
85 Hassan 1928, 106–107; Hornung 1982, 164, 170, 232–234.
86 Hornung 1982, 49–57, 233–236. There are also references in Egyptian literature to gods living outside of Egypt, as in the Middle Kingdom *Tale of the Shipwrecked Sailor*.
87 Hornung 1982, 164, 170; Dousa 2002, 171; Barrett 2011, 316–319.
88 Kockelmann 2008, 79–80.
89 Kockelmann 2008, 68; Barrett 2011, 410.
90 Kockelmann 2008, 49–57. Kockelmann's texts date from the 2nd century BCE through the Roman period. Three are graffiti from Thebes, two are papyrus fragments, and one is an ostrakon.
91 Dousa 2002, 158–160.
92 *CIL* 10, 3800; Bricault 2005, 613, cat. 504/0601, which reads "*una quae es Omnia dea Isis.*" See further: Dousa 2002, 168–169.
93 *SEG* 26, 821; Bricault 2005, 176–178, cat. 114/0202. For commentary, see: Merkelbach 1976; Grandjean 1975.
94 Little is known of the Karamba area of Maroneia. No Egyptian sanctuary has been identified there. For a catalogue of Isiac finds in area, see the relevant plan in: Bricault 2001b. The inscription's date is contested. Grandjean and Bricault argue for a date in the second half of the 2nd century BCE, which is consistent with most of the other inscriptions for this site.
95 Grandjean 1975, 31–44.
96 Grandjean 1975, 44–46.
97 Solmsen 1979, 42–43; Žabkar 1988, 129–132; Versnel 1990, 35; Dousa 2002, 170–173.
98 Bricault 2005, 176–178, cat. 114/0202 = *IThrace* 205; adapted from a translation by G. H. R. Horsley. αὕτη μεθ' Ἑρμοῦ γράμμαθ' εὗρεν | καὶ τῶν γραμμάτων ἃ μὲν ἱερὰ τοῖς μύσταις, ἃ δὲ δημόσια | τοῖς πᾶσιν. αὕτη τὸ δίκαιον ἔστησεν, ἵν' ἕκαστος ἡμῶν || ὡς ἐκ τῆς φύσεως τὸν θάνατον ἴσον ἔσχεν, καὶ ζῆν ἀπὸ τῶν | ἴσων εἰδῆι· αὕτη τῶν ἀνθρώπων οἷς μὲν βάρβαρον, οἷς δ' ἕλλη|νίδα διάλεκτον ἔστησεν, ἵν' ἦι τὸ γένος διαλλάσσον μὴ μό|νον ἀνδράσιν πρὸς γυναῖκας ἀλλὰ καὶ πᾶσι πρὸς πάντας. | σὺ νόμους ἔδωκας, θεσμοὶ δ' ἐκαλοῦντο κατὰ πρώτας· τοι || [γα]ροῦν αἱ πόλεις εὐστάθησαν, οὐ τὴν βίαν νομικὸν ἀλλὰ | [τ]ὸν νόμον ἀβίαστον εὑροῦσαι. σὺ τιμᾶσθαι γονεῖς ὑπὸ | [τ]έκνων ἐποίησας, οὐ μόνον ὡς πατέρων, ἀλλ' ὡς καὶ θεῶν | [φ]ροντίσασα· τοιγαροῦν ἡ χάρις κρείσσων ὅτε τῆς φύσε|ως τὴν ἀνάγκην καὶ θεὰ νόμον ἔγραψεν.
99 Hall 2002, 172–226. Looking towards later periods in Greek antiquity, see: Sartre 2005;

100 Mattingly 2014, 37; Richter 2011; Müller 2016.
100 See, for example, Swain 1996, 17–101; Whitmarsh 2001, 41–56; Richter 2011, 135–147; Spawforth 2011, 59–86. Gleason's emphasis on language is directed through a study of bodily comportment and culturally encoded gender ideals. See, in particular: Gleason 1995, 29–54.
101 This phenomenon is particularly evident in the biography of Favorinus, whose Latin and Greek were mocked by other Second Sophistic gatekeepers. On the problem of ethnicity and language acquisition, see Gell., NA 1.2.3–9, 1.10; Whitmarsh 2001, 90–130.
102 RICIS 114/0202 = IThrace 205. Adapted from a translation by G. H. R. Horsley. σοὶ πρὸς κατοίκησιν | Αἴγυπτος ἐστέρχθη. σὺ μάλιστα τῆς Ἑλλάδος ἐτίμησας τὰς | Ἀθήνας· κεῖθι γὰρ πρῶτον τοὺς καρποὺς ἐξέφηνας· Τριπτόλε|μος δὲ τοὺς ἱεροὺς δράκοντάς σου καταζεύξας ἁρματοφο|ρούμενος εἰς πάντας Ἕλληνας διέδωκε τὸ σπέρμα· τοιγαροῦν | τῆς μὲν Ἑλλάδος ἰδεῖν σπεύδομεν τὰς Ἀθήνας, τῶν δ' Ἀθη||νῶν Ἐλευσῖνα, τῆς μὲν Εὐρώπης νομίζοντες τὴν πόλιν, τῆς | δὲ πόλεως τὸ ἱερὸν κόσμον.
103 The similarities between the Eleusinian Mysteries and Isiac rituals have been noted: Alvar 2008, 11–12, 56–59; Martzavou 2012b.
104 On Middle Platonic intellectuals, see: Dillon 1996. Individual thinkers are known to us mostly through Philostratus' *Lives of the Sophists* and references in Aulus Gellius' *Attic Nights*. See further: Eshleman 2012.
105 See the introduction to Chapter 2 and and the beginning of the section "Constructing Groupness" regarding the scholarly controversies surrounding the use of Apuleius as a source for Isiac religion. Scholars agree that the passage here reflects knowledge of Isiac aretalogies.
106 Apul., *Met.* 11.5.
107 Apul., *Met.* 11.2; adapted from the translation by: Griffiths 1975, 71–73. *Regina caeli, sive tu Ceres alma frugum parens originalis, quae, repertu laetata filiae, vetustae glandis ferino remoto pabulo, miti commonstrato cibo, nunc Eleusiniam glebam percolis; seu tu caelestis Venus, quae primis rerum exordiis sexuum diversitatem generato amore sociasti et aeterna subole humano genere propagato nunc circumfluo Paphi sacrario coleris; seu Phoebi soror, quae partu fetarum medelis lenientibus recreato populos tantos educasti praeclarisque nunc veneraris delubris Ephesi; seu nocturnis ululatibus horrenda Proserpina, triformi facie larvales impetus comprimens terraeque claustra cohibens, lucos diversos inerrans vario cultu propitiaris...quoquo nomine, quoquo ritu, quaqua facie te fas est invocare.*
108 Holliday 2015, 214; Pond Rothman 1975, 22. This tendency continues into Christian art. The sarcophagus of Junius Bassius (4th century CE [?]), for example, features a scene connecting Caelus with the transfer of power from Christ to Peter: Elsner 2003, 82–84.
109 *Met.* 11.5.1: *deorum dearumque facies uniformis*. The whole speech runs through *Met.* 11.5–6.
110 Bradley 2012, 126–146.
111 On the earlier Platonic tradition, see: Vasunia 2001, 216–248.
112 The date of the text is controversial, with some arguing for a date as late as 125–130 CE: Jannoray 1946. Others suggest a date closer to 100–115: Babut 1999, 178, 181; Stadter 1999, 174n4. Griffiths and Brenk agree that the text should be dated to the years just before 120 CE. Brenk, however, believes the text belongs to the latter years of Trajan's reign, while Griffiths is inclined to date it to the beginning of Hadrian's: Griffiths 1970, 16–17; Brenk 2002, 77.
113 Alvar 2008, 39–51; Dunand 1973b, 39–40; Griffiths 1970, 47–51.
114 Plut., *De Is.* 372e–f; Karamanolis 2014.
115 Plutarch 1936, 41 n. a. See also: Alvar 2008, 41–60; Babut 1999.
116 Vasunia 2001, 75–109; Richter 2011, 206–235.
117 Froidefond (1987, 116) believes that Isis' role as the rebuilder of Osiris' body brings her closer to the Platonic definition of the Demiurge. O'Brien (2015, 101–102) agrees that Plutarch's formulation of Isis does not strictly follow Plato's formulation in the *Timaeus*, but rather fulfills the role of Demiurge in Plutarch's cosmology because Plutarch believes the World Soul exists in matter. O'Brien also argues that Isis fulfills portions of the role of the immanent Logos and the Receptacle in Platonic thought, creating an innovative, eclectic philosophical character.
118 Plut., *De Is.* 373b: ὅν ἡ Ἶσις εἰκόνα τοῦ νοητοῦ κόσμου αἰσθητὸν ὄντα γεννᾷ.
119 Plut., *De Is.* 372f, 373a–b. This definition of the receptacle comes from Pl., *Tim.* 49c6–7,

120 Plut., *De Is.* 372d-e: ὅθεν καὶ τῶν ἀγαλμάτων αὐτῆς τὰ μὲν κερασφόρα τοῦ μηνοειδοῦς γεγονέναι μιμήματα, τοῖς δὲ μελανοστόλοις ἐμφαίνεσθαι τὰς κρύψεις καὶ τοὺς περισκιασμοὺς ἐν οἷς διώκει ποθοῦσα τὸν ἥλιον.

121 Plut., *De Is.* 372e: ὑπὸ δὲ τῶν πολλῶν μυριώνυμος κέκληται, διὰ τὸ πάσας ὑπὸ τοῦ λόγου τρεπομένη μορφὰς δέχεσθαι καὶ ἰδέας. See also: Bricault 2006b.

122 Plut., *De Is.* 372f: εἰκὼν γάρ ἐστιν οὐσίας ἐν ὕληι.

123 Hani 1976; Richter 2001; Brenk 2001, 2005; Platt 2011, 81–85.

124 Richter 2001.

125 Platt 2011, 12–13. Vout (forthcoming) has argued that the accretion of ideal images within sanctuaries contributed to their overall sense of sacredness and experience of encountering the divine.

126 Platt 2011, especially 135–169.

127 Brenk 1999; Richter 2001; Sfameni Gasparro 2007; Dousa 2002; Malaise 2005, 15–19.

128 The only cult that approaches the level of frequency observed in the Greek cults is that of Asklepios. See: Moyer 2011, 165; Alvar 2008, 333–335; Renberg 2017. More traditional types of oracles also inspired the foundation of Egyptian cults in Greece. At Istros, for example, the city used a Greek oracle at Kalchedon to determine whether to found a sanctuary of Sarapis: Istria, Archaeological Museum inv. 378, 3rd century BCE; *SEG* 24 (1969), 1091; Bricault 2005, 741, cat. 618/1101.

129 Renberg 2017, 330–392. See also Moyer 2011, 165–174; Alvar 2008, 331–335. On dreams more generally in Greek and Roman literature, see: Platt 2011, 254–287; Renberg 2017.

130 Moyer 2011, 165–168.

131 *IG* 11 4, 1299, lines 29–94.

132 Dunand 1973b, 79–82. The interventionist aspect may not have been as important on Crete, but several inscriptions demonstrate that this trait was highly valued at Thessaloniki and other Egyptian cult centers in Greece.

133 The Maiistas Chronicle includes several pieces of key information, such as the Memphite origins: Apollonios (I)'s and the cult's early foundation in Apollonios (I)'s home, omitted in Apollonios (II)'s more terse account: Moyer 2011, 158.

134 The author was probably a devotee of Sarapis, whose limited Greek made extensive use of Homeric idioms: Engelmann 1975, 25–57.

135 καὶ γάρ τ'ἀμφιαλεῖ Δήλωι ἀρίσημα τέλεσσας / τἀπολλωνίου ἱρὰ καὶ εἰς μέγαν ἤγαγες αἶνον (lines 35–36).

136 Dream oracles and nocturnal visitation are common forms of interaction between divinities and mortals in most ancient religions, but they appear to be especially common in the Egyptian cults during the early Hellenistic period. Regarding dream oracles in the ancient Near East, see: Oppenheim 1956. For Egypt, see: Sauneron 1959. For Greco-Roman instances, see: Hanson 1980; van Straten 1976; Renberg 2017, 330–392.

137 *IG* 11 4, 1299, lines 43–46. These lines are fragmentary, and Engelmann reconstructs them with the problematic term ΑΝΤΙΠΑΤΡΟΙΟ, referring to the man erecting the statue. He opts to follow Merkelbach in arguing that ἀντίπατρος meant the son who succeeds his father in performing a sacred duty, which Moyer and others believe was a common practice on Delos and in Egypt: Engelmann 1975, 32–36; Moyer 2011, 161–165. Renberg (2017, 390n157) does not consider this an instance of ritual incubation because he believes the priest's home and the sanctuary are separate, which is to misunderstand the urban context in which the sanctuary stood. For a reasoned interpretation of the two-statue problem, see: Wilhelm 1934.

138 *IG* 11 4, 1299, lines 56–59, following: Moyer 2011. ἔγρεο· Βαῖνε δὲ μέσσα παστάδος ἀμφὶ θύρευθρα καὶ εἴσιδε γράμμα τυπωθέν τυτθῆς ἐκ βύβλοιο τό σε φρονέοντα διδάξει ὅππηι μοι τέμενος τεύχηις καὶ ἐπικλέα νειόν.

139 Moyer (2011, 169) argues the note may reference Egyptian ticket oracles. See also: Frankfurter 2010, 538–539.

140 *IG* 11 4, 1299, lines 77–80, following: Moyer 2011: μέθες ἄλγος ἀπὸ φρενός· οὔ σέ τις ἀνδρὸς ψῆφος ἀϊστώσει, ἐπεὶ εἰς [ἐ]μὲ τείνεται αὐτόν ἥδε δίκη, τὴν οὔτις ἐμεῦ περιώσιον ἄλλος ἀνὴρ αὐδήσει, σὺ δὲ μηκέτι δάμναο θυμόν.

141 Apollonios and his family likely housed the early versions of the cult in their own home,

142 rendering the sanctuary itself the location of the divine encounter: *IG* 11 4, 1299, lines 14–16. Kleibl (2009, 211–213) notes that the second sanctuary was built over a private home and may have been directly connected to another.

142 Versnel 1990, 1–30; Zanker 2004, 84–99; Squire 2009; Platt 2011, 52–69.

143 τοῦ δ'ἱεροῦ τοὔνομα καὶ σαφῶς ἐπαγγέλλεται καὶ γνῶσιν καὶ εἴδησιν τοῦ ὄντος· ὀνομάζεται γὰρ Ἰσεῖον ὡς εἰσομένων τὸ ὄν, μετὰ λόγου καὶ ὁσίως εἰς τὰ ἱερὰ παρέλθωμεν τῆς θεοῦ.

144 Griffiths 1970, 70–74; Elsner 1995, 41–47; Brenk 2002, 80–81; 2005, Richter 2001; Zanker 2004.

145 On the ear reliefs, see the catalogue in: Gasparini 2016. For footprints, see the relevant entries in: Dunand 1973b; Tzanavari 1993; Christodoulou 2011.

146 See: Gasparini 2016, 566–570, cat. 2–14.

147 Dunand 2000, 90; Gasparini 2016, 556–557.

148 Gasparini 2016, 559–561. On the performance of aretalogies at Kyme, see: Martzavou 2012a, 276.

149 Castiglione 1971; Dunbabin 1990; Christodoulou 2011, 18–22; Takács 2014; Revell 2016. It is unlikely that enough evidence will arise to solve this problem entirely, and at this point their interpretation is a matter of scholarly opinion.

150 Revell 2016.

151 Thessaloniki: Archaeological Museum inv. MΘ 1955: *IG* 10 2, 104; Bricault 2005, 162, cat. 113/0566. Dion: Archaeological Museum inv. MΔ 419, 420, 422, 424; Christodoulou 2011, 18–22. Also, from Thessaloniki: Archaeological Museum inv. MΘ 1955; Despinis et al. 1997–2010, cat. 322. On the different interpretations, see: Christodoulou 2011, 21–22 n. 80, 84 with accompanying bibliography.

152 Takács (2014) and Platt (2011, 11–30) highlight the importance of visual representations and visualizations for epiphanic experience, providing a second dimension through which we can read these reliefs.

153 This version of the index derives on Charles Peirce's initial 19th-century definition. On Peirce's semiotic thought, see: Atkin 2013.

154 Meyer 2017.

155 Platt 2011, 124–169.

156 Bianchi 2011. Tran tam Tinh's *LIMC* article (1990) on Isis, which defines Isis' iconography in a limited and hypercategorized manner, focuses almost exclusively on objects from Italy and Alexandria and is now out of date.

157 Tran tam Tinh 1986, 364; Malaise 2005, 194–195.

158 Mol 2015b; Mazurek 2016.

159 Malaise 2005, 193–197; Elsner 1995, 25–47; Squire 2009, 223–229.

CHAPTER 4

1 One notable exception is a basalt statuette from Hellenistic Delos found in Sarapieion C that featured a hieroglyphic inscription. Though the inscription details a musician's life and identifies the subject as a woman, it is possible that devotees would have seen this statuette as a representation of Isis or another Egyptian goddess. See: Hauvette-Besnault 1881, 313–316; Roussel 1915, 65; Leclant and de Meulenaere 1957; Marcadé 1969, 409; Barrett 2011, 335.

2 Mylonopoulos 2016; Mazurek 2020a. Though Anubis and other deities are mentioned in inscriptions, there is only one known image of Anubis from Roman Greece. The headless example from Gortyna (Iraklion, Archaeological Museum inv. H411, 2nd-century CE adaptation of the 4th-century BCE Richelieu Hermes type; Romeo and Portale 1998, 104–106, cat. 16, plate 7c) depicts the god assimilated to known types of Hermes. If this example follows the roughly contemporary Hermanubis now in the Vatican Museum (from Anzio, 2nd century CE, Vatican Gregorian Egyptian Museum inv. 22840), it may have had an animal head.

3 Many scholars have discussed how sculptors integrated Greek styles into their representations of Isis. See, in particular: Malaise 1972a, 176–181; Tran tam Tinh 1990, 790–795; Bianchi 2011; Plantzos 2011; Mylonopoulos 2016.

4 Malaise 2009; Malaise and Veymiers 2018, 486–492.

5 As I demonstrate in Chapter 5, using Isiac cult costume was an effective way to stand out in the broader landscape of Greek funerary portraiture. Greek colonies in Egypt adopted and adapted Egyptian gods as early as the 6th century BCE. See, with relevant bibliography: Bricault 2006a, 77–83.

6 Scott 2013, 110–136; Mol and Versluys 2015; Hodos 2015; Versluys 2015.
7 This definition is derived from: Brubaker 2004, 34–35, 44–46; Gordon 2013, 149–151.
8 Studying the construction of individual selves in antiquity is difficult, and my use of the term here does not presume that we can access this level of cognition. Rather, I am considering the production of a collective self and subjectivity that resulted from a person's engagement with the cult's rituals, texts, and material culture: Gordon 2013, 146.
9 Gordon 2013, 146–151. My reading of Egyptian religion works from the assumption that many of those who held high-level priesthoods and dedicated sanctuaries were civic and cultural elites familiar with the contemporaneous theological and philosophical debates going on in Athens. See Chapter 2; see also: Alvar 2008, 233–238; Almagor 2013; Gordon 2013, 148–149; Stone 2014, 158–160; Mazurek 2018.
10 Brubaker 2004, 42.
11 Busts were also popular for both deities, but I have elected to omit them here in the interest of brevity. For a fuller survey of Sarapis' types, see: Clerc and Leclant 1994.
12 Iraklion, Archaeological Museum inv. 259. From the *cella* of the Egyptian sanctuary at Gortyna on Crete: Oliverio 1914; Dunand 1973a, 73–82; Tran tam Tinh 1983, 13–16; Romeo and Portale 1998, 33–37; Kleibl 2007, 231–234.
13 Tran tam Tinh 1983, ch. 1.
14 Neither of these attributes would be inappropriate to another deity but seem to appear most frequently in representations of Sarapis.
15 Marble relief of Sarapis *debout* with Artemis of Ephesus: Bricault 2005, 437, cat. 304/0612; Clerc and Leclant 1994, no. 175; Tran tam Tinh 1983, inv. 4B 2, fig. 121. Another marble relief from the baths of Ephesus includes an image of Sarapis *debout* alongside Isis, Anubis, Harpokrates, and Cybele: *I.Ephesos* 5, no. 573; Bricault 2005, 438, cat. 304/0614. A calcite base with Sarapis *debout* and Isis from Xanthos: Kater-Sibbes 1973, no. 417; Tran tam Tinh 1983, no. 3, fig. 93; Clerc and Leclant 1994, no. 125a.
16 Athens, National Archaeological Museum inv. 4546; Machaira 2000, 247, fig. 4.
17 Statue of Sarapis-Neptune: *CIL* 8 1002 = 12462; Tran tam Tinh 1983, no. 45; Bricault 2005, 757, cat. 703/0102. Statue of Sarapis (figure 21): Tunis, Bardo Museum inv. C922; Kater-Sibbes 1973, no. 738; Tran tam Tinh 1983, 246; no. 54, fig. 262; Clerc and Leclant 1994, no. 69.
18 Tran tam Tinh 1983, 1B 24, fig. 38, 1B 25, fig. 39.
19 Relief depicting Isis and Sarapis: Dunand 1973a, plate 44; Tran tam Tinh 1983, 151–152, no. 35, fig. 94; Clerc and Leclant 1994, no. 125b.
20 Athens, National Archaeological Museum inv. 4546; Kater-Sibbes 1973, cat. 357; Tran tam Tinh 1983, cat. 22, fig. 76.
21 Thessaloniki, Archaeological Museum inv. MΘ 837, 1st century BCE; Voutiras 2012.
22 Tran tam Tinh 1983, cat. 310, fig. 100.
23 Athens, Agora Museum inv. S 1068, dated generally to the Roman period. See: Martens 2015.
24 Tran tam Tinh 1983, no. 63, fig. 291.
25 Aghii Deka, Apotheke inv. GO 201, 2nd-century CE. Oliverio 1914, 376; 1915, 309; Romeo and Portale 1998, 112–114, cat. 18, plate 8c; Karetsou and Andreadaki-Vlazaki 2000, 441, cat. 510.
26 Romeo and Portale 1998, 109–115, cat. 17–18.
27 Delos, Archaeological Museum inv. A 1990 +A 2003; Marcadé 1969, 427, plate 58.
28 Nearly all examples of the seated Sarapis type depict the god raising his left arm, almost certainly to hold a scepter. For examples, see: Clerc and Leclant 1994, cat. 1–19.
29 Delos, Archaeological Museum inv. A 1936; Marcadé 1969, 427, plate 58; inv. A 1990 +2003; Roussel 1915, 45, no. 2; Marcadé 1969, 427, plate 58.
30 On display outside of the Archaeological Museum of Corinth. Johnson 1931, 30–31; Kater-Sibbes 1973, cat. 468; D. E. Smith 1977, 218.
31 Cambridge, UK, Fitzwilliam Museum inv. GR.87.1907; Budde and Nicholls 1964, 30, cat. 55, plate 18.
32 Olympia, Archaeological Museum inv. Λ171; Kater-Sibbes 1973, cat. 489.
33 Amphipolis, Archaeological Museum inv. Λ75; Bommas 2005, 68, no. 133; Veymiers 2009, 504–506.
34 Rhodes, Archaeological Museum inv. Γ2772; Fantaoutsaki 2011, 56–57, fig. 14.
35 Tran tam Tinh 1983, 1–5. The cult's origins are similarly fraught with historical and theological arguments, and the bibliography

surrounding the topic is massive. For our purposes, the cult's theological and historical origins are less important than its artistic and geographical ones, but I refer the curious reader to: Fraser 1960; Welles 1962. For a more recent bibliography, see: Milleker 1985, 121–124; Malaise 2005, 127–138; Bricault and Versluys 2014b, 8-19.

36 The principal literary sources are Tac., *Hist.* 4.83–84; Plut., *De Is.* 361f–362a; Clem. Al., *Protr.* 4.48; Rufinus, *Historia Ecclesiastica* 2.23. More dubious is the claim in Pseudo-Callimachus, in ca. 200 CE (*vit. Alex.* 1.33), that the cult of Sarapis was founded by Alexander. Most scholars writing after the 1980s omit this account from the canon of foundational narratives and the cult's early history, probably because the Alexandrian sanctuary to Sarapis cannot predate Ptolemy I. All of these sources significantly postdate the proposed date of the cult's image, which Tran tam Tinh (1983, 1) suggests would have been produced in the late 4th century or early 3rd century BCE.

37 Tac., *Hist.* 4.84.5; Amelung 1903, 177–179.

38 Barat 2010, 35–36, fig. 3.1. The figurine was found with other fragmentary terracottas, including a fragment of a Kore or Isis figurine, next to a building identified as a temple of Sarapis dating to the Hellenistic or Roman period.

39 For example, Pollitt (1990, 91–92) includes Clement's testimony in his standard handbook of Greek artists as evidence for Bryaxis' major works.

40 Stambaugh 1972; Tran tam Tinh 1983; Clerc and Leclant 1994.

41 Stambaugh 1972, 27–35; Mylonopoulos 2016, 116 n. 42.

42 Perry 2005, 112–149; Touchette 2015, 297–305.

43 Mylonopoulos 2016, 106–107, 116–117.

44 Bricault 2001a, 8. See also: Martens 2015.

45 Gauckler and Poinssot 1910, 43, no. C922, plate 23, 1; Kater-Sibbes 1973, no. 738; Tran tam Tinh 1983, no. V4, fig. 262.

46 For example, the marble statuette of Asklepios from Tivoli, now in the Vatican, or the example in Athens (National Archaeological Museum inv. 704; Berger 1982, 66–71).

47 For example, the Egyptian gods of Sarapieion C on 2nd-century BCE Delos received the same types of sacrificial gifts as Asklepios, and it is possible that the two sanctuaries competed for patients: Siard 2009, 159–161. Similarly, in an example to be discussed further in the section "Ideal Sculptures in the Thessaloniki Sarapeum," Voutiras (2012) compares a 1st-century BCE statuette of Sarapis from Thessaloniki (Thessaloniki, Archaeological Museum inv. MΘ 837) to a pair of roughly contemporary statuettes from the Asklepios sanctuary at Marrylos.

48 Bricault and Versluys 2014b, 16-22.

49 Eingartner 1991, 10–32; Nagel 2015; Albersmeier 2018; Malaise and Veymiers 2018.

50 Nagel 2015, 202–203. This difference is reflected in literature as well: Bricault 2004, 549.

51 Delos, Archaeological Museum inv. A2399; Marcadé 1969, 228n4. Additional examples: Delos, Archaeological Museum inv. A 5370, A 5302, A 5373; Marcadé 1969, 432, plate 57. There is also a cult statue of Isis *du Cynthe* still on site in Sarapieion C, dated through epigraphic evidence to 128/127 BCE (*ID* 2044).

52 (1) Rhodes, Archaeological Museum inv. Γ2765, mid-Hellenistic period; Fantaoutsaki 2011, 56–57, fig. 13; Mazurek 2020a, 187, fig. 41. (2) London, British Museum inv. Sc. 2150, ca. 150 BCE; Eingartner 1991, 112–113, cat. 7, fig. 8. (3) Rhodes, Archaeological Museum inv. Γ58, end of the 2nd century or beginning of the 1st century BCE; Gualandi 1976, 67n7; Machaira 2011, 81, cat. 50, plates 64–65. (4) Rhodes, Archaeological Museum inv. Γ2547/B.E. 916; Machaira 2011, 81, cat. 51, plate 66. Gualandi (1976, 165–166, cat. 160, fig. 199) identifies Rhodes Archaeological Museum inv. E425 (dated to the second half of the 2nd century BCE) as Isis, but Machaira (2011, 82, cat. 52, plate 67) argues that it is a nymph.

53 Iraklion, Archaeological Museum inv. ΓΛ. 1116, end of the 2nd century BCE; Karetsou and Andreadaki-Vlazaki 2000, 433–434, cat. 503.

54 Athens, National Archaeological Museum inv. 224, 2nd century BCE; Machaira 2000, 246, fig. 2.

55 Kavala, Archaeological Museum inv. Λ195, mid-2nd century–1st century BCE; Damaskos 2013, 98, cat. 95, plates 204–207; Mazurek 2020b.

56 In relief, from a round altar depicting several Egyptian gods: Eingartner 1991, 110–111, cat. 3, figs. 3–4.

57 Athens, National Archaeological Museum inv. 1617, late 2nd century to early 3rd century CE; Walters 1988, 83, 104–105, plate 34c–d; Eingartner 1991, 121, cat. 31, plate 23; Romiopoulou 1997, no. 104; Kaltsas 2002, 361, cat. 771. Eingartner (1991, 21–23) compares the statue with examples from the Louvre, Lakonia, and the Porta Latina at Rome. Based on the context of its closest comparanda, the Sparta example probably depicts the goddess rather than a devotee.

58 Iraklion, Archaeological Museum inv. ΓΛ. 314, 120–130 CE; Karetsou and Andreadaki-Vlazaki 2000, 436, cat. 506.

59 Dion, Archaeological Museum inv. ΜΔ 410; Christodoulou 2011, 11–16.

60 Fragment of a white marble *Knotenpalla*, preserving only the torso with the knot and remnants of Isis' curled locks; unpublished, on display in the Archaeological Museum of Philippi, 2nd century CE.

61 Marathon, Archaeological Museum inv. 438, mid-2nd century CE; Dekoulakou 2010, 114–116, figs. 11–14; 2011a, 31, fig. 7; Mazurek 2018, 628–629, figs. 22–24.

62 A similar statuette of Anubis, in which he has the body of Hermes, comes from the Sanctuary of the Egyptian Gods at Gortyna and dates to the Antonine period: Iraklion, Archaeological Museum inv. 411; Romeo and Portale 1998, 104–109, cat. 16, plate 7c.

63 Rethymno, Archaeological Museum inv. Λ42; Karetsou and Andreadaki-Vlazaki 2000, 437, cat. 507.

64 In two Hellenistic examples, one from Delos and another from Amphipolis, the costume consists of three garments: a chiton, a knotted mantle, and a hip mantle slung across the waist: Mazurek 2020b.

65 On the various forms and distributions of pharaonic and Greco-Roman *sistra*, see: Klebs 1931; Genaille 1984; Ziegler 1984.

66 On the origin and interpretation of the Isis-locks, also called Libyan locks, see: Malaise 1972a, 176–181; Leclant 1986, 343–348; Albersmaier 2005; Plantzos 2011, 391–392; Nagel 2015, 193–201.

67 Several scholars point to the representations of Ptolemaic queens, who seem to have been identifying with and dressing as Isis, as a key vector in the transmission of the costume to the Mediterranean world. See: Plantzos 2011; Nagel 2015, 200–201; Albersmaier 2018.

68 For pharaonic models, see: Bianchi 1980; Malaise 1992, 1994. On the connections with Ptolemaic queens, see: Albersmaier 2005; 2018, 458–461; Plantzos 2011; Nagel 2015, 199–201.

69 Mazurek 2020a.

70 Eingartner (1991, 33–48) associates this type with the western Mediterranean.

71 Gortyna: Iraklion, Archaeological Museum inv. H 260; Romeo and Portale 1998, 91–98, cat. 14, plates 6c–d. Eingartner also identifies another statue from Gortyna as Isis in the *diplax* with a floral garland and *situla* (Aghii Deka, Apotheke inv. 166, from the Praetorium, 150–160 CE), but the findspot suggests to me that it more likely served as a portrait. See: Porro 1913, 349–352, fig. 9; Eingartner 1991, 142, cat. 95, plate 50.

72 Messene, Archaeological Museum inv. 12000, mid-2nd century CE; Themelis 2011, 100–103.

73 Thessaloniki, Archaeological Museum inv. ΜΘ 843, 2nd century CE; Despinis et al. 1997–2020, vol. 1, 114–115, cat. 87.

74 Several of the *Knotenpalla* examples described above can also be identified as Isis Fortuna: Tran tam Tinh 1990, 794–795; Mazurek 2020b.

75 Dion, Archaeological Museum inv. ΜΔ 5442, ca. 2nd century CE. See: Pandermalis 2016, 23, fig. 9.

76 Three examples from Kerameiai in modern North Macedonia, dating from the 1st century CE to early 3rd century CE: Düll 1977, 411–412, cat. 272–274. Bust of Isis Fortuna from Herakleia, 2nd century CE: Düll 1977, 410, cat. 270. Two possible examples come from Messene. One, a bronze statuette, was found in the fill of the Doric Temple to Messana in the agora: Messene, Archaeological Museum inv. 14613; Themelis 2011, 99. The other, which Themelis reconstructs from a forearm with fruits suggesting a cornucopia, was found among the decorations of the Theater but may have belonged to the Isis sanctuary: Messene, Archaeological Museum inv. 15194; Themelis 2011, 103–104.

77 Themelis 2011, 106–108.

78 Beschi 1988, 858–859.

79 Hdt. 2.59; Tran tam Tinh 1990, 793–794.

80 Peschlow-Bindokat 1972, 127–136.

81 Paris, Louvre inv. Br. 192; Tran tam Tinh 1973, cat. A 14, figs. 36–37. The Isis *lactans*

82 "Die Erwerbungen" 1890, 60.
83 2nd–3rd century CE. See: Collart 1937, 448; Tran tam Tinh 1973, 73, cat. A 24 bis.
84 Berlin, Hoffman Sammlung inv. 572; Tran tam Tinh 1973, 73, cat. A 23, figs. 46–47.
85 Imported Egyptian statuettes from Delos: Marcadé 1952; Leclant 1957. From Rhodes: Fantaoutsaki 2011, 50–60, figs. 15–19.
86 Nagel 2015, 205–211.
87 Bradley 2006, 16–18. More often bodily sections of statues were painted with colors that reflected Greco-Roman understandings and idealization of human skin: red-brown for men and white for women: Stager 2016, 107–110. In my view, it is likely that the bodies of Isiac sculptures were painted in this way. There are statues of Isis in which the goddess's garments are carved in black marble (such as Thessaloniki, Archaeological Museum inv. MΘ 843; Despinis et al. 1997–2020, vol. 1, 116–117, cat. 87), but in these statues, the arms and head are separate pieces of white marble and were likely not painted.
88 Bradley 2006, 12–16.
89 Nagel 2015, 202–204; Mylonopoulos 2016.
90 Similar multivalent readings probably characterized Egyptianizing material culture in Italy, as argued in: Petersen 2012; Barrett 2017a.
91 Nagel 2015.
92 Despinis et al. 1997–2020, vol. 1, 64–66. For more on Tutu, see: Kaper 2003.
93 IG 10 2, 254; Bricault 2005, 153, cat. 113/0545.
94 Dimitriadis 2012; Koukouvou 2012, 109. See also: Steimle 2008, 81–88.
95 Pelekides 1921, 1934; "Chronique des fouilles" 1924; Wrede 1926; Makaronas 1940; Koukouvou 2012. Steimle (2004) has also published a study of the notes of Austrian archaeologist Hans von Schoenebeck, which contains some brief sketches.
96 Makaronas 1940. The plot excavated in 1939 lies below modern Odos Ptolemaion and Odos Antigonidon. Despinis et al. (1997–2020, vol. 1, 114) note that several pieces of Egyptianizing sculpture were connected with the Varelas plot and theorizes that the area might have housed a second Isiac sanctuary.
97 Koukouvou 2017, 268–269. Figure 11.6 provides an example of the Sarapeum's inventories. There was not, however, an official museum space in Thessaloniki until 1925, when the Yeni Cami was converted. Both the Rotunda and the Church of Agia Paraskevi Acheiropoitos were used between 1917 and 1925. Throughout the 1930s there was only one curator and one custodian for the archaeological museum, which further hampered attempts to systematize and document new finds: Daux and Edson 1974, 522–523.
98 Koukouvou 2012, 111, fig. 8.
99 For the discussion of van Schoenebeck's notes, see: Bommas 2002; Steimle 2004; 2008, 131–132. The original notebook is held at the archive of the Deutsches Archäologisches Institut in Berlin, inv. 19.12.1904, gefalled 17.8.1944.
100 Steimle 2004, abb. 1.
101 Düll 1977; Egelhaaf-Gaiser and Steimle 2003, 154–167; Kleibl 2009, 204–207; Salditt-Trappmann 1970, 47–52; Steimle 2004, 298–304.
102 Based on his 2004 study of van Schoenebeck's notes, Steimle (2004, 2006) argues that there is no indication that the finds were grouped in any particular way, much less cached in a crypt. He also criticizes the Thessaloniki Archaeological Museum's model of the sanctuary. He argues too that van Schoenebeck's notes do not actually describe the architecture represented in the model. See also: Falezza 2012, 268.
103 Pelekides 1921; Steimle 2004.
104 Pelekides (1921) does not give enough information to identify the female ideal statue or to allow us to determine which head of Sarapis he is describing. For the altar, see: IG 10 2.1, 84, 103; Despinis et al. 1997–2020 vol. 1, 66–67, figs. 121–124.
105 Despinis et al. 1997–2020, vol. 1, 63–64, cat. 45, figs. 125–126. See: Makaronas 1940, 464, no. 4.
106 Bommas 2005, 98–100; Kleibl 2009, 204–207; Steimle 2008, 99–103.
107 Dekoulakou 2011a, 34; Fantaoutsaki 2011, 52–61; Themelis 2011, 105–108.
108 There is no direct evidence for the date of the sanctuary's foundation, but Vitti believes it was part of the early Hellenistic urban layout. On the sanctuary's foundation, see: Edson

1940, 134; Pelekides 1921, 1934; Vitti 1992, 66; Steimle 2008, 79–80; Kleibl 2009, 207; Koester 2010.
109 Late 3rd-century BCE inscriptions: Thessaloniki, Archaeological Museum inv. MΘ 971; *IG* 10 2, 75; Bricault 2005, 136, cat. 113/0501; Thessaloniki, Archaeological Museum inv. MΘ 969; *IG* 10 2, 94; Bricault 2005, 136–137, cat. 113/0502. 187 BCE inscription: Thessaloniki, Archaeological Museum inv. MΘ 824; *IG* 10 2, 3; Bricault 2005, 137, cat. 113/0503.
110 Wrede 1926; Steimle 2008, 90–92. Steimle suggests that the Hellenistic phase would have been constructed of mud brick but provides no evidence to support this hypothesis.
111 Steimle (2008, 94–95), following Wild (1981, 1824); Kleibl (2009, 207) agrees with Steimle's proposals.
112 For a more detailed treatment of these issues, see: Steimle 2008, 83–103.
113 Woodward 1925, 225–226; Brady 1938, 7, no. 71; Kater-Sibbes 1973, 90, no. 500; Düll 1977, 150, no. 13; Despinis et al. 1997–2020, vol. 1, 113–114, cat. 84. While Brady describes this head as coming from the Thessaloniki Sarapeum, the Museum's inventory indicates that it came from the Varelas plot on Odos Olympou.
114 The arrangement of the hair recalls Corinth, Archaeological Museum inv. S 2378, though the lower curls on the Corinth head are carved in a more detailed manner: Milleker 1985, 132–135, no. 3.
115 Makaronas 1940, 465.
116 Donohue (1997) rejects the idea of cult statues, noting that the concept is never mentioned in the texts of antiquity. She suggests instead that the category is a modern invention. But a wide variety of terms existed to describe statues, and statues could change their purpose and meaning over their lifespan. Statues that we might consider to be votives because of their smaller scale or because of their status as a copy could also receive veneration. In sum, we lack the kind of evidence about ritual engagement that might indicate which statues were considered more important than their neighbors. See further: Mylonopoulos 2010, 1–10.
117 Despinis et al. 1997–2020, vol. 1, cat. 80, figs. 197–200. The inventory card for this object was made long after the head was found.
118 Fullerton 1990, 1–12.
119 Thessaloniki, Archaeological Museum inv. MΘ 837; Despinis et al. 1997–2020, vol. 4, 30–31, cat. 677; Voutiras 2012. Voutiras (2012, 269–270) also notes the statuette's formal similarity with statues of Asklepios from other sites in Thessaloniki and suggests that the statuette imitates a Hellenistic-period cult statue of Sarapis in the sanctuary based on a parallel with the much later assemblage at Gortyna discussed in the subsections "Sarapis" and "Isis."
120 Despinis et al. 1997–2020, vol. 1, 48. Despinis suggests these two heads could have served as two phases of the same statue, but there is no real evidence to suggest they stood on the same body.
121 Makaronas 1940, 465; Despinis et al. 1997–2020, vol. 1, 48–49, cat. 27, figs. 54–57. Neumann (1993) favors a very early Hellenistic or even late Classical date for the head and identifies it as Dionysos, but the techniques used to carve the curls are not consistent with that date or identification.
122 Dillon 2010, 103–134.
123 Isis wears several crowns in Egypt, including the crown of Hathor (horns framing a solar disc), a stepped throne, and several headdresses with the feathers of *ma'at* and other vegetal elements, but the *basileion* is among the most common. See: Tran tam Tinh 1990, 762.
124 Based on the sculptural technique, it is likely that this image was produced in Athens, not Macedonia.
125 Mazurek 2020a, 187–192.
126 Despinis et al. 1997–2020, vol. 1, 114–115.
127 While no other statue of Isis I know of has a similar set of depressions, many heads of Isis do have holes for attaching diadems and other headpieces. See, for example, the statue of Isis *lactans* from Perge, now in Antalya (Museum of Archaeology inv. A 3279), which features a large rectangular cutting near the front of the head: Tran tam Tinh 1973, cat. A-1, figs. 15–16.
128 Harpokrates' gesture alludes to the idea of childhood and rebirth in Egyptian religion. As one of the most popular subjects of Egyptian terracottas, there are innumerable examples of Harpokrates making this gesture in Egyptian art. For relevant examples, see: Frankfurter 1998, 134; Barrett 2011, 180–185,

247–250. For Harpokrates' iconography, see: Hall 1977.
129 Hall 1977, 56; Despinis et al. 1997–2020, vol. 1, 116. Budischovsky (2011, figs. 1–3) has assembled a set of bronzes, almost all without provenance, that also depict the god with the cornucopia and *pshent* crown.
130 Messene, Archaeological Museum inv. 13477: Themelis 2011, 98–99, cat. B, fig. 2. The statuette was found in the area between the theater and the stadium. Because the statue is missing its head, Themelis is not secure in this identification. Other examples were found in the Athenian Agora, such as the bronze statuette Agora Museum inv. B333: Thompson 1950, 332–333, plate 106a; Sharpe 2014, 154–167, cat. 7, figs. 17–8. The Agora example was found with a statuette of Telesphoros in a well inside the Roman-period bath. The two child-gods may have had some sort of relationship in the Roman period: Veymiers 2011, 115–118.
131 *Bull.* 1946–1947, 342–345; Bricault 2005, 55, cat. 104/0206; Dunand 1973b, 153–155.
132 This trend has been noticed in Hellenistic Thessaly, Argos, Boeotia, Delos, and is consistent with epigraphic dedications from around the region: Dunand 1973b, 41–46; Decourt and Tzaifalis 2007, 358; Schachter 2007, 388; Veymiers 2011, 124–127.
133 Despinis et al. 1997–2020, 86, cat. 86. Although the statue's provenance is not recorded in the inventory, it is identified as one of the more significant finds of the 1923 campaign in a *BCH* field report: "Chronique des fouilles" 1924, 497.
134 Romeo and Portale 1998, 33–39; Dekoulakou 2011a. At Marathon, Isis' consort is Osiris, not Sarapis.
135 Tran tam Tinh 1983, 157, cat. 3 16, fig. 106. From Pompeii, 6 2, 14. The painting dates to 62–79 CE.
136 σύνοικον δ'ἔλαβες Σέραπιν, καὶ τὸν κοινὸν ὑμῶν θεμένων γάμον, / τοῖς ὑμετέροις προσώποις ὁ κόσμος ἀνέλαμψεν ἐνομματισθεὶς / Ἡλίωι καὶ Σελήνηι·: Grandjean 1975, 17–18, 54–64. Similar sentiments are expressed in the aretalogies of Kyme (and, by extension, its copy in Thessaloniki, discussed in the section "Synnaoi Theoi"), Ios, Andros (lines 15–17), and Diodorus, though in those texts Isis is described as the wife of Osiris, not Sarapis. Grandjean also makes much of the term κοινόν used to describe the relationship between these two divinities, suggesting a more egalitarian relationship that corresponds to Isis' more prominent position in Greek cults.
137 Thessaloniki, Archaeological Museum inv. ΜΘ 833; Despinis et al. 1997–2020, vol. 1, 107–108, cat. 77, figs. 186–189.
138 Thessaloniki, Archaeological Museum inv. ΜΘ 832; Despinis et al. 1997–2020, vol. 1, 106–107, cat. 76. Despinis also identifies a second fragmentary statue found in a nearby plot as a statue of Artemis and associates it with the Sarapeum: Thessaloniki, Archaeological Museum inv. ΜΘ 1958, Despinis et al. 1997–2020, vol. 2, 17–18, cat. 153. ΜΘ 832 depicts a female *peplophoros* with a short himation crossing from the left shoulder to the right elbow. The head, separately pieced, and the right forearm are missing. This statue displays characteristic 2nd-century CE carving techniques, including the deep undercutting of vertical folds, a thick, Classicizing body, and a doughy feel to the drapery. Because of the long *kolpos* fold on the *peplos* and the way the statue's arms are positioned, Despinis argues that this statue is a copy of a 5th-century BCE original. The life-sized statue, which depicts a Greek goddess, perhaps Artemis or Demeter, is carved from Dokimeion marble. Regarding the Ariccia Artemis, see: Kahil 1984, 638; Giuliano 1985, 160, cat. 41. Although the himation's arrangement and the placement of the hand on the hip more closely follows the Ariccia Artemis type, Despinis argues that the arm positioning on this statue does not correspond exactly with that or any other known type and argues that the statue might also represent Athena or Demeter. He compares the Thessaloniki statue with a statue of Athena from the Athenian Agora and a statue that Despinis identifies as Demeter from Alaoui in North Africa: Gauckler and Poinssot 1910, 50, cat. 971, plate 30, no. 3.
139 Despinis et al. 1997–2020, vol. 1, 104–106, cat. 75. See further: Andronikos 1985; Brinke 1991, 52, 93, 157, cat. G 21.
140 See the examples collected in: Brinke 1991.
141 Andronikos 1985, 12; Pandermalis 1982b, 216; Brinke 1991, 52; Despinis et al. 1997–2020, vol. 1, 105.
142 At Dion, for example, Isis took over a late Classical-period sanctuary of Artemis that

143 Examples: *IG* 10 2, 77 (2nd–1st century BCE, Thessaloniki, Archaeological Museum inv. MΘ 964), *IG* 10 2, 78 (2nd–1st century BCE, Thessaloniki, Archaeological Museum inv. MΘ 951), *IG* 10 2, 80 (2nd–1st century BCE, Thessaloniki, Archaeological Museum inv. MΘ 978), *IG* 10 2, 88 (1st century CE, Thessaloniki, Archaeological Museum inv. MΘ 954).

144 *IG* 10 2, 85 (15/14 BCE, 1st century CE, Thessaloniki, Archaeological Museum inv. MΘ 1953), *IG* 10 2, 88 (1st century CE, Thessaloniki, Archaeological Museum inv. MΘ 954). The last line has been reconstructed to include καὶ συνβώμοις: Bricault 2005, 149, cat. 113/0534.

145 *IG* 10 2, 109 (39/38 BCE, Thessaloniki, Archaeological Museum inv. MΘ 965); *IG* 10 2, 83 (37/36 BCE [?], Thessaloniki, Archaeological Museum inv. MΘ 1950); *IG* 10 2, 84 (ca. 40–35 BCE, 1st century CE, Thessaloniki, Archaeological Museum inv. MΘ 986); *IG* 10 2, 116 (1st century BCE, 1st century CE, Thessaloniki, Archaeological Museum inv. MΘ 1003). The second line has been reconstructed to include ἐν[τεμενίοις – – –]: Bricault 2005, 142, cat. 113/0517.

146 *IG* 2 2, 4962; Lamont 2015, 43–45. Roman emperors were often described as *synnaoi theoi* within Greek temples, as discussed in: Steuernagel 2010.

147 Lamont 2015, 44. These reliefs include a votive relief from the Piraeus Asklepion, ca. 420 BCE, which depicts Asklepios with Hygeia and one of his sons: Copenhagen, Ny Carlsberg Glyptothek inv. 1430; Lamont 2015, 45–46, fig. 5.4.

148 Contra: Veymiers 2018, 50–51.

149 Von Lieven 2016.

150 *IG* 10 2, 254 (1st–2nd century CE, Thessaloniki, Archaeological Museum inv. MΘ 1683). See: Pelekides 1934, fig. 1; Bricault 2005, 154, cat. 113/0545. The sanctuaries at Thessaloniki, Kyme, Kassandreia, and Ios all have "I am Isis" aretalogies, while Maroneia and Andros have what Martzavou and other scholars have called the "You are Isis" type: Martzavou 2012a.

151 *IKyme* 97–108, no. 41, plate 11. See also *IG* 12 Suppl., 98–99; Salač 1927, 378–383, plate 15.

152 ἐγὼ τὸ καλὸν καὶ αἰσχρὸ[ν] διαγεινώσκεσθαι ὑπὸ τῆς Φύσεως ἐποίησα. / ἐγὼ ὅρκου φοβερώτερον οὐθὲν ἐποίησα. / ἐγὼ τὸν ἀδίκως ἐπιβουλεύοντα ἄλλοις ὑποχείριον τῷ ἐπιβου[λ]ευομένῳ παρέδωκα (*IKyme* 41, lines 32–34). In the Maroneia aretalogy, Isis is also given responsibility for justice, though in that text she establishes the laws in order to create equality and prevent violence (lines 30–31, οὐ τὴν βίαν νομικὸν ἀλλὰ [τ]ὸν νόμον ἀβίαστον εὐφοῦσαι; Bricault 2005, 176–178, cat. 114/0202; Grandjean 1975, 16–82.

153 *I.Kyme* 41, lines 32–34, trans. Beard et al. 1998a, sec. 12.4a.

154 Thessaloniki, Archaeological Museum inv. MΘ 996, *IG* 10 2, 61; Bricault 2005, 161, cat. 113/0563; Despinis et al. 1997–2020, vol. 1, 118–119, cat. 88, figs. 230–233. The inscription and statuette date to 182/183 CE.

155 Finkelpearl 1998, 205–209; Bommas 2002, 133–134; Alvar 2008, 188–190; Martzavou 2012a, 270–274.

156 Grandjean 1975, 15; Alvar 2008, 188; Martzavou 2012a, 268; Moyer 2017, 36–37.

157 Tran tam Tinh 1990, 793–795.

158 Plut., *De Is.* 377a–b, trans. F. C. Babbitt (Plutarch 1936, 155–157).

159 On the gesture, see: Tran tam Tinh 1988, 415–416; Malaise 2005, 199–203. In addition to the Harpokrates from Thessaloniki described in the section "Ideal Sculpture in the Thessaloniki Sarapeum," there are examples of this type from elsewhere. Dion: Archaeological Museum inv. MΔ 400; Pandermalis 2016, 111, cat. 27. Messene: Archaeological Museum inv. 13477; Themelis 2011, 97, fig. 2.

160 Pearson 2021.

161 Müller 1969; Pirelli 2006; Clausen 2013.

162 These might include looting in antiquity. Most Egyptian sculptures found in Greece and Italy are small-scale statuettes like the sphinx discussed here. Metal objects and textiles, which are frequently depicted in Pompeian wall painting and, as Pearson (2015) argues, were also commonly imported from Egypt, are often not preserved in Greek contexts.

163 A significant corpus has been identified on Crete: Karetsou and Andreadaki-Vlazaki

2000; Philips 2008. Among the handful of imported Egyptian objects is a black stone statuette of the god Tutu from Thessaloniki, a few small statuettes of women or female deities from Delos, a group of imported Egyptian images from Rhodes, and a Greek-style green basalt statue of a river god from Messene (Archaeological Museum inv. 250). See: Marcadé 1952; Leclant 1957; Themelis 2011, 99, fig. 3.
164 *ID* 1417.
165 Despinis et al. 1997–2020, vol. 1, 64–66.
166 This deity developed in Egypt during the Late Period and became more prominent in the Ptolemaic period. In later Egyptian religion, Tutu is the son of the goddess Neith and appears in both sphinx and human form. The first attestation of Tutu comes from the reign of Apries (589–570 BCE), and the last from the reign of Caracalla: Kaper 2003, 19–33.
167 Despinis et al. 1997–2020, vol. 1, 64–66.
168 Budapest, Museum of Fine Arts inv. 50.958; Picard 1958; Veymiers 2009, 498–504, fig. 17. Similarly, a 2nd-century CE relief from nearby Amphipolis mentions one of Tutu's Greek names, *Totoe Theodaimon Hypnos*, and depicts the god with his characteristic iconography: sphinx head, crocodiles, snake tail, knives for feet, and a scorpion. Though depicting a similar deity, the Amphipolis relief is a Greek and perhaps even a local product and renders even this highly unusual (from a Greek perspective) deity in Greek form, all the way down to his knife-toes.
169 Cline 2005; Versluys 2010, 15–19; Pangiatopoulos 2012; Mol 2015b, 103.
170 G. Parker 2008, 147–202; Swetnam-Burland 2015, 22.

CHAPTER 5

1   A revised version of this chapter was published in *Hesperia*, and I thank editor Jennifer Sacher for her permission to reproduce part of that article here. The reproduction is courtesy of the American School of Classical Studies at Athens.
2   Smyrna (funerary stele of Isias, 2nd century BCE, London, British Museum inv. 1772,0703.1), Syros (1st century or 2nd century CE, now lost), Tanagra (1st century CE, Thebes, Archaeological Museum inv. 28), Phryxou Limen in Bithynia (200–250 CE, Istanbul, Archaeological Museum inv. 3545), Apollonia in Illyria (Fier, Archaeological Museum of Apollonia inv. 125), Caesarea in Mauretania (late 2nd century CE, Cherchell, Archaeological Museum inv. S118), Rome (110–130 CE, Naples, Museo Archeological Nazionale inv. 2929).
3   My definition elaborates on Gell's concept of distributed personhood and Brubaker's concept of identification: Brubaker 2004, 41–43; Gell 1998, 96–115.
4   Brubaker 2004, 28–47.
5   See Chapter 1 and see also: Papaioannou 2016.
6   Many scholars have made similar arguments regarding Roman material culture in the provinces. For a recent scholarly overview, see: Versluys 2014; van Oyen 2017. See also: Webster 2001, 1–9, 190–192; Revell 2005; Versluys 2015.
7   Neer 2011, 49. My treatment of embodiment derives much from: Massumi (2002, 1–15).
8   On the importance of this otherness for creating a global Isiac community, see: Rüpke 2014, 198–205.
9   Rothe (2012, 2013) uses the term frequently in her work on gendered provincial portraiture in Gaul and Germania. For an example from earlier anthropological work, see: Nadig 1986.
10 For example: Heyn 2010; A. M. Smith 2013.
11 In a promotional interview dated February 24, 2017, Rubina Raja says that the Palmyra Portrait Project, based at Aarhus University, has identified over 3,000 Palmyrene funerary reliefs in museums and private collections around the world.
12 There are, of course, exceptions. In Tomb C (T.32), four slabs had only one name in the inscription but held multiple burials. The names of women and children were omitted: de Jong 2017, 117. *Loculi* are not the only type of funerary portraiture used at Palmyra. Reclining portraits appear on sarcophagi, often displayed in groups. Reliefs depicting groups of people banqueting were also popular: Heyn 2016, 186–188.
13 There are two groups of men, priests and caravan merchants, that on the whole prefer what we might characterize as local dress: Heyn 2017, 207. The large sarcophagi from hypogea tombs permitted a freer form of representation, and in these instances, men

14 Colledge argues that representations of women wearing Greek dress appear on grave stelai, a common form of funerary sculpture, in the early part of Palmyra's Roman period, but then notes several features that more closely mimic the so-called local costume: "They drape the cloak in a complex manner and add a veil. Drapery is highly patterned, and hems are 'stiffened' at each side of the women's ankles. Embroidery and jewelry add diversity." These reliefs normally include palm fronds and the *dorsalium* curtain, and occasionally feature a set of circular objects that are not found in Greek art: Colledge 1976, 64.

15 Appian describes it as a *polis* in his account of Marc Antony's raid in 41 BCE: App. *B Civ.* 5.9; A. M. Smith 2013, 21–22. Appian, however, is writing in the mid-2nd century CE, when Palmyra was a well-established urban center.

16 A. M. Smith 2013, 21–28.

17 Portland, Museum of Art inv. 54.3, dated to 150–200 CE: Ronzevalle 1902; Ingholt 1928, 95, cat. PS 65; Colledge 1976, 249, 259; Vermeule 1981, 384, cat. 333; Parlasca 1990, 139, fig. 6; Heyn 2010, 643, cat. 25a, 25b; Krag 2018, 302, cat. 505.

18 More often, husbands and wives, fathers and sons, mothers and sons, or mothers and daughters appear together: Krag 2016, 186. It is also possible that "daughter" is a mistranslation. In a letter dated September 23, 1987, M. J. Geller of the University of Pennsylvania's Museum of Archaeology and Anthropology offers a translation of "mother" for the Palmyrene word *barata* and notes other infelicities in the translation of inscriptions in two other reliefs now held by the Portland Art Museum.

19 While hairstyles might have offered some women an opportunity to differentiate themselves, more often than not most women around the Mediterranean followed the style of the empress or styles that had been in use for generations like the "melon coiffure." In the mid to late 2nd century, when this portrait was made, empresses tended to follow more conservative styles like the one used here. See: P. Stewart 2008, 85–89; Fejfer 2008, 351–359; Dillon 2010, 135.

20 Krag 2016, 186n49.

21 Heyn (2016, 200) is unsure whether the veil-grasping gesture is borrowed from the Roman *pudicitia* pose used in female portraiture throughout the Mediterranean, but the gesture is almost certainly a feminine one. She attaches no special meaning to the looped-over fabric in Balya's left hand. See: Heyn 2010, 635–636.

22 On jewelry in Palmyrene portraiture more generally, see: Mackay 1949; Heyn 2016, 201–203; Krag 2017.

23 Heyn 2017, 212; Krag 2017; 2018, 96–110. Jewelry plays a similar role in female mummy portraits, which suggests a further consistency in its use for provincial subjects. See: Riggs 2005, 398–402.

24 Heyn (2016, 201–204) believes that at least some of this jewelry would have been fashioned locally, which would have further emphasized the economic inequality between those who owned jewelry and those who did not. Still, even in local jewelry, much of the raw material must have been imported – that is, conveyed along the global trade networks that passed through Palmyra.

25 Heyn 2017.

26 Heyn 2016, 200; 2017, 212.

27 The banqueting reliefs and group sarcophagi, of which 141 are preserved, tend to have larger groups of figures. These are normally found in hypogea tombs: Heyn 2016, 186–188.

28 Heyn 2017, 205–206. It is also important to recognize the impact of eastern models on Palmyrene portraiture and sculpture more generally. See: Butcher 2003, 278; Edwell 2008, 33–34; Long 2016, 136–140.

29 R. R. R. Smith 1998, 65–66.

30 De Jong 2017, 65–69.

31 De Jong 2017, 65–70.

32 Because of the paucity of evidence from pre-Roman Syria, it is difficult to determine whether these portrait reliefs are new or if they draw from a preexisting artistic and funerary tradition. Even sculpted grave stelai are not known before the 1st century CE. See: Colledge 1976, 36.

33 These tombs may have followed local traditions visible throughout the former Phoenician territories in North Africa and elite

34 The hypogea often included monumental sarcophagi that depicted large family groups banqueting together. There seems to be a major shift in funerary practices during the mid-2nd century CE: A. M. Smith 2013, 29–30. Smith follows Schmidt-Colinet (1989, 161–163) in his argument that the shift must be related to Hadrian's visit in 129 CE. Andrade (2013, 171–210) argues similarly that Hadrian's policies and visit had a significant impact on Palmyra's expression of Greekness, as well as on its urban landscape.

[Note: entry before 34 continues:] tomb practices in Anatolia and Palestine. See: de Jong 2017, 73–76.

35 Colledge (1976, 67) dates their period of popularity from the mid-1st century through the late 3rd century CE.
36 De Jong 2017, 67–68. The average rectangular mausoleum size in Roman Syria reached 11 m × 11 m × 5 m.
37 De Jong 2017, 169–171.
38 MacMullen 1982; Bodel 2000; de Jong 2017, 141.
39 Heyn 2017, 204.
40 Borg 2000; Riggs 2005, 1–22, 96–174. Alterity is always an option, not a requirement. There are many examples of female portrait mummies in which women are shown wearing Roman clothing. One such example is the Isidora mummy, now on display in Los Angeles (Getty Villa Museum: inv. 81.AP.42, ca. 100 CE). See: Corcoran 1995, vol. 2, nos. 18, 40, 43–44, 63, 66, 158; Thompson 1982, 32–33, nos. 2, 64.
41 Rothe 2012, 2013.
42 Rodgers 2003.
43 While it is safe to say the type was popular in Athens, it is harder to determine whether these reliefs were less popular elsewhere, due to Athens' unusually excellent history of excavation and publication.
44 Other examples within Greece include a relief found on Aigina that probably came from the cemetery on Rheneia (Walters 1988, plate 14d), a mid-1st-century BCE example from Eretria (Walters 1988, 28, no. 167), two examples from Tanagra (Bonnano-Aravantinos 2009, 1152–1155, cat. 1–2, figs. 1–5), and one from a funerary context in Eleusis (Walters 1988, 35–36). Four were found in the area of Piraeus, and another on the island of Salamis (Walters 1988, 37). See: Martzavou 2012b, 69n58.
45 This sense of difference, as argued by Mol (2015b, 91–95), was a critical part of religious experience in mystery cults. For the concept more generally, see: Bachmann-Medick 2017; Pangiatopoulos 2012. On the importance of alterity for creating a global Isiac community, see: Rüpke 2014, 198–205.
46 Boston, Museum of Fine Arts inv. 1971.209. The stele was found at Athens, reportedly in the foundations of a house between the Mint and the Bouleuterion on Stadiou Street in February 1876. It is dated to ca. 160–170 CE, based on the inscription and sculptural technique. Walters believes the relief may have been found in situ: Comstock and Vermeule 1976, 276; Vermeule 1988, 113; Walters 1988, 36.
47 On the hairstyle, see: Stephens 2017. See also: Stephens 2008.
48 Messene, Archaeological Museum inv. 12000, dated to the Trajanic or Hadrianic period; Themelis 2011, 100–103, cat. E, figs. 8a–d. See cover image.
49 Thank you to Ellen Perry for this reference.
50 Athens, National Archaeological Museum inv. 1233. Found in the modern period in the Library of Hadrian along with seven or eight other Isiac funerary reliefs. Dunand 1973a, 147; Walters 1988, 74; Eingartner 1991, 146, cat. 104, plate 65; Romiopoulou 1997, 45, cat. 34; von Moock 1998, 127, cat. 231, plates 31d, 32a–d; Karapanagiotou 2013, cat. 370.
51 Trimble 2011, 55–59.
52 Van Moock and Eingartner date the relief to the Flavian period based on the unnamed woman's hairstyle, but Walters and Dunand prefer a Trajanic date. See note 50 for references. The elaborate, curly hairstyles associated with Flavian women appear in female portraiture into the Hadrianic period. See: Fejfer 2008, 353–355, figs. 276–277.
53 It is very likely these reliefs would have been painted in such a way as to further emphasize their distinctive dress. Color seems to have played a key role in the cult's priesthoods and dress. One well-known priesthood was the *melanophor*, who presumably wore black garments: Eingartner 1991, 60–80. A mid-2nd-century BCE relief from Thessaloniki, dedicated to Osiris by Demetrios in honor of his parents, depicts a man in *melanophor* costume: *IG* 10 2, 107; Despinis et al.

1997–2020, vol. I, cat. 67; Voutiras 2005, 282–285. Barrett (2011, 142–148) also identifies black paint on several Isis figurines from Hellenistic Delos, which may indicate that they were representations of *melanophor* priests. Apuleius further describes cult costumes' variegated color in *Met.* 11.2.

54 Many were found in the area of the modern Plaka, but this concentration may not accurately reflect the distribution of these objects in the Roman period.

55 Most lack a secure findspot. Walters (1988, 91–112) covers the examples from the Agora. For the Kerameikos example, see: von Moock 1998, 157, cat. 384.

56 Von Moock 1998, 42, cat. 48.

57 Parlama and Stampolidis 2000, 196–197, cat. 179. Excavators dated the cemetery containing Mousa's stele from the 1st century BCE to the 1st century CE, while dating the relief itself to ca. 150 CE. In the later 2nd century CE, a larger building was erected on the site, providing a useful *terminus ante quem* for the relief. The use of a floral garland is less common at Athens, though there are a few examples, such as: Athens, National Archaeological Museum inv. 5256; Piraeus, Archaeological Museum inv. 1160. The garland is normally associated with a different costume used in later portraits of Isis devotees or in contemporary portraits from the western Empire: Eingartner 1991, 72–73. No reliefs have yet been associated with the Kotzia Square cemetery, which also dates to the Roman period.

58 Von Moock 1998, 147, cat. 324, plate 49c.

59 Martzavou (2011, 79–80) argues that many of the reliefs found in the Agora may have come from the area of the City Eleusinion, where it is likely that a sanctuary dedicated to Isis once stood. The clustering of reliefs in the Agora, however, is more likely a product of post-depositional processes. There is no evidence of boundary stones for group burials like those on Roman Kos discussed in Chapter 2.

60 Athens, Kerameikos Archaeological Museum inv. P190; dated to the later 2nd century CE. Von Moock 1998, 107, cat. 119, plates 11c–d, 12a–d; Karapanagiotou 2013, cat. 316. Von Moock categorizes the male figure as a "Normaltypus" and the woman as an example of the popular Large Herculaneum Woman type discussed below.

61 Fejfer 2008, 355–356.

62 The differences would not have been as dramatic in the case of devotees wearing the *diplax*, which more closely follows prevailing norms of female dress in Roman-period Athens.

63 It is unclear who decided how an ancient portrait, particularly a funerary portrait, was designed and dedicated. See: A. Stewart 1979, 11–26; R. R. R. Smith 2006, 70–73; P. Stewart 2008, 11–12.

64 On the strong normative drive in Hellenistic and Roman portraiture, particularly for women, see: Dillon 2010, 135–149; Fejfer 2008, 331–369.

65 Among many, see: P. Stewart 2008, 85–107; Alexandridis 2010; Dillon 2010, 1–10.

66 Dillon 2006, 61–98; 2010, 135–159; Lee 2015, 49–51.

67 Vorster 2008, 120–122; Dillon 2010, 157–163; Trimble 2011, 152–203.

68 Beard et al. 1998b, 264–265.

69 Walters (1988, 50–54) and Dunand (1973b, 184) both dismiss the argument that the reliefs could be Isis. The strong similarities with the rest of the funerary reliefs from Roman Athens in typology, technique, and style support this argument.

70 Von Moock's catalogue (1998) contains 577 grave reliefs, of which 74 are identifiable as Isis devotees through costume. Walters' volume (1988) identifies another thirty-four from the Agora excavations. Along with the Metro excavation example, these reliefs constitute about one-sixth of the known funerary stelai from Roman-period Athens, a proportion that is too high if only priestesses are permitted to use this type.

71 Walters 1988, 52. Martzavou (2011, 78) notes that there is a relatively high preponderance of migrant women in the corpus, including five women from Miletus.

72 On Apuleius as a source for Isiac rituals, see the section "Apuleius as a Source for Isiac Rituals" in Chapter 2.

73 Apul., *Met.* 11.24.

74 Martzavou 2012a, 274–275. Epiphanies are normally mediated through material culture, a fact that informed Greek understandings of cult images: Platt 2011, 52–60.

75 Alvar 2008, 342.

76 Elsner 2007, 297. See further: Festugière 1954, 80–84.

77 Transcendence seems to be a key component of this cult and may have been part of its

78 Athens, National Epigraphical Museum inv. 8426. Its date is securely based on its dedicatory inscription, *IG* 2 2, 4702. Both Martzavou (2011, 68–69) and Walters (1988, 31, plate 1a) connect the funerary reliefs with this fragment.

79 Isis sanctuaries are known from the South Slope of the Akropolis, the Roman Agora, the are of the city Eleusinion, and the area of the modern Metropolitan basilica just north of the Akropolis. On the cult in Athens, see: Matricon-Thomas 2012; Muniz Grijalvo 2009. The South Slope sanctuary had a cult image whose head was preserved into the 1980s, but that piece is now lost: Walker, pers. comm., October 2013. See, with accompanying references: Walker 1979; Martzavou 2012b, 68. Figurines and reliefs often refer to image types that are reproduced in the round as ideal images: Kousser 2008, 34–40. There are also many examples of women dressing up as statues or in the guise of the goddess as reproduced in ideal images, including the sacred law from Adania (*LSCG* 64, lines 23–25) that requires devotees to dress as the god: Connelly 2007, 85–86, 106–108; Gawlinski 2008, 156; 2011, 69–71; Platt 2011, 11–15, 40–49.

80 The inscriptions are *IG* 3, 203 (Athens, end of the 2nd century BCE–early 1st century CE), *CIG* 2, 2295 = *ID* 2079 (Delos, 115/114 BCE, now lost, originally from Sarapieion C), and *ID* 2103 (Delos, 114/113 BCE, Delos, Archaeological Museum inv. A 586). Originally from Sarapieion C. See further: Dunand 1973a, 10–11; Baslez 1977, 62, 134; Martzavou 2012b, 68–69; Matricon-Thomas 2012, 51.

81 Thessaloniki, Archaeological Museum inv. MΘ 997, *IG* 10 2, 1; Despinis et al. 1997–2020, vol. 1, 91–93, cat. 67, fig. 150.

82 Voutiras 2005, 283–285. This identification was also suggested in: Malaise and Veymiers 2018, 205–206. In Despinis et al. 1997–2020, vol. 4, 133–134, Voutiras also suggests that a late Hellenistic to early Imperial portrait statue of a young man in a draped himation (Thessaloniki, Archaeological Museum inv. MΘ 836) imitates a 1st-century BCE statuette of Sarapis found in the same sanctuary (Thessaloniki, Archaeological Museum inv. MΘ 837; Despinis et al. 1997–2020, vol. 4, 30–31, cat. 677). I intend to explore this example further in a future publication.

83 Brubaker 2004, 12, 41–42; Mol and Versluys 2015, 451–452.

84 Bell 1997, 99.

85 Mol and Versluys 2015, 456–457.

86 Brubaker 2004, 41–44; Trimble 2011, 192–196.

87 Walters 1988, 56. These include: (1) relief of Kallo and Synpheron, Flavian period (found at 4 Odos Polytechneion in Piraeus, Athens, Ephorate of Classical Antiquities for the City of Athens inv. M761; Walters 1988, 38, 56, plates 13a–d; von Moock 1998, 91, cat. 12); (2) relief found stored in the Library of Hadrian in Athens, late Antonine Period (Athens, National Archaeological Museum inv. Από 235; Walters 1988, 56, cat. 204); (3) relief of Sosipatros and Epiteugma, now in the Archaeological Museum of Lavrio (Dunand 1973a, 147); and (4) an early 3rd-century CE relief of Kleitomenes, found on Paros, reused in a later tomb but probably carved by an Athenian workshop: Orlandos, *ArchEphem* 1960 (1965), 4, plate Θ. Another fragmentary relief (Athens, Agora Museum inv. S 1584, Roman period; Walters 1988, cat. 17, plate 33a) depicts a pattern of drapery consistent with a male subject, but Walters does not identify it as such.

88 Athens, Ephorate of Classical Antiquities for the City of Athens inv. M761; Eingartner 1991, 147, cat. 105, plate 66; von Moock 1998, 91, cat. 12. On the Small Herculaneum type, see: Vorster 2008, 117–119; Dillon 2010, 92–96.

89 Llewellyn-Jones 2003, 54–58, 155–202.

90 Heyob 1975, 81–82; Arnaoutoglou 2003, 155–160; Walters 2000. While the numbers at Athens are higher, the city's unusual preservation may contribute to this prevalence. Still, it is clear that women participated frequently as cult functionaries of many types. Publication of Isiac inscriptions is ongoing, but the proportions of male to female devotees have not changed significantly. See: Martzavou 2012b.

91 Swetnam-Burland 2011, 337–339.

92 Stamatopoulou (2008) dates the stele to the second half of the 3rd century BCE on the letter forms used in the stele's inscriptions.

93 Athens: Agora Museum inv. S 333, mid-1st century CE, though earlier dates into the 2nd century BCE have been proposed. Harrison (1953, 12–14, cat. 3, plate 3) argues that the head was left roughly finished and does not depict the subject with a shaved head. Delos: Archaeological Museum inv. A 5934, mid to late Hellenistic period (Michalowski 1932, 29–30, plates 23–24). The Agora example was found in a late Roman fill, and the Delian example's findspot has been lost, so the dates proposed are stylistic. The Agora example has a rough finish on its head. The Delian example is too worn to determine if the head is shaved or bald, but its face is similar enough to the Athenian head to suggest there was some connection between the two even if they were not direct copies. A third head from Athens, now in Copenhagen, has a similar veristic face and bald head but lacks the priestly fillet: Buschor 1949, fig. 43; Harrison 1953, 14.

94 Veymiers 2018, 36–37.

95 Macr., *Satr.* I, 21, 14. For an overview of scholarly debates on the nature and interpretation of this hairstyle, see: Baecke-Dahmen 2018, 509–517.

96 Christodoulou 2018. These are Dion, Archaeological Museum inv. MΔ 8929 (dated to the Trajanic/Hadrianic period with an early 3rd-century CE reuse) and MΔ 9008 (dated to the reign of Caracalla and reused shortly thereafter). Both were found in the House of Leda and in their second phase may have represented sons of the family that lived there. A portrait of an infant with a similar hairstyle dating to the 1st century CE is now in Athens (National Archaeological Museum inv. 3907; Romiopoulou 1997, 40–42, cat. 22, plates 42, 43).

97 Athens, National Archaeological Museum inv. 1223. Walters (1988, 38n39, 84, plate 38) dates the pieces to 210–220 CE, while Eingartner dates them to 60–90 CE (1991, 146, cat. 103, plate 65; Baecke-Dahmen 2018, 519). Inscription: *IG* 2/3 2, 12752; Bricault 2005, 26, cat. 101/0248.

98 Athens, National Archaeological Museum inv. Θ243; Romiopoulou 1997, 31, cat. 17.

99 Baecke-Dahmen 2018, 527–535.

100 Swetnam-Burland 2011, 339–342.

101 Dekoulakou 2011a, 32–34. Albersmaier (2018, 452–453) notes the prevalence of fringed garments on male figures, most of which she identifies as priests. The person depicted is likely a devotee or possibly a priest of some sort, but there is no way to determine his precise status without more evidence.

102 Naples, Museo Archeologico Nazionale inv. 4991; De Caro 1996, cat. 134; Bonifacio 1997, 28–32, no. 1, plate 1. C. Norbanus Sorex's involvement with the Egyptian cults has been disputed, but van Andriga (2012, 107–108) makes a compelling argument for considering him an active participant in the sanctuary's rituals and a likely devotee of mystery religions more generally.

103 The Iseum at Pompeii was enclosed with high walls and accessible through only one or two doors that could be easily closed. See: van Andriga 2012; Mol and Versluys 2015, 458–459. Swetnam-Burland (2015, 105–135), however, thinks the sanctuary's paintings were directed at a wider audience.

104 This is likely an accident of preservation rather than a mark of the sanctuary's exceptionalism.

105 No inventory number; displayed on site. Found in the north court of Sarapieion C, across from the Iseion: Hauvette-Besnault 1881, 307–308, no. 4; Marcadé 1969, 324, plate 71; Brun-Kyriakidis 2016, 69, fig. 3.

106 Delos, Archaeological Museum inv. A 5932. Found on the "Terrace of the Foreign Gods," in the north court of Sarapieion C across from the Iseion: Hauvette-Besnault 1881, 308, no. 9; Michalowski 1932, plate 37; Marcadé 1969, 319, no. 3; Brun-Kyriakidis 2016, 70, fig. 4.

107 Delos, Archaeological Museum inv. A 4180. May depict Sarapis. Roussel stated that the head came from the basin of the Inopos, but it is not certain that it was originally displayed in Sarapieion C: Roussel 1915, 65, no. 2, fig. 11; Marcadé 1969, 427; Brun-Kyriakidis 2016, 70.

108 Delos, Archaeological Museum inv. A 1803, preserving the forearm and hand at life-sized scale: Roussel 1915, 67, no. 6; Marcadé 1969, 88, plate 6; Brun-Kyriakidis 2016, 71. Brun-Kyriakidis (2016, 68–71) also catalogues several female portraits from Sarapieion C, including the statue of Diodora set up on site and a small female portrait head in marble.

109 Mol 2015b; Mol and Versluys 2015, 458; Nagel 2015, 188–190. Contra: Alvar 2008,

164, the importance of foreign symbolism in Isiac cult does not lessen over the long term: Mazurek 2016, 50–61.
110 Papaioannou 2016. Imperialism is not an even process. Each region experienced Roman rule differently due to its history, environment, culture, politics, economy, and social connectivity. While my own views tend towards a broad Mediterraneanism, the scale of analysis often affects our interpretations of the Roman Mediterranean and the impact of imperial power on any particular region or site. See further: Woolf 1993; Revell 2005, 1–5; Mattingly 2014, 42–49; Müller 2016.
111 This pairing is a common one, but it is not the only option. There are examples of local persistence in dress and hairstyles from around the Mediterranean, as well as examples of both men and women adopting Greco-Roman dress. See further: Webster 2001; Aldhouse Green 2003; Rodgers 2003; Riggs 2005, 96–174.
112 Heyn 2010.
113 Closterman 2007. These types of representational strategies may have continued in use into the 2nd century CE, allowing representations of single women like Lamia Viboulla: no provenance, Piraeus, Archaeological Museum inv. 1160, early Antonine period (Walters 1988, 19, 23, 43, 47, plate 27) to engage with nearby sculptures and inscriptions to nuance a family identity.
114 Mol and Versluys 2015.
115 R. R. R. Smith 1998.

CHAPTER 6

1 A portion of this chapter previously appeared in the *American Journal of Archaeology*. Thanks to editor Jane Carter for her permission to reproduce it here.
2 Alvar 2008; Versluys 2012, 33–36; 2013; 2015; Rüpke 2014, 198–205; Barrett 2019, 32–36. See further the discussion of authenticity in Chapter 3.
3 Scott 2013, 8–9. This approach is based on the premise that sanctuaries can be considered as *places* in the Roman world. In this context, place is a historically situated, subjective, and constructed experience of space related to experiences of topography, geography (both physical and cultural), culture, and power.
4 Bordieu 1985, 723–725; Scott 2010, 13–16; 2013, 8. I consider place to be critical to processes of identification and, most importantly, self-location. These ideas are based in discussions of place in: Rodman 1992; Alcock 1994; Feld and Basso 1996; Cole 2004, 7–29; Scott 2013, 1–14. In particular, Richards' (1999) arguments regarding the religious significance of landscape in the pharaonic Nile Valley inspired my interpretations.
5 Brubaker 2004, 44–45.
6 Latour 2005, 1–17; Collar 2013, 8–17.
7 Brubaker 2004, 44–45.
8 Appadurai 1990.
9 On imagined geographies, see: E. Saïd 1978, 49–73.
10 Versluys 2002, 26–35. See further: Malaise 2005, 210–213.
11 Merrills 2017, 124–131.
12 Barrett 2017b, 295, 310–314.
13 Barrett 2019, 335–336. Barrett also notes that Nilescapes often draw on knowledge about the Nile gleaned from imported objects and travel, as well as on a partial knowledge of Egyptian rituals surrounding the Inundation Festival.
14 Barrett 2019, 250–277.
15 Barrett 2019, 337–342.
16 Versluys 2002, 248–252. Barrett (2019, 348–357) has studied these contexts at Pompeii in more detail.
17 Versluys 2002, 249–251. See also the base of a reclining Nile statue from the temple of Isis on the Campus Martius: Rome, Vatican Museum inv. 2300; Malaise 1972a, 194, cat. Rome 348; Lembke 1994, 214–216, cat. E1; Versluys 2002, 68–69. On the Ostia mosaic: Floriani Squarciapino 1962, 21; Malaise 1972a, 78–82; Mar 2001, 284–285.
18 Floriani Squarciapino 1962, 21; Malaise 1972a, 78–82; Versluys 2002, 45–48; Mar 2001.
19 Most recently, see Swetnam-Burland 2015, 105–141.
20 Barrett 2019, 315–317.
21 Ali Ibrahim and Scranton 1976. The Kenchreai glass panels have been connected with a potential Isis sanctuary, and while it is clear that there was an important sanctuary to Isis at Kenchreai during the Antonine period, the identification of this particular building is probably incorrect: Rife, pers. comm., May 2019; also argued in: Versluys 2002, 219; Veymiers 2018, 48–49.

22 Ali Ibrahim 1976, 104–141; Versluys 2002, 218–219.
23 Ibrahim locates the port scenes specifically in North Africa through exhaustive identification of all of the animals and plants in each scene: Ali Ibrahim 1976, 31–163.
24 Ali Ibrahim 1976, 39–45, cat. 3a–f, drawing 7, figs. 26, 57–58.
25 Naples, Museo Archeologico Nazionale inv. 113195. On this image and the trope more generally, see: Versluys 2002, 138–140, cat. 59, fig. 79; Barrett 2019, 62–67, 81n99, 88–91, 108, fig. 2.4. Ali Ibrahim also identifies a cylindrical marble object of the Antonine period, found near the church of San Vitale in Rome, which features a young boy riding a crocodile sidesaddle, as a close comparison with the figure in the Kenchreai glass panel: Lovatelli 1880, plates 14–16; Ali Ibrahim 1976, 41–42nn30–31. There is also a later mosaic, ca. 400–600 CE, from Thebes, that depicts a Nilotic river landscape complete with ibises, lotuses, snakes, ducks, and a personification of the Nile with a hydria: Versluys 2002, 222–223, cat. 120, fig. 144.
26 The Italian corpus is vast and can be consulted in: Versluys 2002, 43–175, 336–373. More recently, Barrett (2019, 60–136) has reappraised some of the Pompeian material with emphasis on these iconographic and contextual features.
27 Bruneau 1972, 313–314, cat. 335c, fig. 287; Guimer-Sorbets and Nenna 1992, 617, plate 4.1; Versluys 2002, 223–224.
28 Robinson 1965, 293, fig. 20; Versluys 2002, 219–221, cat. 119, figs. 141–142.
29 Touchais 1989, 620, fig. 71; Versluys 2002, 221–222, fig. 143.
30 Vasunia 2001, 92–93.
31 Vasunia 2001, 75–77; Gruen 2011. Swetnam-Burland (2015, 143) notes that Ammianus Marcellinus (22.15.1–31), writing well into the 4th century CE, cites Herodotus as a source and continues to frame his discussion of Egypt in a Herodotean perspective.
32 Manolaraki 2013, 280.
33 Murray 1970, 167–169; Burstein 1996, 598–599.
34 Gruen 2011, 91–99. For example, Diod. 1.67.7, in which Diodorus attempts to differentiate himself from Herodotus, but the work is nevertheless engaged with Herodotean questions. See further: Burton 1972, 20–29. Other scholars have argued that Book I of Diodorus Siculus is an *epitome* of Hecataeus' lost *Aegyptiaca*, including: Murray 1970, 144. More recently, Muntz (2011, 592–594) has argued that Diodorus must have used Herodotus as a key source, and that his attitudes towards Herodotus are much less polemical than previously believed. Though Herodotus eventually fell out of favor as a historical source, particularly in paradoxography, Priestley (2014, 75–87) argues that the general format for this genre relies more on Herodotean precedent than it does on Aristot., *Mir. Ausc.* and other sources that were treated as factual.
35 For example, the bottomless holes of Strabo 17.1.52 (based on Hdt. 2.109), the preservation of sacred knowledge over long stretches of time in hieroglyphic writing described in: Cic., *Rep.* 3.14, Diod. Sic. 1.81, Strabo 17.1.3. See further: Manolaraki 2013, 29–42, 119–132; 2018; Merrills 2017, 174–183.
36 See the preceding paragraphs for Herodotus on the annual flood. On the solar connotations of Horus, see: Plut., *De Is.* 372b–e.
37 For a similar argument regarding kinetic viewer experiences in Roman villas, see: Bergmann 2001.
38 Hall 2002, 11; Kemezis 2014, 390–391.
39 Mandaville 1999.
40 Vlassopoulos 2015, 7–12.
41 Manolaraki 2018, 345–347.
42 Merrills 2017, 282–284; Manolaraki 2018, 360–361.
43 I have argued elsewhere (Mazurek 2018) that the sanctuary also served philosophical functions and helped its viewers explore Middle Platonic metaphysics. I view the interpretation presented here as complementary, and believe that this sanctuary, like most in the ancient world, served several functions and responded to multiple subjectivities.
44 I disagree with Gleason's (2010) formulation of biculturality, but she is correct to note that code-switching was key to Herodes' success. See also: Tobin 1997, 31–67.
45 Most of our biographical information about Herodes Atticus comes from Philostratus' account in the *Lives of the Sophists* (*V S*). Herodes Atticus was born in 101–103 CE and died at age seventy-six (*V S* 565) at some point during the years 177–179 CE. Scholars disagree about Herodes' precise dates, based on

divergent readings of *V S* 588–589. On this controversy, see: Swain 1990, critiquing: Ameling 1983a, 159–161. The precise dates of Herodes' birth and death do not impact my arguments here.

46 Graindor 1930, 20–38. On the relationships of Greek sophists with Roman emperors, see: König 2014, 252–258.

47 At Kephissia, the most significant finds are a familial grave plot that included a series of high-quality portrait busts. This villa is the source of many of the portrait busts now in the National Archaeological Museum of Athens (Götte 2001, plate 64s). First excavated in 1961, the site revealed a portrait of Herodes Atticus, a portrait of Polydeukion, a black marble arm (thought to belong to a statue of Memnon), and the head of a horse (Vanderpool 1961). At Eva Loukou, the primary works are: Spyropoulos 2001, 2006. Strazdins (2022) offers a more nuanced and holistic examination of these sites. While Spyropoulos gives a preliminary overview of the sculptural program at the villa, it is well known from those that have seen the Loukou storerooms informally that a lot of high-quality sculpture has been excavated here, including at least one sphinx and an Egyptianizing head that Siskou compares with the Osiris statues described in the section "Time and Style in the Ideal Sculpture."

48 Based on epigraphic evidence, it seems that the villa extended over most of the plain of Marathon, from the sea to the mountains, reaching at least up through the Avlona Valley and ancient Oinoe. Given the size of the villa, lavish domestic structures and extensive agricultural works must have existed, but at present only a scattered handful of buildings are known. A group of buildings was found in the area called *Mandra tis Grias* on the western slope of Mt. Kotroni, approximately 10 km northwest of the Egyptian sanctuary. This area included an entrance gate called the Arch of Eternal Harmony, an arched gateway flanked by seated portrait statues of Herodes and his wife Regilla. A six-line epigram carved on the eastern pillar of the Arch refers to Regilla's death, providing a *terminus ante quem* for the Arch of about 160 CE: *SEG* 23, 121; Gleason 2010; Geagan 1964, 151; Ameling 1983b, cat. 99; Tobin 1997, 247–249. Further to the north and closer to the village of Oinoe is another structure associated with Herodes' villa. Travlos mapped the building in the 1980s, reconstructing a series of square piers that formed a kind of peristyle with marble benches along the interior, perhaps an atypical bath structure or a social meeting place: Tobin 1997, 266–271; Galli 2002, 198–203.

49 Marcus Aurelius, *Ex Philostrati Vitis Sophistarum*, included in the miscellaneous letters of Marcus Aurelius: Fronto 1920, 294–297. On these letters and their manuscript traditions, see: Fleury 2016.

50 Wright (Philostratus and Eunapius 1922, 156n1) suggests that the text may refer to the urban sanctuary of Sarapis, but Graindor (1930, 187) and Tobin (1997, 261–262) agree that Philostratus must be referring to a site at Marathon. Earlier in the passage (*V S* 552–553), Agathion describes his close connection with the land of Marathon at length: he names the hero Marathon as his father, and Philostratus notes that this hero has a statue on display at Marathon as well. His food comes specifically from the farmers of Marathon and Boeotia. Agathion also makes clear his general disdain for the city of Athens, which he thinks is full of barbarian immigrants who "deteriorate" (παραφθείρονται) the Greek language. It seems unlikely that Philostratus would have set an encounter with his idealized rustic savant in Athens, making the Marathon villa a better candidate for the Egyptianizing Temple of Canobus than Herodes' more urban villa at Kephissia.

51 Strazdins 2019, 257.

52 Whitmarsh (2001, 105–108) and Gray (2006, 362–365) connect this story to a longer heroic tradition of the male rustic in Attic literary and artistic culture.

53 Herodes had a particularly strong connection to Marathon: he was born there, his family claimed descent from Miltiades, the Athenian victor at Marathon, and in his will he asked to be buried there (*V S* 565). While there are examples of sanctuaries located on private estates but open to the public (Xen., *Ana.* 5.3.7–23), this seems to have been a special provision extended for festivals and not a general rule. Thank you to Caitlín Barrett for this reference.

54 Though in published accounts this structure is only referred to as a cistern, Dekoulakou believes that it referenced the Canopeum at

Hadrian's Villa in Tivoli: pers. comm., July 2019. See further: Oikonomakou 2005.

55 Athens, National Archaeological Museum, Egyptian Collection inv. 1, Vavritsas 1968, 230–234; Dekoulakou 2011a, 25–28; Siskou 2011, 92, cat. 4, figs. 9a–e.

56 Marathon, Archaeological Museum inv. BE1: Siskou 2011, 89, cat. 1, figs. 1a–g.

57 Marathon, Archaeological Museum inv. BE2: Dekoulakou 2010, 113–114, fig. 10.

58 Previous research analyzed the sanctuary based on excavations up to 1968: Tobin 1997, 255–263; Galli 2002, 178–193. Dekoulakou's subsequent excavations revealed over half of the sanctuary and resulted in a radically revised ground plan and a significant expansion of the sculptural corpus, rendering the earlier studies obsolete.

59 My description of the sanctuary at Marathon is based on excavator Dekoulakou's descriptions: Dekoulakou 1999, 2003, 2010, 2011a, 2011b. Earlier results of 1960s salvage-work appear in: Vavritsas 1968. Additionally, I received tours of the site from excavators Dekoulakou in June 2013 and Fotiadi in 2019. At present, the complex opens directly onto the beach, though Fauvel's 1792 drawings indicate remains of buildings to the east that are still visible underwater. No systematic excavations have been done to determine whether these buildings belong to the sanctuary or to Herodes' villa, but Dekoulakou and Fotiadi believe they are part of the villa.

60 Βιβούλλιος Πολυ/δεύκης Ἡρώδου ε/[ταῖ]ρος καὶ τραφεὶς/[ἐκ το]ύτου *vel* [ὑπ'α]ὐτοῦ εὐσεβεί/[ας ἕ]νεκα: SEG 59 233, Dekoulakou 2011a, 37–38, figs. 19, 20. The inscription was found inside the building's cryptoporticus, probably not in situ. Though normally Polydeukion dedicates under the diminutive form of his name, Πολυδευκίων, he and many of his family members also use the name Polydeukes. On the names related to the Vibulli, see: Ameling 1983b, 167.

61 Tobin 1997, 233.

62 Götte 2003, 549–557; Dekoulakou 2011a, 39–40.

63 Galli 2002, 191.

64 I have argued for identifying the site as a sanctuary for similar reasons in: Mazurek 2018, 632.

65 SEG 59 198. The first line of the text is lost, and most of the text is fragmentary. Reconstructed by Dekoulakou (2011a, 36, figs. 16–17; 2011b, 34–35) and based on unpublished advice from Rizakis, following IG 14 1103. Another fragmentary inscription from the site (Dekoulakou 2011a, 37, fig. 18) includes the text – – –]Σ ΙΕΡΟ[– – –, further evidence that the site supported religious activities.

66 These lamps are not fully published, but some are studied in Fotiadi 2011. Dekoulakou (2011a, 27n18) identifies most of them as Alpha Globule Lamps, referencing Perlzweig (1961, plate 14).

67 Dekoulakou (2003; 2011a, 34–35) indicates that most of the lamps from Room B have similarly oversized proportions. See further: Podvin and Veymiers 2008, 66–67; Fotiadi 2011, 65n2. Fotiadi's corpus includes lamps signed with the names Minkianos, Agemonos, Apollophano(s?), Sytyxianos, Kreskentos, Loukios, and Sposianos. These workshops were prolific, with 2nd-century examples known from Athens, Corinth, and Patras. The Loukios workshop is active from the end of the 1st century through the 2nd century CE, and the Sposianos workshop from the first half of the 2nd century through the beginning of the 3rd century CE. The iconography of the discs is consistent, but it is not clear whether these lamps were made from the same mold. Because of the wide range of possible dates, Fotiadi (2011, 65, 75–77nn46–47) also argues that the Marathon lamps could have been commissioned after the 160s CE.

68 Fotiadi 2011, 74.

69 It seems that much of the site's freestanding and architectural sculpture was destroyed in a later period. There are two large lime kilns on the site and several large piles of ash and marble fragments. It is possible that later dedications were destroyed, though it would be curious if only the material from the initial use phase survived. I thank Pelly Fotiadi for sharing her insights about the dating of these lamps.

70 Maikidou 2015, 28; Dekoulakou 2017. The study of these coins is ongoing, though some have been dated to the reigns of Constantine II (337–347 CE) and Theodosius II (402–450 CE). It is not clear whether the coins' findspot represents a primary or secondary deposition. This new evidence disproves my earlier

71 suggestion that the sanctuary may have been used only during the lifetime of Herodes Atticus: Mazurek 2018, 631–632.

71 While the monumentality of the East Court's entrance pylon suggests that this was the primary path for visitors, devotees could have entered the West Court directly through its North, South, and West Pylons. Visitors coming from the bath complex (about 40 m south of the sanctuary's southern wall) may have used the South Pylon to enter. Because the areas to the north and west of the sanctuary have not been investigated, it is not clear whether there were monuments that would have encouraged visitors to enter from those sides. There are cuttings for the insertion of single-leafed doors at all the pylons that could have regulated these access points: Dekoulakou 2011a, 26–27.

72 Dekoulakou 2011a, 26.

73 Plut., *De Is.* 359b. In this passage, Plutarch lists the island of Philae as a possible location of the true tomb of Osiris. Versluys and Meyboom have suggested that some of the Nilotic mosaics and paintings depict the tomb of Osiris at Philae: Meyboom 1995, 61–63; Versluys 2002, 279–285.

74 The pylons are preserved only at a height of approximately 1 m. The veneers are reconstructed based on the presence of a fine mortar on the brick surface: Dekoulakou 2011a, 25.

75 Dekoulakou 2011a, 32–34, fig. 13.

76 P. Fotiadi, pers. comm., July 2019.

77 For the lintel found in 1968, see: Petrakos 1995, 79, fig. 32. For the fragments found in Dekoulakou's excavations, see: Dekoulakou 2011a, 25, fig. 11; 2011b, 26–27. A similar insignia appears on a flat stone panel on Delos: Archaeological Museum inv. A 6994. On the floor of the corridor was preserved a cache of nineteen lamps datable to the late 2nd century CE, and in one of the rooms was found a small assemblage of coins datable to the 4th–5th century CE.

78 It is difficult to determine if the structure resembled a pyramid or if the other Egyptianizing features in the sanctuary prompt us to reconstruct a pyramid. Excavators Dekoulakou and Fotiadi believe the structure could have been a *naiskos* on a stepped platform, inaccessible to visitors. The architectural and archaeological evidence here is not clear enough to determine the building's precise shape, except that its limestone conglomerate core was covered in revetments of some kind.

79 On the pyramid tombs of Rome, see: van Aerde 2015, 165–170. Van Aerde (2015, 169, fig. 64) does describe a potential pyramid under excavation along the Via Appia that seems similar, but that structure is made of a concrete core in a pyramidal shape and does not appear stepped.

80 Ricke 1965, 3–18. Mari and Sgalambro (2007, 99–103) have also argued that the obelisk of Antinoos (also known as the Barberini obelisk) now displayed on the Pinchian Hill in Rome, was originally part of the Egyptianizing complex at Hadrian's Villa at Tivoli they call the Antinoeion. For a detailed textual argument against this identification, see: Renberg 2010, 181–191.

81 Length, ca. 1.4 m; height, 0.65 m: Dekoulakou 2011a, 31, figs. 9–10. A second, unpublished sphinx was found at the site out of context.

82 A similar statue was found at Eva Loukou: Karusu 1969, 262–263, plate 84, figs. 2–3. On Herodes' villa at the site, see further: Spyropoulos 2006; Strazdins 2022.

83 Marathon, Archaeological Museum inv. 438: Dekoulakou 2010, 114–116; 2011a, 30–31, fig. 7.

84 See further: Nagel 2015; Albersmeier 2018, 458–463.

85 The crook and flail are common attributes of Osiris, as seen in a drawing of the god in a Book of the Dead section from Akhmin that dates to the Ptolemaic period: Russman 2001, cat. 105. The present statue has likely reinterpreted this iconography without care for its original meaning, much like the adapted "ankh" included in the Isis statue from the Iseum at Pompeii: Swetnam-Burland 2015, fig. 121b.

86 Malaise 1972b, 329–330; Foertmeyer 1989; Versluys 2002, 423; Barrett 2019, 104–106.

87 Siskou 2011, 89, cat. 2; Dekoulakou 2011a, 27. In terms of technique and style, the statues have much in common with the Antonine-period grave reliefs from Athens discussed in Chapter 5: Walters 1988, 75–81; Dekoulakou 2010, 117–120.

88 South Pylon: Marathon, Archaeological Museum inv. 414; Dekoulakou 2010, 111–112, figs. 2–5; 2011a, 28–29, fig. 3. West Pylon: Marathon, Archaeological Museum

89 There is no statue base preserved outside the East Pylon and inside the East Court, and it is not clear whether another pair stood outside the East Pylon. Further, the statue fragments found outside the South Pylon indicate that the exterior pairs were carved on a larger scale.

90 Since this costume has no antecedents in Greek art, it may reference Egyptian iconography, where long-sleeved dresses are more common: Ashton 2001, 39, 41–42; Dekoulakou 2010, 114. The costume may have been popularized in Ptolemaic sculpture. Cleopatra VII appears in this garment in a 1st-century BCE statue: Roullet 1972, cat. 180, fig. 203.

91 See: Malaise 1972a, 176–177; Bianchi 2011, 482–493.

92 The use of the term "syncretism" is controversial. C. Stewart (1999, 40–42, 56–58), however, has argued convincingly that an increasing scholarly awareness of colonialist viewpoints allows us to reconsider the term as a non-pejorative way of describing intercultural and religious mixtures. In Stewart's view, syncretism is an ideal term for exploring the interrelationships between religion and culture. Isis commonly had syncretized forms and epithets that allowed her to fill roles formerly occupied by local deities. For the practice in Isiac religion and its problems in contemporary scholarship, see: Leclant 1986, 341–343; Malaise 2005, 193–197; Moyer 2011, 146–153; Woolf 2014, 86–92.

93 This headdress contains three sheaves of wheat rather than the two normally seen in Isis-Demeter images. The same variant of Isis with three sheaves of wheat in her headgear also appears on some of the lamps studied in: Fotiadi 2011, 70–72. Fotiadi describes this as one of many iconographic idiosyncrasies found throughout the sanctuary.

94 Touchette 2015, 292. Zagdoun (1989) has applied this term to Classical Greek art as well, but most other scholars of the style, including Fullerton (1990) and Hallett (2012), reserve it for Roman works: Elsner 2017.

95 Hallett 2012, 84–86; Touchette 2015, 293–296.

96 Elsner 2017, 458–462.

97 Most notably, several ideal sculptures from the Iseum of Pompeii used archaizing forms: van Andriga 2012.

98 Barrett 2019, 283–294.

99 Pearson 2015, 46–47. Pearson's work also demonstrates that many other kinds of luxury objects from Egypt were integrated into Roman wall painting, calling into question the assumption that most of these images were fantastic or imagined.

100 Manolaraki 2013, 6. On ideas of time in Second Sophistic Greece and their cultural and political education, see: Strazdins 2021.

101 Mazurek 2018, 629n88. This type of essentializing action is a key part of E. Saïd's (1978, 49–73) Orientalism.

102 On the importance of materiality to the study of *Aegyptiaca*, see: Mol 2012.

103 North Pylon statue: Marathon, Archaeological Museum inv. BE1; Siskou 2011, 89, cat. 1, figs. 1a–g. West Pylon statue: Marathon, Archaeological Museum inv. 546; Siskou 2011, 89, cat. 3, figs. 4a–3. South Pylon statue: Marathon, Archaeological Museum inv. 415; Siskou 2011, 89, cat. 2, figs. 2a–e. Fragments from exterior of South Pylon: Marathon, Archaeological Museum inv. 413 a, b, c; Siskou 2011, 92, cat. 5–8, figs. 10a–e. The male statues from the North Pylon and the fragments from the South Pylon have fewer details in their rendering of the body than the West Pylon and National Archaeological Museum images. The last two examples have incised irises, clear depictions of nipples on the chest, an incised groove on the throat, and more careful modeling of the fists, abdominal muscles, and back pillar: Siskou 2011, 83. On stylistic eclecticism, see: Perry 2005, 112–149; Swetnam-Burland 2015, 53–61; Versluys 2015, 154.

104 Fischer (1975) argued that these are folded over or rolled pieces of cloth or papyrus.

105 The funerary stele of Lamia Biboullia dates to the second half of the 2nd century CE, depicting the deceased with a similarly fleshy oval face and broad bodily proportions: Piraeus, Archaeological Museum 1168; Walters 1988, plate 27. The Osiris statue, however, has a more rigid posture that recalls Archaic *kouroi* and their Egyptian precedents. On Egyptian influence on Archaic sculpture, see: Davis 1981.

106 The inclusion of Sarapis' *kalathos* headdress indicates that we are looking at a god rather than an idealized Egyptian king. In Egyptian art, the division between the two is not

107 Epigraphic dedications include examples from Delos Sarapieion C: *IG* 11 4, 1234 (before 166 BCE); Thessaloniki: *IG* 10 2, 107 (2nd century BCE); Euboia: *IG* 12 Suppl., 565 (1st century BCE); Gomphoi: *SEG* 2, 359; Volos, Athanasakio Archaeological Museum inv. E838 (1st–2nd century CE). Some Roman literary texts mention Osiris and his mythology, including Diodorus Siculus' account of Osiris' feud with Typhon (1.88), Stat. *Theb.* (1.718–719), Luc. *Pharsalia* 8.831–834, and Plutarch's *De Iside*. See: Manolaraki 2013, 252–257.

108 No statues or images of Osiris are known from Greek sanctuaries. A statue base for a now-lost statue of Osiris has been found at Fiesole, and a few imported bronzes found in Italy depict Osiris in his mummiform type. The Herakleitos mosaic from a villa in Piccolo Aventino in Rome, however, may depict him in anthropomorphic form: Siskou 2011, 83–87, with accompanying bibliography. In Tib. 7.43–49, he is described as human in form, performing dances and other active movements not possible for a mummiform god.

109 Richter 2001, 191–195.

110 *V S* 564, Gell., *NA* 1.26. On the problem of Herodes' age for this encounter with Plutarch, see: Dillon 1988, 114; 1996, 237–238; Mazurek 2018, 612n4, 614.

111 As argued in: Mazurek 2018. Calvenus Taurus regularly invited his students to his home for philosophical instruction and discussion (Gell., *NA* 7.13), and Herodes had a smaller group of favorite students call the Klepsydrion that dined with him after lectures (*V S* 585–586). See further: Eshleman 2012, 131–135. Herodes often invited his students to his villa at Kephissia (Gell., *NA* 1.2.1, 18.10), and there are mentions of Herodes bringing students to Marathon in later periods of his life (Fronto 1920, 2:294–297). Admittedly, viewers who were not familiar with the Egyptian cults or Egyptian deities more generally may not have been concerned about the differences between Sarapis and Osiris.

112 Rome, Vatican Museums, Gregorian Egyptian Museum inv. 22795. Mari and Sgalambro (2007, 97–98) have argued that the statue should be relocated to their proposed Antinoeion. The text of the Pincian Obelisk identifies Antinoos as Osiris-Antinoos, son of Re, and if this statue were displayed in the same complex, as Mari and Sgalambro claim, it is likely that viewers would have interpreted this image as Osiris. For a translation of the text, see: Boatwright 1987, 243–246; Meyer et al. 1994; Grenier 2008, 1–36.

113 Based on this comparison, Gazda (1980) and Vout (2005, 92–93) have suggested that the male statues from the Marathon sanctuary could represent Antinoos or Polydeukion as a parallel to Antinoos. The stylistic differences between the more naturalistic Tivoli examples and the more archaistic Marathon statues suggest a difference in subject. Further, the Marathon statues lack portrait features that would support identification as either Antinoos or Polydeukion. See: Siskou 2011, 83–88.

114 Contra: Siskou 2011.

115 There are examples of imported Egyptian statuettes that depict male figures in the *shendyt* kilt and *nemes* headdress, including a faience example from the House of Octavius Quarto at Pompeii (Pompeii inv. 2898), that could have also served as models. See: Tronchin 2006, 45–52; Barrett 2019, 260–261, fig. 6.6.

116 Dekoulakou 2011b, 32, figs. 11–12. Fragments of two other Horus falcons were found at the site out of context, bringing the total known number to five. Dekoulakou does not describe the distribution of the hawks, but Fotiadi discussed these findspots with me in July 2019 and suggested that the falcons may have flanked each side of the staircase. This reconstruction would coincide with the way the type was used at the Ptolemaic Temple of Horus at Edfu.

117 Still on site. See: Watterson 1998, color plate 9.

118 Examples of this Harpokrates type were found in the Egyptian sanctuaries at Dion (Archaeological Museum inv. MΔ 400, 100–125 CE; Pandermalis 2016, 111, cat. 27); Thessaloniki (Archaeological Museum inv. MΘ 844, 3rd century CE; Despinis et al. 1997–2020, vol. 1, 115–116, cat. 86, figs. 221–225), and Messene (Messene, Archaeological Museum inv. 1344, 16696, Hadrianic period; Themelis 2011, 97, 108).

There are other examples of this type in other media, however, that may have informed Herodes' decision. Horus-falcons appeared in at least two sanctuaries in the Greek islands: four examples of Horus depicted as a falcon, probably produced in Egypt, were found in the Egyptian sanctuary at Rhodes Town, and the temple inventories of Sarapieion C on Delos include mentions of objects depicting bird-headed gods, notably a hawk-headed statue and an earring depicting a Horus-falcon with the Egyptian double crown: (Rhodes, Archaeological Museum inv. Γ2762, Γ2750; Fantaoutsaki 2011, 57–59, figs. 15–16). On the Delian examples, see: Hamilton 2000, 235; Hatzidakis 2003, 338, 657, 438n657; Barrett 2011, 188n643. Herodes may have also looked to Italy, where examples of Horus in bird form are known from the wall paintings of the north wall of the Black Room at Boscotrecase and a silver cup from the Palaestra at Pompeii (New York, Metropolitan Museum of Art inv. 20.192.10; Swetnam-Burland 2015, 55, fig. 1.18); Naples (Naples, Museo Archeologico Nazionale inv. 640, probably from the Praedia of Julia Felix; Swetnam-Burland 2015, 170, fig. 4.16b).

119 Find announced in *La Repubblica* with photographs, but not yet published: Grattoggi 2014. The article suggests that Mari identified the site as a temple of Isis based on this find, and a sphinx discovered in 2006. He cites the Marathon Horus statuette as comparanda for the Tivoli example, but the arrangement of the wings is different enough that this, too, should be considered more of a free copy or adaptation.

120 As Barrett (2019, 341–352) argues, Tivoli draws upon a long tradition of incorporating Egyptianizing themes into domestic architecture, and it is likely that Herodes was familiar with these precedents as well. The close personal connections between Herodes and the Imperial family discussed in the section "The Sophist's Nile at Marathon" make it likely that the Marathon villa was meant to allude more concretely to the Tivoli structures. The identification of the so-called Antinoeion is contested. For the original identification, see: Mari 2004; Mari and Sgalambro 2007; and for a refutation, see: Grenier 2008, 37–46; Renberg 2010, 181–191. The primary argument against the identification of the structure as an Antinoeion is philological evidence, namely Epiphanus, *Ancoratus* 106.9, as discussed in: Boatwright 1987, 241; and Clem. Alex., *Protr.* 491–493, discussed in Renberg (2010, 185), which suggests that Antinoos was buried at Antinoopolis in Egypt. I find Mari and Sgalambro's archaeological evidence more compelling than Renberg's philological arguments, but even if it is not the actual tomb of Antinoos, the structure identified as an Antinoeion features a program of Egyptianizing sculpture and architectural ornament that would provide a useful source of inspiration for Nilotic art and architecture.

121 SHA *Hadr.* 26.5. There has been considerable debate about the veracity of the *Historia Augusta* as a source for topographic knowledge, but Long (2002) has demonstrated that increased attention to vocabulary shifts in 4th-century Latin and advances in archaeological research have indicated that the *HA* is more reliable as a topographical source for Rome, especially Antonine and Severan Rome, than has been previously assumed. Even still, Macdonald and Pinto (1995, 6–8) are reluctant to identify these toponyms with any particular structure within the villa. On the connection between the villa's topography and expressions of global rule, see further: von Stackelberg 2009, 85; Barrett 2019, 331–335.

122 Barrett 2019, 334.

123 Regarding ongoing use after Hadrian's death, see: MacDonald and Pinto 1995, 198–205. Thank you to Tolly Boatwright for her assistance on this point. On Herodes' relationship with Marcus Aurelius, see: Graindor 1930, 66–68, 76–79, 120–131; Tobin 1997, 8–9, 35–48, 52, 291; Eshleman 2012, 126–131.

124 Barrett 2019, 333–334. See further: Versluys 2012, 34; Swetnam-Burland 2015, 155–167.

125 Dekoulakou 2011a, 38–39, figs. 21, 22. Dekoulakou is publishing this statue separately in a forthcoming essay. There was also a bronze female portrait statue, which remains unpublished and is undergoing restoration: I. Dekoulakou, pers. comm., June 2013.

126 Bust of Herodes Atticus (Paris, Louvre inv. NIII2536, Fejfer 2008, figs. 229, 232). Bust of Marcus Aurelius (Paris, Louvre inv. NIII2535, Fejfer 2008, figs. 227, 230, 231). Bust of Lucius Verus (Oxford, Ashmolean Museum

127 All three date to the mid-2nd century CE: Fittschen 2001.
128 Dekoulakou (2011b, fig. 2) reconstructs these excavations in an area to the immediate southeast of the East Court. See further: Biddle 1993, 120; Fittschen 2001; Galli 2002, 192n765.
129 Fittschen 2001, 71–73. Fittschen and Dekoulakou believe the trio of busts was found close to Room A: Dekoulakou 2011a, 38–39.
130 Fittschen 2001; Dekoulakou 2010. Based on the carving style and forms of constructing the busts' bases, Fittschen connects the Marathon bust group with other portraits of Polydeukion and Herodes Atticus produced by the same workshop, including examples of Herodes Atticus now in Basel (Antikenmuseum inv. BS 280), Athens (National Archaeological Museum inv. 4810, 4811), and Polydeukion in Berlin (Staatliche Museum inv. 413) and London (Soane's Museum, findspot unknown), mostly from findspots in Attika.
131 On the *kosmetai* portraits and the image of the Greek intellectual in the 2nd century CE, see: R. R. R. Smith 1998, 78–81; D'Ambra 2005, 207–212.
132 Most notably in the *ethne* reliefs of the Sebasteion of Aphrodisias and the "Eastern Victory Type" of Antonine imperial portraiture type, known from Hierapytna, Gortyna, Kissamos, and the Athenian Agora, that depicts Roman emperors stomping on barbarians. See: Gergel 2004, 377–386; R. R. R. Smith 2013, 71–122.
133 This is a common trope in Philostratus, but that author is careful to nuance the relationship between Greek intellectual elite and emperor by noting the uneasy power imbalance between the two: König 2014, 258.
134 Bommas 2012, 192–193.
135 Early travelers to the region described the area as the "marsh of Marathon" or "island" and the site is still referred to as *Mikro Elos*, or "little marsh," in Modern Greek. See: Dekoulakou 2011a, 25. The trade in North African wild animals (Mackinnon 2006) could have provided Herodes with animals to contribute further to a Nilotic atmosphere.
136 Sotiriadis 1926, 36–37. The canal is no longer visible and was likely destroyed in the 1960s during the construction of the Golden Coast Hotel in the area north of the sanctuary.
137 Wild 1981, 30–47; Kleibl 2009, 113–114. This phenomenon may be temporal as well as regional. Wild notes that water crypts are very popular in Hellenistic sanctuaries but decline in frequency in the Roman period.
138 Kleibl 2007; 2009, 108–114. See also: Wild 1981, 25–53, 71–85.
139 Fantaoutsaki 2011, 52–55; Themelis 2011, 105–106; Veymiers 2011, 124–125.
140 Though not part of the sanctuary, a spring house stood immediately behind the Athenian South Slope sanctuary and could have provided water to the Isiac community: Walker 1979, 245, fig. 1.
141 Wild 1981, 26–34; Kleibl 2007; 2009, 102–105.
142 Barrett 2011, 119–250; 2019, 60–113.
143 Delos: *ID* 2155, 2160 (restored), Roussel 1914/1915, cat. 179 (lost, bronze plaque), *ID* 2087, 2088. See also: Malaise 2005, 30; Siard 2007. Corinth: Steatite jar with Osiris Hydreios in relief; Williams 1985, 80, cat. 49, fig. 17. See further: Wild 1981, 101–128. Thessaloniki: Thessaloniki, Archaeological Museum inv. MΘ 1950, *IG* 10 2, 83 (marble plaque).
144 Underneath the base for Aphrodite Hypolympidia discussed in Chapter 2 flowed a constant stream of water that fed a small reservoir underneath her statue base: Pandermalis 1982a, 730–731.
145 Mylonopoulos 2008, 63–66; Pandermalis 2016, 23. Nielson (2002, 224–225) incorrectly identifies the feature as a processional *dromos*. Similarly, the garden at the Casa di Octavius Quarto at Pompeii uses a long linear water feature in its Nilotic garden assemblage: Platt 2002; von Stackelberg 2009, 101–125; Mol 2015a, 392–446.
146 Pandermalis 1997, 25, 73; 2000, 89. Bulls: Dion, Archaeological Museum inv. MΔ 398, MΔ 5448.
147 Pandermalis 2000, 89; Mylonopoulos 2008, 65–66. On the cult of Apis, see further: Dunand and Zivie-Coche 2004, 214–220; Malaise 2005, 128–129; Bricault 2013, 58–61.
148 Rhodes, Archaeological Museum inv. Γ2775; Fantaoutsaki 2011, 61, fig. 21. The Rhodes statuette is found in the crypt, but this may not have been its original display context. On the Apis bull's significance in Hellenistic Egypt, see: Thompson 1988, 10–29. For his significance in Greco-Roman cults of Isis, see: Malaise 2005, 41–45.

149 Oliverio 1914, 377; Salditt-Trappmann 1970, 66; Wild 1981, 72–76.
150 Wild (1981, 73–74), referencing Plut., *De Iside* 372c. See further: Merkelbach 1963, 38; Griffiths 1970, 450.
151 A *boophore* who could have performed such a rite is commemorated in a 2nd-century CE list of cult functionaries in the Sarapeum at Thessaloniki: *IG* 10 2, 244; Bricault 2005, 160, cat. 113/0561.
152 Di Vita 1999, 10–14, figs. 3–9. Di Vita (1999, 14–18, fig. 10) reconstructs the 4th-century CE architrave inscription as [T. P]ACTUME [IUS – – – – – –]CRES UC / CONS [——], which he connects with T. Pactumeius Magnus, a Roman aristocrat and bureaucrat whose family was transferred to Crete, perhaps to the territory of Knossos, and served as a prefect of Egypt under Marcus Aurelius. The inscription may refer to one of his descendants.
153 *I.Cret.* 4, 249; Bricault 2005, 374, cat. 203/0607; Karetsou and Andreadaki-Vlazaki 2000, 380, cat. 422.
154 Di Vita 1999, 30–31. Di Vita's reconstruction would require the 4th-century Pactumeius architrave to replace Flavia Philyra's 2nd-century CE one.
155 It is not clear exactly how many elements or which combinations could produce a recognizably Nilotic aesthetic. I expect that it would depend on a variety of social, artistic, spatial, and sensorial factors that would be almost impossible to reconstruct with the current evidence.
156 Mukerji 1997, 18. For a complementary analysis of Pompeiian gardens, see: Barrett 2019, 50–140.

CHAPTER 7

1 Gordon 2014; Versluys 2013; Mol 2015b.
2 Bonnet et al. 2009; Mol 2015b.
3 In Eretria (Kleibl 2009, 198–200, cat. A6), two fountains are contained within the temple precinct. At Athens (Kleibl 2009, 183–185, cat. A1), there is a spring house that lies a bit to the northeast of the sanctuary, housing a natural water source in use since the Mycenaean period. See further: Bruneau 1975, 46, 50–52; Walker 1979.
4 Barrett 2019, 333–346.
5 Kemezis 2014; Dench 2017, 100–103.
6 Jennings 2011, 21–31.
7 Gasparini and Gordon (2018) have recently pointed out the importance of historicizing stereotypes and ethnic thinking on broader time scales, and a more detailed study of local and temporally specific histories of Isiac cults could offer important insights into the lived experiences of Isiac cults. Even still, their typology offers only two historical divisions and a handful of ideological divisions with which to analyze the material discussed here.
8 This effect has been observed for ancient Christianity and is a fundamental facet of Judaism. See further: Rebillard 2012.
9 See, for example, a votive relief (Rome, Musei Capitolini inv. 4371) that depicts Isis-Demeter standing while holding a torch.
10 There are no known examples of Isis wearing such a headdress. There is a fragmentary example of a 2nd-century CE Anubis statue found on Delos that, according to a reconstruction by Perdrizet, depicts the god with a dog's head on a human body that also carries palm leaves and a caduceus. Marcadé (1952, 123, fig. 22) is skeptical of this reconstruction, however, and the statue is very partial and abraded.
11 There is precedence for using a human "epiphany" in the guise of the goddess. In Hdt. 1.61.3, Pisistratus dresses a woman named Phye as Athena and drives her into Athens. According to Herodotus' account, the Athenians judged Phye to be the real goddess and are fooled, an encounter that Platt (2011, 15–16) describes as an epiphany.
12 Harrison 2015, 3–7.

BIBLIOGRAPHY

Throughout the book, ancient works are abbreviated according to the *Oxford Classical Dictionary*, 4th ed. Modern journals and book series are abbreviated according to the *American Journal of Archaeology*, with the exception of Brill's *Religions of the Greco-Roman World* series, which is abbreviated as *RGRW*.

"Chronique des fouilles et découvertes archéologiques dans l'Orient hellénique." 1924. *BCH* 48, 446–515.

"Die Erwerbungen der ägyptischen Abteilung der Königl. Museen im Jahre 1889." 1890. *ZÄS* 281–282, 54–62.

Adams, A. 1989. "The Arch of Hadrian at Athens." In *The Greek Renaissance in the Roman Empire: Papers from the Tenth British Museum Classical Colloquium*, edited by S. Walker and A. Cameron, 10–16. London: Institute of Classical Studies.

Albersmaier, S. 2005. "Griechisch-römische Bildnisse der Isis." In *Ägypten, Griechenland: Rom. Abwehr und Berührung*, edited by H. Beck, 310–315. Frankfurt am Main: Das Städel.

Albersmeier, S. 2018. "The Garments of the Devotees of Isis." In *Individuals and Materials in the Greco-Roman Cult of Isis: Agents, Images, and Practices*, *RGRW* 187, edited by V. Gasparini and R. Veymiers, 448–469. Leiden: Brill.

Alcock, S. E. 1994. "Minding the Gap in Hellenistic and Roman Greece." In *Placing the Gods: Sanctuaries and Sacred Space in Ancient Greece*, edited by S. E. Alcock and R. Osborne, 247–262. Oxford: Clarendon Press.

Alcock, S. E. 1995. *Graecia Capta: The Landscapes of Roman Greece*. Cambridge: Cambridge University Press.

Aldhouse Green, M. 2003. "Poles Apart? Perceptions of Gender in Gallo-British Cult-Iconography." In *Roman Imperialism and Provincial Art*, edited by S. Scott and J. Webster, 95–118. Cambridge: Cambridge University Press.

Alexandridis, A. 2010. "Neutral Bodies? Female Portrait Statue Types from the Late Republic to the Second Century C.E." In *Material Culture and Social Identities in the Ancient World*, edited by S. Hales and T. Hodos, 252–282. Cambridge: Cambridge University Press.

Ali Ibrahim, L., and R. L. Scranton. 1976. *The Panels of Opus Sectile in Glass, Kenchreai 2*. Leiden: Brill.

Almagor, E. 2013. "Dualism and the Self in Plutarch's Thought." In *Religious Dimensions of the Self in the Second Century CE*, edited by J. Rüpke and G. Woolf, 3–22. Tübingen: Mohr Siebeck.

Alston, R. 1996. "Conquest by Text: Juvenal and Plutarch on Egypt." In *Roman Imperialism: Post-colonial Perspectives*, edited by J. Webster and J. N. Cooper, 99–109. Leicester: School of Archaeological Studies, Leicester University.

Alvar, J. 2008. *Romanising Oriental Gods: Myth, Salvation and Ethics in the Cults of Cybele, Isis and Mithras*, *RGRW* 165. Translated by R. Gordon. Leiden: Brill.

Alvar, J. 2018. "Social Agentivity in the Eastern Mediterranean Cult of Isis." In *Individuals and Materials in the Greco-Roman Cults of Isis*, *RGRW* 187, edited by V. Gasparini and R. Veymiers, 221–247. Leiden: Brill.

Ameling, W. 1983a. *Herodes Atticus*, Vol. 1, *Biographie*. Zürich: Hildesheim.

Ameling, W. 1983b. *Herodes Atticus*, Vol. 2, *Inschriftenkatalog*. Zürich: Hildesheim.

Amelung, W. 1903. "Le Sarapis de Bryaxis." *RA* 42, 177–204.

Anderson, G. 1993. *The Second Sophistic: A Cultural Phenomenon in the Roman Empire*. London: Routledge.

Ando, G. 2000. *Imperial Ideology and Provincial Loyalty in the Roman Empire*. Berkeley: University of California Press.

Ando, C. 2005. "Interpretatio Romana." *CP* 100(1), 41–51.

Andrade, N. 2013. *Syrian Identity in the Greco-Roman World*. Cambridge: Cambridge University Press.

Andronikos, M. 1985. "Ἡ Ἀφροδίτη τῆς Θεσσαλονίκης." *AEphem* 1985, 1–32.

Antonaccio, C. 2003. "Hybridity and the Cultures within Greek Culture." In *The Cultures within Ancient Greek Culture: Contact, Conflict, Collaboration*, edited by C. Dougherty and L. Kurke, 57–74. Cambridge: Cambridge University Press.

Antonaccio, C. 2004. "Siculo-Geometric and the Sikels: Ceramics and Identity in Eastern Sicily." In *Greek Identity in the Western Mediterranean: Papers in Honour of Brian Shefton, Mnemosyne Suppl.* 246, edited by K. Lomas, 55–82. Leiden: Brill.

Antonaccio, C. 2005. "Excavating Colonization." In *Ancient Colonization: Analogy, Similarity and Difference*, edited by H. Hurst and S. Owen, 93–110. Bristol: Duckworth Press.

Antonaccio, C. 2013. "Networking the Middle Ground? The Greek Diaspora, Tenth to Fifth Century BC." *Archaeological Review from Cambridge* 28(1), 241–256.

Appadurai, A. 1990. "Disjuncture and Difference in the Global Cultural Economy." *Public Culture* 2(2), 1–24.

Arnaoutoglou, I. 2003. *Thusias heneka kai sunousias: Private Religious Associations in Hellenistic Athens*. Athens: Academy of Athens.

Arnaoutoglou, I. 2018. "*Isiastai Sarapiastai*: Isiac Cult Associations in the Eastern Mediterranean." In *Individuals and Materials in the Greco-Roman Cults of Isis: Agents, Images, Practices, RGRW* 187, edited by V. Gasparini and R. Veymiers, 248–282. Leiden: Brill.

Ashton, S.-A. 2001. *Ptolemaic Royal Sculpture from Egypt: The Interaction between Greek and Egyptian Traditions*. Oxford: Oxbow.

Assmann, J. 1997. "Magic and Theology in Ancient Egypt." In *Envisioning Magic: A Princeton Seminar and Symposium, Numen Series* 75, edited by P. Schäfer and H. Kippenberg, 1–18. Leiden: Brill.

Assmann, J. 2001. *The Search for God in Ancient Egypt*. Ithaca, NY: Cornell University Press.

Assmann, J. 2009. *Egyptian Solar Religion in the New Kingdom: Re, Amun, and the Crisis of Polytheism*. Translated by A. Alcock. New York: Routledge.

Atkin, A. 2013. "Peirce's Theory of Signs." In *The Stanford Encyclopedia of Philosophy*, edited by E. Zalta. https://plato.stanford.edu/archives/sum2013/entries/peirce-semiotics.

Aupert, P. 1976. "Chronique des fouilles en 1975." *BCH* 100, 591–745.

Babut, D. 1999. "Sur Soclaros de Chéronée et sur le nombre des enfants de Plutarque: méthodologie d'une mise au point." *RPh* 73, 175–189.

Bachmann-Medick, D. 2017. "Alterity – A Category of Practice and Analysis: Preliminary Remarks." *On Culture: The Open Journal for the Study of Culture* 4. https://nbn-resolving.org/urn:nbn:de:hebis:26-opus-133874.

Baecke-Dahmen, A. 2018. "Roman Children and the 'Horus Lock' between Cult and Image." In *Individuals and Materials in the Greco-Roman Cults of Isis: Agents, Images, and Practices, RGRW* 187, edited by V. Gasparini and R. Veymiers, 509–538. Leiden: Brill.

Bagnall, R. 1997. "The People of the Roman Fayum." In *Portraits and Masks: Burial Customs in Roman Egypt*, edited by M. L. Bierbrier, 7–15. London: British Museum Press.

Bagnall, R., and B. W. Frier. 1994. *The Demography of Roman Egypt*. Cambridge: Cambridge University Press.

Baldassarri, P. 1995. "Augusto Soter: Ipotesi sul monopteros dell'Acropoli ateniese." *Ostraka* 4, 69–84.

Barat, C. 2010. "La ville de Sinope, réflexions historiques et archéologiques." *Ancient Civilizations from Scythia to Siberia* 16, 25–64.

Barrett, C. E. 2011. *Egyptianizing Figurines from Delos*, Columbia Studies in the Classical Tradition 36. Leiden: Brill.

Barrett, C. E. 2017a. "Egypt in Roman Visual and Material Culture." In *Oxford Handbooks Online in Classical Studies*, edited by G. Williams. Oxford: Oxford University Press.

Barrett, C. E. 2017b. "Recontextualizing Nilotic Scenes: Interacting Landscapes in the Garden of the Casa dell'Efebo, Pompeii." *AJA* 121(2), 293–332.

Barrett, C. E. 2019. *Domesticating Empire: Egyptian Landscapes in Pompeian Gardens*. Oxford: Oxford University Press.

Barth, F. 1969. *Ethnic Groups and Boundaries. The Social Organization of Culture Difference*. Boston: Little Brown.

Baslez, M. F. 1977. *Recherches sur les conditions de pénétration et de diffusion des religions orientales à Délos, IIe–Ier avant notre ère*, Collection de l'École Normale Supérieure des Jeunes Filles 9. Paris: De Boccard.

Beall, S. M. 2001. "Homo fandi dulcissimus: The Role of Favorinus in the 'Attic Nights' of Aulus Gellius." *AJP* 122(1), 87–106.

Beard, M., J. North, and S. Price. 1998a. *Religions of Rome*, Vol. 2, *A Sourcebook*. Cambridge: Cambridge University Press.

Beard, M., J. North, and S. Price. 1998b. *Religions of Rome*, Vol. 1, *A History*. Cambridge: Cambridge University Press.

Bell, C. 1992. *Ritual Theory, Ritual Practice*. Oxford: Oxford University Press.

Bell, C. 1997. *Ritual: Perspectives and Dimensions*. Oxford: Oxford University Press.

Berger, E. 1982. "Zwei neue Skulpturenfragmente im Basler Ludwig-Museum: Zum Problem des 'Asklepios Giustini.'" In *Praestant interna: Festschrift für Ulrich Hausmann*, edited by B. F. Löringhoff, 63–71. Tübingen: Verlag Ernst Wasmuth.

Bergmann, B. 2001. "Meanwhile, Back in Italy ... Creating Landscapes of Allusion." In *Pausanias: Travel and Memory in Roman Greece*, edited by J. F. Cherry and S. E. Alcock, 154–166. Oxford: Oxford University Press.

Beschi, L. 1988. "Demeter." *LIMC* 4, 844–892. Zürich: Artemis Verlag.

Bianchi, R. S. 1980. "Not the Isis Knot." *Bulletin of the Egyptological Seminar* 2, 9–31.

Bianchi, R. S. 2011. "Images of Isis and Her Cultic Shrines Reconsidered: Towards an Egyptian Understanding of the *interpretatio graeca*." In *Nile into Tiber: Egypt in the Roman World – Proceedings of the IIIrd International Conference of Isis Studies, Faculty of Archaeology, Leiden University*, RGRW 159, edited by L. Bricault, M. J. Versluys, and P. G. P. Meybook, 470–504. Leiden: Brill.

Biddle, N. 1993. *Nicholas Biddle in Greece: The Journals and Letters of 1806*. Edited by R. A. McNeal. University Park: Pennsylvania State University Press.

Binder, W. 1969. *Der Roma-Augustus Monopteros auf der Akropolis in Athen und sein typologischer Ort*. Stuttgart: Universität Karlsruhe.

Bingen, J. 2007. *Hellenistic Egypt: Monarchy, Society, Economy, Culture*. Berkeley: University of California Press.

Birley, A. R. 1997. *Hadrian: The Restless Emperor*. London: Routledge.

Boatwright, M. T. 1987. *Hadrian and the City of Rome*. Princeton, NJ: Princeton University Press.

Boatwright, M. T. 2000. *Hadrian and the Cities of the Roman Empire*. Princeton, NJ: Princeton University Press.

Bodel, J. 2000. "Dealing with the Dead: Undertakers, Executioners, and Potter's Fields in Ancient Rome." In *Death and Disease in the Ancient City*, edited by V. M. Hope and E. Marshall, 128–151. London: Routledge.

Bøgh, B. 2015. "Beyond Nock: From Adhesion to Conversion in the Mystery Cults." *History of Religions* 54(3), 260–287.

Bommas, M. 2002. "Apostel Paulus und die ägyptischen Heiligtümer Makedoniens." In *Ägyptische Mysterien*, edited by J. Assman and M. Bommas, 127–141. Munich: Fink.

Bommas, M. 2005. *Heiligtum und Mysterium. Griechenland und seine ägyptischen Gottheiten*. Mainz am Rhein: von Zabern.

Bommas, M. 2012. "The Iseum Campense as a Memory Site." In *Memory and Urban Religion in the Ancient World*, edited by M. Bommas and J. Harrisson, 177–212. London: Bloomsbury Academic Press.

Bonifacio, R. 1997. *Ritratti romani da Pompei*. Rome: Bretschneider.

Bonnano-Aravantinos, M. 2009. "Stele funerarie di età romana da Tanagra con raffigurazione di personaggi legati alla sfera religiosa." Αρχαιολογικό Έργο Θεσσαλίας και Στερεάς Ελλάδας 2006(2), 1151–1165.

Bonnet, C., V. Pirenne-Delforge, and D. Praet, eds. 2009. *Les religions orientales dans le monde grec et romain: Cent ans après Cumont 1906–2006 – Bilan historique et historiographique*. Brussels: Belgian Historical Institute of Rome.

Bordieu, P. 1977. *Outline of a Theory of Practice*. Translated by R. Nice. Cambridge: Cambridge University Press.

Bordieu, P. 1985. "The Social Space and the Genesis of Groups." *Theory and Society* 14(6), 723–744.

Bordieu, P. 1990. *The Logic of Practice*. Translated by R. Nice. Stanford, CA: Stanford University Press.

Borg, B. E. 2000. "The Face of the Elite." *Arion* 8(1), 63–96.

Borg, B. E. 2011. "Who Cared about Greek Identity? Athens in the First Century BCE." In *The Struggle for Identity: Greeks and Their Past in the First Century BCE*, edited by T. A. Schmitz and N. Wiater, 213–235. Stuttgart: Franz Steiner Verlag.

Bowditch, P. L. 2011. "Tibullus and Egypt: A Postcolonial Reading of Elegy 1.7." *Arethusa* 44(1), 89–122.

Bowie, E. L. 1970. "Greeks and Their Past in the Second Sophistic." *PastPres* 46, 3–41.

Bradley, K. 2012. *Apuleius and Antonine Rome: Historical Essays*. Toronto: University of Toronto Press.

Bradley, M. 2006. "Colour and Marble in Early Imperial Rome." *Cambridge Classical Journal* 52, 1–22.

Brady, T. A. 1938. *Repertory of Statuary and Figured Monuments Relating to the Cult of the Egyptian Gods*. Columbia: University of Missouri.

Brélaz, C., and J. Demaille. 2017. "Traces du passé macédonien et influences de l'hellénisme dans les colonies de Dion et de Philippes." In *L'Héritage grec des colonies romaines d'Orient. Interactions culturelles dans les provinces hellénophones de l'empire romain*, edited by C. Brélaz, 119–158. Paris: De Boccard.

Bremmer, J., and A. Erskine. 2010. "Getting in Contact: Concepts of Human–Divine Encounter in Classical Greek Art." In *The Gods of Ancient Greece: Identities and Transformations*, edited by J. Bremmer and A. Erskine, 106–126. Edinburgh: Edinburgh University Press.

Bremmer, J. N. 2014. *Initiation into the Mysteries of the Ancient World*. Berlin: de Gruyter.

Brenk, F. 1999. "'Isis is a Greek word': Plutarch's Allegorization of Egyptian Religion." In *Plutarco, Platón y Aristóteles: Actas del V Congreso Internacional de la I.P.S. Madrid-Cuenca, 4–7 de mayo de 1999*, edited by A. Pérez Jiménez, J. García López, and R. M. Aguilar, 227–238. Madrid: Ed. Clásicas.

Brenk, F. 2001. "In the Image, Reflection and Reason of Osiris: Plutarch and the Egyptian Cults." In *Misticismo y Religiones Místéricas en la Obra de Plutarco. Actas del VII Simposio Español sobre Plutarco, Palma de Mallorca, 2–4 Nov. 2000*, edited by A. Pérez Jiménez and F. C. Bordoy, 83–98. Madrid-Málaga: Ediciones Clásicas & Charta Antiqua.

Brenk, F. 2002. "Religion under Trajan: Plutarch's Resurrection of Osiris." In *Sage and Emperor: Plutarch, Greek Intellectuals, and Roman Power in the Time of Trajan (98-117 A.D.)*, edited by P. A. Stadter and L. van der Stockt, 73–92. Leuven: Leuven University Press.

Brenk, F. 2005. "Plutarch's Middle-Platonic God: About to Enter or Remake the Academy." In *Gott und die Götter bei Plutarch: Götterbilder-Gottesbilder-Weltbilder*, edited by R. Hirsch-Luipold, 27–49. Berlin: de Gruyter.

Brenk, F. 2007a. "Osirian Reflections: Second Thoughts on the Isaeum Campense at Rome." In *With Unperfumed Voice: Studies in Plutarch, in Greek Literature, Religion and Philosophy, and in the New Testament Background*, 383–395. Stuttgart: Steiner.

Brenk, F. 2007b. "The Isis Campensis of Katja Lembke." In *With Unperfumed Voice: Studies in Plutarch, in Greek Literature, Religion, and Philosophy, and in the New Testament Background*, 371–382. Stuttgart: Steiner.

Bricault, L. 2001a. "Les anubophores." *Bulletin de la Société Égyptologique de Genève* 24, 29–42.

Bricault, L. 2001b. *Atlas de la diffusion des cultes isiaques: IVe s. av. J.-C.- IVe s. apr. J.-C.* Paris: Académie des inscriptions et belles-lettres.

Bricault, L. 2004. "La diffusion isiaque: une esquisse." In *Fremdheit-Eigenheit: Ägypten, Griechenland und Rom, Austausch und Verständnis*, edited by P. C. Bol and G. Kaminski, 548–556. Munich: Prestel.

Bricault, L. 2005. *Recueil des inscriptions concernant les cultes isiaques: RICIS*, Vols. 1–3. Paris: De Boccard.

Bricault, L. 2006a. *Isis, dame des flots.* Liège: C.I.P.L.

Bricault, L. 2006b. "Du nom des images d'Isis polymorphe." In *Religions orientales – culti misterici. Neue perspektiveren – nouvelles perspectives – prospettive nuove*, edited by C. Bonnet and J. Rüpke, 75–94. Stuttgart: Franz Steiner Verlag.

Bricault, L. 2008. "Supplément au *RICIS*." In *Bibliotheca Isiaca I*, edited by L. Bricault, 77–130. Bordeaux: Éditions Ausonius.

Bricault, L. 2013. *Les cultes isiaques dans le monde gréco-romain: Documents réunis, traduits et commentés.* Paris: Les Belles Lettres.

Bricault, L. 2014. "*RICIS* Supplément III: Compléments aux inscriptions déjà publiées dans le RICIS et ses deux premiers Suppléments." In *Bibliotheca Isiaca III*, edited by L. Bricault and R. Veymiers, 139–208. Bordeaux: Éditions Ausonius.

Bricault, L., and M. J. Versluys, eds. 2012. *Egyptian Gods in the Hellenistic and Roman Mediterranean: Image and Reality between Local and Global.* Palermo: Salvatore Sciascia Editore.

Bricault, L., and M. J. Versluys, eds. 2014a. *Power, Politics and the Cults of Isis: Proceedings of the Vth International Conference of Isis Studies, Boulogne-sur-Mer, RGRW* 180. Leiden: Brill.

Bricault, L., and M. J. Versluys. 2014b. "Isis and Empires." In *Power, Politics and the Cults of Isis: Proceedings of the Vth International Conference of Isis Studies, Boulogne-sur-Mer, RGRW* 180, edited by L. Bricault and M. J. Versluys, 3–35. Leiden: Brill.

Bricault, L., and R. Veymiers, eds. 2011. *Bibliotheca Isiaca II.* Bordeaux: Éditions Ausonius.

Brinke, M. 1991. *Kopienkritische und typologische Untersuchungen zur statuarischen Überlieferung der Aphrodite Typus Louvre-Neapel.* Hamburg: Verlag Dr. Kovac.

Broadbent, M. 1968. *Studies in Greek Genealogy.* Leiden: Brill.

Brubaker, R. 2004. *Ethnicity without Groups.* Cambridge, MA: Harvard University Press.

Brubaker, R. 2009. "Ethnicity, Race, and Nationalism." *Annual Review of Sociology* 35 (21), 21–42.

Brun-Kyriakidis, H. 2016. "L'Exposition des statues-portraits dans le Sarapieion C de Délos." In *Eikones: Portraits en contexte – Recherches nouvelles sur les portraits grecs du Ve au Ier s. av. J-C*, edited by R. von den Hoff and F. Queyrel, 65–88. Venosa: Osanna Edizioni.

Bruneau, P. 1970. *Recherches sur les cultes de Délos à l'époque hellénistique et à l'époque impériale. BÉFAR* 217. Paris: De Boccard.

Bruneau, P. 1972. *Les mosaïques, Délos* 29. Paris: De Boccard.

Bruneau, P. 1973. "Le quartier de l'Inopus à la fondation du Sarapieion A dans un 'lieu plein d'ordure.'" In *Études déliennes publiées à l'occasion du centième anniversaire du début des fouilles de l'École française d'Athènes à Délos*, edited by A. Plassart, 111–136. Paris: De Boccard.

Bruneau, P. 1975. *Le sanctuaire et le culte des divinités égyptiennes à Érétrie, ÉPRO* 45. Leiden: Brill.

Bruneau, P. 1990. "Deliaca (VIII)." *BCH* 114, 553–567.

Bubelis, W. S. 2012. "Inheritance, Priesthoods, and Succession in Classical Athens: The Hierophantai of the Eumolpidai." In *Families in the Greco-Roman World*, edited by R. Laurence and A. Strömberg, 95–105. London: Continuum.

Budde, L., and R. Nicholls. 1964. *A Catalogue of the Greek and Roman Sculpture in the Fitzwilliam*

Museum. Cambridge: Cambridge University Press.

Budischovsky, M.-C. 2011. "Petits bronzes d'Égypte gréco-romaine: Harpocrate à la *cornucopia*, Harpocrate sur le bélier." In *Bibliotheca Isiaca II*, edited by L. Bricault and R. Veymiers, 163–168. Bordeaux: Éditions Ausonius.

Burkert, W. 2002. "Mysterien der Ägypter in griechischer Sicht: Projektionen im Kulturkontakt." In *Ägyptische Mysterien*, edited by J. Assmann and M. Bommas, 9–26. Munich: Wilhelm Fink Verlag.

Burstein, S. M. 1996. "Images of Egypt in Greek Historiography." In *Ancient Egyptian Literature: History and Forms, Probleme der Ägyptologie 10*, edited by A. Loprieno, 591–604. Leiden: Brill.

Burstein, S. M. 2008. "Greek Identity in the Hellenistic Period." In *Hellenisms: Culture, Identity, and Ethnicity from Antiquity to Modernity*, edited by K. Zacharia, 59–78. London: Ashgate.

Burton, A. 1972. *Diodorus Siculus Book I: A Commentary, ÉPRO 29*. Leiden: Brill.

Buschor, E. 1949. *Das hellenistische Bildnis*. Munich: Biederstein Verlag.

Bussels, S. 2012. *The Animated Image: Roman Theory on Naturalism, Vividness and Divine Power*. Leiden: Akademie Verlag.

Butcher, K. 2003. *Roman Syria and the Near East*. Los Angeles, CA: J. Paul Getty Museum.

Calhoun, C. 2003. "The Variability of Belonging: A Reply to Rogers Brubaker." *Ethnicities* 3(4), 558–568.

Camia, F., and A. Corcella. 2018. "Hadrian, the Olympieion, and the Foreign Cities." In *What's New in Roman Greece? Recent Work on the Greek Mainland and the Islands in the Roman Period*, edited by F. Camia et al., 477–486. Athens: National Hellenic Research Foundation/Institute of Historical Research.

Canducci, D. 1990. "I 6475 cateci greci dell'Arsinoite." *Aegyptus* 70, 211–255.

Canducci, D. 1991. "I 6475 cateci greci dell'Arsinoite: Prosopografia." *Aegyptus* 71, 121–216.

Carbon, J.-M. 2016. "The Festival of the Aloulaia, and the Association of the Alouliastai. Notes Concerning the New Inscription from Larisa/Marmarini." *Kernos* 29, 185–208.

Castiglione, L. 1971. "Zur Frage der Sarapis-Füße." *Zeitschrift für ägyptische Sprache und Altertumskunde* 97(1), 30–43.

Chang, R. S. 2002. "Critiquing 'Race' and Its Uses: Critical Race Theory's Uncompleted Argument." In *Crossroads, Directions, and a New Critical Race Theory*, edited by F. Valdes, J. M. Culp, and A. P. Harris, 87–96. Philadelphia, PA: Temple University Press.

Chaniotis, A. 2013. "Staging and Feeling the Presence of God: Emotion and Theatricality in Religious Celebrations in the Roman East." In *Panthée: Religious Transformations in the Roman Empire, RGRW 177*, edited by L. Bricault and C. Bonnet, 169–189. Leiden: Brill.

Cho, S., K. W. Crenshaw, and L. McCall. 2013. "Toward a Field of Intersectionality Studies: Theory, Applications, and Praxis." *Signs* 38(4), 785–810.

Christodoulou, P. 2011. "Les reliefs votifs du sanctuaire d'Isis à Dion." In *Bibliotheca Isiaca II*, edited by L. Bricault and R. Veymiers, 11–22. Bordeaux: Ausonius Éditions.

Christodoulou, P. 2018. "New Hairstyle, New Identity: Two Busts of Boys with *cirrus* from Dion." In Γλυπτική και κοινωνία στη ρωμαϊκή Ελλάδα: καλλιτεχνικά προϊόντα, κοινωνικές προβολές, edited by P. Karanastasi and T. Stefanidou-Tiveriou, 163–180. Thessaloniki: University Studio Press.

Chuvin, P., and J. Yoyotte. 1986. "Documents relatifs au culte pélusien de Zeus Casios." *RA* 1986, 41–63.

Claridge, A. 1999. "L'Hadrianeum in Campo Marzio: storia dei rinvenimenti e topografia antica nell'area di Piazza di Pietra." In *Provinciae fideles: il fregio del tempio di Adriano in Campo Marzio*, edited by M. Sapelli, 117–127. Milan: Electa.

Clausen, K. B. 2013. "Domitian between Isis and Minerva: The Dialogue between the 'Egyptian' and Graeco-Roman' Aspects of the Sanctuary of Isis at Beneventum." In *Egyptian Gods in the Hellenistic and Roman*

Mediterranean: Image and Reality between Local and Global, edited by L. Bricault and M. J. Versluys, 93–122. Palermo: Salvatore Sciascia Editore.

Clerc, G., and J. Leclant. 1994. "Sarapis." *LIMC* 7, 666–692. Zürich: Artemis Verlag.

Cline, E. 2005. "The Multivalent Nature of Imported Objects in the Ancient Mediterranean World." In *Emporia: Aegeans in the Central and Eastern Mediterranean – Proceedings of the 10th International Aegean Conference / 10e Rencontre égéenne internationale, Aegeum 25*, edited by R. Laffineur and E. Greco, 45–51. Liège and Austin, TX: Université de Liège and University of Texas.

Closterman, W. E. 2007. "Family Ideology and Family History: The Function of Funerary Markers in Classical Attic Peribolos Tombs." *AJA* 111(4), 633–652.

Cole, S. G. 2004. *Landscapes, Gender and Ritual Space*. Berkeley: University of California Press.

Coles, A. 2017. "Between Patronage and Prejudice: Freedman Magistrates in the Late Roman Republic and Empire." *TAPA* 147 (1), 179–208.

Collar, A. 2013. *Religious Networks in the Roman Empire: The Spread of New Ideas*. Cambridge: Cambridge University Press.

Collart, P. 1937. *Philippes, ville de Macédoine depuis ses origines jusqu'à la fin de l'époque romaine*. Paris: De Boccard.

Colledge, M. A. R. 1976. *The Art of Palmyra*. London: Thames and Hudson.

Comstock, M. B. V., and C. C. Vermeule. 1976. *Sculpture in Stone: The Greek, Roman and Etruscan Collections*. Boston: Museum of Fine Arts.

Concannon, C. W. 2014. *"When You Were Gentiles": Specters of Ethnicity in Roman Corinth and Paul's Corinthian Correspondence*. New Haven, CT: Yale University Press.

Concannon, C. W. 2021. "'Honor Flits Away as Though It Were a Dream': Statues, Honor, and Favorinus' Corinthian Oration." *CP* 116(1) 61–75.

Connelly, J. B. 2001. "Reclaiming the Theatrical in the Second Sophistic." *Helios* 28(1), 75–96.

Connelly, J. B. 2007. *Portrait of a Priestess: Women and Ritual in Ancient Greece*. Princeton, NJ: Princeton University Press.

Corcoran, L. H. 1995. *Portrait Mummies from Roman Egypt I–IV Centuries A.D.: With a Catalog of Portrait Mummies in Egyptian Museums*. Chicago: University of Chicago Press.

Crenshaw, K. W. 1988. "Race, Reform and Retrenchment: Transformation and Legitimation in Antidiscrimination Law." *Harvard Law Review* 101(7), 1331–1387.

Crenshaw, K. W. 1991. "Mapping the Margins: Intersectionality, Identity Politics, and Violence against Women of Color." *Stanford Law Review* 43(6), 1241–1299.

D'Ambra, E. 2005. "*Kosmetai*, the Second Sophistic, and Portraiture in the Second Century." In *Periklean Athens and Its Legacy: Problems and Perspectives*, edited by J. Barringer and J. M. Hurwit, 201–216. Austin: University of Texas Press.

Daly, L. W. 1950. "Roman Study Abroad." *AJP* 71(1), 40–58.

Damaskos, D. 2013. Κατάλογος γλυπτών του Αρχαιολογικού Μουσείου Καβάλας. Thessaloniki: Αρχαιολογικό Ινστιτούτο Μακεδονικών και Θρακικών σπουδών.

Darnell, J. C. 2004. *The Enigmatic Netherworld Books of the Solar–Osirian Unity: Cryptographic Compositions in the Tombs of Tutankhamun, Ramesses VI and Ramesses IX*. Fribourg: Academic Press.

Daux, G., and C. Edson. 1974. "I G X, 2 1: Prolegomena, Epilegomena." *BCH* 98, 551–552.

Davis, W. 1981. "Egypt, Samos, and the Archaic Style in Greek Sculpture." *JEA* 67, 61–81.

De Caro, S. 1996. *The National Archaeological Museum of Naples*. Napoli: Electa.

De Jong, L. 2017. *The Archaeology of Death in Roman Syria*. Cambridge: Cambridge University Press.

De Souza, M. 2003. "Religiosus ou les métamorphoses du 'religieux' dans le monde romain de la fin de la République à l'Empire chrétien II siècle av. J.-C. – Début du Ve siècles apr. J.-C." *Bulletin du Centre d'études*

Médiévales d'Auxerre 7. http://doi:10.4000/cem.3552.

Decourt, J.-C., and A. Tziafalis. 2007. "Cultes et divinités isiaques en Thessalie: identité et urbanisation." In *Nile into Tiber: Egypt in the Roman World – Proceedings of the IIIrd International Conference of Isis Studies, Faculty of Archaeology. Leiden University, RGRW 159*, edited by L. Bricault, M. J. Versluys, and P. G. P. Meybook, 329–363. Leiden: Brill.

Dekoulakou, I. 1999. "Νέα στοιχεία από την ανασκαφή του Ιερού των Αιγυπτίων Θεών στον Μαραθώνα." *Archaeologika Analekta ex Athenon* 27–34, 113–124.

Dekoulakou, I. 2003. "Λύχνος με παράσταση Σάραπη και Ίσιδος από το ιερό των Αιγυπτίων θεών στον Μαραθώνα." In *Επιτύμβιον*, edited by G. Neumann, 213–222. Athens: Benaki Museum.

Dekoulakou, I. 2010. "Statues of Isis from the Sanctuary of the Egyptian Gods at Marathon." In *Μαραθών: Η μάχη και ο αρχαίος δήμος*, 109–133. Athens: A. Kardamitsa.

Dekoulakou, I. 2011a. "Le sanctuaire des dieux égyptiens à Marathon." In *Bibliotheca Isiaca II*, edited by L. Bricault and R. Veymiers, 23–46. Bordeaux: Ausonius Éditions.

Dekoulakou, I. 2011b. "The Egyptian Sanctuary at Marathon." In *Proceedings of the Second Hellenistic Studies Workshop at Alexandria, 4–11 July 2010*, edited by K. Savvopoulos, 24–44. Alexandria: Bibliotheca Alexandrina.

Dekoulakou, I. 2017. "ΜΠΡΕΞΙΖΑ ΜΑΡΑΘΩΝΟΣ." *Ergon* 2017, 11–16.

Demaille, J. 2008. "Les *P. Anthestii*: une famille d'affranchis dans l'élite municipale de la colonie romaine de Dion." In *La fin du statut servile? Affranchissement, libération, abolition. Volume I*, edited by J. Annequin and M. Garrido-Hory, 285–202. Besançon: Presses Universitaires de Franche-Comté.

Dench, E. 2017. "Ethnicity, Culture, and Identity." In *The Oxford Handbook of the Second Sophistic*, edited by W. A. Johnson and D. S. Richter, 99–114. Oxford: Oxford University Press.

Despinis, G., T. Stefanidou-Tiveriou, and E. Voutiras, eds. 1997–2020. *Catalogue of Sculpture in the Archaeological Museum of Thessaloniki*, Vols. 1–4. Thessaloniki: National Bank Cultural Foundation.

Di Vita, A. 1999. "Di un singolare doccione a testa di coccodrillo e del tempio o dei templi delle divinità egizie a Gortina." *ASAtene*, 72–73, 7–33.

Díaz-Andreu, M., and S. Lucy. 2005. "Introduction." In *The Archaeology of Identity: Approaches to Gender, Age, Status, Ethnicity, and Religion*, edited by M. Díaz-Andreu and S. Lucy, 1–12. London: Routledge.

Dillon, J. 1996. *The Middle Platonists, 80 B.C. to A.D. 220*. Ithaca, NY: Cornell University Press.

Dillon, J. M. 1988. "'Orthodoxy' and 'Eclecticism': Middle Platonists and Neo-Pythagoreans." In *The Question of "Eclecticism": Studies in Later Greek Philosophy*, edited by J. M. Dillon and A. A. Long, 104–126. Berkeley: University of California Press.

Dillon, S. 2006. *Ancient Greek Portrait Sculpture: Contexts, Subjects, and Styles*. Cambridge: Cambridge University Press.

Dillon, S. 2010. *The Female Portrait Statue in the Greek World*. Cambridge: Cambridge University Press.

Dimitriadis, V. S. 2012. "Thessaloniki in the Crucial Decade of 1912–1922." In *Archaeology behind the Battle Lines: In Thessaloniki of the Turbulent Years 1912–1922*, edited by P. Adam-Veleni and A. Koukouvou, 44–47. Thessaloniki: Archaeological Museum of Thessaloniki.

Donohue, A. A. 1997. "The Greek Images of the Gods. Considerations on Terminology and Methodology." *Hephaistos* 15, 31–45.

Dousa, T. E. 2002. "Imagining Isis: On Some Continuities and Discontinuities in the Image of Isis in Greek Hymns and Demotic Texts." In *Acts of the Seventh International Conference of Demotic Studies: Copenhagen, 23–27 August 1999*, edited by K. Ryholt, 149–184. Chicago: University of Chicago Press.

Dow, S. 1937. "The Egyptian Cults in Athens." *HTR* 30(4), 183–232.

Düll, S. 1977. *Die Götterkulte nordmakedoniens in römischer Zeit: Eine kultische und typologische*

Untersuchung anhand epigraphischer, numismatischer und archäologischer Denkmäler. Munich: Wilhelm Fink Verlag.

Dunand, F. 1967. "Sur une inscription isiaque de Mégalapolis." *ZPE* 1, 219–224.

Dunand, F. 1973a. *Le culte d'Isis dans le bassin oriental de la Méditerranée, Vol. 2, Le culte d'Isis en Grèce*, ÉPRO 26. Leiden: Brill.

Dunand, F. 1973b. *Le culte d'Isis dans le bassin oriental de la Méditerranée*, Vol. 3, *Le culte d'Isis en Asie Mineure, Clergé et rituel des sanctuaires isiaques*, ÉPRO 26. Leiden: Brill.

Dunand, F. 2000. *Isis, mère des dieux*. Paris: Errance.

Dunand, F., and C. Zivie-Coche. 2004. *Gods and Men in Egypt: 3000 BCE to 395 CE*. Translated by D. Lorton. Ithaca, NY: Cornell University Press.

Dunbabin, K. M. D. 1990. "Ipsa deae vestigia ... Footprints Divine and Human on Greco-Roman Monuments." *JRA* 3, 85–109.

Edson, C. 1940. "Macedonica." *HSCP* 51, 125–136.

Edwell, P. 2008. *Between Rome and Persia: The Middle Euphrates, Mesopotamia and Palmyra under Roman Control*. London: Routledge.

Egelhaaf-Gaiser, U. 2000. *Kulträume im römischen Alltag: Das Isisbuch des Apuleius und der Ort von Religion im kaiserzeitlichen Rom*. Stuttgart: Franz Steiner Verlag.

Egelhaaf-Gaiser, U., and C. Steimle. 2003. "Religion in der römischen Provinz Makedonien." In *Römische Reichs- und Provinzialreligion – Globalisierungs- und Regionalisierungsprozesse in der antiken Religionsgeschichte: Ein Forschungsprogramm stellt sich vor*, edited by H. Cancik, J. Rüpke, and F. Fabricius, 154–167. Erfurt: Religionswissenschaft, Philosophische Fakultät.

Eingartner, J. 1991. *Isis und ihre Dienerinnen in der Kunst der römischen Kaiserzeit*, Mnemosyne Suppl. 115 Leiden: Brill.

Elsner, J. 1995. *Art and the Roman Viewer: The Transformation of Art from the Pagan World to Christianity*. Cambridge: Cambridge University Press.

Elsner, J. 2001. "Structuring 'Greece.' Pausanias' *Periegesis* as a Literary Construct." In *Pausanias: Travel and Memory in Roman Greece*, edited by S. E. Alcock and J. F. Cherry, 3–20. Oxford: Oxford University Press.

Elsner, J. 2003. "Inventing Christian Rome: the Role of Early Christian Art." In *Rome the Cosmopolis*, edited by C. Edwards and G. Woolf, 71–99. Cambridge: Cambridge University Press.

Elsner, J. 2007. *Roman Eyes: Visuality and Subjectivity in Art and Text*. Princeton, NJ: Princeton University Press.

Elsner, J. 2012. "Material Culture and Ritual: State of the Question." In *Architecture of the Sacred: Space, Ritual, and Experience from Classical Greece to Byzantium*, edited by B. Westcoat and R. G. Ousterhout, 1–26. Cambridge: Cambridge University Press.

Elsner, J. 2017. "Visual Ontologies: Style, Archaism, and Framing in the Construction of the Sacred in the Western Tradition." In *The Frame in Classical Art: A Cultural History*, edited by V. Platt and M. Squire, 457–501. Cambridge: Cambridge University Press.

Engelmann, H. 1975. *The Delian Aretalogy of Sarapis*. ÉPRO 44. Leiden: Brill.

Engels, D. 1990. *Roman Corinth: An Alternative Model for the Classical City*. Chicago: University of Chicago Press.

Engels, J. 2010. "Macedonians and Greeks." In *A Companion to Ancient Macedonia*, edited by J. Roisman and I. Worthington, 81–98. Malden, MA: Wiley-Blackwell.

Eshleman, K. 2008. "Defining the Circle of Sophists: Philostratus and the Construction of the Second Sophistic." *CP* 103(4), 395–413.

Eshleman, K. 2012. *The Social World of Intellectuals in the Roman Empire: Sophists, Philosophers, and Christians*. Cambridge: Cambridge University Press.

Falezza, G. 2012. *I santuari della Macedonia in età romana: Persistenze e cambiamenti del paesaggio sacro tra II secolo A.C e IV secolo D.C*. Rome: Edizioni Quasar.

Fantaoutsaki, C. 2011. "Preliminary Report on the Excavation of the Sanctuary of Isis in Ancient Rhodes: Identification, Topography, and Finds." In *Bibliotheca Isiaca*

II, edited by L. Bricault and R. Veymiers, 47–64. Bordeaux: Ausonius Éditions.

Fantuzzi, M. and R. Hunter. 2004. *Tradition and Innovation in Hellenistic Poetry*. Cambridge: Cambridge University Press.

Feil, E. 1992. "From the Classical *Religio* to the Modern *Religion*: Elements of a Transformation between 1550 and 1650." In *Religion in History: The Word, the Idea, the Reality*, edited by M. Despland and G. Vallée, 31–43. Waterloo, ON: Wilfrid Laurier University Press.

Fejfer, J. 2008. *Roman Portraits in Context*. Mainz am Rhein: de Gruyter.

Feld, S., and K. H. Basso. 1996. "Introduction." In *Senses of Place*, edited by S. Feld and K. H. Basso, 3–12. Santa Fe, NM: School of American Research Press.

Festugière, A. J. 1949. "À propos des arétalogies d'Isis." *HTR* 42(4), 209–234.

Festugière, A. J. 1954. *Personal Religion among the Greeks*. Berkeley: University of California Press.

Finkelpearl, E. 1998. *Metamorphosis of Language in Apuleius: A Study of Allusion in the Novel*. Ann Arbor: University of Michigan Press.

Fischer, H. G. 1975. "An Elusive Shape within the Fisted Hands of Egyptian Statues." *Metropolitan Museum Journal* 10, 9–21.

Fischer-Bovet, C. 2015. "Social Unrest and Ethnic Coexistence in Ptolemaic Egypt and the Seleucid Empire." *PastPres* 229, 3–45.

Fittschen, K. 2001. "Eine Werkstatt attischer Porträtbildhauer im 2 Jh. n. Chr." In *Griechenland in der Kaiserzeit: Neue Funde und Forschungen zu Skulptur, Architektur und Topographie – Kolloquium zum sechzigsten Geburtstag von D. Willers*, edited by C. Reusser, 71–77. Bern: Institut für klassische Archäologie der Universität Bern.

Fleury, P. 2016. "Marcus Aurelius' Letters." In *A Companion to Marcus Aurelius*, edited by M. van Ackern, 62–76. Malden, MA: Wiley-Blackwell.

Flinterman, J.-J. 1995. *Power, Paideia and Pythagoreanism: Greek Identity, Conceptions of the Relationship between Philosophers and Monarchs, and Political Ideas in Philostratus' Life of Apollonius*. Amsterdam: J. C. Gieben.

Floriani Squarciapino, M. 1962. *I culti orientali ad Ostia, ÉPRO* 3 Leiden: Brill.

Flowers, M. 2000. "From Simonides to Isocrates: The Fifth-Century Origins of Fourth-Century Panhellenism." *ClAnt* 19(1), 65–101.

Flüchter, A., and J. Schöttli. 2015. "Introduction." In *The Dynamics of Transculturality: Concepts and Institutions in Motion*, edited by A. Flüchter and J. Schöttli, 1–26. Cham, Switzerland: Springer.

Foertmeyer, V. A. 1989. "Tourism in Graeco-Roman Egypt." PhD dissertation, Princeton University.

Fotiadi, P. 2011. "Ritual Terracotta Lamps with Representations of Sarapis and Isis from the Sanctuary of the Egyptian Gods at Marathon: The Variation of 'Isis with Three Ears of Wheat.'" In *Bibliotheca Isiaca II*, edited by L. Bricault and R. Veymiers, 65–77. Bordeaux: Ausonius Éditions.

Fowden, G. 1986. *The Egyptian Hermes. A Historical Approach to the Late Pagan Mind*. Cambridge: Cambridge University Press.

Fowler, H. N., and R. Stillwell. 1932. *Introduction, Topography, Architecture, Corinth 1*. Cambridge, MA: Harvard University Press.

Frankfort, H. 1948. *Ancient Egyptian Religion: An Interpretation*. Mineola, NY: Dover Publications.

Frankfurter, D. 1998. *Religion in Roman Egypt: Assimilation and Resistance*. Princeton, NJ: Princeton University Press.

Frankfurter, D. 2010. "Religion in Society: Graeco-Roman." In *A Companion to Ancient Egypt*, edited by A. B. Lloyd, 526–546. Malden, MA: Blackwell.

Fraser, P. M. 1960. "Two Studies on the Cult of Sarapis in the Hellenistic World." *OpAth* 3, 1–53.

Froidefond, C. 1971. *Le mirage égyptien dans la littérature grecque d'Homère à Aristote*. Aix-en-Provence: Imprimerie Louis-Jean.

Froidefond, C. 1987. "Plutarque et le platonisme." *ANRW* II 36(1), 184–233.

Fronto. 1920. *Correspondence*, Vol. 2, Loeb Classical Library 113. Translated by C. R. Haines. Cambridge, MA: Harvard University Press.

Fullerton, M. D. 1990. *The Archaistic Style in Roman Statuary*, Mnemosyne Suppl. 110. Leiden: Brill.

Galli, M. 2002. *Die Lebenswelt eines Sophisten: Unterschungen zu den Bauten und Stiftungen des Herodes Atticus*. Mainz am Rhein: von Zabern.

Gasparini, V. 2011. "Isis and Osiris: Demonology vs. Henotheism?" *Numen* 58(5–6), 697–728.

Gasparini, V. 2016. "Listening Stones: Cultural Appropriation, Resonance, and Memory in the Isiac Cults." In *Vestigia: Miscellanea di studi storico-religiosi in onore di Filippo Coarelli ne suo 80 anniversario*, edited by V. Gasparini, 555–574. Stuttgart: Franz Steiner Verlag.

Gasparini, V. 2018. "Les acteurs sur scène: Théâtre et théâtralisation dans les cultes isiaques." In *Individuals and Materials in the Greco-Roman Cults of Isis: Agents, Images, and Materials*, RGRW 187, edited by V. Gasparini and R. Veymiers, 714–746. Leiden: Brill.

Gasparini, V., and R. Gordon. 2018. "Egyptianism: Appropriating 'Egypt' in the 'Isiac Cults' of the Graeco-Roman World." *ActaArchHung* 581, 571–606.

Gauckler, P., and M. L. Poinssot. 1910. *Catalogue du Musée Alaoui*. Paris: Ernest Leroux.

Gawlinski, L. 2008. "'Fashioning' Initiates: Dress at the Mysteries." In *Reading a Dynamic Canvas: Adornment in the Ancient Mediterranean World*, edited by C. S. Colburn and M. C. Heyn, 146–169. Newcastle: Cambridge Scholars Publishing.

Gawlinski, L. 2011. *The Sacred Law of Andania: A New Text with Commentary*. Berlin: de Gruyter.

Gazda, E. 1980. "A Portrait of Polydeukion." *Bulletin of the Museums of Art and Archaeology, University of Michigan* 3, 1–13.

Geagan, D. J. 1964. "A New Herodes Epigram from Marathon." *AM* 79, 149–156.

Geagan, D. J. 1997. "The Athenian Elite: Romanization, Resistance, and the Exercise of Power." In *The Romanization of Athens: Proceedings of an International Conference Held at Lincoln, Nebraska April 1996*, edited by M. C. Hoff, 19–32. Oxford: Oxbow.

Geary, P. 2002. *The Myth of Nations: The Medieval Origins of Europe*. Princeton, NJ: Princeton University Press.

Gell, A. 1998. *Art and Agency: An Anthropological Theory*. Oxford: Clarendon Press.

Genaille, N. 1984. "Sistrum, diffusion gréco-romaine." In *Lexikon der Ägyptologie V*, edited by W. Helck and E. Otto, 963–965. Wiesbaden: Otto Harrassowitz.

Gergel, R. A. 2004. "Agora S166 and Related Works: The Iconography, Typology, and Interpretation of the Eastern Hadrianic Breastplate Type." In *XAPIΣ: Essays in Honor of Sara A. Immerwahr*, edited by A. P. Chapin, 371–409. Princeton, NJ: ASCSA.

Gettel, E. 2018. "Recognizing the Delians Displaced after 167/6 BCE." In *Displacement and the Humanities: Manifestos from the Ancient to the Present*, edited by E. Isayev and E. Jewell. Special issue. *Humanities* 7(4). https://doi.org/10.3390/h7040091.

Giridharadas, A. 2018. "What Is Identity?" *New York Times*, 1 September.

Giuliano, A. 1985. *Museo Nazionale Romano I*, Vol. 8. Rome: De Luca.

Giuman, M. 1999. "Metamorfosi di una dea: Da Artemide ad Iside in un santuario di Dion." *Ostraka* 8, 427–446.

Gleason, M. 1995. *Making Men: Sophists and Self-presentation in Ancient Rome*. Princeton, NJ: Princeton University Press.

Gleason, M. W. 2010. "Making Space for Bicultural Identity: Herodes Atticus Commemorates Regilla." In *Local Knowledge and Microidentities in the Imperial Greek World*, edited by T. Whitmarsh, 125–162. Cambridge: Cambridge University Press.

Gordon, R. 2013. "Individuality, Selfhood, and Power in the Second Century: The Mystagogue as a Mediator of Religious Options." In *Religious Dimensions of the Self in the Second Century CE*, edited by J. Rüpke and G. Woolf, 146–172. Tübingen: Mohr Siebeck.

Gordon, R. 2014. "Coming to Terms with the 'Oriental' Religions of the Roman Empire." *Numen* 61, 657–672.

Gordon, R. 2016. "On the Problems of Initiation." *JRA* 29, 720–725.

Götte, H. R. 2001. *Athens, Attica, and the Megarid: An Archaeological Guide*. New York: Routledge.

Götte, H. R. 2003. "Zum Bildnis des Polydeukion: Stiltendenzen athenischer Werkstatten im 2. Jahrhundert n. Chr." In *Romanisation und Resistenz in Plastik, Architektur und Inschriften der Provinzen des Imperium Romanum: Neue Funde und Forschungen – Akten des VII – Internationalen Colloquiums über Probleme des Provinzialrömischen Kunstschaffens*, edited by P. Noelke, 549–557. Mainz am Rhein: von Zabern.

Graindor, P. 1930. *Un milliardaire antique: Herode Atticus et sa famille.* Cairo: Imprimerie Misr.

Grand-Clément, A. 2018. "Du blanc, du noir et de la bigarrure: le jeu des couleurs dans les représentations d'isiaques." In *Individuals and Materials in the Greco-Roman Cults of Isis: Agents, Images, Practices, RGRW 187*, edited by V. Gasparini and R. Veymiers, 340–365. Leiden: Brill.

Grandjean, Y. 1975. *Une nouvelle arétalogie d'Isis à Maronée, ÉPRO 49.* Leiden: Brill.

Grattoggi, S. 2014. "'Scoperto il tempio di Iside': Tivoli, gli scavi nella Palestra hanno riportato alla luce statue e capitelli." *La Repubblica*, 4 December.

Gray, C. L. 2006. "The Bearded Rustic of Roman Attica." In *City, Countryside, and the Spatial Organization of Value in Classical Antiquity*, edited by R. Rosen and I. Sluiter, 349–368. Leiden: Brill.

Grenier, J.-C. 1989. "La décoration statuaire du 'Serapeum' du 'Canope' de la Villa Adriana: Essai de reconstitution et d'interprétation." *MÉFRA* 101(2), 925–1019.

Grenier, J.-C. 1999. "Le 'Sérapeum' et le 'Canope': une 'Égypte' monumentale et une 'Méditerranée.'" In *Hadrien: Trésors d'une villa impériale*, edited by J. Charles-Gaffiot and H. Lavagne, 75–79. Milan: Electa.

Grenier, J.-C. 2008a. "Hadrian's Canopus." In *The She-Wolf and the Sphinx: Rome and Egypt from History to Myth – Rome, Museo Nazionale di Castel Sant'Angelo*, edited by E. Lo Sardo, 112–117. Rome: Electa.

Grenier, J.-C. 2008b. *L'Osiris Antinoos.* Montpellier: CNRS Université Paul Valéry. www.enim-egyptologie.fr/cahiers/1/Grenier_Antinoos.pdf.

Griffiths, J. G. 1970. *Plutarch's De Iside et Osiride.* Swansea: University of Wales Press.

Griffiths, J. G. 1975. *The Isis-Book Metamorphoses, Book XI, ÉPRO 39.* Leiden: Brill.

Gruen, E. S. 1986. *The Hellenistic World and the Coming of Rome.* Berkeley: University of California Press.

Gruen, E. S. 2011. "Egypt in the Classical Imagination." In *Rethinking the Other in Antiquity*, edited by E. S. Gruen, 76–114. Princeton, NJ: Princeton University Press.

Gruen, E. S. 2013a. "Did Ancient Identity Depend on Ethnicity? A Preliminary Probe." *Phoenix* 67(1–2), 1–22.

Gruen, E. S. 2013b. "Did Romans Have an Ethnic Identity?" *Antichthon* 47, 1–17.

Gualandi, G. 1976. "Sculture di Rodi." *ASAtene* 54, 7–260.

Guimer-Sorbets, A.-M., and M.-D. Nenna. 1992. "L'emploi du verre, de la faïence et de la peinture dans les mosaïques de Délos." *BCH* 116, 607–632.

Habicht, C. 1997. *Athens from Alexander to Antony.* Translated by D. L. Schneider. Cambridge, MA: Harvard University Press.

Hall, E. 1989. *Inventing the Barbarian: Greek Self-definition through Tragedy.* Oxford: Oxford University Press.

Hall, E. S. 1977. "Harpocrates and Other Child Deities in Ancient Egyptian Sculpture." *JARCE* 14, 55–58.

Hall, J. 1997. *Ethnic Identity in Greek Antiquity.* Cambridge: Cambridge University Press.

Hall, J. 2001. "Contested Ethnicities: Perceptions of Macedonia within Evolving Definitions of Greek Identity." In *Ancient Perceptions of Greek Ethnicity*, edited by I. Malkin, 159–186. Cambridge: Cambridge University Press.

Hall, J. M. 2002. *Hellenicity: Between Ethnicity and Culture.* Chicago: University of Chicago Press.

Hallett, C. 2012. "The Archaic Style in Sculpture in the Eyes of Ancient and Modern Viewers." In *Making Sense of Greek Art*, edited by V. Coltman, 70–100. Exeter: University of Exeter Press.

Hamilton, R. 2000. *Treasure Map: A Guide to the Delian Inventories.* Ann Arbor: University of Michigan Press.

Hani, J. 1976. *La religion égyptienne dans la pensée de Plutarque*. Paris: Les Belles Lettres.

Hanson, J. S. 1980. "Dreams and Visions in the Graeco-Roman World and Early Christianity." *ANRW II* 32(2), 1395–1427.

Harrison, E. B. 1953. *Portrait Sculpture, Agora I*. Princeton, NJ: American School of Classical Studies at Athens.

Harrison, S. J. 2004. *Apuleius: A Latin Sophist*. Oxford: Oxford University Press.

Harrison, S. J. 2015. "Lucius in *Metamorphoses* Books 1–3." In *Characterisation in Apuleius' Metamorphoses: Nine Studies*, edited by S. Harrison, 3–14. Newcastle-upon-Tyne: Cambridge Scholars Publishing.

Harrisson, J. 2012. "Isis in the Greco-Roman World: Cultural Memory and Imagination." In *Memory and Urban Religion in the Ancient World*, edited by M. Bommas and J. Harrisson, 213–236. London: Bloomsbury Academic Press.

Hartog, F. 1988. *The Mirror of Herodotus: The Representation of the Other in the Writing of History*. Translated by J. Lloyd. Berkeley: University of California Press.

Hassan, S. 1928. *Hymnes religieux du Moyen Empire*. Cairo: Service des Antiquités de l'Egypte.

Hatzfeld, J. 1975. *Les trafiquants italiens dans l'Orient hellénique*. New York: Arno Press.

Hatzidakis, P. J. 2003. *Delos*. Athens: Latsis Foundation.

Hauvette-Besnault, A. 1881. "Fouilles de Délos." *BCH* 6, 295–352.

Helbig, W. 1963. *Führer durch die öffentlichen Sammlungen klassischer Altertumer in Rom*, Vols. 1–4. Tübingen: E. Wasmuth.

Heyn, M. C. 2010. "Gesture and Identity in the Funerary Art of Palmyra." *AJA* 114(4), 631–661.

Heyn, M. C. 2016. "Status and Stasis: Looking at Women in the Palmyrene Tomb." In *The World of Palmyra*, edited by A. Kropp and R. Raja, 194–206. Copenhagen: Royal Danish Academy of Arts and Letters.

Heyn, M. C. 2017. "Western Men, Eastern Women? Dress and Cultural Identity in Roman Palmyra." In *What Shall I Say of Clothes? Theoretical and Methodological Approaches to the Study of Dress in Antiquity*, edited by M. Cifarelli and L. Gawlinski, 210–217. Boston: American School of Classical Studies at Athens.

Heyn, M., and R. Raja. 2018. "Male Dress Habits in Roman Period Palmyra." In *Fashioned Selves: Dress and Identity in Antiquity*, edited by M. Cifarelli, 41–53. Oxford: Oxbow Books.

Heynen, H. 2006. "Questioning Authenticity." *National Identities* 83, 287–300.

Heyob, S. K. 1975. *The Cult of Isis among Women in the Graeco-Roman World*, ÉPRO 51. Leiden: Brill.

Hodos, T. 2009. "Local and Global Perspectives in the Study of Social and Cultural Identities." In *Material Culture and Social Identities in the Ancient World*, edited by S. Hales and T. Hodos, 3–31. Cambridge: Cambridge University Press.

Hodos, T. 2015. "Global, Local, and in between: Connectivity and the Mediterranean." In *Globalisation and the Roman World: World History, Connectivity, and Material Culture*, edited by M. Pitts and M. J. Versluys, 240–254. Cambridge: Cambridge University Press.

Hodos, T. 2017. "Globalization: Some Basics – Introduction." In *The Routledge Handbook of Archaeology and Globalization*, edited by T. Hodos, 3–11. Oxford: Routledge.

Hoff, M. C. 1989. "Civil Disobedience and Unrest in Augustan Athens." *Hesperia* 58(3), 267–276.

Hoff, M. C. 1992. "Augustus, Apollo, and Athens." *MusHelv* 49(4), 223–232.

Holliday, P. 2015. "Roman Art and the State." In *A Companion to Roman Art*, B. Borg, 195–214. Malden, MA: Wiley Blackwell.

Hölscher, T. 2008. "The Concept of Roles and the Malaise of 'Identity': Ancient Rome and the Modern World." In *Role Models in the Roman World: Identity and Assimilation*, edited by S. Bell and I.-L. Hansen, 41–56. Ann Arbor: University of Michigan Press.

Hornung, E. 1982. *Conceptions of God in Ancient Egypt: The One and the Many*. Translated by J. Baines. Ithaca, NY: Cornell University Press.

Hornung, E. 1994. "Altägyptische Wurzeln der Isismysterien." In *Hommages à Jean Leclant*, Vol. 3, edited by C. Berger, G. Clerc, and N. Grimal, 287–293. Cairo: Institut français d'archéologie orientale.

Hudson McLean, B. 1996. "Place of Cult in Voluntary Associations and Christian Churches on Delos." In *Voluntary Associations in the Graeco-Roman World*, edited by J. S. Kloppenborg and S. G. Wilson, 186–226. London: Routledge.

Huskinson, J. 2000. "Looking for Culture, Identity, and Power." In *Experiencing Rome: Culture, Identity, and Power in the Roman Empire*, edited by J. Huskinson, 3–27. London: Routledge.

Huzar, E. G. 1961–1962. "Roman–Egyptian Relations on Delos." *ClJ* 57, 169–178.

Ingholt, H. 1928. *Studier over Palmyrensk Skulptur*. Copenhagen: C. A. Reitzels Forlag.

James, S. A. 2014. "The Last of the Corinthians? Society and Settlement from 146 to 44 BCE." In *Corinth in Contrast: Studies in Inequality, Novum Testamentum Suppl.* 155, edited by S. J. Friesen and S. A. James, 17–38. Leiden: Brill.

Jannoray, J. 1946. "Inscriptions delphiques d'époque tardive. Inscriptions de Lébadée." *BCH* 70, 247–262.

Jennings, J. 2011. *Globalizations and the Ancient World*. Cambridge: Cambridge University Press.

Jennings, J. 2017. "Distinguishing Past Globalizations." In *The Routledge Handbook of Archaeology and Globalization*, edited by T. Hodos, 12–28. London: Routledge.

Jentel, M. O. 1981. "Aigyptos." *LIMC* 1, 378–380. Zürich: Artemis Verlag.

Johnson, F. P. 1931. *Sculpture 1896–1923, Corinth* 9, Vol. 1. Princeton, NJ: American School of Classical Studies in Athens.

Jones, C. P. 1999. *Kinship Diplomacy in the Ancient World*. Cambridge, MA: Harvard University Press.

Jones, C. P. 2008. "Multiple Identities in the Age of the Second Sophistic." In *Paideia: The World of the Second Sophistic*, edited by B. Borg, 13–21. Berlin: De Gruyter.

Jones, S. 1997. *The Archaeology of Ethnicity*. London: Routledge.

Jones, S. 2010. "Negotiating Authentic Objects and Authentic Selves: Beyond the Deconstruction of Authenticity." *Journal of Material Culture* 15(2), 181–203.

Jördens, A. 2012. "Status and Citizenship." In *The Oxford Handbook of Roman Egypt*, edited by C. Riggs, 247–260. Oxford: Oxford University Press.

Kahil, L. 1984. "Artemis." *LIMC* 2, 618–753. Zürich: Artemis Verlag.

Kaltsas, N. 2002. *Sculpture in the National Archaeological Museum, Athens*. Translated by D. Hardy. Los Angeles: Getty Publications.

Kaper, O. E. 2003. *The Egyptian God Tutu: A Study of the Sphinx-God and Master of Demons*. Leuven: Peeters.

Karamanolis, G. 2014. "Plutarch." In *The Stanford Encyclopedia of Philosophy*, edited by E. N. Zalta. https://plato.stanford.edu/entries/plutarch/.

Karapanagiotou, A. 2013. Γυναίκα και κοινωνική προβολή στην Αθήνα: η μαρτυρία των επιτύμβιων αναγλύφων της ύστερης Ελληνιστικής και της Αυτοκρατορικής περιόδου. Volos: Ministry of Education, Religion, Culture, and Athletics.

Karetsou, A., and M. Andreadaki-Vlazaki. 2000. ΚΡΗΤΗ ΑΙΓΥΠΤΟΣ. Πολιτισμικοί δεσμοί τριών χιλιετιών: Κατάλογος. Iraklion: Ministry of Culture.

Karivieri, A. 2018. "*Varius, Multiplex, Multiformis* – Greek, Roman, Panhellenic: Multiple Identities of the Hadrianic Era and Beyond." In *Gender, Memory, and Identity in the Roman World*, edited by J. Rantala, 283–300. Amsterdam: Amsterdam University Press.

Karusu, S. 1969. "Die Antiken vom Kloster Luku in der Thyreatis." *RM* 76, 253–265.

Kater-Sibbes, G. J. F. 1973. *Preliminary Catalogue of Sarapis Monuments, ÉPRO* 36. Leiden: Brill.

Kemezis, A. M. 2014. "Greek Ethnicity and the Second Sophistic." In *A Companion to Ethnicity in the Ancient Mediterranean*, edited by J. McInerney, 390–404. Malden, MA: John Wiley & Sons.

Kennell, N. 1988. ΝΕΡΩΝ ΠΕΡΙΟΔΟΝΙΚΗΣ. *AJP* 109(2), 239–251.

Keulen, W. 2015. "*Lubrico virentis aetatulae*: Lucius as Initiate *Metamorphoses* Book 11." In *Characterisation in Apuleius' Metamorphoses*, edited by S. J. Harrison, 29–55. Newcastle-upon-Tyne: Cambridge Scholars Publishing.

Kindt, J. 2012. *Rethinking Greek Religion*. Cambridge: Cambridge University Press.

King, C. 2003. "The Organization of Roman Religious Beliefs." *ClAnt* 22(2), 275–312.

Klebs, L. 1931. "Die verschiedenen Formen des Sistrums." *ZÄS* 67(1), 60–63.

Kleibl, K. 2007. "Water-Crypts in Sanctuaries of Graeco-Egyptian Deities of the Graeco-Roman Period in the Mediterranean Region." In *Proceedings of the Fourth Central European Conference of Young Egyptologists*, edited by K. Endreffy and A. Gulyás, 1–17. Budapest: Chaire d'Égyptologie, Université Eötvös Loránd de Budapest.

Kleibl, K. 2009. *Iseion: Raumgestaltung und Kultpraxis in den Heiligtümern gräco-ägyptischer Götter im Mittelmeerraum*. Worms am Rhein: Wernersche Verlagsgesellschaft.

Kockelmann, H. 2008. *Praising the Goddess: A Comparative and Annotated Re-edition of Six Demotic Hymns and Praises Addressed to Isis*. Berlin: De Gruyter.

Koester, H. 2010. "Egyptian Religion in Thessalonike: Regulation for the Cult." In *From Roman to Early Christian Thessalonike: Studies in Religion and Archaeology*, edited by L. Nasrallah, C. Bakirtzis, and S. J. Friesen, 133–150. Cambridge, MA: Harvard University Press.

König, J. 2001. "Favorinus' 'Corinthian Oration' in Its Corinthian Context." *PCPS* 47, 141–171.

König, J. 2014. "Images of Elite Community in Philostratus: Re-reading the Preface to the Lives of the Sophists." In *Roman Rule in Greek and Latin Writing: Double Vision, Impact of Empire* 18, edited by J. M. Madsen and R. Rees, 246–270. Leiden: Brill.

Koukouvou, A. 2012. "The Sarapieion. A Sanctuary of Egyptian Gods Rises from the City's Ashes." In *Archaeology behind the Battle Lines: In Thessaloniki of the Turbulent Years 1912–1922*, edited by P. Adam-Veleni and A. Koukouvou, 108–112. Thessaloniki: Archaeological Museum of Thessaloniki.

Koukouvou, A. 2017. "The Formation of the Collection of the Archaeological Museum of Thessaloniki and the Exhibition 'Archaeology behind the Battle Lines': A Dialogue." In *Archaeology behind the Battle Lines: The Macedonian Campaign 1915–1919 and Its Legacy*, edited by A. Shapland and E. Stefani, 261–280. London: Routledge.

Kousser, R. M. 2008. *Hellenistic and Roman Ideal Sculpture: The Allure of the Classical*. Cambridge: Cambridge University Press.

Krag, S. 2016. "Females in Group Portraits in Palmyra." In *The World of Palmyra*, edited by A. Kropp and R. Raja, 180–193. Copenhagen: Royal Danish Academy of Sciences and Letters.

Krag, S. 2017. "Changing Identities, Changing Positions: Jewelry in Palmyrene Funerary Portraits. In *Positions and Professions in Palmyra*, edited by T. Long and A. H. Sørensen, 36–51. Copenhagen: Royal Danish Academy of Sciences and Letters.

Krag, S. 2018. *Funerary Representations of Palmyrene Women: From the First Century BC to the Third Century AD*. Turnhout: Brepols.

Kravaritou, S. 2016. "Sacred Space and the Politics of Multiculturalism in Demetrias Thessaly." In *Hellenistic Sanctuaries between Greece and Rome*, edited by M. Melfi and O. Bobou, 128–151. Oxford: Oxford University Press.

Kropp, A. J. M., and R. Raja. 2014. "The Palmyra Portrait Project." *Syria* 91, 393–408.

Kyriakidis, E., ed. 2007. *The Archaeology of Ritual*. Los Angeles: Cotsen Institute of Archaeology.

Lamont, J. 2015. "Asklepios in the Piraeus and the Mechanisms of Cult Appropriation." In *Autopsy in Athens: Recent Archaeological Research on Athens and Attica*, edited by M. Miles, 37–50. Oxford: Oxbow Books.

Landskron, A. 2006. "Repräsentantinnen des *Orbis Romanus* auf dem sog – Partherdenkmal von Ephesos: Personifikationen und Bildpropaganda." In *Das Partherdenkmal von*

Ephesos: Akten des Kolloquiums Wien, 27–28 April 2003, edited by W. Seipel, 102–128. Wien: Kunsthistorisches Museum.

Lateiner, D. 1989. *The Historical Method of Herodotus*. Toronto: University of Toronto Press.

Latour, B. 2005. *Reassembling the Social: An Introduction to Actor-Network Theory*. Oxford: Oxford University Press.

Le Dinahet-Couilloud, M.-T. 1974. *Les Monuments funéraires de Rhénée: Délos 30*. Paris: De Boccard.

Leclant J., and L. de Meulenaere. 1957. "Une statuette égyptienne à Délos." *Kêmi* 14, 34–42.

Leclant, G. 1986. "Isis, déesse universelle et divinité locale, dans le monde gréco-romain." In *Iconographie classique et identités régionales*, edited by L. Kahil and C. Augé, 341–353. Athens: École francaise d'Athenes; Paris: De Boccard.

Lee, M. M. 2015. *Body, Dress, and Identity in Ancient Greece*. Cambridge: Cambridge University Press.

Lembke, K. 1994. *Das Iseum Campense in Rom: Studien über den Isiskult unter Domitian*. Heidelberg: Verlag Archäologie und Geschichte.

Libby, B. B. 2011. "Moons, Smoke, and Mirrors in Apuleius' Portrayal of Isis." *AJP* 132(2), 301–322.

Lichterman, P., R. Raja, A.-K. Rieger, and J. Rüpke. 2017. "Grouping Together in Lived Ancient Religion: Individual Interacting and the Formation of Groups." *Religion in the Roman Empire* 31, 3–10.

Llewellyn-Jones, L. 2003. *Aphrodite's Tortoise: The Veiled Women of Ancient Greece*. Swansea: Classical Press of Wales.

Long, J.-F. 2002. "Bygone Rome in the *Historia Augusta*." *Syllecta Classica* 13, 180–236.

Long, T. 2016. "Facing the Evidence: How to Approach the Portraits." In *The World of Palmyra*, edited by A. Kropp and R. Raja, 135–149. Copenhagen: Royal Danish Society of Sciences and Letters.

Lovatelli, E. C. 1880. "Di una antica base marmorea con rappresentanze del Nilo." *BCom* 8, 185–197.

Lowenthal, D. 1992. "Authenticity? The Dogma of Self-Delusion." In *Why Fakes Matter: Essays on Problems of Authenticity*, edited by M. Jones, 184–192. London: British Museum Press.

Lowenthal, D. 2013. *The Past Is a Foreign Country: Revisited*. Cambridge: Cambridge University Press.

Lupu, E. 2004. *Greek Sacred Law: A Collection of New Documents*, RGRW 152. Leiden: Brill.

Luraghi, N. 2008. *The Ancient Messenians: Constructions of Ethnicity and Memory*. Cambridge: Cambridge University Press.

Luraghi, N. 2014. "The Study of Greek Ethnic Identities." In *A Companion to Ethnicity in the Ancient Mediterranean*, edited by J. McInerney, 228–241. Malden, MA: Wiley Blackwell.

MacDonald, W. L., and J. A. Pinto. 1995. *Hadrian's Villa and Its Legacy*. New Haven, CT: Yale University Press.

Machaira, V. 2000. "Ἶσις και Σαράπις στο Αιγαίο." In ΚΡΗΤΗ – ΑΙΓΥΠΤΟΣ: Πολιτισμικοί δεσμοί τριών χιλιετιών, edited by A. Karetsou, 244–249. Athens: Karon Editions.

Machaira, V. 2011. Ἑλληνιστικά γλυπτά της Ῥόδου: Κατάλογος, Vol. 7. Athens: ΚΕΝΤΡΟΝ ΕΡΕΥΝΗΣ ΤΗΣ ΑΡΧΑΙΟΤΗΤΟΣ, ΑΚΑΔΗΜΙΑ ΑΘΗΝΩΝ.

Mackay, D. 1949. "The Jewelry of Palmyra and its Significance." *Iraq* 112, 160–182.

Mackil, E. 2012. *Creating a Common Polity: Religion, Economy, and Politics in the Making of the Greek Koinon*. Berkeley: University of California Press.

Mackinnon, M. 2006. "Supplying Exotic Animals for the Roman Amphitheatre Games: New Reconstructions Combining Archaeological, Ancient Textual, Historical and Ethnographic Data." *Mouseion* 62, 137–161.

MacMullen, R. 1982. "The Epigraphic Habit in the Roman Empire." *AJP* 103, 175–187.

Maikidou, D. 2015. *The Statues of Isis in the Sanctuary of the Egyptian Gods: Meaning and Context in a Global Roman World*. MA dissertation, Leiden University.

Makaronas, C. 1937. "ΝΕΑ ΕΙΔΗΣΕΙΣ ΕΚ ΔΙΟΥ ΤΟΥ ΠΙΕΡΙΚΟΥ Η ΘΕΣΙΣ ΤΟΥ ΙΕΡΟΥ ΤΟΥ ΔΙΟΣ." *ArchEphem*, 2, 527–533.

Makaronas, C. 1940. "Χρονικά Αρχαιολογικά." *Makedonika* 1, 464–496.

Malaise, M. 1972a. *Inventaire préliminaire des documents égyptiens découverts en Italie*, ÉPRO 21. Leiden: Brill.

Malaise, M. 1972b. *Les conditions de pénétration et de diffusion des cultes égyptiens en Italie*, ÉPRO 23. Leiden: Brill.

Malaise, M. 1992. "À propos de l'iconographie 'canonique' d'Isis et des femmes vouées à son culte." *Kernos* 5, 329–361.

Malaise, M. 1994. "Note sur le noeud isiaque." *Göttinger Miszellen* 143, 105–108.

Malaise, M. 2005. *Pour une terminologie et une analyse des cultes isiaques*. Brussels: Académie royale de Belgique.

Malaise, M. 2007. "Les hypostoles: Un titre isiaque, sa signification et sa traduction iconographique." *ChrÉg* 82(163–164), 302–322.

Malaise, M. 2009. "Le basileion, une couronne d'Isis: Origine et signification." In *Elkab and Beyond: Studies in Honour of Luc Limme*, edited by W. Claes and H. de Meulenaere, 439–455. Leuven: Peeters.

Malaise, M., and R. Veymiers. 2018. "Les dévotes isiaques et les atours de leur déesse." In *Individuals and Materials in the Greco-Roman Cults of Isis: Agents, Images, and Practices*, RGRW 187, edited by V. Gasparini and R. Veymiers, 470–508. Leiden: Brill.

Malkin, I. 1998. *The Returns of Odysseus: Colonization and Ethnicity*. Berkeley: University of California Press.

Malkin, I. 2011. *A Small Greek World: Networks in the Ancient Mediterranean*. Oxford: Oxford University Press.

Malmberg, S. 2011. "Rev. Revell, Roman Imperialism and Local Identities." *EJA* 141–142, 334–336.

Mandaville, P. G. 1999. "Territory and Translocality: Discrepant Idioms of Political Identity." *Millennium: Journal of International Studies* 28(3), 653–673.

Manolaraki, E. 2013. *Noscendi Nilum cupido: Imagining Egypt from Lucan to Philostratus*. Berlin: De Gruyter.

Manolaraki, E. 2018. "Domesticating Egypt in Pliny's *Natural History*." In *After 69 CE: Civil War in Flavian Literature*, edited by L. Donovan Ginsberg and D. Krasne, 341–361. Berlin: De Gruyter.

Mar, R. 2001. *El santuario de Serapis en Ostia*. Tarragona: Universitat Rovira i Virgili.

Marcadé, J. 1952. "À propos des statuettes hellénistiques on aragonite du Musée de Délos." *BCH* 76, 96–135.

Marcadé, J. 1969. *Au musée de Délos: Étude sur la sculpture hellénistique en ronde bosse découverte dans l'île*, BÉFAR 215. Paris: De Boccard.

Mari, Z. 2004. "L'Antinoeion di Villa Adriana." *RenPontAcc* 76, 263–314.

Mari, Z., and S. Sgalambro. 2007. "The Antinoeion of Hadrian's Villa: Interpretation and Architectural Reconstruction." *AJA* 111 (1), 83–104.

Martens, B. A. 2015. "Sarapis as Healer in Roman Athens: Reconsidering the Identity of Agora S 1068." In *Autopsy in Athens: Recent Archaeological Research on Athens and Attica*, edited by M. M. Miles, 51–65. Oxford: Oxbow.

Martin, S. R. 2017. "Ethnicity and Greek Art History in Theory and Practice." In *Theoretical Approaches to the Archaeology of Ancient Greece*, edited by L. C. Nevett, 143–163. Ann Arbor: University of Michigan Press.

Martzavou, P. 2010. "Les cultes isiaques et les italiens entre Délos, Thessalonique et l'Eubée." *Pallas* 84, 181–205.

Martzavou, P. 2011. "Priests and Priestly Roles in the Isiac Cults: Women as Agents in Religious Change in Late Hellenistic and Roman Athens." In *Ritual Dynamics in the Ancient Mediterranean: Agency, Emotion, Gender, Representation*, edited by A. Chaniotis, 61–84. Stuttgart: F. Steiner.

Martzavou, P. 2012a. "Isis Aretalogies, Initiations, and Emotions: The Isis Aretalogies as a Source for the Study of Emotions." In *Unveiling Emotions: Sources and Methods for the Study of Emotions in the Greek World*, edited by A. Chaniotis, 267–291. Stuttgart: F. Steiner.

Martzavou, P. 2012b. "Priests and Priestly Roles in the Isiac Cults: Women as Agents in Religious Change in Late Hellenistic and

Roman Athens." In *Ritual Dynamics in the Ancient Mediterranean: Agency, Emotion, Gender, Representation*, edited by A. Chaniotis, 61–84. Stuttgart: F. Steiner.

Martzavou, P. 2018. "What Is an Isiac Priest in the Greek World?" In *Individuals and Materials in the Greco-Roman Cults of Isis: Agents, Images, and Materials*, RGRW 187, edited by V. Gasparini and R. Veymiers, 127–155. Leiden: Brill.

Massumi, B. 2002. *Parables for the Virtual: Movement, Affect, Sensation*. Durham, NC: Duke University Press.

Matricon-Thomas, E. 2012. "Le culte d'Isis à Athènes: entre aspect 'universel' et spécificités locales." In *Egyptian Gods in the Hellenistic and Roman Mediterranean: Image and Reality between Local and Global*, edited by L. Bricault and M. J. Versluys, 41–66. Palermo: Salvatore Sciascia Editore.

Mattingly, D. J. 2004. "Being Roman: Expressing Identity in a Provincial Setting." *JRA* 17, 5–25.

Mattingly, D. J. 2014. "Identities in the Roman World: Discrepancy, Heterogeneity, Hybridity, and Plurality." In *Roman in the Provinces: Art on the Periphery of Empire*, edited by L. R. Brody and G. L. Hoffman, 35–60. Boston: McMullen Museum of Art.

Mazurek, L. 2016. "Material and Textual Narratives of Authenticity? Creating Cabotage and Memory in the Hellenistic Eastern Mediterranean." In *Across the Corrupting Sea: Post-Braudelian Approaches to the Ancient Eastern Mediterranean*, edited by C. W. Concannon and L. A. Mazurek, 39–61. London: Routledge.

Mazurek, L. A. 2018. "The Middle Platonic Isis: Text and Image in the Sanctuary of the Egyptian Gods at Herodes Atticus' Marathon Villa." *AJA* 122(4), 611–644.

Mazurek, L. A. 2020a. Fashioning a Global Goddess: Critiquing the Local through Hellenistic Images of Isis. In *Mediterranean Archaeologies of Insularity in the Age of Globalization*, edited by A. Kouremenos and J. M. Gordon, 179–207. Oxford: Oxbow Books.

Mazurek, L. A. 2020b. "An Isis Statuette from Amphipolis in Context." In *Bibliotheca Isiaca IV*, edited by L. Bricault and R. Veymiers, 85–93. Bordeaux: Éditions Ausonius.

McCoskey, D. E. 2012. *Race: Antiquity and Its Legacy*. New York: Bloomsbury Academic.

Merkelbach, R. 1962. *Roman und Mysterium in der Antike*. Munich; Berlin: C. H. Beck.

Merkelbach, R. 1963. *Isisfeste in griechisch-römischer Zeit: Daten und Riten*. Meisenheim am Glan: A. Hain.

Merkelbach, R. 1973. "Zwei Texte aus dem Sarapeum zu Thessalonike." *ZPE* 10, 45–54.

Merkelbach, R. 1976. "Zum neuen Isistext aus Maroneia." *ZPE* 23, 234–235.

Merrills, A. 2017. *Roman Geographies of the Nile: From the Late Republic to the Early Empire*. Cambridge: Cambridge University Press.

Meskell, L. 2003. "Memory's Materiality: Ancestral Presence, Commemorative Practice and Disjunctive Locales." In *Archaeologies of Memory*, edited by R. M. van Dyke and S. E. Alcock, 34–55. Malden, MA: Blackwell.

Meskell, L. 2004. *Object Worlds in Ancient Egypt: Material Biographies Past and Present*. Oxford: Berg.

Méthy, N. 1996. "La divinité suprême dans l'oeuvre d'Apulée." *RÉL* 74, 247–269.

Méthy, N. 1999a. "*Deus exsuperantissimus*: une divinité nouvelle? À propos de quelques passages d'Apulée." *AntCl* 68, 99–117.

Méthy, N. 1999b. "La communication entre l'homme et la divinité dans les *Métamorphoses* d'Apulée." *ÉtCl* 67(1), 43–56.

Méthy, N. 1999c. "Le personnage d'Isis dans l'oeuvre d'Apulée: essai d'interprétation." *RÉA* 101, 125–142.

Meyboom, P. G. P. 1995. *The Nile Mosaic of Palestrina: Early Evidence of Egyptian Religion in Italy*, RGRW 121. Leiden: Brill.

Meyer, H., G. Grimm, and D. Kessler. 1994. *Der Obelisk des Antinoos: Eine kommentierte Edition*. Munich: Fink.

Meyer, M. 2017. "The *Martyria* of the Strife for Attica: *Martyria* of Changes in Cult and Myth – Space and Time in the West Pediment of the Parthenon." In *Time and Space in Ancient Myth,*

Religion and Culture, edited by A. Bierl, M. Christopoulos, and A. Papachrysostomou, 181–196. Berlin: De Gruyter.

Michalowski, C. 1932. *Les portraits hellénistiques et romains, Délos 13*. Paris: De Boccard.

Millar, F. 1981. "The World of the Golden Ass." *JRS* 71, 63–75.

Milleker, E. J. 1985. "Three Heads of Sarapis from Corinth." *Hesperia* 54(2), 121–135.

Mol, E. 2012. "The Perception of Egypt in Networks of Being and Becoming: A Thing Theory Approach to Egyptianising Objects in Roman Domestic Contexts." *Theoretical Roman Archaeology Journal*, 117–131. http://doi.org/10.16995/TRAC2012_117_131.

Mol, E. 2015a. *Egypt in Material and Mind: The Use and Perception of Aegyptiaca in Roman Domestic Contexts of Pompeii*. PhD dissertation, University of Leiden.

Mol, E. 2015b. "Romanising Oriental Cults? A Cognitive Approach to Alterity and Religious Experience in the Roman Cults of Isis." In *Romanisation des dieux orientaux? Transformations religieuses dans les provinces balkaniques à l'époque romaine: Nouvelles découvertes et perspectives – Proceedings of the International Symposium Skopje, 18–21 September 2013*, edited by A. Nikoloska and S. Müskens, 89–111. Skopje: University of Leiden.

Mol, E. 2017. "Object Ontology and Cultural Taxonomies: Examining the Agency of Style, Material, and Objects in Classification through Egyptian Material Culture in Pompeii and Rome." In *Materialising Roman Histories*, edited by A. van Oyen and M. Pitts, 169–189. Oxford: Oxbow.

Mol, E., and M. J. Versluys. 2015. "Material Culture and Imagined Communities in the Roman World." In *A Companion to the Archaeology of Religion in the Ancient World*, edited by R. Raja and J. Rüpke, 451–461. Malden, MA: John Wiley & Sons.

Montevecchi, O. 1970. "Nerone a una polis e ai 6475." *Aegyptus* 50, 5–33.

Moormann, E. M. 2018. "Ministers of Isiac Cults in Roman Wall Painting." In *Individuals and Materials in the Greco-Roman Cults of Isis: Agents, Images, and Practices, RGRW 187*, edited by V. Gasparini and R. Veymiers, 366–383. Leiden: Brill.

Morgan, C. 1991. "Ethnicity and Early Greek States: Historical and Material Perspectives." *PCPS* 37, 131–163.

Morgan, C. 2003. *Early Greek States beyond the Polis*. London: Routledge.

Moyer, I. 2008. "Notes on Re-reading the Delian Aretalogy of Sarapis (IG XI.4 1299)." *ZPE* 166, 101–107.

Moyer, I. 2011. *Egypt and the Limits of Hellenism*. Cambridge: Cambridge University Press.

Moyer, I. 2016. "Isidorus at the Gates of the Temple." In *Greco-Egyptian Interactions: Literature, Translation, and Culture, 500 BC–AD 300*, edited by I. Rutherford, 209–244. Oxford: Oxford University Press.

Moyer, I. 2017. "The Memphite Self-revelations of Isis and Egyptian Religion in the Hellenistic and Roman Aegean." *Religion in the Roman Empire* 3, 318–343.

Moyer, I., and J. Dieleman. 2010. "Egyptian Literature." In *A Companion to Hellenistic Literature*, edited by J. J. Clauss and M. Cuypers, 429–447. Malden, MA: Blackwell.

Mukerji, C. 1997. *Territorial Ambitions and the Gardens of Versailles*. Cambridge: Cambridge University Press.

Müller, C. 2016. "Globalization, Transnationalism, and the Local in Ancient Greece." In *Oxford Handbooks Online: Classical Studies, Social and Economic History*, edited by G. Williams. Oxford: Oxford University Press.

Müller, H. W. 1969. *Il culto di Iside nell'antica Benevento: catalogo delle sculture provenienti dai santuari egiziani dell'antica Benevento nel Museo del Sannio*. Benevento: Museo del Sannio.

Muniz Grijalvo, E. 2009. "The Cult of the Egyptian Gods in Roman Athens." In *Les religions orientales dans le monde grec et romain: Cent ans après Cumont 1906–2006*, edited by C. Bonnet and V. Pirenne, 325–341. Brussels: Belgian Historical Institute at Rome.

Muntz, C. E. 2011. "The Sources of Diodorus Siculus, Book 1." *CQ* 61(2), 574–594.

Muntz, C. E. 2017. *Diodorus Siculus and the World of the Late Roman Republic*. New York: Oxford University Press.

Murray, O. 1970. "Hecataeus of Abdera and Pharaonic Kingship." *JEA* 56, 141–171.

Mylonopoulos, I. 2008. "The Dynamics of Ritual Space in the Hellenistic and Roman East." *Kernos* 21, 49–79.

Mylonopoulos, I. 2010. "Divine Images versus Cult Images: An Endless Story about Theories, Methods, and Terminologies." In *Divine Images and Human Imaginations in Ancient Greece and Rome*, RGRW 170, edited by I. Mylonopoulos, 1–19. Leiden: Brill.

Mylonopoulos, I. 2016. "Hellenistic Divine Images and the Power of Tradition." In *Hellenistic Sanctuaries between Greece and Rome*, edited by M. Melfi and O. Bobou, 106–127. Oxford: Oxford University Press.

Nadig, M. 1986. *Die verborgene Kultur der Frau: Ethnopsychoanalytische Gespräche mit Bäuerinnen in Mexiko – Subjektivität und Gesellschaft im Alltag von Otomi-Frauen*. Frankfurt: Fischer Taschenbuch Verlag.

Nagel, S. 2015. "The Goddess's New Clothes: Conceptualising an 'Eastern' Goddess for a 'Western' Audience." In *The Dynamics of Transculturality: Concepts and Institutions in Motion*, edited by A. Flüchter and J. Schlöttli, 187–217. New York: Springer Publishing.

Neer, R. T. 2011. *The Emergence of the Classical Style in Greek Sculpture*. Chicago: University of Chicago Press.

Neumann, G. 1993. "Ein weiblicher Kopf in Thessaloniki." *AM* 108, 213–224.

Nielson, I. 2002. *Cultic Theatres and Ritual Drama*, Aarhus Studies in Mediterranean Antiquity 4. Aarhaus: Aarhaus University Press.

Nigdelis, P. 2010. "Voluntary Associations in Roman Thessalonike: In Search of Identity and Support in a Cosmopolitan Society." In *From Roman to Early Christian Thessalonike: Studies in Religion and Archaeology*, edited by L. Nasrallah, C. Bakirtzis, and S. J. Friesen, 13–47. Cambridge: Cambridge University Press.

O'Brien, C. S. 2015. *The Demiurge in Ancient Thought*. Cambridge: Cambridge University Press.

Oikonomakou, M. 2005. "Νέα ευρήματα από τον Μαραθώνα και την Νέα Μάκρη." In *Αττική 2004 Ανασκαφές, Ευρήματα, Νέα Μουσεία*, edited by V. Vasilopoulou, 41–43. Athens: B' Ephorate of Prehistoric and Classical Antiquities.

Oliver, J. H. 1965. "Attic Text Reflecting the Influence of Cleopatra." *GRBS* 6(4), 291–294.

Oliverio, G. 1914. "Scoperta del santuario delle divinità egizie in Gortina." *ASAtene* 1: 376–377.

Oppenheim, A. L. 1956. *The Interpretation of Dreams in the Ancient Near East, with a Translation of an Assyrian Dream-Book*. Philadelphia: American Philosophical Society.

Opsomer, J. 1998. *In Search of the Truth: Academic Tendencies in Middle Platonism*. Brussels: Paleis der Academiën.

Opsomer, J. 2005. "Demiurges in Early Imperial Platonism." In *Religionsgeschichtliche Versuche und Vorarbeiten: Gott und Götter bei Plutarch, Götterbilder – Gottesbilder – Weltbilder*, edited by R. Hirsch-Luipold, 51–99. Berlin: De Gruyter.

Pachis, P. 2003. "The Hellenistic Age as an Age of Propaganda: The Case of Isis' Cult." In *Theoretical Frameworks for the Study of Graeco-Roman Religions: Adjunct Proceedings of the XVIIIth Congress of the International Association for the History of Religions*, edited by L. H. Martin and P. Pachis, 97–125. Thessaloniki: University Studio Press.

Pandermalis, D. 1971. "ΑΝΑΣΚΑΦΗ ΔΙΟΥ." *ArchDelt* B2, 400–402.

Pandermalis, D. 1982a. "Ein neues Heiligtum in Dion." *AA* 1982, 727–735.

Pandermalis, D. 1982b. "Μνημεῖα καὶ τέχνη κατὰ τὴν περίοδο τῆς Ρωμαιοκρατίας." In *Μακεδονία: 4000 χρόνια ελληνικής ιστορίας και πολιτισμού*, edited by M. Sakellariou, 208–221. Athens: ΕΚΔΟΤΙΚΗ ΑΘΗΝΩΝ.

Pandermalis, D. 1984. "Οι επιγραφές του Δίου." In *Πρακτικά του Η' διεθνούς συνεδρίου ελληνικής και λατινικής επιγραφικής*, 271–277. Athens: Ministry of Culture.

Pandermalis, D. 1997. *Dion: The Archaeological Site and the Museum*. Translated by D. Hardy. Athens: Adam Editions.

Pandermalis, D. 2000. *Discovering Dion*. Athens: Adam Editions.

Pandermalis, D. (ed.) 2016. *Gods and Mortals at Olympus: Ancient Dion, City of Zeus*. New York: Onassis Foundation.

Pangiatopoulos, D. 2011. "The Stirring Sea: Conceptualizing Transculturality in the Late Bronze Age Eastern Mediterranean." In *Intercultural Contacts in the Ancient Mediterranean: Proceedings of the International Conference of the Netherlands-Flemish Institute in Cairo*, edited by R. Duistermaat and I. Regulski, 31–52. Leuven: Peeters.

Pangiatopoulos, D. 2012. "Encountering the Foreign: De-constructing Alterity in the Archaeologies of the Bronze Age Mediterranean." In *Materiality and Social Practice: Transformative Capacities of Intercultural Encounters*, edited by J. Maran and P. W. Stockhammer, 51–60. Oxford: Oxbow Books.

Papaioannou, M. 2016. "A *Synoecism* of Cultures in Roman Greece." In *Beyond Boundaries: Connecting Visual Cultures in the Provinces of Ancient Rome*, edited by S. E. Alcock, M. Egri, and J. F. D. Frakes, 31–46. Los Angeles: Getty Publications.

Papanikolaou, D. 2009. "The Aretalogy of Isis from Maroneia and the Question of Hellenistic 'Asianism.'" *ZPE* 168, 59–70.

Parker, G. 2008. *The Making of Roman India*. Cambridge: Cambridge University Press.

Parlama, L., and N. C. Stampolidis. 2000. *Athens: The City Beneath the City: Antiquities from the Metropolitan Railway Excavations*. Athens: Goulandris Foundation, Museum of Cycladic Art.

Parlasca, K. 1990. "Palmyrenische Skulpturen in Museen an der amerikanischen Westküste." In *Roman Funerary Monuments in the J. Paul Getty Museum*, Vol. 1, edited by M. True and G. Kock, 133–144. Los Angeles: J. Paul Getty Museum.

Pearson, S. 2015. "Egyptian Airs: The Life of Luxury in Roman Wall Painting." PhD dissertation, University of California, Berkeley.

Pearson, S. 2021. *The Triumph and Trade of Egyptian Objects in Rome*. Berlin: De Gruyter.

Pelekides, S. 1921. "Chroniques des fouilles et découvertes archéologiques dans l'Orient hellénique." *BCH* 45, 540–541.

Pelekides, S. 1934. "Ἀπό τήν πολιτεία καί τήν κοινωνία τῆς ἀρχαίας Θεσσαλονίκης." *Παράρτημα* 2, 48–56.

Pensabene, P. 2009. "Canopo di Villa Adriana: Programmi tematici, marmi e officine nell'arredo statuario." *ASAtene* 87(3), 381–424.

Perlzweig, J. 1961. *Lamps of the Roman Period: First to Seventh Century after Christ*, Agora 7. Princeton, NJ: American School of Classical Studies at Athens.

Perry, E. 2005. *The Aesthetics of Emulation in the Visual Arts of Ancient Rome*. Cambridge: Cambridge University Press.

Peschlow-Bindokat, A. 1972. "Demeter und Persephone in der attischen Kunst des 6. bis 4. Jahrhunderts." *JdI*, 60–157.

Petersen, L. H. 2012. "Collecting Gods in Roman Houses: The House of the Gilded Cupids VI.16.7, 38 at Pompeii." *Arethusa* 45, 319–332.

Petersen, L. H. 2016. "The Places of Roman Isis: Between Egyptomania, Politics, and Religion." In *Oxford Handbooks Online Classical Studies*, edited by G. Williams. Oxford: Oxford University Press.

Petrakos, V. 1995. *Marathon*. Athens: Archaeological Society of Athens.

Pfeiffer, S. 2018. "Comments on the Egyptian Background of the Priests' Procession during the Navigium Isidis." In *Individuals and Materials in the Greco-Roman Cults of Isis: Agents, Images, and Materials*, RGRW 187, edited by V. Gasparini and R. Veymiers, 672–689. Leiden: Brill.

Philips, J. 2008. *Aegyptiaca on the Island of Crete in Their Chronological Context: A Review*, 2 Vols. Wien: Verlage der Österreichischen Akademie der Wissenschaften.

Philostratus and Eunapius. 1922. *The Lives of the Sophists*, Loeb Classical Library 134. Translated by W. C. Wright. London and New York: William Heinemann and G. P. Putnam's Sons.

Picard, C. 1958. "La Sphinge tricéphale dite 'panthée', d'Amphipolis et la démonologie égypto-alexandrine." *MMAI* 50, 49–54.

Pingiatoglu, S. 2010. "Cults of Female Deities at Dion." *Kernos* 23, 179–192.

Pirelli, R. 2006. "Il culto di Iside a Benevento." In *Egittomania: Iside e il mistero*, edited by S. De Caro, 129–143. Milan: Electa.

Pitts, M. 2007. "The Emperor's New Clothes? The Utility of Identity in Roman Archaeology." *AJA* 111(4), 693–713.

Pitts, M., and M. J. Versluys, eds. 2015a. *Globalisation and the Roman World: World History, Connectivity, and Material Culture*. Cambridge: Cambridge University Press.

Pitts, M., and M. J. Versluys. 2015b. "Globalisation and the Roman World: Perspectives and Opportunities." In *Globalisation and the Roman World: World History, Connectivity, and Material Culture*, edited by M. Pitts and M. J. Versluys, 3–31. Cambridge: Cambridge University Press.

Plantzos, D. 2011. "The Iconography of Assimilation: Isis and Royal Imagery on Ptolemaic Seal Impressions." In *More than Men, Less than Gods: Studies on Royal Cult and Imperial Worship – Proceedings of the International Colloquium Organized by the Belgian School at Athens*, edited by P. Ioassif and A. Chankowski, 389–416. Leuven: Peeters.

Platt, V. 2002. "Viewing, Desiring, Believing: Confronting the Divine in a Pompeian House." *Art History* 25(1), 87–112.

Platt, V. 2007. "'Honour Takes Wing': Unstable Images and Anxious Orators in the Greek Tradition." In *Art and Inscriptions in the Ancient World*, edited by Z. Newby and R. Leader-Newby, 247–271. Cambridge: Cambridge University Press.

Platt, V. 2011. *Facing the Gods: Epiphany and Representation in Graeco-Roman Art, Literature, and Religion*. Cambridge: Cambridge University Press.

Plutarch. 1936. *Moralia*, Vol. 5, Loeb Classical Library 306. Translated by F. C. Babbitt. Cambridge, MA: Harvard University Press.

Podvin, J. C., and R. Veymiers. 2008. "À propos des lampes corinthiennes à motifs isiaques." In *Bibliotheca Isiaca I*, edited by L. Bricault, 63–68. Bordeaux: Éditions Ausonius.

Pollitt, J. J. 1990. *The Art of Ancient Greece: Sources and Documents*. Cambridge: Cambridge University Press.

Pond Rothman, M. S. 1975. "The Panel of the Emperors Enthroned on the Arch of Galerius." *Byzantine Studies* 2(1), 19–40.

Porro, G. G. 1913. "Il pretorio di Gortina." *BdA* 7(10), 349–360.

Preston, R. 2001. "Roman Questions, Greek Answers: Plutarch and the Construction of Identity." In *Being Greek under Rome: Cultural Identity, the Second Sophistic, and the Development of Empire*, edited by S. Goldhill, 86–122. Cambridge: Cambridge University Press.

Priestley, J. 2014. *Herodotus and Hellenistic Culture: Literary Studies in the Reception of the Histories*. Oxford: Oxford University Press.

Raja, R., and J. Rüpke. 2015. "Archaeology of Religion, Material Religion, and the Ancient World." In *A Companion to the Archaeology of Religion in the Ancient World*, edited by R. Raja and J. Rüpke, 1–26. Malden, MA: Wiley.

Rebillard, É. 2010. *The Care of the Dead in Late Antiquity*. Ithaca, NY: Cornell University Press.

Rebillard, É. 2012. *Christians and Their Many Identities in Late Antiquity: North Africa, 200–450 CE*. Ithaca, NY: Cornell University Press.

Renberg, G. 2010. "Hadrian and the Oracles of Antinous *SHA* Hadr. 14.7; with an Appendix on the So-Called Antinoeion at Hadrian's Villa and Rome's Monte Pincio Obelisk." *MAAR* 55, 159–198.

Renberg, G. 2017. *Where Dreams May Come: Incubation Sanctuaries in the Greco-Roman World*, 2 Vols., *RGRW* 184. Leiden: Brill.

Revell, L. 2005. *Roman Imperialism and Local Identities*. Cambridge: Cambridge University Press.

Revell, L. 2016. "Footsteps in Stone: Variability within a Global Culture." In *Beyond Boundaries: Connecting Visual Cultures in the Provinces of Ancient Rome*, edited by S. E. Alcock, M. Egri, and J. F. D. Frakes, 206–221. Los Angeles, CA: Getty Publications.

Richards, J. E. 1999. "Conceptual Landscapes in the Egyptian Nile Valley." In *Archaeologies of*

Landscape: Contemporary Perspectives, edited by W. Ashmore and A. B. Knapp, 83–100. Malden, MA: Blackwell.

Richter, D. S. 2001. "Plutarch on Isis and Osiris: Text, Cult, and Cultural Appropriation." *TAPA* 131, 191–216.

Richter, D. S. 2011. *Cosmopolis: Imagining Community in Late Classical Athens and the Early Roman Empire*. Oxford: Oxford University Press.

Ricke, H. 1965. *Das Sonnenheiligtum des Königs Userkaf, Band I, Der Bau*. Cairo: Schweizerisches Institut für ägyptische Bauforschung und Altertumskunde.

Rife, J. L. 2010. "Religion and Society at Roman Kenchreai." In *Corinth in Context: Comparative Studies on Religion and Society*, Novum Testamentum Suppl. 134, edited by S. J. Friesen, D. N. Schowalter, and J. C. Walters, 391–432. Leiden: Brill.

Riggs, C. 2005. *The Beautiful Burial in Roman Egypt*. Oxford: Oxford University Press.

Rizakis, A. 1998. "*Incolae-paroikoi*: populations et communautés dépendantes dans les cités et les colonies romaines de l'Orient." *RÉA* 100 (3–4), 599–617.

Rizakis, A. 2002. "L'émigration romaine en Macédoine et la communauté marchande de Thessalonique: perspectives économiques et sociales." In *Les Italiens dans le monde grec. IIe siècle av. J.C.-Ier siècle ap. J.-C. Actes de la Table Ronde, École Normale École Normale Superior*, edited by C. Müller and C. Hasenohr, 108–132. Paris: De Boccard.

Rizakis, A. 2003. "Recrutement et formation des élites dans les colonies romaines de la province de Macédoine." In *Les élites et leur facettes: Les élites locales dans le monde hellénistique et romain*, edited by M. Cébeillac-Gervasoni and L. Lamoine, 107–130. Rome: École française de Rome.

Robinson, H. S. 1965. "Excavations at Ancient Corinth, 1959–1963." *Klio* 46, 289–305.

Rodgers, R. 2003. "Female Representation in Roman Art: Feminising the Provincial 'Other.'" In *Roman Imperialism and Provincial Art*, edited by S. Scott and J. Webster, 69–94. Cambridge: Cambridge University Press.

Rodman, M. C. 1992. "Empowering Place: Multilocality and Multivocality." *American Anthropologist* 94(3), 640–656.

Romano, D. 2003. "City Planning, Centuriation, and Land Division in Roman Corinth: Colonia Laus Iulia and Corinthiensis and Colonia Iulia Flavia Augusta Corinthiensis." In *Corinth: The Centenary 1896–1996*, Corinth 20, edited by C. K. Williams and N. Bookidis, 279–301. Princeton, NJ: American School of Classical Studies at Athens.

Romeo, I. 2002. "The Panhellenion and Ethnic Identity in Hadrianic Greece." *CP* 97(1), 21–40.

Romeo, I., and E. C. Portale. 1998. *Le sculture, Gortina 3*. Padova: Bottega d'Erasmo.

Romiopoulou, K. 1997. Ελληνορωμαϊκά γλυπτά του Εθνικού Αρχαιολογικού Μουσείου. Δημοσιεύματα του αρχαιολογικού δελτίου 61. Athens: Ταμείο Αρχαιολογικών Πόρων και Απαλλοτριώσεων.

Ronzevalle, S. 1902. "Notes d'épigraphie palmyerienne." *Revue Biblique Internationale* 1902, 413–416.

Rose, C. B. 2005. "The Parthians in Augustan Rome." *AJA* 109(1), 21–75.

Rothe, U. 2012. "The 'Third Way': Treveran Women's Dress and the 'Gallic Ensemble.'" *AJA* 116(2), 235–252.

Rothe, U. 2013. "Whose Fashion? Men, Women, and Roman Culture as Reflected in the Dress in the Cities of the Roman North-West." In *Women and the Roman City in the Latin West*, Mnemosyne Suppl. 360, edited by E. Hemelrijk and G. Woolf, 243–270. Leiden: Brill.

Roullet, A. 1972. *The Egyptian and Egyptianizing Monuments of Imperial Rome*, ÉPRO 20. Leiden: Brill.

Roussel, P. 1913. "Le Sénatus-consulte de Délos." *BCH* 37, 310–322.

Roussel, P. 1915/1916. *Les cultes égyptiens à Délos du IIIe au Ier siècle av. J-C*. Nancy: Imprimerie Berger-Levrault.

Rowlandson, J. 2013. "Dissing the Egyptians: Legal, Ethnic, and Cultural Identities in Roman Egypt." In *Creating Ethnicities and*

Identities in the Roman World, edited by A. Gardner and E. Herring, 213–247. London: Institute of Classical Studies.

Rüpke, J. 2014. *From Jupiter to Christ: On the History of Religion in the Roman Imperial Period*. Translated by D. M. B. Richardson. Oxford: Oxford University Press.

Rüpke, J. 2016. *On Roman Religion: Lived Religion and the Individual in Ancient Rome*. Ithaca, NY: Cornell University Press.

Rüpke, J. 2018. "Theorising Religion for the Individual." In *Individuals and Materials in the Greco-Roman Cults of Isis*, RGRW 187, edited by V. Gasparini and R. Veymiers, 61–73. Leiden: Brill.

Russman, E. 2001. *Eternal Egypt: Masterworks of Ancient Art from the British Museum*. Berkeley: University of California Press.

Saïd, E. 1978. *Orientalism*. New York: Vintage Books.

Saïd, S. 2001. "The Discourse of Identity in Greek Rhetoric from Isocrates to Aristides." In *Ancient Perceptions of Greek Ethnicity*, edited by I. Malkin, 275–299. Cambridge, MA: Center for Hellenic Studies.

Salač, A. 1927. "Inscriptions de Kyme d'Éolide, de Phocée, de Tralles et de quelques autres villes d'Asie Mineure." *BCH* 51, 374–400.

Salditt-Trappmann, R. 1970. *Tempel der ägyptischen Götter in Griechenland und an der Westküste Kleinasiens*, ÉPRO 15. Leiden: Brill.

Sapelli, M. 1999. *Provinciae fideles: il fregio del Tempio di Adriano in Campo Marzio*. Rome: Electa, Soprintendenza Archeologica di Roma.

Sartre, M. 2005. *The Middle East under Rome*. C. Porter and E. Rawlings, trans. Cambridge, MA: Belknap Press.

Sauneron, S. 1959. "Les songes et leur interprétation dans l'Égypte ancienne." In *Les songes et leurs interprétation*, edited by A.-M. Esnoul, 17–61. Paris: Seuil.

Sauneron, S. 1962. *Les fêtes religieuses d'Esna aux derniers siècles du paganisme*. Cairo: L'Institut français d'archéologie orientale.

Schachter, A. 2007. "Egyptian Cults and Local Elites in Boiotia." In *Nile into Tiber: Egypt in the Roman World – Proceedings of the IIIrd International Conference of Isis Studies, Faculty of Archaeology, Leiden University*, RGRW 159, edited by L. Bricault, M. J. Versluys, and P. G. P. Meybook, 364–391. Leiden: Brill.

Schmidt-Colinet, A. 1989. "L'Architecture funéraire de Palmyre." In *La Syrie de l'époque achéménide à l'avènement de l'Islam, Archéologie et histoire de la Syrie 2*, edited by J.-M. Dentzer and W. Orthmann, 447–456. Saarbrücken: Saarbrücker Druckerei und Verlag.

Scott, M. 2010. *Delphi and Olympia: The Spatial Politics of Panhellenism in the Archaic and Classical Periods*. Cambridge: Cambridge University Press.

Scott, M. 2013. *Space and Society in the Greek and Roman Worlds*. Cambridge: Cambridge University Press.

Scroggs, R., and K. I. Groff. 1973. "Baptism in Mark: Dying and Rising with Christ." *JBL* 92 (4), 531–548.

Sfameni Gasparro, G. 2007. "The Hellenistic Face of Isis: Cosmic and Savior Goddess." In *Nile into Tiber: Egypt in the Roman World – Proceedings of the IIIrd International Conference of Isis Studies, Faculty of Archaeology, Leiden University*, RGRW 159, edited by L. Bricault, M. J. Versluys, and P. G. P. Meybook, 40–72. Leiden: Brill.

Sfameni Gasparro, G. 2016. "Il culto di Iside nel mondo ellenistico-romano: tra diffusione e creazione continua: per un nuovo modello interpretativo." *Mare Internum* 8, 13–20.

Sfameni Gasparro, G. 2018. "Identités religieuses isiaques: pour la définition d'une catégorie historico-religieuse." In *Individuals and Materials in the Greco-Roman Cults of Isis: Agents, Images, and Practices*, RGRW 187, edited by V. Gasparini and R. Veymiers, 74–107. Leiden: Brill.

Sharpe, H. 2014. "Bronze Statuettes from the Athenian Agora: Evidence for Domestic Cults in Roman Greece." *Hesperia* 83(1), 143–187.

Shear, J. L. 2007. "Reusing Statues, Rewriting Inscriptions and Bestowing Honours in Roman Athens." In *Art and Inscriptions in the Ancient World*, Z. Newby and R. Leader-Newby, 221–246. Cambridge: Cambridge University Press.

Shear, T. L. 1981. "Athens: From City-State to Provincial Town." *Hesperia* 50(4), 356–377.

Sherk, R. K. 1957. "Roman Imperial Troops in Macedonia and Achaea." *AJP* 78(1), 52–62.

Siard, H. 1998. "La crypte du Sarapieion A de Délos et le procès d'Apollônios." *BCH* 122, 469–489.

Siard, H. 2007. "L'Hydreion du Serapieion C de Délos: la divinsation de l'eau dans un sanctuaire isiaque." In *Nile into Tiber: Egypt in the Roman World – Proceedings of the IIIrd International Conference of Isis Studies, Faculty of Archaeology, Leiden University, RGRW* 159, edited by L. Bricault, M. J. Versluys, and P. G. P. Meybook, 418–445. Leiden: Brill.

Siard, H. 2009. "Le Sarapieion C de Délos: Architecture et cultes." *RA* 2009, 155–161.

Siskou, L. 2011. "The Male Egyptianizing Statues from the Sanctuary of the Egyptian Gods at Marathon." In *Bibliotheca Isiaca II*, edited by L. Bricault and R. Veymiers, 79–96. Bordeaux: Ausonius Éditions.

Slim, H. 1996. "Africa: Rome, and the Empire." In *Mosaics of Roman Africa: Floor Mosaics from Tunisia*, edited by M. E. M. Blanchard-Lemée and M. Ennaïfer, 17–36. Translated by K. D. Whitehead. New York: George Braziller.

Slim, H., and L. Slim. 1996. *Vie et artisinat à Thysdrus/El Jem, ville d'Africa, IIe–IIIe siècles*. Nice: Imprimerie Marc.

Smart, N. 1983. *Worldviews: Cross-cultural Explorations of Human Belief*. New York: Scribner's.

Smith, A. M. 2013. *Roman Palmyra: Identity, Community, and State Formation*. Oxford: Oxford University Press.

Smith, D. E. 1977. "The Egyptian Cults at Corinth." *HTR* 70(3–4), 201–231.

Smith, J. Z. 1998. "Religion, Religions, Religious." In *Critical Terms for Religious Studies*, edited by M. C. Taylor, 269–284. Chicago: University of Chicago Press.

Smith, M. 2017. *Following Osiris: Perspectives on the Osirian Afterlife from Four Millennia*. Oxford: Oxford University Press.

Smith, R. R. R. 1988. "*Simulacra Gentium*: The *Ethne* from the Sebasteion at Aphrodisias." *JRS* 78, 50–77.

Smith, R. R. R. 1991. *Hellenistic Sculpture: A Handbook*. London: Thames and Hudson.

Smith, R. R. R. 1998. "Cultural Choice and Political Identity in Honorific Portrait Statues in the Greek East in the Second Century A.D." *JRS* 88, 56–93.

Smith, R. R. R. 2006. "The Use of Images: Visual History and Ancient History." In *Classics in Progress: Essays on Ancient Greece and Rome*, edited by T. P. Wiseman, 59–103. Oxford: Oxford University Press.

Smith, R. R. R. 2013. *The Marble Reliefs from the Julio-Claudian Sebasteion*. Darmstadt: von Zabern.

Solmsen, F. 1979. *Isis among the Greeks and Romans*. Cambridge, MA: Oberlin College Press.

Sotiriadis, G. 1926. "The New Discoveries at Marathon." *Classical Weekly* 20, 83–84.

Spalinger, A. 2008. "The Rise of the Solar-Osirian Theology in the Ramesside Age: New Points d'Appui." In *Mythos and Ritual: Festschrift für Jan Assman zum 70. Geburtstag*, edited by B. Rothöhler and A. Manisali, 257–275. Berlin: LIT Verlag.

Spawforth, A. J. S. 2011. *Greece and the Augustan Cultural Revolution*. Cambridge: Cambridge University Press.

Spawforth, A. J. S., and S. Walker. 1985. "The World of the Panhellenion: 1. Athens and Eleusis." *JRS* 75, 78–104.

Spyropoulos, G. 2001. *Drei Meisterwerke der griechischen Plastik aus der Villa des Herodes Atticus zu Eva-Loukou*. Frankfurt am Main: Peter Lang.

Spyropoulos, G. 2006. *Η ΕΠΑΥΛΗ ΤΟΥ ΗΡΩΔΗ ΑΤΤΙΚΟΥ ΣΤΗΝ ΕΥΑ-ΛΟΥΚΟΥ ΚΥΝΟΥΡΙΑΣ*. Athens: ΟΛΚΟΣ.

Squire, M. 2009. *Image and Text in Graeco-Roman Antiquity*. Cambridge: Cambridge University Press.

Squire, M. 2011. *The Iliad in a Nutshell: Visualizing Epic on the Tabulae Iliacae*. Cambridge: Cambridge University Press.

Stadter, P. A. 1999. "*Philosophos kai Philandros*: Plutarch's View of Women in the Moralia and the Lives." In *Plutarch's Advice to the Bride and Groom and a Consolation to His Wife*, edited by S. A. Pomeroy, 173–182. Oxford: Oxford University Press.

Stager, J. 2016. "The Materiality of Color in Ancient Mediterranean Art." In *Essays in Global Color History: Interpreting the Ancient Spectrum*, edited by R. B. Goldman, 97–120. Piscataway, NJ: Gorgias Press.

Stamatopoulou, M. 2008. "Ouaphres Horou, an Egyptian Priest of Isis from Demetrias." In *Essays in Classical Archaeology for Eleni Hatzivassiliou, 1977–2007*, edited by D. Kurtz, 249–257. Oxford: Beazley Archive and Archaeopress.

Stambaugh, J. E. 1972. *Sarapis under the Ptolemies*, ÉPRO 25. Leiden: Brill.

Steimle, C. 2004. "Neue Erkenntnisse zum Heiligtum der ägyptischen Götter in Thessaloniki. Ein unveröffentlichtes Tagebuch des Archäologen Hans von Schoenebeck." *AEMΘ* 16, 291–306.

Steimle, C. 2006. "Das Heiligtum der ägyptischen Götter in Thessaloniki und die Vereine in seinem Umfeld." In *Religions orientales – culti misterici: Neue Perspektiven – nouvelles perspectives – prospettive nuove*, edited by C. Bonnet, 27–38. Stuttgart: F. Steiner.

Steimle, C. 2008. *Religion im römischen Thessaloniki: Sakraltopographie, Kult und Gesellschaft 168. Chr.–324 n. Chr.* Tübingen: Mohr Siebeck.

Stephens, J. 2008. "Ancient Roman Hairdressing: On Hairpins and Needles." *JRA* 21, 110–132.

Stephens, J. 2017. *The 'Juno' Hairstyle of Empress Sabina*. www.youtube.com/watch?v=74AT7oNC9xQ.

Stern, H. 1965. "L'image du mois d'octobre sur une mosaïque d'El-Djem." *JSav* 1, 117–131.

Steuernagel, D. 2010. "*Synnaos Theos*: Images of Roman Emperors in Greek Temples." In *Divine Images and Human Imaginations in Ancient Greece and Rome*, RGRW 170, edited by I. Mylonopoulos, 241–256. Leiden: Brill.

Stewart, A. 1979. *Attika: Studies in Athenian Sculpture of the Hellenistic Age, Society for the Promotion of Hellenic Studies Suppl. 14*. London: Society for the Promotion of Hellenic Studies.

Stewart, A. 2012. "Hellenistic Freestanding Sculpture from the Athenian Agora, Part 1: Aphrodite." *Hesperia* 81(2), 267–342.

Stewart, C. 1999. "Syncretism and Its Synonyms: Reflections on Cultural Mixture." *Diacritics* 29(3), 40–62.

Stewart, P. 2008. *The Social History of Roman Art*. Cambridge: Cambridge University Press.

Stone, D. 2014. "Identity and Identification in Apuleius' *Apology*, *Florida*, and *Metamorphoses*." In *Apuleius and Africa*, edited by B. T. Lee and E. Finkelpearl, 154–173. New York: Routledge.

Strazdins, E. 2019. "The King of Athens: Philostratus' Portrait of Herodes Atticus." *CP* 114, 238–264.

Strazdins, E. 2022. *Controlling the Future: Commemoration and Temporality in Imperial Greek Culture*. Oxford: Oxford University Press.

Swain, S. 1990. "The Promotion of Hadrian of Tyre and the Death of Herodes Atticus." *CP* 85(3), 214–216.

Swain, S. 1996. *Hellenism and Empire: Language, Classicism, and Power in the Greek World AD 50–250*. Oxford: Clarendon Press.

Swetnam-Burland, M. 2010. "The Egyptian Obelisk in the Augustan Campus Martius." *ArtB* 92(3), 135–153.

Swetnam-Burland, M. 2011. "'Egyptian' Priests in Roman Italy." In *Cultural Identity in the Ancient Mediterranean*, edited by E. S. Gruen, 336–353. Los Angeles: J. Paul Getty Museum.

Swetnam-Burland, M. 2015. *Egypt in Italy: Visions of Egypt in Roman Imperial Culture*. Cambridge: Cambridge University Press.

Syme, R. 1933. "Some Notes on the Legions under Augustus." *JRS* 23, 14–33.

Syme, R. 1979. "Problems about Janus." *AJP* 100(1), 188–212.

Takács, S. A. 2014. "Divine and Human Feet: Records of Pilgrims Honouring Isis." In *Pilgrimage in Graeco-Roman and Early Christian Antiquity: Seeing the Gods*, edited by J. Elsner, 353–369. Oxford: Oxford University Press.

Te Riele, G.-J. 1978. "Une nouvelle loi sacrée en Arcadie." *BCH* 102, 325–331.

Thakur, S. 2007. "Identity under Construction in Roman Athens." In *Negotiating the Past in* the Past: Identity, Memory, and Landscape in Archaeological Research, edited by N. Yoffee, 104–127. Tucson: University of Arizona Press.

Themelis, P. 2011. "The Cult of Isis at Ancient Messene." In *Bibliotheca Isiaca II*, edited by L. Bricault and R. Veymiers, 97–109. Bordeaux: Ausonius Éditions.

Thompson, D. J. 1988. *Memphis under the Ptolemies*. Princeton, NJ: Princeton University Press.

Thompson, D. L. 1982. *Mummy Portraits in the J. Paul Getty Museum*. Malibu: J. Paul Getty Museum.

Thompson, H. A. 1950. "Excavations in the Athenian Agora: 1949." *Hesperia* 18, 313–337.

Tilg, S. 2014. *Apuleius' Metamorphoses: A Study in Roman Fiction*. Oxford: Oxford University Press.

Tobin, J. 1997. *Herodes Attikos and the City of Athens: Patronage and Conflict under the Antonines*. Amsterdam: J. C. Gieben.

Too, Y. L. 1996. "Statues, Mirrors, Gods: Controlling Images in Apuleius." In *Art and Text in Roman Culture*, edited by J. Elsner, 133–152. Cambridge: Cambridge University Press.

Too, Y. L., ed. 2001. *Education in Greek and Roman Antiquity*. Leiden: Brill.

Topper, K. 2012. *The Imagery of the Athenian Symposium*. Cambridge: Cambridge University Press.

Totti, M. 1985. *Ausgewählte Texte der Isis- und Sarapis Religion*. Hildesheim: Olms.

Touchais, G. 1989. "Chronique des fouilles et découvertes archéologiques en Grèce en 1988." *BCH* 113, 581–700.

Touchette, L.-A. 2015. "Archaism and Eclecticism." In *The Oxford Handbook of Roman Sculpture*, edited by E. Friedland and M. Gunow Sobocinski, 292–306. Oxford: Oxford University Press.

Tran tam Tinh, V. 1973. *Isis lactans: Corpus des monuments gréco-romains d'Isis allaitant Harpocrate*, ÉPRO 37. Leiden: Brill.

Tran tam Tinh, V. 1983. *Sérapis débout: corpus des monuments de Sérapis débout et étude iconographique*, ÉPRO 37. Leiden: Brill.

Tran tam Tinh, V. 1986. "L'acculturation des divinités grecques en Égypte." In *Iconographie classique et identités régionales: colloque international, Paris, 26 et 27 mai 1983*, edited by P. Linant de Bellefonds, 355–364. Paris: de Boccard.

Tran tam Tinh, V. 1988. "Harpokrates." *LIMC* 4, 415–445. Zürich: Artemis Verlag.

Tran tam Tinh, V. 1990. "Isis." *LIMC* 7, 761–795. Zürich: Artemis Verlag.

Trimble, J. 2011. *Women and Visual Replication in Roman Imperial Art and Culture*. Cambridge: Cambridge University Press.

Tronchin, F. C. 2006. "An Eclectic Locus Artis: The Casa di Octavius Quartio at Pompeii." PhD dissertation, Boston University.

Tweed, T. A. 2008. *Crossing and Dwelling: A Theory of Religion*. Cambridge, MA: Harvard University Press.

Tzanavari, K. 1993. "Η Λατρεία των Αιγυπτίων θεών στη Βέροια." In *ΑΡΧΑΙΑ ΜΑΚΕΔΟΝΙΑ V: Ανακοινώσεις κατά το πέμπτο διεθνές συμπόσιο Θεσσαλονίκη, 10-15 Οκτωβρίου 1989*, Vol. 3, Ίδρυμα Μελετών Χερσονήσου του Αίμου 240, 1671–1682. Thessaloniki: Ιδρυμα Μελετών Χερσονήσου του Αίμου.

Vallois, R. 1944. *L'architecture hellénique et hellénistique à Délos jusqu'à l'éviction des Déliens (166 av. J.-C.)*. BÉFAR 157. Paris: De Boccard.

Van Aerde, M. E. J. J. 2015. "Egypt and the Augustan Cultural Revolution: An Interpretive Archaeological Overview." PhD dissertation, University of Leiden.

Van Andriga, W. 2012. "Statues in the Temples of Pompeii: Combinations of Gods, Local Definition of Cults and the Memory of the City." In *Historical and Religious Memory in the Ancient World*, edited by B. Dignas and R. R. R. Smith, 83–118. Oxford: Oxford University Press.

Van Bremen, R. 2003. "Family Structures." In *A Companion to the Hellenistic World*, edited by A. Erskine, 313–330. Malden, MA: Blackwell.

Van Eck, C., and M. J. Versluys. 2015. "The Biography of Cultures: Style, Objects, and Agency." *Les Cahiers de l'École du Louvre* 7, 2–22.

Van Oyen, A. 2017. "Material Culture in the Romanization Debate." In *The Diversity of*

Classical Archaeology, edited by A. Lichtenberger and R. Raja, 287–302. Turnhout: Brepols.

Van Straten, F. T. 1976. "Daikrates' Dream: A Votive Relief from Kos and Some Other *kat'onar* Dedications." *BaBesch* 31, 11–38.

Vandebeek, G. 1946. *De interpretatio graeca van de Isisfigur*. Leuven: Catholic University of Leuven.

Vanderlip, V. F. 1972. *The Four Greek Hymns of Isidorus and the Cult of Isis*. Toronto: A. M. Hakkert.

Vanderpool, E. 1961. "News Letter from Greece." *AJA* 65(3), 299–303.

Vandorpe, K. 2012. "Identity." In *The Oxford Handbook of Roman Egypt*, edited by C. Riggs, 260–276. Oxford: Oxford University Press.

Vasunia, P. 2001. *The Gift of the Nile: Hellenizing Egypt from Aeschylus to Alexander*. Berkeley: University of California Press.

Vavritsas, A. K. 1968. "Ειδήσεις εκ Μαραθώνος: News from Marathon." *Αρχαιολογικά Χρονικά* 1968, 230–234.

Veligianni, C. 1986. "Hypostoloi und Trierarchos auf einer neuen Inschrift aus Amphipolis." *ZPE* 62, 241–246.

Vermeule, C. C. 1981. *Greek and Roman Sculpture in America: Masterpieces in Public Collection in the United States and Canada*. Berkeley: University of California Press.

Vermeule, C. C. 1988. *Sculpture in Stone and Bronze: Additions to the Collections of Greek, Etruscan, and Roman Art, 1971–1988*. Boston: Museum of Fine Arts.

Versluys, M. J. 2002. *Aegyptiaca Romana: Nilotic Scenes and the Roman Views of Egypt*, RGRW 144. Leiden: Brill.

Versluys, M. J. 2010. "Understanding Egypt in Egypt and beyond." In *Isis on the Nile: Egyptian Gods in Hellenistic and Roman Egypt – Proceedings of the IVth International Conference of Isis Studies*, RGRW 171, edited by L. Bricault and M. J. Versluys, 7–38. Leiden: Brill.

Versluys, M. J. 2012. "Making Meaning with Egypt: Hadrian, Antinous and Rome's Cultural Renaissance." In *Egyptian Gods in the Hellenistic and Roman Mediterranean: Image and Reality between Local and Global*, edited by L. Bricault and R. Veymiers, 25–40. Palermo: Salvatore Sciascia Editore.

Versluys, M. J. 2013. "Orientalising Roman Gods." In *Panthée: Religious Transformations in the Graeco-Roman Empire*, RGRW 177, edited by L. Bricault and C. Bonnet, 235–259. Leiden: Brill.

Versluys, M. J. 2014. "Understanding Objects in Motion: An *Archaeological Dialogue* on Romanization." *Archaeological Dialogues* 21(1), 1–20.

Versluys, M. J. 2015. "Roman Visual Material Culture as Globalising Koine." In *Globalisation and the Roman World*, edited by M. Pitts and M. J. Versluys, 141–174. Cambridge: Cambridge University Press.

Versluys, M. J. 2016. "Exploring Aegyptiaca and Their Material Agency throughout Global History." In *The Routledge Handbook of Globalisation and Archaeology*, edited by T. Hodos, 74–89. London: Routledge.

Versluys, M. J. 2017. *Visual Style and Constructing Identity in the Hellenistic World*. Cambridge: Cambridge University Press.

Versnel, H. S. 1990. *Ter Unus: Isis, Dionysos, Hermes – Three Studies in Henotheism, Studies in Greek and Roman Religion* 6/1. Leiden: Brill.

Veymiers, R. 2009. "Les cultes isiaques à Amphipolis: *Membra disjecta* IIIe s. av. J.-C.-IIIe s. apr. J.-C." *BCH* 133, 471–520.

Veymiers, R. 2011. "Les cultes isiaques à Argos: Du mythe à l'archéologie." In *Bibliotheca Isiaca II*, edited by L. Bricault and R. Veymiers, 111–130. Bordeaux: Ausonius Éditions.

Veymiers, R. 2014. "La présence isiaque dans le Péloponnèse: Sur les traces des lieux de culte." *RA* 2014, 143–151.

Veymiers, R. 2018. "Agents, Images, Practices." In *Individuals and Materials in the Greco-Roman Cults of Isis: Agents, Images, and Practices*, RGRW 187, edited by V. Gasparrini and R. Veymiers, 1–60. Leiden: Brill.

Vial, C. 1984. *Délos indépendante*. BCH Suppl. 10. Paris: De Boccard.

Vitti, M. 1992. "Per una definizione dell'impianto urbano di Salonicco da Cassandro a Galerio." *Faventia* 14(2), 55–85.

Vlassopoulos, K. 2013. *Greeks and Barbarians.* Cambridge: Cambridge University Press.

Vlassopoulos, K. 2015. "Ethnicity and Greek History: Re-examining Our Assumptions." *BICS* 58(2), 1–13.

Von Lieven, A. 2016. "Translating Gods, Interpreting Gods: On the Mechanisms behind the *Interpretatio Graeca* of Egyptian Gods." In *Greco-Egyptian Interactions: Literature, Translation, and Culture, 500 BC–AD 300*, edited by I. Rutherford, 61–82. Oxford: Oxford University Press.

Von Moock, D. W. 1998. *Die figürlichen Grabstelen Attikas in der Kaiserzeit: Studien zur Verbreitung, Chronologie, Typologie und Ikonographie.* Mainz: von Zabern.

Von Stackelberg, K. 2009. *The Roman Garden: Space, Sense, and Society.* New York: Routledge.

Vorster, C. 2008. "Greek Origins: The Herculaneum Women in the pre-Roman World." In *The Herculaneum Women: History, Context, Identities*, edited by J. Daehner, 113–140. Los Angeles: The J. Paul Getty Museum.

Vout, C. 2005. "Antinous, Archaeology and History." *JRS* 95, 80–96.

Vout, C. Forthcoming. "The Crowded Stuff of Sanctuaries." In *The Stuff of the Gods: The Material Aspects of Religion in Ancient Greece*, edited by M. Haysom, M. Milli and J. Wallensten. Athens: Swedish Insitute at Athens and British School at Athens.

Voutiras, E. 2005. "Sanctuaire privé: culte public? Le cas du Sarapieion de Thessalonique." In *Ἴδιαι καὶ δημοσίαι: Les cadres "privés" et "publics" de la religion grecque antique*, edited by V. Dasen and M. Piéart, 473–493. Liège: Centre international d'étude de la religion grecque.

Voutiras, E. 2012. "Ὄρθιος Σάραπις ἀπό τη Θεσσαλονίκη." In *Κλασική παράδοση καὶ νεωτερικά στοιχεία στην πλαστική της ρωμαϊκῆς Ελλάδας*, edited by T. Stefanidou-Tiveriou and P. Karanastasi, 265–272. Thessaloniki: University Studio Press.

Walbank, F. W. 1981. *The Hellenistic World.* Cambridge, MA: Harvard University Press.

Walbank, M. E. H. 1997. "The Foundation and Planning of Early Roman Corinth." *JRA* 10, 95–130.

Walker, S. 1979. "A Sanctuary of Isis on the South Slope of the Acropolis." *BSA* 74, 243–258.

Walters, E. J. 1988. *Attic Grave Reliefs that Represent Women in the Dress of Isis*, Hesperia Suppl. 22. Princeton, NJ: ASCSA.

Walters, E. J. 2000. "Predominance of Women in the Cult of Isis in Roman Athens: Funerary Monuments from the Agora Excavations and Athens." In *De Memphis à Rome: Actes du Ier colloque international sur les etudes isiaques*, RGRW 140, edited by L. Bricault, 63–91. Leiden: Brill.

Waterfield, R. 2014. *Taken at the Flood: The Roman Conquest of Greece.* Oxford: Oxford University Press.

Watterson, B. 1998. *The House of Horus at Edfu: Ritual in an Ancient Egyptian Temple.* Stroud: Tempus Publishing.

Webster, J. 2001. "Creolizing the Roman Provinces." *AJA* 105(2), 209–225.

Welles, C. B. 1962. "The Discovery of Sarapis and the Foundation of Alexandria." *Historia* 11, 271–298.

White, M. L. 2005. "Favorinus' 'Corinthian Oration': A Pique Panorama of the Hadrianic Forum." In *Urban Religion in Roman Corinth: Interdisciplinary Approaches*, edited by D. N. Schowalter and S. Friesen, 61–110. Cambridge, MA: Harvard Theological Studies.

Whitmarsh, T. 2001. *Greek Literature in the Roman Empire: The Politics of Imitation.* Oxford: Oxford University Press.

Whitmarsh, T. 2013. "Resistance Is Futile? Greek Literary Tactics in the Face of Rome." In *Les grecs héritiers des romains: huit exposés suivis de discussions*, edited by P. Schubert, P. Ducrey, and P. Derron, 57–85. Geneva: Fondation Hardt.

Whitmarsh, T. 2015. *The Second Sophistic.* Oxford: Oxford University Press.

Wild, R. A. 1981. *Water in the Worship of Isis and Sarapis*, ÉPRO 87. Leiden: Brill.

Wilhelm, A. 1934. "Zu dem Gedichte des Maiistas IG XI 1299." *Symbolae Osloenses* 13 (1), 1–18.

Williams, C. 1985. "Corinth 1984, East of the Theater." *Hesperia* 54(1), 55–96.

Winkler, J. J. 1985. *Auctor and Actor: A Narratological Reading of Apuleius' Golden Ass*. Berkeley: University of California Press.

Woodward, A. M. 1925. "Archaeology in Greece, 1924–1925." *JHS* 45(2), 210–228.

Woolf, G. 1993. "The Unity and Diversity of Romanisation." *JRA* 5, 349–352.

Woolf, G. 1994. "Becoming Roman, Staying Greek: Culture, Identity, and the Civilizing Process in the Roman East." *PCPS* 40, 116–143.

Woolf, G. 2007. "A Sea of Faith?" In *Mediterranean Paradigms and Classical Antiquity*, edited by I. Malkin, 126–143. New York: Routledge.

Woolf, G. 2014. "Isis and the Evolution of Religions." In *Power, Politics, and the Cults of Isis: Proceedings of the Vth International Conference of Isis Studies, Boulogne-sur-Mer, RGRW* 180, edited by L. Bricault and M. J. Versluys, 62–92. Leiden: Brill.

Wrede, W. 1926. "Archäologische Funde des Jahres 1925: Griechenland." *AA* 1926, 430.

Yans, V. 2006. "On 'Groupness.'" *Journal of American Ethnic History* 25(4), 119–129.

Žabkar, L. V. 1988. *Hymns to Isis in Her Temple at Philae*. Hanover, CT: University Press of New England.

Zagdoun, M.-A. 1989. *La sculpture archaïsante dans l'art hellénistique et dans l'art romain du Haut-Empire, BÉFAR* 259. Paris: de Boccard.

Zanker, G. 2004. *Modes of Viewing in Hellenistic Poetry and Art*. Madison: University of Wisconsin Press.

Ziegler, C. 1984. "Sistrum." In *Lexikon der Ägyptologie V*, edited by W. Helck and E. Otto, 959–962. Wiesbaden: Otto Harrassowitz.

INDEX

Actium, Battle of, 8, 45, 65
Aelius Aristides, 22, 189
agency, 7, 15, 30, 33, 55, 62, 190–191, 207
  of material culture, 14
  of sculptures, 10
Agrippa, Marcus, 8–9
Alexandria, 65, 94
alterity, 86, 120, 123, 129–130, 133, 137, 143, 151, 188, 193
Ambrakia, 52
Amorgos, 90
Amphipolis, 46, 53–54, 69, 96–97, 228
animals, 36, 63, 65, 149–150, 178, 180–183, 185
  bulls, 180–182
  crocodiles, 65, 147, 149–150, 182, **182**
Anthestii. See Family
Antoninus Pius, 152
Anubis, 36, 38–39, 49, 55, **96**, 103, 114, 116–117, 216, 220, 243
Aphrodisias, 1
Aphrodite, 71, 104, **106**, 113, 115–116, 166, 180
  Aphrodite-Isis, 38
  Hypolympidia, 47, **48–49**
Apis, 67, 180
Apollo, 114
Apollonius of Tyre, 22
Apuleius, 17
  Metamorphoses, 33, 35–36, 39–40, 44, 55, 76–78, 131, 135, 194
  Platonism, 34
archaism, 28, 47, 97, 105, 108, 163, 169–171, 173, 189
architecture, sanctuary, 13, 45, 47, 104, 146, 152, 158–163, **159**, **161**, 183, 185, 187
aretalogy, 34, 42, 55–57, 70–76, 113–116, 187, 191
  Andros, 55, 70, 74
  Chalkis, 111
  Ios, 55, 70
  Kassandreia, 55, 70
  Kyme, 55, 70, 74, 114–115, 170
  Maroneia, 55, 70, 74–75, 78, 102, 112, 115, 170
  Medinet Madi, 71–72, 74
  Telmessos, 55, 70
  Thessaloniki, 55, 70, 114
Argos, 53, 69, 179

army, Roman, 8, 129
Artemis, 45, 71–72, **105**, 112
Asia Minor, 5, 10, 55, 57, 59, 70, 90, 224
Asklepios, 19, 94–95, 114, 219, 225
associations, 25, 37–40, 56
  Anoubiasts, 38–39
  Anubophores, 38
  Dekaists, 37
  Diakonoi, 52
  Enatists, 37
  Eranists, 52
  Hieraphoroi, 38
  Hypostoliasts, 38
  Isiastai, 38
  Navarchs, 54
  Osiriasts, 52
  Pyrophoroi, 38
  Sarapiastai, 38
  Stoliasts, 38
  Therapeutes, 37, 52
  wives of the colonists and foreigners, 48
Athena, 10, 74, 85, 102, **105**, 112–114, **113**
Athens, 7–8, 10–13, 19, 22, **30**, 37–38, 53, 61, 75, 91, 129–136, 139, 188, 192, 207, 213
  Agora, 9, 133, 139, 226, 231
  Akropolis, 9, 85, 179, 232
  Arch of Hadrian, 10
  Areopagus, 63
  Kerameikos, 133, 143
  Parthenon, 8–9
  Temple of Augustus and Roma, 9–10
  Temple of Olympian Zeus, 11, **12**, 133, 201
Augustus, 7–10, 64, 77
authenticity, 69, 86

beliefs, 32
Bellona, 77
Beneventum, 65, 117
boats, 54, 62, 150
boundaries, 6, 14, 17, 21, 25, 31, 37–38, 41, 44, 57, 60, 69, 86, 152
Brubaker, Rogers, 4, 15, 30, 32
Bryaxis, 94
Bubastis, 115

275

calendars, 34–37, **36**, 40
Calvenus Taurus, 172
Carthage, 78
Cassius Dio, 10, 22, 64
Ceres, 76–77
Chalkis childbirth, 39, 77
children, 22–23, 48, 74, 111, 117, 139–140
Cicero, 7
cista, 36, **100**, 100, 227
Clement of Alexandria, 94
Cleopatra, 8, 65, 239
colonies, 8, 11, 13, 45, 47, 50
color, 23, 107, 149, 230
conquest, of Greece, 7–9
Corinth, 7–8, 23, 33, 150, 193
Crete, 5, 96

Delos, 8, 37–39, 46, 51, 53, 55, **68**, 91, 96, **97**, 99, 136, 139, 172, 179, 188, 228
    Chronicle of Sarapieion A, 60, 67–70, 189
    Maison de Fourni, 150
    Sarapieion A, 39, **83**
    Sarapieion B, 92, 189
    Sarapieion C, 39, 46, 118, 141, 208, 222, 241
Delphi, 100
Demeter, 71–72, 78, 87, 94, 100, 102, 113, 116, 226
Demetrias, 53, 69, 203
demotic, 73
deterritorialization, 66, 72, 77, 80, 86, 184, 189–190, 192
Diana, 77
diaspora, 53–54
Dio Chrysostomus, 22, 64
Diodorus Siculus, 55, 63–64, 74, 235, 240
Dion, 8, 31, 45–52, **46**, **48–49**, 56, 83–84, 96–97, 99, 139, **146**, 180–182, **181**, 188, 227, 240
Dionysius of Halicarnassus, 22
Dionysos, 63, 72
domestication, 58, 66, 176, 189
Domitian, 65, 131
dreams, 54, 68, 80–81, 86, 209
dress, 24, 121
    of devotees, 29, 36, 38–41, 53, 122, 131–134, 144, 188, 193
    Diplax, **3**, 97, **98**, 231
    of Greco-Roman men, 124, 126–127, 132–133
    of Isis, 1, 79, 88, 101, 166
    Knotenpalla, 96, 117, 131, 137, 142, 163
    of male devotees, 137–142, **138**
    of provincial women, 124–130
    and ritual, 36, 41–44
    of Sarapis, 90

ear reliefs, 83
Edfu, Temple of Horus, 174
Egypt, Ptolemaic, 19–21
Eleusis, 75–78, 94, 230
Ephesus, 77, 90, 201
Epidauros, 38, 114

epiphany, 45, 60, 80–86, 116, 193
Eretria, 38, 53–54, 188, 230
Eros, 111, 115, 117, 174
ethnicity, 3–4, 13–16, 25, 61, 69, 123, 186–187, 189–192
ethnos, 18
Eva Loukou, 153, 238
exoticism, 2, 28, 37, 64, 88–89, 97–98, 117, 148, 175, 178, 184, 190

family, 26, 125, 187, 191
    Anthestii, 45–51
    of devotees, 45–52, 67, 137, 143, 219
    of the gods, 26, 59, 74, 112, 114–115
    Herennii, 50–52
    Salarii, 54
Faustina the Younger, 153
Favorinus, 23–25, 218
festivals, 35–37, 40, 56
    Isia, 36, 41
    Navigium Isidis, 36, 39, 54
footprint reliefs, **51**, 51, **83–86**
freedmen, 46, 50, **84**
Fronto, 64

garlands, 98
geography, 5, 13, 23, 27, 60, 86, 146, 151, 175, 187, 192
globalization, 16, 60, 77, 87, 126, 190, 194
Gortyna, 54, **88**, 90–91, **92**, 98, **98**, **179**, 179, 181–182, **182**, 188
Greekness, 3, 5–6, 17–25, 28, 44, 86, 101, 123–124, 129–130, 134, 143, 151, 170, 186–187, 192, 194
    language, 18, 20, 22–23, 25, 74–75, 77, 115, 193
groupness, 25, 30–32, 41, 45, 57, 186–187
gymnasium, 20

Hades, 94
Hadrian, 10–12, 21, 230
    Antinoos, 66
    Panhellenion, 11–13
    Villa at Tivoli, 28, 66, 152, 172–173, **173**, 175, 184
hairstyle, 1, 24, 29, 42, 88, 90, 94–95, 97, 107, 110, 117, 122, **124**, 126, 131, 133, 163, 166
    bald, 139
    Horus-lock, 139
Harpokrates, 55, 71–72, 100, 103, 110–112, **111**, 117, 174, 216
Hecataeus, 151
Hecate, 77
henotheism, 72–73, 114
Hera, 71, 74
Herakles, 63
Herculaneum, **100**
Herennii. *See* family
Hermanubis, 39, 51, 220
Hermes, 72, 74, 115, 170
Herodes Atticus, 127, 152–153, 172, 175–178, **176**, 184
    Polydeukion, 153–158, **156**, 176–177

Herodotus, 18, 59, 61–63, 65, 84, 100, 150, 243
Historia Augusta, 175
Horus, 71, 74, 139, 151, 173, **174**, 211
Hydreion, 54
Hygeia, 116

ideal sculpture, 3, 47–49, **48**, 53, 69, **90–100**, **91–92**, **96–98**, 100, **105–106**, 108–111, 113, 165–171, **165–166**, **174**, 192
imports, 27, 88, 117–119, 188
initiation, 29, 31, 35, 56, 135–136, 143, 210
inscriptions, bilingual, 47
integration, 20, 54
intersectionality, 16, 186, 191
Inventio Osiris, 182
Isis, epithets
    Isis Aphrodite, 166, **168**
    Isis Demeter, 100, 166, **167**, 193
    Isis Dikaiosyne, 135–136
    Isis Lochia, 51
    Isis Orgia, 42, 104
    Isis *Pelagia*, 131
    Isis Tyche/Fortuna, 99, 212
    Isis *unica*, 73, 164
Isis, sculptural types
    Diplax. *See* Dress
    Isis lactans, 100–101, **100**
    Isis Tyche/Fortuna, **99**
    Knotenpalla. *See* Dress
Isocrates, 19, 61
Italians, 46, 50, 54

jewelry, 124, 126
Juno, 77

kalathos, 90, 94, 172
Kenchreai, 34–35, 41, 76–77, **149**, 149
Kephissia, 153
Kerberos, **88**, 90
Kos, 5, 38, 52
    group burial, 38
Kronos, 71, 74, 170

lamps, 36, 38, 154, 156, 162, **165**, 238–239
landscape, 13
laws, 19–22, 114
    Egyptian, 63
    Isis as lawgiver, 74
Lucian, 84
Lucius Verus, 176, 178

Marathon, 27, 96, 106, 140, 147, 153–179, **154**, **158**, **160–162**, **166–167**, **171**, **174**, **176**, 183, 188
Marcus Aurelius, 8, 153, 175–176, **177**, 243
Maroneia, 52, 83, 170
materiality, 5, 13–15, 26, 82, 94, 101, 152, 170, 187, 194, 196
Megalopolis, 29, 39

memory, 7, 14
Memphis, 63, 66–67, 70, 114
Messene, 98–100, 106, 111, 131, 179, 210, 227–228, 240
Middle Platonism, 172, 178, 235
migration, 2, 6, 19–20, 31, 46, 53–56, 189–190
mosaics, **1**, **36**, 65, 147–150, 161
mystes, 42
myth, 3, 23, 26, 36, 43, 63, 66, 72, 151, 173, 189
    and ethnicity, 14, 17–19
    of Osiris, 78–79
    and ritual, 193
    of Sarapis, 93–94
myth, of origin, 11, 66, 85
myth-history, 10–13, 17, 25, 54, 59–61, 69, 75–76, 87, 102, 114–116, 146, 169–170, 183, 188–189

Nemesis, 77
Nero, 9, 21
Nile River, 61, 63–66, 146, 180, 185, 190
Nilometers, 179, 183, 188
nilotic, 146
    in art, **149**
    in Greek sanctuaries, 28
    Landscape, 148, 183, 188, 190
    Literary depictions, 61–67
    in Pompeiian wall painting, 65–66, **66**, 147–152, 183, 189

obelisks, 161, 240
Opous, 54, 56
oracles, 65, 219
Oropos, 9
Orpheus, 63
Osiris, 41, **42**, 65–67, 71–74, 78–79, 136, **154**, **166**, 170, **171**, 180, 207, 211, 213, 238
    Mystes, 42
    Osiris-Antinoos, 172, **173**
Ostia, 149

paideia, 17, 19, 22–23, 25, 153, 177–178
Palmyra, 122–129, **123**, **125**, **128**
Panhellenion, 12, 190
Panhellenism, 8, 19
Paphos, 77
Patras, 8, 150
Pausanias, 13, 39, 94, 189
Persian Wars, 9, 18–19, 23
personifications, 1, 64, 77, 150, 193, 235
Philae, 70, **160**, 238
Philippi, 96–97, 99, 179, 189
    Battle, 8
Philostratus, 22, 24, 153
Piraeus, 114, 230
plants, 65–66, 147, 149–150, 152, 178, 185
Pliny the Elder, 119, 151
    Historia Naturalis, 94, 152
Pliny the Younger, 64

Plutarch, 17, 22–23, 36, 64, 189
    De Iside et Osiride, 42, 55, 66, 78–80, 82, 93, 114, 117, 170, 172, 181
    Platonism, 78–80, 172
Pluto, 94
Polydeukion, 236, *See* Herodes Atticus
polysemy, 79–80, 86–87, 102, 116, 166
Pompeii, 16, 46, 57, 65, 112, **147**, 169, 202, 210, 241–242
    Casa del Medico, 65, 149
    Iseum, **139**, 141, 149, 215, 238–239
portrait sculpture, 9, 23, **24**, 27, 47–50, **49**, 129, **140–141**, 155, 159, 171–178, **176**, 184
    funerary reliefs, 4, **30**, 100, **121**, 122–136, **123**, **125**, **132–133**, **138**, **142**, 188, 192
    Large Herculaneum Woman, 132–134
    verism, 139
    of women, 50, 112
portraits, mummy, 129
Poseidon, 85, 92, 216
priest, 20, 36–37, 41, 53, 67, 115, 131, 139, **139**, 156, 219, 228, 233
    Melanophor, 37, 230
    Pterophor, 36
    Pyrophoros, 38
    stoliasts, 46
    Trierarch, 46
    Zakoros, 39
priestesses, 29, 53–54, 135, 138
processions, 33–34, 36–37, 41, 131, 148, 242
Prometheus, 115, 170
Proserpina, 77
Provinces, Roman, 7–13, 15, 27, 121–122, 129, 178, 183–185
Ptolemaic queens, 97

regulations, 39–40
religion, definition of, 32, 57, 187
Rhodes, 5, 38, 96–97, 106, 179, 181, 228
Romanization, 15
Rome, **1**, 36, 42, 46, 65, 113, 126, 161, 178, 235
    Hadrianeum, 1
    Iseum Campanese, 65

Sarapis, sculptural types, 172
    début (standing), **88**, 90–91
    Sarapis-Asklepios, **95**, **95–96**
    seated, **88**, 91–92
Second Sophistic, 2, 17, 23, 25, 44, 55, 75–76, 78, 151, 189
Selene, 74
self-fashioning, 4, 27, 120–122, 143–144, 186
self-location, 4, 27, 40, 145–147, 184–186, 188

self-understanding, 4, 26–27, 40, 89, 126, 137, 186, 188
sex, 39–40, 62, 65
sexuality, 115, 166
Sinope, 93
sistrum, 1, 36, 42, 97–98, 131, 134
situla, 36, 42, 97–98, 131
Sparta, 63, 96–97
sphinx, 102, **102**, 104, 118, **162**, 162, 190
Strabo, 7, 22, 65, 148
style, 26, 101–102, 116, 118, 171, 187
Suetonius, 65
Synnaoi theoi, 114

Tacitus, 65, 93, 131
Teithras, 39
temporality, 61, 86, 151, 169–170, 178, 183, 189–190
Thasos, 38, 101, 213
Thera, 179
Thessaloniki, 36–39, 42, **43**, 46, 51, 54, 83, 90–91, 97, **103**, **105**, **107–111**, **113**, 117, **118**, 136, 172, 179, 192, 240, 243
    Arch of Galerius, 77, 91, 104
Thysdrus, 1, 36
Tibullus, 64–65
Tithorea, 39, 213
Tralles, 42
transcultural, 60, 75, 102, 135, 143–144, 190–191
Triptolemos, 75
Tutu, 102, 118

universalism, 27, 72, 76, 78–80, 94, 119
universality, 56, 60, 72, 75–76, 78–79, 86, 116, 187, 190

Venus, 76–77, 115
Vespasian, 65
viewership, 17, 60, 80, 85, 102, 106, 116, 129, 137, 143, 160

wall painting, 16, 34, 60, 65, **66**, 112, **139**, **147**, 148–150, 161, 202, 227, 239
water, 28, 36, 45, 69, 85, 148, 178, **180–182**, 185, 188
water crypts, 28, 105–106, 147, 179–183, **179**, 189
    basins, 45, 160, 179–180, 189
women, 18, 37, 50, 74, 110, 129–134
    and alterity, 27, 125, 129, 142
    and cult practices, 36, 39
    in the cultic community, 47–50, 138
    and ethnicity, 123
    in the family, 126
    and inversion, 62–63

Zeus, 92, 94

For EU product safety concerns, contact us at Calle de José Abascal, 56–1°,
28003 Madrid, Spain or eugpsr@cambridge.org.

www.ingramcontent.com/pod-product-compliance
Ingram Content Group UK Ltd.
Pitfield, Milton Keynes, MK11 3LW, UK
UKHW050108230326
469255UK00017B/246